THE BRITISH SUPERHERO

THE BRITISH SUPERHERO

Chris Murray

University Press of Mississippi / Jackson

www.upress.state.ms.us
The University Press of Mississippi is a member of the
Association of American University Presses.

Copyright © 2017 by University Press of Mississippi
All rights reserved
Manufactured in the United States of America

First printing 2017

∞

Library of Congress Cataloging-in-Publication Data

Names: Murray, Christopher, 1975– author.
Title: The British superhero / Chris Murray.
Description: Jackson : University Press of Mississippi, 2017. | Includes bibliographical references and index.
Identifiers: LCCN 2016030090 (print) | LCCN 2016042247 (ebook) | ISBN 9781496807373 (hardback) | ISBN 9781496807380 (epub single) | ISBN 9781496807397 (epub institutional) | ISBN 9781496807403 (pdf single) | ISBN 9781496807410 (pdf institutional)
Subjects: LCSH: Comic books, strips, etc.—Great Britain—History and criticism. | Comic books, strips, etc.—Social aspects—Great Britain—History. | Superheroes in literature. | BISAC: SOCIAL SCIENCE / Popular Culture. | LITERARY CRITICISM / Comics & Graphic Novels. | HISTORY / Europe / Great Britain.
Classification: LCC PN6735 .M87 2017 (print) | LCC PN6735 (ebook) | DDC 741.5/941—dc23
LC record available at https://lccn.loc.gov/2016030090

British Library Cataloging-in-Publication Data available

For Gill and Kaitlyn

CONTENTS

ix   List of Figures

xiii   Acknowledgments

3   Introduction

19   Chapter 1: Penny Dreadfuls, Story Papers, and Protosuperheroes (1825–1935)

56   Chapter 2: False Starts and Minor Triumphs (1936–1949)

105   Chapter 3: From Marvelmen to Pop Art (1950–1961)

149   Chapter 4: Mergers and Marvels (1962–1980)

193   Chapter 5: Revisionism and the British Invasion (1981–1993)

231   Chapter 6: Contemporary British Superheroes (1994–present)

275   Conclusion

283   Notes

291   Bibliography

299   Index

LIST OF FIGURES

Chapter One

Fig. 1: "Dicky the Bird-Man," by Jack B. Yeats, in *Comic Cuts* #1051 (Amalgamated Press, July 2, 1910).
Fig. 2: The Scarlet Bat—The Winged Avenger, in *Film Fun Annual* (Amalgamated Press, 1943).
Fig. 3: The Flaming Avenger, in *The Rover* #372 (DC Thomson, 1933).
Fig. 4: Karga the Clutcher, in *The Skipper* #162 (DC Thomson, 1933).
Fig. 5: The Black Sapper, by Jack Glass, in *The Rover* #384 (DC Thomson, 1929).

Chapter Two

Fig. 6: *Triumph* #772, cover art by Jock McCail (Amalgamated Press, August 5, 1939).
Fig. 7: Derickson Dene, in *Triumph*, by Nat Brand, aka Len Fullerton (Amalgamated Press, 1939).
Fig. 8: *Triumph* #772 (Amalgamated Press, August 5, 1939).
Fig. 9: Superman origin from American daily newspaper strips (McClure Syndicate, 1939).
Fig. 10: Superman page from *Triumph* (1939).
Fig. 11: Page from *Superman* #3 (National Periodicals, Winter 1939), originally published as a newspaper strip, "Superman and the Runaway" (McClure Syndicate, June to July, 1939).
Fig. 12: The second series of Superman in *Triumph* #807 (Amalgamated Press, 1940).
Fig. 13: The Amazing Mr X in *The Dandy* #272 (DC Thomson, 1944).
Fig. 14: Mr Muscle, Britain's Superman, by Denis Gifford, in *Dynamic Comics* (International Comics, 1945).
Fig. 15: Streamline, by Denis Gifford, in *Streamline* #1 (Cardal Publishing, 1947).

Fig. 16: *Super-Duper Comics* #4, by Dennis M. Reader (Cartoon Art Productions of Glasgow, 1947).
Fig. 17: *Marsman Comics*, by Paddy Brennan (Cartoon Art Productions of Glasgow, 1948).
Fig. 18: Wonderman—The Atomic Marvel, by Mick Anglo, in *Wonderman* #4 (Paget, 1948).
Fig. 19: The Tornado, with art by Bob Monkhouse, in *Oh Boy! Comics* #2 (Paget, 1948).
Fig. 20: Stuporman!, by Bob Monkhouse, in *Oh Boy! Comics* (Paget, 1948).
Fig. 21: Captain Might—The Nemesis of Crime, by Denis Gifford, in *Amazing Comics*, 1949 (Modern Fiction Ltd, 1949).

Chapter Three

Fig. 22: *Slick Fun Album*, featuring Superstooge, by Harry Banger (Gerald Swan Ltd, 1956).
Fig. 23: *Captain Zenith*, by Mick Anglo (Martin and Reid Ltd, 1950).
Fig. 24: Electroman, in *Electroman Comics* (King-Ganteaume/Scion, 1951).
Fig. 25: Mr Apollo, in *Dynamic Thrills* (Gerald Swan Ltd, 1952).
Fig. 26: *Masterman Comic*, by Joe Colquhoun (Streamline, 1952).
Fig. 27: *Marvelman* #65 (L. Miller and Son, 1954).
Fig. 28: *Captain Miracle* #3, by Mick Anglo (Anglo Features, 1961).
Fig. 29: Eduardo Paolozzi's *I was a Rich Man's Plaything* (1947).
Fig. 30: Richard Hamilton's *Just What Is It That Makes Today's Homes So Different, So Appealing?* (1956).

Chapter Four

Fig. 31: Gadgetman and Gimmick Kid, by Nevio Zeccara, in *Lion* (IPC, 1966).
Fig. 32: *Fantastic Four* #30, by Stan Lee and Jack Kirby (Marvel, 1964).
Fig. 33: *Pow!* and *Wham!* #63 (Odhams, March 30, 1968).
Fig. 34: Johnny Future, in *Fantastic*, by Luis Bermejo.
Fig. 35: *The Purple Hood* #1, by Michael Jay (Spencer, 1967).
Fig. 36: *Pow!* annual (Odhams, 1971).
Fig. 37: "Electro," with art by Jose Ortiz, in *Pow!* annual (Odhams, 1971).
Fig. 38: Captain Britain advertisement on the back cover of *Mighty World of Marvel* #210 (Marvel UK, 1976).
Fig. 39: Spring-Heeled Jackson, by Dave Gibbons, in *Hotspur* #941 (DC Thomson, 1977).
Fig. 40: Supercats, by Romero, in *Spellbound* #56 (DC Thomson, 1977).

List of Figures   xi

Fig. 41: *The Mighty Apocalypse*, by David Hornsby (self-published, 1977).
Fig. 42: The first appearance of Bananaman in *Nutty*, by John Geering (DC Thomson, 1980).

Chapter Five

Fig. 43: Captain Britain, by Alan Davis, in *Marvel Super-Heroes* #387 (Marvel UK, 1982).
Fig. 44: Marvelman, by Alan Moore and Garry Leach, in *Warrior* #1 (Quality Communications, 1982).
Fig. 45: *Zenith*, by Grant Morrison and Steve Yeowell (Fleetway, 1987).
Fig. 46: *Marshal Law: Super Babylon*, by Pat Mills and Kevin O'Neill (Dark Horse, 1992).
Fig. 47: "The Superhero's Day Off," in *Oink!* #49, by Lew Stringer and Dave Gibbons (Fleetway, 1988).
Fig. 48: *How to Be a Superhero*, written by Mark Leigh and Mike Lepine, with illustrations by Steve Dillon (Penguin Books, 1990).

Chapter Six

Fig. 49: *Brit Force* #6, by Russ Leach (CM Comics, 1994).
Fig. 50: *The Standard*, by John Lees and Jon Rector (ComixTribe, 2008).
Fig. 51: *Meteor*, by Letty Wilson (Panels Comics, 2015).
Fig. 52: *Alpha*, by Chris Murray and Phillip Vaughan (UniVerse, 2016).
Fig. 53: "The Amazing Alpha," by Chris Murray and Norrie Millar (UniVerse, 2016).
Fig. 54: "Pop Goes the Art World," by Chris Murray and Letty Wilson (UniVerse, 2016).
Fig. 55: "Alpha vs Doc Holiday and his Goons," by Chris Murray and Elliot Balson (UniVerse, 2016).
Fig. 56: The Amazing Mr X, redesigned for the *Digital Dandy* (DC Thomson, 2012).
Fig. 57: Saltire, by Phillip Vaughan. Saltire created by John Ferguson (Diamondsteel Comics, 2015).
Fig. 58: *SuperBob*, directed by Jon Drever (Grain Media, 2015).

ACKNOWLEDGMENTS

No project like this is completed without the support of a great many individuals. Special thanks must go to friends and colleagues at the University of Dundee: Brian Hoyle, Phillip Vaughan, Keith Williams (who took an aspiring young comics scholar under his wing many years ago), Laura Findlay, Jennifer Barnes, Jo George, Nicole Deveranne, Matthew Jarron, Ana Salzberg, Daniel Cook, Jennifer Byers, Daria Wall, Jim Stewart, Claire Milne, and Mayra Crowe. A great deal is owed to my Deans, David Finkelstein and Jim Livesey, who have been hugely supportive over the years. I am incredibly indebted to my students, who continue to inspire me with their passion and talents: Norrie Millar, Damon Herd, Stephen O'Donnell, Calum Laird, Hannah Rose, William Grady, Kelly Kanayama, Rebecca Horner, Megan Sinclair, Callum Paterson, Adleen El-Ammar, Rossi Gifford, Elliot Balson, Letty Wilson, Madeline Gangnes, Erin Keepers, Jessica Burton, and Claire Roe. Many thanks also to the staff at the University Press of Mississippi, especially Vijay Shah, Katie Keene, and Lisa McMurtray, who showed great patience during the delays that came with accepting the mantle of parenthood.

In the course of writing this book, I have met and corresponded with many fellow comics historians, scholars, and creators, notably Peter Hansen, Lew Stringer, Terry Hooper, John McShane, Grant and Kristan Morrison, Frank Quitely, John and Clare Ferguson, Alex Ronald, John Lees, Roger Sabin, Billy Grove, Joan Ormrod, Mel Gibson, Dave Huxley, Dave Gibbons, Cam Kennedy, Monty Nero, Ken Fudge, Ian Kennedy, and Dan McDaid. Thanks also to DC Thomson staff, including Dan McGachey, Mike Stirling, David Powell, and especially Morris Heggie, to whom I owe many a pint. Massive thanks to my partner in crime and fellow editor of *Studies in Comics*, Julia Round. Thanks are also due to the British Film Institute, whose staff was enormously helpful on my trips to the Denis Gifford

Collection, and the Carnegie Trust, whose support made possible several vital research trips. Also, George Corderio, proprietor of Dundee's *Black Hole* comic shop, and for my money the most important man in Dundee. Finally, I must acknowledge the tremendous support of my family: my wife Gill and my daughter Kaitlyn, my mother Marlyn, my sister Tracy, and my brother Gavin, as well as Lisa, Gary, Alistair, Alison, Claire, Jessica, and Emily-Rose. Special thanks go to my father Chris and my uncles Stuart, Dougie, and Alastair, who gave me my first comics all those years ago.

Professor Chris Murray
Dundee, Scotland

THE BRITISH SUPERHERO

INTRODUCTION

The idea of the British superhero is often considered to be a contradiction in terms. Superheroes belong to America. They soar between the skyscrapers of the great American cities, both real and imagined, from New York to Metropolis, Chicago to Gotham. They represent the ideals of "truth, Justice, and the *American* Way." Moreover, while superheroes are popular all over the world, nowhere is the association between the genre and the comics medium as close as it is in America. However, the origins of the superhero run deep and come from many different sources. America may be the world leader in terms of the production of superhero comics, but superheroes have appeared in a great many countries around the world. Many of these international superheroes owe much to American characters like Superman and Batman, but there are also fascinating and quite different variations on the superhero in each of these countries. Rather than being the product of political and cultural hegemony, superheroes have emerged from a range of national contexts and have become a transnational phenomenon across a range of media. Indeed, as editors Shane Denson, Christina Meyer, and Daniel Stein point out in the introduction to their book *Transnational Perspectives on Graphic Narratives* (2013), "comics and other forms of graphic narrative are predisposed towards crossing national borders and cultural boundaries because of their unique visual-verbal interface that seems to translate more readily—though not without transformation and distortion—across cultures than do monomedial forms of literature, nonnarrative artworks, or even such visual narrative media as film."[1]

Whereas American superheroes have often been patriotic and emblems of traditional "wholesome" values (themselves bound up in a complex mythology and discourse of national identity), British superheroes, or American superhero comics created by British creators, have often worked against the assumptions and conventions of the genre, forming a countertradition that subverts the superhero, employs a mode of parody, and in some instances offers a satirical critique of the genre and its politics. Therefore, the "transformation and distortion" that Denson, Meyer, and Stein point to is exactly the focus of this book. As comics writer and artist Dave Gibbons, the co-creator of *Watchmen* (1986), attests, "superheroes in British comics have always been a bit strange. We've never gone for the full-on American model. They are always slightly odd and mutated."[2] This mutation is partly based on differences in cultural and industrial contexts, differing attitudes toward power and authority, and the fact that there is a particularly strong history of satire and parody in British comics that can be traced back through Ally Sloper comics and the prints and cartoons produced by Hogarth, Gillray, and Rowlandson. When British creators have produced superhero stories, the best ones have offered something more than a pale imitation of the "American model," often in the form of parody, mixing the heroic adventure narrative with humor, or undermining it somehow. This book will explore the nature of British superheroes and consider the place of the genre within British comics history and the ways in which these comics have offered a commentary on the American superhero. It argues that the superhero genre is a blend of several influences and that in British comics these influences were often quite different from those in America. This resulted in some alternate approaches to the figure of the superhero, which has produced some of the "oddness" to which Gibbons refers.

As this book will show, the British subversion of the superhero genre goes back to the 1930s, but the best-known and most often cited examples of this appeared in the early to mid-1980s, when British writers and artists had a significant influence on American superhero comics, forming the first wave of the so-called British Invasion, which was followed in the early 1990s by a second wave.[3] The appropriation of the superhero genre by British comics creators afforded them the opportunity to mobilize the superhero as a discursive construct for the purposes of political commentary, challenging the commonly understood politics of the superhero (which are usually seen as conservative, moralistic, and masculine) through satire and parody that reflected British attitudes towards America but were also a mirror of attitudes towards Britain itself. In many ways, this is similar to the reworking of the American Western film by Italian directors in the 1960s in what became known as "spaghetti westerns." As Jeffrey Richards notes in his introduction to Christopher Frayling's book on spaghetti westerns, such films "represented an extraordinary and potent crossfertilization of American and European cultures."[4]

A similar argument can be made for the long but largely forgotten history of British superhero comics, which subverted the genre and undermined its assumptions, tropes, and conventions. Therefore, what many British superheroes show is that the superhero genre does not need to merely conform to or mirror dominant ideological concerns; it can also act as a site of opposition to them. Superheroes are simultaneously constructions of certain power formulations and one of the mechanisms by which creators working within popular genres can critique power. This came to the fore in the 1980s in the revisionist approach adopted in Frank Miller's *The Dark Knight Returns* (1986); Alan Moore and Dave Gibbons's *Watchmen* (1986); *Zenith* (1987–1993), by Grant Morrison and Steve Yeowell; and *Marshal Law* (1987–1992), by Pat Mills and Kevin O'Neill. Of these, only the first, *The Dark Knight Returns*, was produced by American creators. The others are by British comics creators, although only *Zenith* was issued by a British publisher, the others being released by American publishers. These texts subverted the superhero genre and challenged perceptions of it, with complex narrative structures and characters who were troubled, even psychotic, as opposed to heroic and all-powerful. These were undoubtedly landmark texts in the history of the superhero genre, but they did not spring out of nowhere; rather, they were linked to a longer tradition of appropriation and subversion of the superhero that was not exclusively British but in which British comics creators played a significant part. Arguably this is related to the close, and sometimes tense, relationship between the British and American comics industries, but it is perhaps also a function of the complex political and cultural relationship between the two countries.

On the surface the best of friends and enjoying what was termed a "special relationship" by Winston Churchill, Britain and America have always been caught up in a complex political dynamic, from the Declaration of Independence and the American Revolution through to the present day. As historian Ronald Hyam notes in *Britain's Declining Empire* (2006), the British attitude toward America in the nineteenth century was summarized by Lord Derby's 1880 remark that America was "forty Englands rolled into one," and as Hyam points out, this concealed a sense of competition, and even fear, that made the bond more of an uncomfortable relationship than a special one.[5] At around the same time that the superhero genre was emerging, the decline of the British Empire was set against the ascendency of its former colony to the status of superpower.[6] This entrenched a certain amount of mutual suspicion, as well as some shared political interests and a high degree of cultural exchange.[7] This was seen in the propaganda and popular culture of the 1940s. In Britain, Americans were portrayed as boorish and vulgar "Yanks" but as basically good-natured and friendly. This was a source of much humor, but in the end the message was clear: for all their cultural differences from the British, Americans were brave and steadfast allies. Because of the greater discrepancy between American and Soviet standards, during the war there was a greater need to justify the alliance with the Soviet Union, so films and comics often focused on the Soviets rather than Britain. However, when British (or more precisely, English) characters did appear in American comics, they were often stereotypically upper class and eccentric, but beneath that they were brave and loyal friends (until after the war, when British actors were increasingly cast as Hollywood villains).

In the postwar years, the military necessities of the Cold War ensured a continued American presence in Britain, but the stereotypes seen in popular culture held sway in political attitudes, too. American administrations saw the British as elitist and imperialist, even in the face of a crumbling empire, while Whitehall saw Americans as crass and vulgar cousins, with more than a dash of idealism and naïveté.[8] The former colony now, in a sense, occupied its old colonial master, both in cultural and military terms, creating a still greater bond but also several tensions. This may well have been the relationship that American politicians had actively sought for several decades, with a degrading of Britain's influence as a world power forcing it into a coalition with America. Churchill's framing of the situation was in some ways simply putting the best face on what was an economic, military, and political inevitability. This relationship had consequences for comics, with American comics coming into Britain via US military bases, but it was also reflected more broadly in British popular culture and the penetration of American culture into it, which was just one part of the postwar global dominance of American popular culture and brands. When the superhero genre took off in the late 1930s, America already exercised an extraordinary degree of cultural dominance on the global stage, with the products of American popular culture leading several creative industries, notably filmmaking. American newspaper strips were another major international success, being syndicated across the United States and translated and distributed worldwide. These films, comics, magazines, and products made American culture seem glamorous and aspirational in sharp contrast to the poverty and deprivation of postwar Britain.

The industrial context and production standards also point to key differences between American and British comics. British comics were larger (usually tabloid format) but with fewer pages and were usually black and white, or with cover pages in color, or with single colors on some interior pages. The economies of scale were never really in favor of full color in British comics, whereas in American comics, the larger market allowed for color. Other key differences were that British comics were usually weekly, as opposed to monthly or bimonthly American comics, and were usually anthologies, with short two-to-six page stories, as opposed to the format of American comics, where individual stories would be around eight to nine pages long, until the comics went to whole issue stories (often over twenty pages long) and centered on a single character or a related group of characters. Indeed, the anthology format is still the norm in British comics. These differences were a point of enlightening debate between British comics artist and historian Denis Gifford and Jerry DeFuccio, an editor at *Mad Magazine* in America in the 1950s. They were engaged in a transatlantic exchange of comics, with Gifford sending DeFuccio British comics, most of which were completely unknown in America, and DeFuccio sending hard-to-find American comics to Gifford. In a letter dated November 22, 1957, DeFuccio replied to Gifford, saying,

> Generally I found the [British] comics rather vapid and disappointing. I guess it's because I've grown used to seeing colour and superior artwork in our own publications. Some of the British comics pages are no more than "teasers," they don't present enough to the reader in one instalment. There is one item I really liked in the most recent parcel to arrive. It's called Blackshirt and the signature on the story is Bill Ladey. I like this artist's angle shots. He seems to have been influenced by our comic artist Irv Novick who did a masked hero called The Shield years ago.[9]

From this correspondence it is clear that there were many differences between British and American comics cultures but also significant dialogue between them as well. At the Incontro Sul Fumetto (Conference on Comic Strips) held in Bologna, Italy, as part of the 1977 Children's Book Fair, Gifford gave an address titled "From Beau Ogleby to Bristow: The International Strip in Great Britain." Referring to the rise of American comic strips in the 1930s he said,

> The American strip was taking over the world [in the 1930s]. Two possible reasons for this suggest themselves. The American strip has more vitality, is more personal to the artist, more creative and original, than its British counterpart. This is because in the field of the comic book[,] British publishers

restrict their product to a juvenile audience. The average cutoff point is the age of eleven. Thus artists and writers working in the medium are forced to follow a confined editorial attitude not found in the freer fields of [American comics]. In the area of the newspaper strip, Britain has found more success: Jeff Hawke, Tiffany Jones, and even the extremely native Andy Capp and Bristow, are known and enjoyed around the world. . . . The second reason for the international success of American strips is the perfection of the syndication system. . . . It was [the expansion of the American syndicates overseas] that virtually wiped out the international expansion of the British comic strip.[10]

The marketing strategies employed by each industry were also very different. It would be highly unusual for a new British comic to launch without a free gift (a mask, badge, or toy), whereas such gifting was never part of American comics culture. Finally, whereas superhero and humor comics were dominant genres in America, humor, adventure, war, sports, and girls comics were much more popular in Britain than superheroes. But superhero comics eventually made inroads into the British market, and American reprints became increasingly important in Britain, displacing some homegrown content.

What Is a Superhero?

In general terms, a superhero fights against injustice using extraordinary means. In *Superhero: The Secret Origin of a Genre* (2006), Peter Coogan argues that the superhero is

> a heroic character with a selfless, pro-social mission; with superpowers-extraordinary abilities, advanced technology, or highly developed physical, mental, or mystical skills; who has a superhero identity embodied in a code-name and iconic costume, which typically express his biography, character, powers, or origin (transformation from extraordinary person to superhero); and who is generically distinct, i.e. can be distinguished from characters of related genres (fantasy, science fiction, detective, etc.) by a preponderance of generic conventions. Often superheroes have dual identities, the ordinary one of which is usually a closely guarded secret.[13]

However, there are many other tropes and conventions at work, and often stories revolve around what Richard Reynolds calls the moment of "extra-effort."[14] Superheroes can never win simply because they have superhuman abilities. Instead, when faced with seemingly insurmountable odds, the superhero must tap hidden reserves of power or moral conviction in order to overcome evil. In this sense the superhero story is a morality tale, and functions as a parable about power and identity. Given this, it is clear that the superhero is just one example in a long line of hero archetypes. There have always been characters like this whose feats have inspired others, from the heroes of ancient myth, such as Gilgamesh and Hercules, to folk heroes such as Robin Hood and Paul Bunyan. However, despite its appearance as monolithic and conservative, the superhero genre has never been as stable and uniform as it appears. Though Superman and Batman were both published by National Periodicals (later known as DC Comics), Batman was in some ways a reaction against Superman. Whereas Superman was utopian and about modernity and the future, Batman was dystopian and gothic, rooted in the past and especially the tragedy of his origin—the murder of his parents.

If the generic models for Superman were science fiction and romance, for Batman they were crime and horror. And then there was Wonder Woman, also from National Periodicals, who introduced a more overt influence from mythology and fables and reacted against the gender politics of the rest of the genre, mainly Superman and Batman. Rather than hegemonic, the genre was always divided against itself, and examples come from just one company, National Periodicals, over a relatively short span of time. Widening things out, it is clear that Timely's (later Marvel's) Captain America was quite different in tone from National's comics, and Fawcett's Captain Marvel was quite different from all of them. Also, the idea of the superhero was quickly parodied, notably in cartoons like *Mighty Mouse*, which appeared in 1942. In the 1960s, the Marvel Comics revolution very consciously shifted the definition of the superhero, reacting against the wholesome comics of its rival DC by presenting characters who were brash, argumentative, and hip. If the focus is pulled back even further, it is clear that there is no real uniformity to the idea of the superhero. Indeed, one of the many misperceptions about the genre is that it is fixed and monolithic and that the characters are simple cyphers for conservative values, white privilege, and masculine power. While there may be a strong element of that in many superhero stories, they are usually about identity and transformation, and the thing that seems to define the superhero on the surface (physical power) is ultimately shown to be inadequate, with a deeper ethical, emotional or intellectual strength being required to win the day.[15] However, providing a definition of the genre and the superhero is no easy thing.

Taking the first appearance of Superman in *Action Comics* #1 as a template, Reynolds offers a definition of the superhero based on the seven elements that he identifies as crucial to the character type. These are,

1. The hero is marked out from society. He often reaches maturity without having a relationship with his parents.
2. At least some of the superheroes will be like earthbound gods in their level of powers. Other superheroes of lesser powers will consort easily with these earthbound deities.
3. The hero's devotion to justice overrides even his devotion to the law.
4. The extraordinary nature of the superhero will be contrasted with the ordinariness of his surroundings.
5. Likewise, the extraordinary nature of the hero will be contrasted with the mundane nature of his alter ego. Certain taboos will govern the actions of these alter egos.
6. Although ultimately above the law, superheroes can be capable of considerable patriotism and moral loyalty to the state, though not necessarily to the letter of its laws.
7. The stories are mythical and use science and myth indiscriminately to create a sense of wonder.[16]

On this basis, the superhero would appear to be quite a reasonably straightforward character. The superhero exists in a world where fantastic powers and/or feats of skill are deployed in a fight against evil and injustice, but once closer scrutiny is applied, it becomes more complex. Superheroes frequently don costumes to conceal their identities, but some do not, and most have powers such as incredible strength, invulnerability, and flight, but this varies from character to character. Some may be invisible or telepathic, or can shrink to the atomic level, or run faster than the speed of light. Any power that can be imagined has most likely been held by a superhero at some point, and that is not even taking into account some of the more exotic and fantastical superpowers, such as time travel and superbreath. Some superheroes have no superpowers at all, like Batman, who uses gadgets and technology and is a highly skilled combatant with the resources of a billionaire at his disposal. Even though Batman does not have superpowers in the traditional sense, he does endure the kind of physical stresses and injuries that no human would be able to subject themselves to without serious harm. He is routinely shot and stabbed and performs high impact feats of gymnastics, jumping from rooftops and swinging from a rope high above

Gotham's streets. It is clear that a normal human body could not endure this in the real world. His fantastic feats are not attributed to superpowers as such, but rather skill, physical toughness, and willpower, but if that is the case, is a character such as Judge Dredd, or a hero from an action film, also a superhero? Clearly not.

This presents a problem for any definition of the superhero. The abilities and powers of the superhero are not enough to define the genre. Nor is there a tone, mood, or setting that defines the genre, in the way that tone or mood usually defines a horror story or romance or setting defines a Western. Instead, the superhero genre is a combination of many different genres and operates in an accumulative way, superimposing itself on other genres. It blends myth, parables, and epic narratives with numerous popular genres, including science fiction, crime, the Western, and horror, along with a dash of romance, to create a supergenre. The key term here is the prefix "super," meaning to move above and beyond or to exceed expectations. The superhero genre is not a stable or fixed category, but is continually moving beyond categorization, expanding its parameters, and actively resisting rigid or all-encompassing definitions. To a certain extent this is true of all genres, but it is especially the case with the superhero genre, which places transformation at the center of its concerns.

In *The Hero with a Thousand Faces* (1949), Joseph Campbell described what he called the "monomyth," a narrative pattern that is found throughout the cultures of the world and describes the journey of the hero. He says, "A hero ventures forth from the world of common day into a region of supernatural wonder: fabulous forces are there encountered and a decisive victory is won: the hero comes back from this mysterious adventure with the power to bestow boons on his fellow man."[17] In *The American Monomyth* (1977) and *The Myth of the American Superhero* (2002), Robert Jewett and John Shelton Lawrence revise Campbell's ideas in line with the politics of American exceptionalism (the notion that America is inherently superior to other nations based on ideas of manifest destiny and the supposedly revolutionary principles of the Constitution). Whereas Campbell describes the journey from the world into a supernatural otherworld, Jewett and Lawrence argue that the American monomyth operates as follows: "A community in a harmonious paradise is threatened by evil; normal institutions fail to contend with this threat; a selfless superhero emerges to renounce temptations and carry out the redemptive task; aided by fate, his decisive victory restores the community to its paradisiacal condition; the superhero then recedes into obscurity."[18] The superhero genre, Jewett and Lawrence claim, is an example of the American monomyth in that it reflects a certain predisposition towards utopian thinking and the association of America with paradise.

While the original superhero is often said to be Superman, who gave his name to the genre, the origin of the superhero is much more complex than would appear. The superheroes that emerged in comics from the late 1930s to the early 1940s were most directly related to characters that had appeared in newspaper adventure strips and pulp novels, such as Tarzan, by Edgar Rice Burroughs. Partly based on Tarzan, Lee Falk's The Phantom appeared in newspaper strips and was one of the key prototypes of the superhero. Then there were the science-fiction heroes like Buck Rogers and Flash Gordon, as well as the heroes of film and radio serials. Arguably, even E. C. Segar's Popeye was a forerunner of the superhero, and there were several characters in nineteenth-century popular culture in both Britain and America who fit most definitions of a superhero. Likewise, the master criminals from these stories very much prefigure the supervillain. All these elements contributed to the formation of the superhero, so rather than the superhero appearing fully formed in the shape of Superman, the genre emerged as an act of distillation, a concentration of preexisting elements. This is why traces of the superhero are found everywhere in the decades leading up to that moment of "creation." In truth, what Jerry Siegel and Joe Shuster did was to refine and name something that already existed although not fully conceptualized. This does not minimize their creativity or importance, but their achievements should not obscure the many other creators who helped to shape the concept of the superhero over a longer period of time. In effect, the idea of the superhero was not created in one moment, but rather was slowly shaped, and although American publishers were the most active and influential, not all of the material that pointed the way toward the superhero concept was American.

Therefore, the superhero was a blend of influences from the start, and given this, it is clear why there is no single definition of the superhero that satisfies all criteria or refers to a single, all-encompassing superhero archetype. What makes Superman special is not so much that he was supposedly first, but rather the way in which he brought ideological force to the idea of the superhero and visualized the concept in a powerful way. His origin story mythologized the American experience, especially that of the immigrant, making the superhero narrative a near-perfect metaphor for America's view of itself, and the superhero an icon of national identity, binding together notions of patriotism and manifest destiny. From the messianic protector, to the patriotic defender of liberty, to the troubled vigilante, superheroes were quite diverse, even in the early years, reflecting the tensions and contradictions bound up in this highly ideological figure. Moreover, Superman has changed considerably from the character he was in those early stories to the character that is known today. Again, the key point is that superhero comics change with the times, reflecting changing political circumstances.

The politics of the American superhero were certainly shaped by the Great Depression (although this book argues for a prehistory of the genre that can be traced back into the nineteenth century), but they were also greatly influenced by subsequent political imperatives. Many superhero comics adopted a propagandist role during World War II, and some tackled the "Red Menace" during the Cold War. Then there was a widespread renewal of their wartime propagandist role in the wake of 9/11.[19] That is not to say all superhero comics conformed to these values, but a significant proportion of them did, and certainly enough to justify the perception that the genre had certain political leanings. Rightly or wrongly the superhero is still seen as a powerful emblem of American national identity and purpose and a symbol for the global power it wields. They personify heroism and dramatize political concerns and are therefore a lens through which to view the operation of ideology, which often distorts complexity into apparently simple oppositions of good and evil.

The superhero is therefore a very appealing target for satire and parody, mocking the simple fabular logic that appears to rule the world of most superheroes. However, what is often overlooked in the attempt to situate the superhero genre in terms of its historical relationship to other genres or as a publishing or multimedia phenomenon is the extent to which the genre, or this supergenre, is itself a mode of parody. In *Parody: Ancient, Modern, and Post-modern* (1993), Margaret A. Rose observes that the definition of parody has never remained stable; citing Fred W. Householder Jr. (1944), she notes that an early Aristotelian definition holds parody to be a work of short length using epic language and meter but with a trivial, satirical, or mock heroic subject.[20] The American superhero echoes Romance literature with its questing knights, or classical mythology with its superhuman gods, or any number of heroic narratives, then subverts them into the adventures of caped characters wearing costumes inspired by circus strongmen. These works may be regarded as relatively trivial, or having a mock-heroic element, but in order for this to work completely, the creators of these superhero characters would have to have had these targets in mind. (Parody often has this problem, that in order to be effective, the readership or audience have to be somewhat aware of the targets.)

It may be argued that there were elements of parody and the mock heroic in some superhero comics from the 1930s and 1940s (there are elements of this in Plastic Man and Captain Marvel, for example), but what is being played with there is the model of the superhero that had recently been created. Superman and Batman, along with Wonder Woman, Captain America, and many other superheroes from the 1940s, are not exactly "mock epics" or trivial in their concerns, as they address important issues such as the war, patriotism, and heroism in a way that is quite "straight." There is an element of parody in the superhero genre, but that need not always imply mockery. Indeed, as Linda Hutcheon indicates, in Greek "para" can mean "beside" as well as "against," so the imitation of another mode or form can sometimes been taken as a sign of intimacy between them, suggestive of an "accord" or "simulation."[2] Hutcheon also argues that parody is always ideologically suspect because of its doubling techniques, but that it can be thought of as "the inscription of the past in the present."[22] The superhero genre is one that is replete with doublings, layered on top of one another, and the kind of continual reinscription Hutcheon describes has certainly become a key part of the genre, which is a palimpsest. The British superhero is therefore a parody of a parody, or at least, often parodies or reinscribes a genre and characters that are themselves decipherable as parody or reinscriptions of previous models, which are either being imitated or are being mocked. This doubling (for it is at least that, although several more layers may be uncovered) makes the superhero a complex construct, and the British superhero even more so; this itself may account for its "odd and mutated" nature.

Media scholar John Fiske's point about the role of parody in popular culture is a useful one in this regard. He argues that parody is often used in an excessive and clichéd way to draw attention to its difference from "reality" in order to make clear that an engagement with real world politics is taking place and to construct a space in which those issues can be dramatized for rhetorical effect.[23] In his view, the idea that popular texts present clichéd stories or operate within generic conventions is neither a barrier to thinking of them as politically sophisticated nor to allowing them to be used as part of a debate about important issues. This is a sort of alienation effect, in which irony and parody provide enough distance from the real to inscribe a critique of it within popular texts. Indeed, some of the most subversive superhero stories are often those that switch the apparently simple, eternal world of the superhero for one of consequences and change, and this has been a common strategy of British comics creators—bringing the superhero into the "real world" and establishing an overt critique of the genre by highlighting its absurdities. British superhero stories often have a kind of parodic doubling, and excess of meaning, above and beyond the excess seen in American superhero comics. The superhero genre may in fact be a parody of the epic hero narrative expressed through an image of the mythic paradigms of the American Dream and manifest destiny, filtered through the frontier myth, and mixed with a range of genres, but when that is reinscribed in a British context, is all of this distilled into a satire of American politics as expressed through its popular culture? In some of the cases explored in this book, that may well be the case, and this is an example of the distortion that Denson, Meyer, and Stein regard as a function of transnational dialogue between cultures and what Gibbons refers to as a "mutation," with this implying a degree of critique. In other cases, the "parody" at work comes closer to the other definition, with simulation and appropriation resulting in a less confrontational approach.

Aside from these issues of parody and appropriation, the fact that this book sets out to investigate the British superhero necessitates some discussion of what it is meant by "British." For the purposes of the argument set out here, "British" refers to the United Kingdom, which is to say England, Wales, Scotland, and Northern Ireland. However, it should be noted that how "united" these countries are is a matter of debate. The long-standing union of these entities arguably creates an identity that is British, but the constituent parts still have strong national identities. For many in Scotland, Ireland, and Wales, England is seen as the dominant, and potentially oppressive, partner, having the biggest population by far. But then, there is a north-south divide in England that operates along class lines. The stereotype is that southern England is middle class and northern England is working class and deprived and perhaps has more in common with Scotland in that respect. Many Scots and the Irish have particular objections to the Union on the grounds that they see themselves as colonized subjects. The uprisings in Ireland and the calls for independence, which turned to a bloody terrorism campaign waged on the British mainland and in Ireland, furthered divisions. In recent years, there have been less violent calls for independence, or at least more autonomy from London, from Scotland in particular. Added to this, Britain's relationship to Europe is a hugely contentious issue. While some British people see themselves as European as well as British, for others the two identities are incompatible. So the notion of what it means to be British is a complex one. However, while knowledge of the rivalry between England and Scotland is useful when considering the competitiveness between AP/ICP/Fleetway in London and DC Thomson in Dundee, in the main this book does not go into detail about these issues.

The focus of this book is on the relationship between British and American comics and the treatment of the superhero in Britain, but there were many precursors to the superhero in British popular culture, especially in the mass print culture of the nineteenth century, and as will be seen in Chapter One, they were quite different from their American counterparts. By the early twentieth century, much of the British comics industry was dominated by Amalgamated Press, a publisher that defined the history of British comics from the late nineteenth century to the 1930s and yet was also instrumental in bringing an American style of storytelling into British comics, along with its great rival, DC Thomson. One of the most important factors driving the success of comics in both Britain and America in the late nineteenth and early twentieth centuries was the emergence of a new audience—children and teenagers. Many periodicals targeted younger readers in the 1930s, when the superheroes appeared in comics, but in Britain the main focus was on humor and adventure stories. Perhaps for this reason, when American superhero comics were first reprinted in Britain in the late 1930s, they were viewed as something of a curiosity, and it took a while for them to establish themselves. They did not fit the preexisting genres and styles of British comics, although many creators were influenced by American comics, and several faltering attempts were made to establish British superheroes throughout the 1940s, as explored in Chapter Two. The older British influences persisted in various ways, making the British superheroes of the late 1940s and the 1950s a hybrid of British and American traditions.

By this time, several British superheroes had become established and some enjoyed a degree of success, but there were complex publishing obstacles to negotiate, which included strong competition from other genres, paper rationing, bans on American imports, controversies about the supposedly ill effect of American horror comics and other "American-style" comics, attempts to disguise British comics as American ones, and imports of Australian reprints of American material. What many of the British superheroes lacked was the grand prosocial mission that Coogan describes or a sense of manifest destiny in their do-gooding. Also, it was more common for the British costumed characters to be villains or mysterious figures with ambiguous motives rather than heroes. In contrast, the forces of law and order would also often be rather conventional persons such as detectives or policemen as opposed to exciting costumed adventurers.

These parodic elements and subversions of genre conventions partly came from the dominant role humor played in British comics. This association was made all-the-stronger due to the fact that the more visual style of storytelling that was seen as the "American style" was most often applied to humor comics in Britain, so on a formal level American superhero comics "looked funny" to British eyes. Another factor was that the adventure genre in British periodicals was closely associated with the boy's weeklies, which contained prose stories with some spot illustrations as opposed to the more visually orientated American style that emerged from the newspaper strips. This created dissonance between genre and form, so attempts to showcase American superhero comics, or to copy them, encountered a barrier. In time this would change, but to a certain extent British readers, publishers, and creators, at least prior to the 1950s, arguably found it hard to identify with the American-style superhero in a British context, which is partly why attempts to create British superheroes were so fraught with difficulty and were met with failure. As Chapter Three will show, American superheroes were often popular in Britain when imports or reprints were available, but the relationship between British and American comics, as seen through the lens of the superhero, was a complex one, mediated by political and cultural differences as well as by different readerships, expectations, and publishing practices, with elements of parody creeping in. Chapters Four, Five, and Six will trace the course of this relationship from the 1970s to the present.

The British superheroes have always been there alongside the highly popular reprints of American comics, mimicking the confidence and bravado of their cousins across the Atlantic or offering a pointed critique of the politics of the American superhero, revealing much about the political and cultural relationship between Britain and America. This relationship was partly about the competition between the two industries, with reprinted or imported American material threatening to strangle the indigenous market at certain points and British publishers and creators either emulating the popular American material or producing work that satirized it. The impulse to parody American comics, and particularly superheroes, came from the different approach to notions of heroism and national identity in each culture, but also from a feeling that these comics cultures were in competition with one another (albeit in a rather asymmetrical contest). As Dave Gibbons has said, "[British superheroes] are like American superheroes seen through a weird distorting lens," which was perhaps the same one described by Denson, Meyer, and Stein as a function of the transnational border crossing as the genre moved between cultures.[24] This book aims to understand the processes and political pressures that led to this distortion and to reveal a new understanding of the British superhero.

Chapter 1

PENNY DREADFULS, STORY PAPERS, AND PROTOSUPERHEROES (1825–1935)

Long before superhero comics appeared in America, a tradition of periodical adventure stories existed on both sides of the Atlantic. In Britain, the Victorian popular press was particularly lively, and a huge number of weekly and monthly publications appeared. They catered to a wide audience, although many of the most successful titles were aimed at adolescent boys. There were many kinds of stories featured in these publications, from detective fiction to tales of war and exploration, and some of the archetypes that would later feature in British superhero comics were formed here. These publications were not comics as such but, rather, were mainly prose stories with an illustrated cover and sometimes with some internal illustrations. These types of serial publications were enormously successful, and they created a new kind of popular literature for a new readership (which was mainly working class). Over the course of the nineteenth century, these serial adventures came in two forms, mainly distinguished by their content. There were the "story papers," sometimes known as boy's weeklies, that were usually wholesome adventure stories, and there were "penny bloods" or "penny dreadfuls," which drew more overtly on gothic literature and were therefore much more gory and sensational. This chapter will examine these publications, their relationship with similar publications in America, and the heroic and villainous characters that appeared therein, with a particular focus on certain characters who, in retrospect, can be seen as protosuperheroes and villains. In many ways, these publications established the market and audience for adventure comics in Britain and influenced the emergence of a similar market in America, where dime novels and pulp magazines, which flourished there—along with newspaper strips—would later influence the rise of superhero comics.

The Emergence of British Comics

For the most part, the publications that were available in the early years of the nineteenth century offered stories that were intended to be morally educational, emphasizing good behavior and respect for parents. The idealized children who appeared in these stories, whom the children were supposedly to emulate, may have been a parent's notion of the perfect child, but they were somewhat pious. However, the publication of William Clarke's *The Boy's Own Book: A Complete Encyclopedia of all the Diversions, Athletic, Scientific, and Recreative, of Boyhood and Youth* in 1828 marked an important change of direction. First published in London, it sold out its initial print run in a matter of months and was reprinted for the American market in Boston the following year, also to great success. The book was an illustrated compendium of rules for games and sporting activities, illusions, magic tricks, and puzzles, as well as containing information about nature and animals. This was a marked difference from previous publications for children, largely because it was actually aimed at children rather than at parents. Whereas previous publications operated on the assumption that parents would want to buy educational and improving reading material for their children, *The Boy's Own Book* found a new balance between education and entertainment. This proved to be so popular that the book went through many editions over the course of the century and provoked a series of imitators. As sports historian Robert William Henderson observes, *The Boy's Own Book* "was a tremendous contrast to the juvenile books of the period, which emphasized piety, morals and instruction of mind and soul; it must have been received with whoops of delight by the youngsters of [Britain and America]."[1]

In September 1832, just a few years after *The Boy's Own Book* appeared, *The Boys' and Girls' Penny Magazine* became the first hugely successful story paper for children. *The Penny Magazine*, published weekly by W. Howden in London, which was based in the Strand, ran from September 1832 until March 1833. As the name suggests, it cost a penny, and each issue was eight pages long and had a prominent illustration on the front cover. The stories were aimed at a pre-teen readership and were often based on fairy tales, but the magazine had a very broad appeal and did particularly well with its Christmas issue, which reportedly sold 835,000 copies. Clearly, there was a huge, largely untapped market, and publishers took note. Soon there were several similar story papers offering prose stories with some illustrations rather than compendia of games and sporting activities. The story papers marked a significant advance in juvenile publications and appeared at a time when the serialization of novels was a huge publishing phenomenon.

Indeed, in the 1830s the serialization of novels by the likes of Charles Dickens reached new heights of success and popularity. Dickens's serialized novels initially appeared in 1836, the first being *The Pickwick Papers*, published by Chapman and Hall, which was based in the Strand alongside W. Howden, publisher of *The Boys' and Girls' Penny Magazine*. At this time, the Strand and nearby Fleet Street (where the newspaper publishers were based) were the center of British publishing, and Holywell Street, which ran parallel to the Strand at the east end of the street, was the center of the Victorian pornography industry, so literature, journalism, popular entertainment for children, and pornography sat alongside each other at the heart of London. It was a very exciting time for publishers who clamored to cater to the demands of the public. These demands were partly driven by the fact that about this time the concept of reading for leisure was becoming established as a new working-class pastime, and publishers were discovering the considerable profits that could be made by producing cheaply made serials and weekly publications for this readership. Before long the publishers recognized that the adolescent male readership was a particularly lucrative one and began producing adventure story papers that catered directly to this market.

In Britain the humor tradition that wove through Hogarth, Gillray, Rowlandson, *The Glasgow Looking Glass*, and *Punch*, delivered one of its first superstar characters in 1867 in the form of Ally Sloper, one of the earliest recurring fictional characters in comics. He first appeared in the British magazine *Judy* (which was a response to *Punch*) and was created by Charles H. Ross, and his French wife, the actress and cartoonist Emilie de Tessier (working under the pseudonym Marie Duval). As Roger Sabin notes,

> Sloper was created by Charles Ross, formerly a writer of penny dreadfuls, though his wife Marie Duval soon took over cartooning duties and was certainly important in developing the character.... Sloper was possibly influenced by Dickens's Mr Micawber and maybe certain characters in *Punch* (e.g. the cockney "Arry"), but soon developed his own conniving charm and became the most popular feature of [*Judy*].[2]

As with Töpffer's Mr Wooden Head, there is a suggestion of influence from Combes and Rowlandson's Dr Syntax, but rather than being a pompous upper class buffoon Ally Sloper is a working class buffoon with ideas above his station. This enormously popular character appeared in his own comic, *Ally Sloper's Half Holiday* (1884), and for three decades he was widely merchandised and appeared in film versions. Sabin points out that there is some evidence that Sloper may even have been the inspiration for Charlie Chaplin's "little tramp" character, as Chaplin was born in London in 1889 and in a revealing interview with journalist Victor Thompson in 1957 he noted that he enjoyed reading comics as a boy. He said,

> Ah, those comics. The wonderfully vulgar paper for boys [*Illustrated Chips*] with "Casey Court" pictures, and the 'Adventures of Weary Willie and Tired Tim,' two famous tramps with the world against them. There's been a lot said about how I evolved the little tramp character who made my name. Deep, psychological stuff has been written about how I meant him to be a symbol of all the class war, of the love-hate concept, the death-wish and what-all. But if you want the simple Chaplin truth behind the Chaplin legend, I started the little tramp simply to make people laugh and because those other old tramps, Weary Willie and Tired Tim, had always made me laugh.[3]

Sloper was also an influence on W. C. Fields, whose routines involved him performing as a drunken misanthrope. Clearly there was a strong transatlantic connection at work here, again pointing to a complex transnational relationship between texts, media and artists.

One of the key British publishers of the time was James Henderson, who released *Funny Folks* in 1874 and then *Scraps* in 1883. A strong transatlantic connection was evident in the latter title, which reprinted (some might say plagiarized) material from American publications such as *Puck* and *Life*. Seeing the success of Ally Sloper comics, *Funny Folks*, and *Scraps*, a young journalist named Alfred Harmsworth, who had been a writer for Henderson, revolutionized British comics by introducing weekly publications such as *Comic Cuts* and *Illustrated Chips*, both of which ran from 1890 to 1953. Crucially, Harmsworth was looking toward America for inspiration as well as at his competitors, as seen in the first issue of *Comic Cuts*, which—following the example of *Scraps*—opened with an issue that simply reprinted American material. *Comic Cuts* and *Illustrated Chips* were enormously successful, and Harmsworth soon shifted his attention to finding original British strips. He was also committed to making his publications cheaper, charging half a penny and thereby undercutting the penny publications, including the penny dreadfuls that had dominated the market.

This, along with his notable success in establishing a range of newspapers and magazines, led to Harmsworth's setting up Amalgamated Press in 1901. This would firmly establish the marketplace for British comics and make Harmsworth, or Lord Northcliffe as he became, extremely wealthy and powerful. Amalgamated Press became the largest publisher of periodicals in the world, led by Harmsworth's unfailing business instinct.[4] His innate sense of what the buying public wanted resulted in his being a pioneer not only in comics but also in tabloid journalism, in the latter field creating *The Daily Mail* and *The Daily Mirror*. Whereas America had Pulitzer and Hearst, Britain had Harmsworth, and all three would have a huge influence on the development of comics.

For several decades, Amalgamated Press defined the look and format of British comics, in which images typically were arranged in a grid, accompanied by text underneath. In many cases, the images merely illustrated the descriptions given in the text. This mode was shared by American publications for most of the nineteenth century, but their newspaper strips became much more dynamic and visually appealing toward the end of the century, which greatly influenced American comics. Strips like Richard F. Outcault's *The Yellow Kid* (1895–1898) show a transition from one form to the other, significantly advancing the use of word balloons. But by the time Winsor McCay was creating *Little Nemo in Slumberland* (1905–1926), text had become secondary to fantastic, striking visuals and experimental use of form. The influence of McCay and others, like George Herriman in his *Krazy Kat* (1913–1944), took American newspaper strips in a new direction, perhaps influenced by cinema and later animation, and this meant less dependency on blocks of text to tell the story. This was made possible by the very profitable market for syndicated newspaper strips to fill the funnies and by the support from magnates like William Randolph Hearst and Joseph Pulitzer. The paper quality, reproduction techniques, and space given to the American funnies provided a much better platform than the one in Britain, and America took the lead, producing the best comic art in the world at this time, with humor the dominant mode.[5] The influence of American comics was considerable. Indeed, the reason the medium is known as "comics" in the Anglo-American world is that this was the time when the medium was at the height of its popularity, and newspaper strips (or comics or funnies) where humor was the main genre were the dominant mode. But there were other successful branches of serial publication—the penny dreadfuls, boy's weeklies, and pulp magazines—and it is in these publications that protosuperheroes began to appear.

The adventure publications aimed at adolescent male readers became known as the boy's weeklies, and they dominated publishing for younger readers throughout the late nineteenth and early twentieth centuries before being displaced by comics in the 1930s. However, the origins of the boy's weeklies is very much tied up with the penny bloods (later known as penny dreadfuls)—appearing in the 1830s—which were decidedly less morally upstanding and much more sensationalistic, featuring prominent villains, many of whom proved to have a considerable influence on later British comics. The penny dreadfuls drew on one of the most successful and popular publishing sensations of the age—gothic literature. Given the widespread popular appeal of the gothic and its exploration of horror and sexuality, it was no surprise that in pursuit of adolescent male readers, publishers set juvenile publications on a direct collision course with the gothic. This resulted in some of the most thrilling and disturbing popular entertainment of the time, which played a considerable part in shaping the popular adventure genre that would go on to influence the development of the superhero.

Penny Dreadfuls

The term *penny dreadful* describes a type of lurid and sensational publication that became popular in the 1830s and often featured stories about real criminals or else reprinted popular gothic novels, often in the form of unauthorized versions. They were originally known as penny bloods in reference to their frequently violent content, becoming known as penny dreadfuls in the 1860s. These pulp periodicals featured highwaymen, pirates, and other disreputable types like Dick Turpin or supernatural creatures like Spring-Heeled Jack, while others were based on popular melodramas or were torn from the headlines of newspapers. This, along with the fact that they sold for a penny, was the key to their success, as they were relatively affordable and highly entertaining. They appeared weekly and were usually around eight pages long with striking covers, which were often sensational and carried strong suggestions of sex and violence. They served the urban working classes' need for cheap, entertaining reading material. Later, in the 1880s, paper quality improved slightly, the typical page count rose to sixteen, and the quality of the illustrations improved, but the subject matter was the most important thing, and the more lurid the better.

However, despite their reputation, the periodicals that were lumped together under the term *penny dreadful* were actually quite diverse, covering several genres, but it was the ones that had a particular emphasis on crime and horror that gained the most attention. This focus on crime stemmed from a long tradition of "murder pamphlets" and other texts that gave detailed accounts of murders or other shocking crimes and often took the form of narratives based on (supposedly) transcribed confessions given by criminals shortly before execution. Variations on this theme had been popular for centuries, and there was a ready market for them. The emphasis on low crimes, dastardly deeds, and the activities of the authorities to ensnare criminals made for good entertainment value, much of it highly exaggerated to maximize public appeal.[6]

The other influence came from fashionable literature of the time, namely, gothic fiction. The huge popularity of the "literature of sensation" was linked to the murder pamphlets in that both reveled in gory accounts of murder and crime, but gothic literature added a concern with the supernatural, which sprung from myths and folklore. When serial publications became highly popular in the early nineteenth century, all of these influences were clearly in evidence, and while they initially appealed to a broad audience, as the century wore on they focused more on adolescent male readers and increasingly drew on gothic literature. As E. S. Turner notes in *Boys Will Be Boys* (1948), a study of boy's adventure stories of the nineteenth and early twentieth centuries,

> Popular fiction of the early nineteenth century was steeped in darkness and diablerie. Spectres gliding in a green phosphorescence, hags picking over the bones of charnel houses, deathsheads in closets, heirs to great estates chained in dungeons, forests stuffed with robbers and werewolves, graves creaking open in the moonlight to let the vampires out—these were the stock-in-trade of the Gothic, and the bogus Gothic, novelist. The vogue for these romantic horrors had been set by Horace Walpole (*The Castle of Otranto*), Ann Radcliffe (*The Mysteries of Udolpho*) and Matthew Gregory Lewis (*The Monk*): and there were plenty of pens ready to imitate, translate, paraphrase or purloin for the benefit of the literate fringe of the working classes.[7]

Many penny dreadfuls were, therefore, essentially pirate versions of gothic stories or a mode of subgothic. So despite the success and popularity of the more wholesome story papers in the early years of the nineteenth century, their rather safe adventures stories soon faced fierce competition from the even cheaper and far more sensationalistic penny dreadfuls. These were particularly popular among older children, who were drawn to the more challenging and controversial content; the readership, however, was in no way limited to a particular age group, although as Turner points out, "the first 'penny dreadfuls' were not aimed at the juvenile market, but the scalp-tingling subject matter readily seduced the young from their lukewarm loyalty to *Robinson Crusoe* and *Quintin Durward*."[8]

The publisher most closely associated with the penny dreadfuls was Edward Lloyd, who had great success with a range of penny publications. Indeed, the first penny blood was *Lives of the Most Notorious Highwaymen, Footpads, &c*, published by Lloyd in 1836. It is believed that Lloyd himself coined the term *penny blood*, and he was certainly behind the drive toward ever more violent and gory stories featuring murderers and thieves, both real and imagined. However, Lloyd found even greater success in the 1840s with *Lloyd's Illustrated London Newspaper* (later to become *Lloyd's Weekly Newspaper*), and he eventually abandoned penny bloods to concentrate on his more reputable publications. However, when he was creating penny bloods, he did so with a keen business sense. It was noted by Thomas Frost in his *Forty Years' Recollections* (1860) that Lloyd and his editorial team often tried out stories on the office boy or a servant or young factory worker. If they enjoyed the stories, then then knew they were reaching their core demographic.[9] Lloyd also gathered a team of writers in his Salisbury Square offices, near Fleet Street, the heart of publishing in Britain; these included Thomas Peckett Prest and James Malcolm Rymer, the co-creators of *Sweeney Todd*.[10] These writers, who formed the Salibsury Square School, were put to work imagining blood-curdling scenarios for serialized gothic stories in between plagiarizing works by Dickens, only slightly altering titles and character names. Their stories were published anonymously, and in any case, there was no easily enforceable law against literary piracy, so Lloyd and his team enjoyed great commercial success. Their output was prodigious, as there were so many periodicals to service all at once, and as far as the penny dreadfuls were concerned, no scenario or disturbing detail that they could concoct was too much for the eager readers. Indeed, the spirit of competitive gory one-upmanship that was fostered among the writers led to horrors far in excess of much gothic literature.

One example of the extremes that the penny dreadful would reach was *Varney the Vampire, or The Feast of Blood* (1845–1847), by the extremely prolific James Malcolm Rymer. This was one of the most famous and blood-soaked penny dreadfuls of the time. It very much drew on the gothic tradition, but its biggest claim to fame comes from the fact that it had a huge influence on Bram Stoker's *Dracula* (1897), which was written fifty years later. *Varney the Vampire* is, rather than Stoker's more well-known text, the origin point for many of the tropes associated with the figure of the modern vampire. The sensational images that accompanied the text were a very important aspect of the serial's success. Varney would be shown assaulting a beautiful young woman while she lay in bed, with obvious sexual overtones, and the descriptions given in the text also made clear the sexual nature of these attacks.

Rymer and Prest were also responsible for *The String of Pearls: A Romance*, which introduced Sweeney Todd. It was published weekly by Lloyd across eighteen parts in *The People's Periodical* and *Family Library* (1846–1847). It is likely that Rymer and Prest took turns, writing alternating parts. It was later collected as a book under the title *The String of Pearls: The Barber of Fleet Street, A Domestic Romance* (1850). In many ways this was, like *Varney the Vampire*, the archetypal penny dreadful, being overtly sensationalistic and depicting immoral, taboo-breaking violence. In the case of *Varney the Vampire*, it was rape (or a thinly disguised version of it), and in *The String of Pearls* it was cannibalism, which was another very popular theme for penny dreadfuls. Here were two villains, Varney and Sweeney Todd, who were possessed of supernatural powers or unhuman appetites but whom the reading public were rooting for. In comparison, the characters who pursued them, the upholders of law and order, were boring. Very rarely did the heroes match up to the appeal of the villains. As Dave Gibbons notes, "It was a trope in British comics that the lead character would be a villain. Usually there would be a bumbling policeman whose job it was to catch the criminal, but the main focus was on the bad guy." This trope can be traced right back to the penny dreadfuls.[11]

Another highly successful writer of penny dreadfuls was G. W. M. Reynolds, who came from a distinguished military family and who himself received a military education. He turned to writing when he took possession of his inheritance on the death of his parents in 1829 and established himself as one of the most widely read authors in English of his day. He was the editor and a writer for *The London Journal* when it was established in 1845. It was one of the most popular magazines in Britain in the nineteenth century, but his interests in sensational literature led him to a hugely successful career as a writer of serialized fiction. His *Wagner, the Wehr-Wolf* (1845), was another example of the penny dreadful's debt to gothic horror.

This story followed the title character, Wagner, through his transformation into a werewolf following a pact made with the devil.

However, Reynolds found greater success when he moved away from explicit gothic horror and focused on crime and detection. His most famous long works were *The Mysteries of London* (1844–1846) and its sequel, *The Mysteries of the Court of London* (1848–1856). These works, which borrowed heavily from Eugène Sue's serialized novel *Les Mystères de Paris* (The Mysteries of Paris, 1842–1843), which established the "city mystery" genre, mixed the sensational aspects of the gothic novel with more down-to-earth matters of urban poverty and crime. The emphasis on working-class life, the seedy underworld, and the explicit portrayal of sexual themes made Reynolds's work more relevant to his readers than most literature of the day. His writing was extremely popular with lower- and middle-class readers, perhaps because his characters were not simply evil or degraded but were instead a reflection of their environment. This approach derived from Reynolds's own radical politics (he was a prominent socialist and Chartist), and his use of lurid descriptions of crime and violence were targeted at addressing social problems, but he also gave readers what they wanted—an entertaining story that did not preach to them. Importantly, the illustrations were also striking and helped to sell the stories, which were popular in both Britain and America. Indeed, the city mystery genre really took off in American serial publication, and soon similar stories appeared featuring cities throughout the United States. Again, in Reynolds's work there were few obvious heroes but several villains for whom the reader is encouraged to have some sympathy. This was a pattern that would define many penny dreadfuls and establish a long-running trait in British popular fiction, including the boy's weeklies and comics of the twentieth century, where heroes were frequently much less interesting than villains.

Naturally, the rise of the penny dreadful could not be sustained indefinitely, and in time a backlash would emerge.[12] In the 1860s, when the term *penny dreadful* started to replace *penny blood*, a new type of story appeared. These stories were less influenced by the gothic novel and were much less political and explicit in terms of sex and violence. Their readership was also narrower as they targeted younger male readers, and while these stories were still referred to as "penny dreadfuls," the term *penny blood* could hardly be applied to them. These were sanitized and much closer to the likes of *The Boys' and Girls' Penny Magazine*. This was largely because a fear emerged that penny dreadfuls might be influencing young minds. The questions asked of the penny dreadfuls are all too familiar: Were these read at the expense of more "improving" stories? Did they sensationalize violence and crime? Were they responsible for perceived rises in what was later called juvenile delinquency? Such questions have always haunted comics, and all mediums associated with children have been scapegoats for wider social problems at some point. As with later moral panics, children's popular culture was attacked because it is easier to blame that material than it is to address the underlying economic and social causes. The penny dreadfuls might not have contained the best written or improving of stories, but they were a huge success among the poor but literate classes in urban and industrial centers and were passed around and shared, so their reach was considerably greater than their print runs.

There were those who argued that these publications were not just dreadful but morally harmful due to their focus on criminals and salacious subjects and educationally harmful because they were badly written. These objections were couched in terms of concern for the poor, but the fear of penny dreadfuls was more likely driven by anxiety over their influence and the potential for political subtexts to spark revolution, or at least to reveal social inequalities. However, the penny dreadfuls also had notable supporters, such as G. K. Chesterton, who argued that the claim the penny dreadfuls encouraged juvenile delinquency was ridiculous, pointing out that the notion that these publications lacked literary merit was misguided on two fronts, first, because the criminal exploits detailed in them were also to be found in literary works, and second, because "literary worth" was secondary to the function of fiction, which was to inspire the imagination. In *The Defendant* (1901), he argued that the dreadfuls were in no way lacking in that regard.[13] Even Thomas Wright, in his investigations of the working-class culture of the time, argued that they did not necessarily lead to crime, although he noted that they had usurped the place of "the natural reading for boys" which would make them more cultured than reading the penny dreadfuls.[14] As Kevin Carpenter notes in his introduction to *Penny Dreadfuls and Comics* (1983),

> The phrase "penny dreadful" encapsulates an attitude and an over-simplification. It was invented as a term of abuse to denigrate penny-part novels and cheap weekly periodicals, devoted mainly to tales of sensation and adventure and illustrated with lurid woodcuts, which were published for the amusement of working-class youth from the 1860s on.... There was general agreement amongst teachers, clergymen, magistrates and journalists that the penny dreadful glorified crime; that its boy-readers were tempted into a

life of degradation and theft; that the amount of this garbage on the market was enormous; and that some kind of suppression should be placed on these publications. These were received truths, and few people actually bothered to examine the story-papers they assailed with such fury. Certainly, some of these booklets were shocking enough, brutal and inhuman, and deserved to be called "dreadful." But the expression "penny dreadful" became a term of blanket condemnation, applied to the whole field of popular juvenile fiction which was scarcely justifiable.[15]

Carpenter also points out that one of those who attacked the penny dreadful was Edward Salmon, who wrote in his *Juvenile Literature As It Is* (1888) that penny dreadfuls were "degrading and debilitating" and would lead to the "moral and material ruin of the working class."[16] However, despite the fact that the publications were cheap and often crude, their influence was considerable. Indeed, Robert Louis Stevenson, author of *The Strange Case of Dr Jekyll and Mr Hyde* and *Kidnapped* (both 1886), was by his own admission addicted to penny dreadfuls as a youth, and they clearly influenced his own writing.[17] Moreover, these publications likely increased literacy by making available reading material in which working-class readers were interested and actively sought out. However, as far as their critics were concerned, the "dreadfulness" of such publications was less to do with aesthetic quality or production standards and much more to do with the fact that some of them were aimed at working-class and adolescent readers and were therefore politically volatile, potentially stoking fires of discontent among the masses.[18] Whether or not this was the case, the majority of the penny dreadfuls certainly rejected the modesty and piety of mainstream popular fiction and featured rebellious, even villainous characters, who were sometimes portrayed sympathetically. This, then, may have been the crucial point. The penny dreadfuls were not pious and moralistic, did not preach to the working classes, offered representations of poverty and crime that were relevant to their lives and experience, and portrayed characters who rebelled against law and order. Rather than being harmful to the working classes, the penny dreadfuls were threatening to the status quo and a site of potential revolutionary discord. The supernatural or criminal characters portrayed were compelling, and unlike American adventure stories and comics, where good and evil were much more clearly delineated, the moral ambiguity in these stories persisted in British popular culture long after the penny dreadfuls were gone.

Renewed attacks on violent and lurid serial publications came from Lord Shaftsbury in an 1878 lecture to the Religious Tract Society, where he warned of the "frightful issues" that were brought into the homes of the poor and the privileged alike by these publications. In this speech he invoked the image of the penny dreadful as a monster or murderer, saying that they were "creeping" into homes and "penetrating" them with insidious ideas.[19] Such texts were seen by Shaftsbury as a place for liberal sentiments to grow, and so it was often attacked by conservative forces. It was no surprise, then, that concern over the effect of the penny dreadfuls was accompanied by a move to supplant them with sanitized and politically conservative replacements. This trend toward morally sound material was seen in the publication of the first successful boy's weekly by Samuel Beeton, who offered *The Boy's Own Magazine*, launched in 1855 and running until 1890. By the mid-1850s, other publications aimed at adolescents that were rather more wholesome had started to appear. As Stefan Dziemianowicz notes in his introduction to *Penny Dreadfuls*, his 2014 collection of stories,

> Like the Gothic novel, the penny dreadful enjoyed a brief but spectacular interval of popularity. By the 1850s, penny dreadfuls had given way to penny papers for boys, such as *The Boy's Own Paper*, *Boys of England*, and *The Young Gentleman's Journal*. Writers continued to produce serial stories for these penny papers, but the luridness of their content was greatly toned down, much to the relief of worried parents and protectors of public morality.[20]

Another exemplar of this change was *The Boys of England*, a story paper that appeared in 1866, created by Edwin J. Brett, a former publisher of penny bloods. Indeed, his were more bloody than most, with stories such as the controversial "The Wild Boys of London" (1866), which featured a gang of wild children who lived in the sewers and stole dead bodies. He made a fortune with such tales. In stark contrast, *The Boys of England* was directed at a younger readership and featured schoolboy heroes such as Jack Harkaway. This character proved to be a runaway hit. A runaway from school, he nevertheless adhered to a strict code of honor and duty. So popular was the character, created by Bracebridge Hemyng, that he had a considerable following on both sides of the Atlantic. Harkaway was a far cry from "The Wild Boys of London," Dick Turpin, or Varney the Vampire. Here was a hero whose values were pure and whose love of adventure took him around the world. He was the kind of idealistic imperialist schoolboy that Joseph Conrad would undermine forever in his novel *Heart of Darkness* (1899).

In Harkaway, the reader encounters all the moral certitude and spirit of boundless enthusiasm that is drained from Marlow over the course of his colonial experience in Conrad's novel. Still, Harkaway was a hero that the readers of *The Boys of England* could aspire to emulate. With publications like this, the emphasis shifted from villains and monsters to do-gooding heroes. More wholesome entertainment came in the form of *The Boy's Own Paper*, which appeared in 1879, produced by the Religious Tract Society with the aim of instilling Christian values in young men.[21] This publication was inspired by Lord Shaftsbury's lecture to the Society the previous year. The Society clearly took his warning seriously, and *The Boy's Own Paper* was a huge success. A host of copycat titles soon followed. The boy's weeklies had arrived.

Boy's Weekly Story Papers

Part of the appeal of the penny dreadfuls was that the stories featured in these publications were of the "blood and thunder" variety. They were hugely entertaining and kept the reader gripped and desperate for the next installment. When the dreadfuls were on the wane in the 1860s, publishers were desperate to hold onto readers while also appearing responsive to demands for more responsible subject matter. The strategy that many adopted was to keep the "blood and thunder" tone and the spirit of high adventure but to reduce the gore and make the protagonists heroes rather than villains or monsters. The characters in the boy's weeklies were therefore usually quite simple types—heroic adventurers who were, for the most part, upstanding, moral, and noble and dastardly villains (though rarely murderous ones) who were criminals or savages. The stories promoted masculine behavior and imperialist values, celebrating the empire as an opportunity for adventure in the colonies or at war.[22] Occasionally, the villains would be a bit more inventive, but in the main the characters, like the stories, were quite predictable and repetitive. The stories were calculated to be exciting above all else, and despite claims that they were improving literature, there was little in the way of characterization, nuance, or literary qualities in these stories, and what little was present was not as important as keeping the reader gripped and returning each week for the next installment.

The goal of the boy's weeklies was to provide content that was more exciting and spirited than the earlier story papers aimed at younger children, which were full of games and puzzles, while also being much less sensational, and therefore less supposedly harmful than the penny dreadfuls. Stefan Dziemianowicz observes that in America, "The boy's papers were the forerunners of the nickel weeklies dime novels popular at the end of the nineteenth century," and that in both Britain and America they were "more wholesome publications [which] tended to feature stories with young heroes who triumphed over circumstance through pluck and luck, as well as cowboys, crime-solvers, and real historical figures."[23] As Kelly Boyd notes in *Manliness and the Boy's Story Paper in Britain: A Cultural History, 1855–1940* (2003),

> The boy's story paper formed the central core of young male reading from the middle of the nineteenth century to the Second World War. Jammed full of adventure tales, school stories, detective thrillers and science fiction, leavened with the occasional non-fiction feature, story papers served to entertain the average boy and provide him with a world view. They were cheap, easily purchased, traded, abandoned and lost . . . but between 1855 and 1940 they were the established leisure activity of millions of boys in a day when comics had yet to be invented.[24]

Boyd also observes that the story papers, while "quick to respond to events of the day, allowing their popular characters to take part in important movements in society" and "expert at adapting themselves to the changing tastes of their readers," were also inherently conventional, "[echoing] the conservatism of schoolboys eager to understand the world and fit into it rather than reshape it."[25] Whereas the villains of penny dreadfuls could be transgressive and, in the hands of writers like Reynolds, could serve as a call to arms to the poor and exploited, the boy's weeklies were politically neutered and, as Boyd suggests, were aimed at maintaining the status quo. This point is also made by George Orwell in his 1940 essay "Boy's Weeklies," where he says,

> There is no clear reason why every adventure story should necessarily be mixed up with snobbishness and gutter patriotism. For, after all, the stories in the *Hotspur* and the *Modern Boy* are not Conservative tracts; they are merely adventure stories with a Conservative bias. It is fairly easy to imagine the process being reversed. It is possible, for instance, to imagine a paper as thrilling and lively as the *Hotspur*, but with subject-matter and "ideology" a little more up to date.[26]

In spite of this, readers clearly found something aspirational and inspirational in these publications, and there was a fierce battle for the attention of this young readership, which resulted in the penny dreadfuls being on the wane by the early 1890s. However, Harmsworth wanted to put an end to any lingering competition from penny dreadfuls, so he aimed to put them out of business completely while also undercutting any competition from the other boy's weeklies. Therefore, he published even cheaper weeklies such as *Halfpenny Marvel*, *The Union Jack*, and *Pluck*. These featured morally uplifting tales, at least at first. Soon they were almost as lurid and sensationalistic as the penny dreadfuls had been, only cheaper. In the end, these "Ha'penny dreadfullers" effectively drove the penny dreadfuls out of business, not because they offered a more wholesome alternative, but because they undercut them. Harmsworth's weekly story papers began to assert greater dominance in the field, and soon he created a range of comics to accompany them, including the long-running *Comic Cuts* in 1890. As noted earlier, the first issue reprinted American comic strips that had already been published by Harmsworth's former employer, James Henderson, in his comic *Scraps*. However, after publishing an advertisement calling for comics creators to provide new content, Harmsworth was soon publishing original British material. He followed *Comics Cuts* with *Illustrated Chips* in the same year. Both ran until 1953, inspiring a host of imitators along the way. Harmsworth's gambit of cutting the price to a half penny had worked, and his company, Amalgamated Press, took a premier place in the emerging comics industry.

Harmsworth's weekly story papers introduced the character of Sexton Blake, a detective very much in the mold of Sherlock Holmes who went on to become a considerably successful character. Created by Harry Blyth, Sexton Blake appeared in 1893 in Harmsworth's halfpenny story paper *The Marvel*, just six years after the first Sherlock Holmes story was published. Some of the similarities between the two characters were striking: they were both private detectives who offered their services as consultants; they often worked with the police; both resided in Baker Street in London; and both had companions, Dr Watson in Holmes's case and Tinker in Blake's (although Tinker was a later addition, appearing in 1904). Whereas Watson served as narrator and was an experienced military man, Tinker was a much younger man who was something of a sidekick. In the Blake stories, the Dr. Watson role was displaced onto Detective Inspector Coutts, who served as Blake's main contact with the police. Blake was certainly less of an eccentric than Holmes, but both were recognized as geniuses. However, one of the key differences between Holmes and Blake was that Blake changed considerably over the course of his stories, largely due to the fact that while Holmes's stories were written by one man, Arthur Conan Doyle, Sexton Blake's adventures were written by almost two hundred different writers.

While Sexton Blake had first appeared in *The Marvel* in 1893, it was his place in Harmsworth's *Union Jack*, which started in 1894, that brought him to a large readership. *Union Jack* ran till 1933, and Sexton Blake was a permanent feature in it. When *Union Jack* folded, Blake survived by making the move to *Detective Weekly*, which ran until the 1940s, when it became a victim of wartime paper shortages. Although Sherlock Holmes is now a household name, for a long time Sexton Blake was the more popular and well-known character. Indeed, such was his popularity that in 1915 the Sexton Blake Library was started. This was a series of novel-length stories that ran until 1968. Also, several comics featuring Blake ran through the 1960s to the late 1970s. His adventures were popular with an international readership and were widely translated. There were also a great many adaptations into film and television between 1909 and 1960, along with several stage plays. Blake also had a popular radio series in the 1930s. While Blake was not a superhero, his stories firmly established some of the tropes of the genre through a range of strange and exotic villains and master criminals. Indeed, after the turn of the century, Blake's villains threatened to outshine him, and by the 1920s many of them were, in effect, supervillains. Examples include Count Bonali (who appeared in 1920), a criminal whose eyes glowed, allowing him to see in the dark; Dr Satira (1926), an evil genius who could control animals; and Mr Mist (1928), a disfigured inventor who created an invisibility ray and used it to commit crimes. These are just a few of the bizarre master criminals with supernatural abilities who appeared in Sexton Blake stories. Any one of these could very reasonably be called supervillains, the only problem being that they were not matched by a superhero. Blake was a genius detective and extraordinary in any number of ways, but he was no superhero.

With the success of Sexton Blake and several major publications, Harmsworth's Amalgamated Press expanded again in the early years of the twentieth century with *The Gem* (1907–1939) and *The Magnet* (1908–1940), which meant that Harmsworth's publications practically cornered the market for story papers. There was some competition from publisher Trapp Holmes, who produced *Smiles, Funny Cuts,* and *Vanguard,* but in the end Harmsworth won out. However, *Vanguard* was notable for its focus on stories set in schools, and this had a lasting impact. Such was the success of Harmsworth's line that *Boys' Friend Library,* which ran from 1906 to 1940, collected stories that had been previously published in story papers such as *The Gem, Magnet,* and *The Boy's Friend*. Like most boy's story papers, Harmsworth's magazines dealt with a range of subjects and a number of genres, from schoolboy adventures to war stories, historical tales, fantasy, and science fiction. Some were straitlaced and dramatic, while others were played for laughs. The stories in *Gem* and *Magnet* were mainly the work of one man, Charles Hamilton, an incredibly prolific writer who created a huge number of school stories, including the popular Greyfriars School stories that featured the obnoxious and comically overweight schoolboy, Billy Bunter, which Hamilton wrote for *The Magnet* under one of his pen names, Frank Richards. The legacy of the school genre was the huge popularity of child characters in British comics, and this perhaps explains why the American superhero Captain Marvel, whose alter ego was a young boy, was copied so much in Britain in the postwar years (see Chapter Three).

The popularity of the boy's weeklies continued to grow throughout the early twentieth century, but despite the fact that the most extreme content associated with the penny dreadfuls was gone, these publications were still a source of anxiety to some, who set about using these weeklies as convenient scapegoats for a range of social problems. In *Boy Life and Labour: The Manufacture of Inefficiency* (1914), Arnold Freeman undertook a study of young boys in the workforce in Birmingham over a period of several years, charting their activities and cultural interests in an attempt to discover why some of the boys were deteriorating in character and employability. When he turned his attention to what he called "Cheap Literature," he found that

> of all the boys . . . questioned scarcely any patronised the public libraries; very few indeed read any better-class literature. The bulk of them, as do many boys of the middle classes, read what are called "penny dreadfuls" and "halfpenny comics." These can be bought second-hand very cheaply indeed; they are freely circulated from one boy to another, and are read to the exclusion of almost all other literature, except perhaps Sporting and Police News in the Mail. There is a widespread impression that this literature is of a most pernicious character; but, it certainly seems to me that its evil influence has been exaggerated, and that it is not so harmful to the boy as either the Picture Palace or the Music Hall. . . . Working-boys are not greatly interested in things of real life; they want sensation, excitement, melodrama; they love romance, no matter how fantastic or far-fetched. Their imaginations are prepared for any flight of fancy; their instincts are all agog for anything that is lurid or weird or bloodthirsty; and the literature that is prepared for them makes the most direct appeal to these boyish instincts. The boy, tired with a real life that presents little enough of romance, finds a vent for all the emotional stirrings.[27]

Other notable criticisms came from author George Orwell in "Boy's Weeklies," where he noted that the politics of these publications were completely ossified.

> [In the Boy's Weeklies] there is no political development whatever. The world of the *Skipper* and the *Champion* is still the pre-1914 world of the *Magnet* and the *Gem*.... And except that Americans are now admired instead of being laughed at, foreigners are exactly the same figures of fun that they always were. If a Chinese character appears, he is still the sinister pigtailed opium-smuggler of Sax Rohmer; no indication that things have been happening in China since 1912—no indication that a war is going on there, for instance. If a Spaniard appears, he is still a "dago" or a "greaser" who rolls cigarettes and stabs people in the back; no indication that things have been happening in Spain. Hitler and the Nazis have not yet appeared, or are barely making their appearance. There will be plenty about them in a little while, but it will be from a strictly patriotic angle (Britain versus Germany), with the real meaning of the struggle kept out of sight as much as possible. As for the Russian Revolution, it is extremely difficult to find any reference to it in any of these papers.... The clock has stopped at 1910. Britannia rules the waves, and no one has heard of slumps, booms, unemployment, dictatorships, purges or concentration camps.[28]

However, the publishers knew that the readers' desire for sensation, excitement, and melodrama meant potentially huge profits if they could appeal to those desires. Attracted by this eager audience, other publishers stepped into the field of adventure comics. In the early 1920s, the hugely successful publications of Amalgamated Press suddenly faced competition from Scotland. Dundee-based publisher DC Thomson unleashed what would become known as "The Big Five": *Adventure* (1921–1961), followed by *The Wizard* (1922–1963), *The Rover* (1922–1961), *The Skipper* (1930–1941), and *The Hotspur* (1933–1959). With a slightly rougher sensibility, these came to dominate the market, presenting a challenge to the Amalgamated Press titles and eventually overtaking them. DC Thomson even challenged Sexton Blake with its own detective, Dixon Hawke, who was based in Glasgow and appeared in the Dixon Hawke Library from 1919 and in *Adventure* and *The Sunday Post* newspaper. Amalgamated Press fought back with *The Champion* (1922–1955) and its sister publication, *The Triumph* (1924–1940), but Amalgamated Press struggled to compete and the two eventually merged in

1942 as DC Thomson continued to go from strength to strength. Part of the reason for The Big Five's success was that they responded to the American pulp magazines and superior American adventure comic strips of the time and seemed a bit more "rough and tumble" than the sanitized English boy's weeklies. This did not mean a return to the sensibilities of the penny dreadfuls, but The Big Five did offer a harder edge and were more obviously influenced by American films and pulp literature. In time they would also feature characters who were arguably early versions of superheroes and villains.

Protosuperheroes and Villains

Several protosuperhero types appeared in newspaper strips. Perhaps the most notable was Hugo Hercules, one of the first superpowered heroes, who was created by William H. D. Koerner. This character appeared in the comics supplement of the *Chicago Tribune* from September 1902 to January 1903. Hugo Hercules had prodigious strength and used his powers for good. He had no costume or secret identity, or pro-social mission, as Coogan might put it, but he never failed to help someone in need. And he had a catchphrase: "just as easy." By the late 1920s, several story papers had comic strip sections, and comics often included prose stories of the kind found in the story papers.

As time went on, the balance started to shift in favor of the comics, as text stories started to give way to them, and by the early 1960s the story papers were all but gone, or in the case of DC Thomson's Big Five, some of them were relaunched as comics. This was a marked difference with America, where the story papers had turned into dime novels and pulp magazines, which developed in a different direction than the funnies and comic books, appealing to an older readership. The American comic book industry emerged from the newspaper strips, whereas in Britain comics had grown up alongside the weeklies. Therefore, while the adventure genre in American comics came directly out of the newspaper strips, in Britain the adventure genre in comics emerged from the story papers. A notable American exception was Superman, who was inspired by Tarzan, Buck Rogers, and The Phantom newspaper strips and has often been linked to a pulp novel, *The Gladiator* (1930), by Philip Wylie, although the creators of Superman denied that connection. Moreover, Superman was first conceived of as a prose story, "Reign of the Superman" (where he was the villain), before being prepared as a newspaper strip proposal and finally appearing in a comic book. But this was the exception to the rule. The success of Superman was in part because the character was unlike most other characters appearing in comics. In Britain, the influence of story papers and penny dreadfuls on the emergence of superhero prototypes was more profound.

One of the most popular DC Thomson heroes to emerge from the story papers was Morgyn the Mighty, who originally appeared in a text story in *The Rover* #304 (February 1928) before featuring as an illustrated strip in the first issue of *The Beano* (1938).[29] The Morgyn stories in *The Rover* were heavily inspired by Tarzan stories, comics, and films, again demonstrating the close transnational and transatlantic relationship at work. Tarzan had first appeared in serialized stories in 1912 and in a book in 1914. Films followed, starting in 1918, but the most famous films starred Johnny Weissmuller; the first, *Tarzan of the Apes*, appeared in 1932. Morgyn was supposedly the strongest man in the world, and while not a superhero as such, he was indicative of the way DC Thomson's story papers were going. Usually filled with stories of cowboys, soldiers, or Royal Canadian Mounted Police, these weeklies started to move toward material highly influenced by American pulps and films. There was also a French influence in the form of Fantomas (who appeared in French crime fiction in 1911 and in films from 1913 onward). Fantomas was a prototypical master criminal and, crucially, the main character. In many of these kinds of stories, and in the great penny dreadful tradition, the heroes would be rather uncharismatic detective types and the villains much more interesting. Characters like Spring-Heeled Jack (who came right out of the penny dreadfuls) and The Winged Man, with their frightening, almost demonic appearances, were marked as morally compromised and frightening characters. Science fiction was also featured in several weeklies, showing the influence of popular literature, film, radio serials, and comic strips such as Buck Rogers and Flash Gordon. While texts like these were not about superheroes, it is clear that these adventure heroes influenced what was to come.

Some of the most common protosuperhero types appearing in the story papers were of the flying man variety, although they were not all heroic adventurers. "Dicky the Bird-Man," which started in *Comic Cuts* #1051, July 2, 1910, and ran until August 13 of that year, was created by the famed Irish painter Jack B. Yeats, who was the son of John Butler Yeats and brother of poet William Butler Yeats. Before committing himself fully to painting in 1917, Yeats had a considerable career in comics. He drew illustrations for *The Boy's Own Paper* and wrote articles for *Punch* using the pseudonym W. Bird. Starting in 1893, he created a parody of Sherlock Holmes called "Chubblock Homes," which appeared in *Comic Cuts* from 1893 to 1894 and

Fig. 1: "Dicky the Bird-Man," by Jack B. Yeats, in *Comic Cuts* #1051 (Amalgamated Press, July 2, 1910).

Funny Wonder from 1894 to 1897. His Dicky the Bird-Man was described as a "winged avenger" who protects the weak and oppressed, though his story was not the adventure series that this description makes it sound like.

Yeats was known for creating wacky characters, and Dicky the Bird-Man was no exception—a spritely old man with a set of artificial wings, who in one typical story rescues an ostrich from a hunter by disguising himself using a few feathers (see Figure 1). The character seemed to be an extrapolation from real life flying men such as Otto Lilienthal, the German aviation pioneer known as the Glider King, who flew gliders closely modeled on bird's wings in the 1890s. While Lilienthal's experiments ended in tragedy with his death in 1896, Yeats's strip is lighthearted fun. In this sense, Yeats was a pioneer in what this book argues is a key element of British comics: parody. On the other hand, "The Winged Man," which appeared in the short-lived Amalgamated Press publication *The Wonder* (1913–1914), was an adventure story quite dark in its tone, telling "the story of a strange genius who, possessed of wonderful powers of invention, sets forth to deal out justice to the evil-doers of the modern world."[30] With huge, black bat-like wings, the mind of an inventor, and a mission to bring justice to the world, The Winged Man appears to be a superhero in all but name.

However, his motives (and therefore superhero status) are not as clear as the prologue to the story implies. In his first appearance, in a story called "The Winged Man: 'Twixt Midnight and Dawn," the reader is introduced to a character who is described as "a weird and wonderful being [who] suddenly appears from out of the unknown." More precisely, his base seems to be on the "bleak Yorkshire coast in a subterranean mysterious lair which he regards as his home, and which his dwarf-like servant man, Ghat, keeps in order for him." Like Batman, who would appear twenty-five years later, The Winged Man is often on the wrong side of the law, a vigilante pursued by the police. Danby Druce, a "world-famous detective [who] has vowed to capture the Winged Man," joins forces with Professor Hexmider, an inventor who provides Druce with a pair of wings similar to those used by The Winged Man so that he can face him in aerial combat. Things become even more complex when the beautiful Mary Evanson attempts suicide and is rescued by Druce. He falls in love with her but does not know that The Winged Man, too, is in love with her. "The Winged Man" had almost all the ingredients of a superhero story, with the costume, secret identity, and hidden base, the only difference being that the focus of the story is not the hero (the detective) but the antagonist, The Winged Man himself, who is a vigilante. If Danby Druce had invented the suit to fight crime he would be a superhero, but the only reason he adopts a flying suit is so he can catch the Winged Man and return things to the status quo and to curtail the activities of the more interesting character, the mysterious and morally ambiguous Winged Man. A few years after The Winged Man there was Batsowl, a similar character who appeared in a text story in *Illustrated Chips* in 1918. He was Desmond Devance, a meek aristocrat by day who when night falls transforms into a costumed crime fighter with bat-like wings that enable him to fly and also can be used as a cape, adding to his air of mystery. In effect, the essence of what would become Batman was in evidence over thirty years before the character appeared in American comics.

In the same vein as The Winged Man and Batsowl was DC Thomson's Captain Q, who appeared in an illustrated text story in *Wizard* (August 23, 1930), with the first series running for nineteen weeks. This story saw the masked hero "fluttering" through the air on battery-powered bat wings, pursued by a detective. Then there was The Night Hawk, who appeared in *The Nelson Lee Library* as a backup feature in the 1930s. He was Thurston Kyle, a scientist who partnered with a sidekick called Sparrowhawk to fight crime in armored flying suits. Shade the Shadower, another mystery flying man, appeared in *Illustrated Chips* (1933), flying over the "lonely marshes on his mission of justice!" Later there was The Scarlet Bat–The Winged

A great shout went up from the crowd below as the wounded Scarlet Bat appeared at the window of the lofty building. Moonlight lit its red figure clearly when the weird shape strove to clamber through the window, and, as the police came over the roof, the Scarlet Bat leapt into thin air !

Fig. 2: The Scarlet Bat–The Winged Avenger, in *Film Fun Annual* (Amalgamated Press, 1943).

Avenger, who appeared in the 1943 *Film Fun* annual. The illustrations that accompanied The Scarlet Bat story were particularly effective, with some atmospheric images of the character flying through the air or surrounded by the police (see Figure 2). These illustrations were more dynamic than most produced for the story papers, and indeed, some looked quite cinematic. Clearly there was an appetite for these winged adventurers throughout the 1930s and into the 1940s, and so when reprints of American superheroes such as Batman and Hawkman later appeared, they were not entirely without precedent, although the American comics offered heroes, whereas the British protosuperheroes were mystery men and not always heroic in their motives or actions.

Another British predecessor to the masked hero was The Black Whip, who appeared in *The Ranger* (Amalgamated Press, 1931, and reprinted in *Boy's Friend Library* #381, 1933). He was Buck Sinclair, a member of the secret service who uses his skills with a whip to fight on behalf of the British government. Here was a character modeled on Zorro, the flamboyant hero of American pulp stories by New York–based writer Johnston McCulley. Created in 1919, Zorro was by 1931 the star of several films, and The Black Whip clearly draws upon them. Also in 1931, *Wizard* presented The Green Ray, a masked character who could performs incredible feats with a lantern that emits a magical green ray. This was remarkably similar to the superhero Green Lantern, created by writer Bill Finger and artist Martin Nodell, in *All-American Comics* #16 (July 1940) and published by National Periodicals, though a connection seems unlikely (though not impossible). The year 1931 also saw the appearance of The Hooded Protectors, who appeared in stories in *The Nelson Lee Library* and tied into the popularity of school genre. The Hooded Protectors were students at St Frank's School who formed a secret society to protect their school. They were led by Nipper (Richard Hamilton), the assistant of Nelson Lee, a detective character. In previous stories (from about six years earlier), Nipper had been a costumed adventurer, The Hooded Unknown (aka The Phantom Protector). Another superhero prototype was The Flaming Avenger, who appeared in *The Rover* in 1933. This hero was Mat Selwood, a radio shop owner who created his own suit of armor in order to fight crime some thirty years before Marvel comics presented the definitive armored Avenger, Iron Man, in *Tales of Suspense* #39 (March 1963). Selwood's suit had a built-in flamethrower, hence the name Flaming Avenger, and looked like a medieval suit of armor crossed with a diving suit and Ned Kelly's armor (see Figure 3).

In the same year another armored hero, called The Iron Man, appeared in *Illustrated Chips* and *The Skipper* featured Karga the Clutcher, a masked man who "makes the sparks fly" and has a metal hand, prefiguring The Steel Claw, who appeared in IPC comics in the 1960s and 1970s (see Figure 4). By this point, even humor comics like *Comic Cuts* had an adventure thriller or Western story on their back page. Some of the most popular stories featured the daring detective Kenton Steel. In one story from 1937, he tackles a notorious diamond thief known as The Phantom, who wears a black mask and wields a futuristic ray gun. This was arguably yet another case of the villain being more interesting than the hero. Clearly there were many characters

44   Penny Dreadfuls, Story Papers, and Protosuperheroes (1825–1935)

Fig. 3: The Flaming Avenger, in *The Rover* #372 (DC Thomson, 1933). The Rover © DC Thomson & Co Ltd.

in British story papers and comics who could be described as prototype superheroes or villains, but on balance there were more protosupervillains than there were superheroes.

One of the most intriguing and lasting of the protosupervillians was DC Thomson's The Black Sapper, who first appeared in a text story in *The Rover* #384 (August 1929). The illustrations for The Black Sapper were provided by DC Thomson staff artist Jack Glass, who was known for his distinctive, heavily inked style. The character of the Sapper was reminiscent of the mysterious villain Fantomas and was a mysterious villain who used a "land submarine" to burrow through the earth. The first story opens with

FREE INSIDE—THE CHASE-ME-CHARLIE PUZZLE

Fig. 4: Karga the Clutcher, in *The Skipper* #162 (DC Thomson, 1933). The Skipper © DC Thomson & Co Ltd.

the mysterious theft of a new invention (an air-replenishing apparatus) created by Commander Ben Breeze, formerly of the Royal Navy, who is described as a "world-famed war submarine hero." As Breeze is about to unveil a model of his invention to Royal Navy officers, he finds it has been stolen from under his nose, with only a hole left in the floor of the vault and a note from The Black Sapper to taunt them. Breeze is assisted in his pursuit by his cousin and sidekick, the young Danny Blair, described as "not yet seventeen." Together they track down the thief and confront his armed gang with nothing but their fists and a fire extinguisher as weapons. While Breeze and Blair were the upstanding heroes, by far the more interesting character was the Sapper. Described as "very short and slim [and] dressed entirely in black, even to a black mask over his face," The Black Sapper was an archetypal supervillain, even down to his bizarre technology and superpowers. When Breeze grapples with the Sapper, grabbing him by the shoulders, "a surprising thing happened. The shoulders beneath his fingers hardened, muscles seemed to grow beneath the thin clothing, muscles as strong as steel and as slippery as glass." At the end of the first story line (*The Rover* #402, December 28, 1929), The Black Sapper escapes using his land submarine, leaving Breeze and Danny to contemplate the threat this terrorist poses to "the whole civilised world" (see Figure 5). Breeze concludes, "The world could be held to ransom."

The Sapper returned in *The Rover* #411 (March 1, 1930) in a story that ran until *The Rover* #430 (July 12, 1930). The Sapper then reappeared in individual installments now and again in 1931. Formally, The Black Sapper stories were typical of the boy's weekly story papers, which is to say that they were prose stories each accompanied by a header image on the first page of each installment and with some spot illustrations throughout that usually had text descriptions alongside the image. The Black Sapper would prove to be a long-running character and would, when he reappeared in the 1960s, change from being a villain to a hero. So there were clearly superhero and villain prototypes in British serial publications in the decades before the genre was supposedly invented, but the American pulp magazines, as might be expected, came a lot closer to the mark.

American Pulps

American pulp magazines appeared in 1894 and were popular through to the 1950s. They were the successors to dime novels, which were more or less the equivalent to penny dreadfuls and story papers.[31] As Julian C. Chambliss and William L. Svitavsky argue in "The Origin of the Superhero: Culture, Race and Identity in US Popular Culture, 1890–1940," in *Ages of Heroes, Eras of Men: Superheroes and the American Experience* (2013), the American dime novel had become a "publishing success during the Civil War as soldiers found the melodramatic stories a diversion from wartime fears [and in peacetime as] concerns about the city displaced the agrarian-oriented view of daily life, the dime novels reflected these concerns by including the urban detective as protagonist."[32] The dime novels were usually adventure stories, and often Western or crime stories, directed at a male readership, whereas American story papers, like their British equivalents, were intended for a

Fig. 5: The Black Sapper, by Jack Glass, in *The Rover* #384 (DC Thomson, 1929). The Rover © DC Thomson & Co Ltd.

more general readership, and many were designed to appeal to families. Given the close relationship between British and American publishing, it is no surprise that there was considerable crossover, with American dime novels and later pulp magazines being reprinted in Britain. Indeed, when *Amazing Stories*, the first American science-fiction magazine, was launched in 1926, it was imported into the British market from the first issue, and several other American magazines were available in Britain in the form of imports or in repackaged form for the British market. Naturally, this soon began to influence British publications, as did the dominance of American films and newspaper strips.

Costumed adventurers were commonplace in American pulps in the 1920s, and as noted, one of the most popular of the masked men was Zorro, who may have been inspired by the 1890 Spring-Heeled Jack penny dreadful (Zorro in turn inspiring *The Black Whip*). Like Zorro, this version of Spring-Heeled Jack was a masked nobleman who fought injustice, sometimes slicing an "S" into walls with his sword, just as Zorro slices a "Z" as a calling card. There were also several "science hero" types, such as Frank Reade and his son, Frank Reade Jr., who were super inventors, creating robotic marvels. These stories began in the late 1860s, and Frank Reade Jr. was featured in serialized stories that appeared in the story paper *The Boys of New York* in the 1880s.

From these influences in dime novels and story papers came a new generation of heroes in the pulp fiction of the 1930s, and a number of these characters had mysterious powers and abilities. One of the most famous examples was The Shadow, a mysterious crime fighter with a disguise and strange psychic powers. This character first appeared in July 1930 as the narrator of the Street and Smith Detective Story Hour radio series. The mysterious figure of The Shadow, with his distinctive voice and memorable introduction ("Who knows what evil lurks in the hearts of men? The Shadow knows!") became very popular with the radio audience, and he soon appeared in his own magazine in April 1931 to meet the public's demand for stories about this enigmatic figure. These were mainly written by Walter B. Gibson under the pen name Maxwell Grant, who fleshed out the character and his world. *The Shadow Magazine* was a considerable success, so much so that the character quickly outgrew his role as a narrator for Detective Story Hour. Indeed, in 1937 The Shadow got his own radio program, and a young Orson Welles became the voice of The Shadow for a time. The show was a success and continued for a long while after Welles left in 1938, running until 1954. The Shadow also appeared in a syndicated newspaper strip, adapting the pulp stories to comic strip format, and in his own comic, both appearing in mid-1940. He has appeared in several comics since the 1940s, with a notable series in the 1970s. The Shadow inspired several imitators in pulp magazines and comics, including The Black Bat, Green Lama, The Phantom Detective, and Doc Savage and was one of the key influences on the development of early superheroes such as Batman.

The Black Bat appeared in *Black Bat Detective Mysteries*, a pulp magazine that ran for six issues starting in 1933 and running into 1934. These stories were written by Murray Leinster, one of the pen names used by William Fitzgerald Jenkins. In 1939 a character with the same name, and possibly influenced by the earlier series, was introduced by Thrilling Publications in *Black Book Detective*. These stories, written by Norman A. Daniels under the name G. Wayman Jones, set out an origin story for the crime fighter which revealed that he had been scarred and blinded and disfigured by an acid attack in a courtroom. Variations on this were later used as the origin stories for Doctor Mid-Nite in 1941, Batman's nemesis Two-Face when he first appeared in 1942, and Marvel's Daredevil in 1964. The second Black Bat and Batman were published at around the same time, leading to claims of plagiarism from both publishers and threats of legal action. Lawsuits were averted because National Periodicals editor Whitney Ellsworth, who had previously worked for the Black Bat's publishers, made peace between the rival publishers.

Indeed, rather than copying one another, it is more likely that both creative teams were influenced by the first Black Bat pulp stories from 1933 or any number of "bat avenger"–type stories that had been around for decades. The Phantom Detective also appeared in 1933, and like The Black Bat was published by Thrilling Publications. The character was created by D. L. Champion and was a masked detective and master of disguise. Richard Curtis Van Loan was an orphaned millionaire playboy who had served as a fighter pilot during the World War I before becoming a famous detective with a secret identity. This series was notable for inspiring the Bat-Signal. In one of the stories, The Phantom Detective's confidant, Frank Havens, places a beacon on the roof of the newspaper building that he owns so that it can signal the hero. The notion that this served as the model for the Bat-Signal is supported by the fact that Jack Schiff and Mort Weisinger, two editors on Batman comics, had previously worked as editors on The Phantom Detective. Doc Savage was another character influenced by The Shadow, but rather than emerging from a rival publisher, he was another Street and Smith character, designed to capitalize on their success with The

Shadow. This character was raised by a team of scientists to be the perfect human being, possessing no superpowers as such but with his mind and body honed to hear at superhuman level. *Doc Savage* magazine appeared in March 1933 and ran until 1949. He also appeared as a backup feature in The Shadow comic before starring in his own self-titled comic. There he became something closer to a superhero. As with The Shadow, there have been many versions of Doc Savage in comics, with the character passing between several publishers.

The Green Lama appeared in a story in *Double Detective Magazine* (April 1940), written by Kendell Foster Crossen using the pen name Richard Foster. This was intended as a rival to The Shadow. Like the Phantom Detective, The Green Lama (aka Jethro Dumont) was a millionaire who had inherited his fortune from his parents, very much like Bruce Wayne. He recovers from his grief at the loss on his parents by studying Buddhism in Tibet, where he acquires supernatural powers. These are supplemented by powers gained through science. His abilities are therefore born out of both spiritual and scientific knowledge. Returning to America, he quickly abandons his plans to reform American society through his Buddhist teaching and instead resolves to use his powers to fight crime. Between 1940 and 1943 the character appeared in comics, also written by Crossen.

Clearly the characters who appeared in the American dime novels and story papers were similar to those that appeared in their British equivalents, but as the pulps developed, a range of characters arose who were the precursors of the superheroes—crime fighters with strange powers and near superhuman abilities. As noted, in British boy's papers, similar costumed adventurers were appearing, usually flying men or crime fighters in armor or with advanced technology. However, in the British story papers these characters were sometimes villains, and the heroes were somewhat conventional and boring in comparison, which may have been a hangover from the penny dreadfuls, where the protagonists were often villains but were sometimes presented sympathetically. In contrast, the Western genre's dominance in the dime novels, combined with America's distorted mythology of the West as presented through its popular culture, made for more straightforward heroes whose rugged masculinity and heroic defense of innocents against Indians and outlaws established the archetypes for the superhero. This set up some crucial differences between the representation of heroes in Britain and in America, and as the political fortunes of each country reversed in regard to world power, with the fall of the British Empire and the rise of America to superpower status following World War II, these differences were magnified, while at the same time the influence of American popular culture was felt all the more strongly in Britain. However, despite these converging influences, some of the first treatments of the superhuman came from science-fiction literature.

The Coming Race, The Gladiator, and Odd John

Edward Bulwer-Lytton wrote *The Coming Race* (sometimes known as *Vril, the Power of the Coming Race*) in 1871. It told of explorers discovering an ancient underground civilization, the Vril-Ya, who are far in advance of human society, having mastered a force called Vril. (The concept of Vril became something of a fad in the late nineteenth century, with many products claiming to increase one's Vril.) The Vril-Ya live in an underground utopia and are identified as the "coming race" which, it is suggested, will one day use its superhuman abilities to conquer the Earth, not out of malice but because it is their evolutionary destiny. Vril allows them to fly, heal miraculously, bring inanimate objects to life, and destroy cities. As the narrator says, "Only, the more I think of a people calmly developing, in regions excluded from our sight and deemed uninhabitable by our sages, powers surpassing our most disciplined modes of force, and virtues to which our life, social and political, becomes antagonistic in proportion as our civilisation advances, the more devoutly I pray that ages may yet elapse before there emerge into sunlight our inevitable destroyers."[33]

The Vril-Ya are among the first superbeings in literature, but others later emerged. Philip Wylie's *The Gladiator* (1930) is famously said to have been one of the influences on Superman (though this was denied by his creators). It tells the story of Hugo Danner, who had been granted superpowers through experiments conducted by his father while he was still in the womb. He defeats the school bully, takes part in wrestling matches, and fights in World War I. His fantastic qualities include super strength, super speed, and bulletproof skin, but they bring him neither fame nor happiness, but rather misery as he is not accepted by society. Toward the end of the story, Hugo befriends a scientist who tells him that he has missed his purpose by hiding his powers and trying to gain acceptance. The scientist explains that Hugo's time would have been better spent trying to make other beings like himself and to work together to take over the world, setting themselves up as the master race and eliminating everything that they find objectionable. Distraught over this prospect, Hugo climbs a mountain alone and asks whether he has the right to question God. As if in answer, a lightning bolt strikes him and kills him instantly. Whether this is a freak accident or divine judgment is not clear, but the story ends with the scientist vowing to continue with the plan. In an introduction to the book, Wylie said,

> A temperamental consciousness of material force brought Hugo Danner into being. The frustration of my own muscles by things, and the alarming superiority of machinery started the notion of a man who would be invincible. I gave him a name and planned random deeds for him. I let him tear down Brooklyn Bridge and lift a locomotive. Then I began to speculate about his future and it seemed to me that a human being thus equipped would be foredoomed to vulgar fame or to a life of fruitless destruction. He would share the isolation of geniuses and with them would learn the inflexibility of man's slow evolution. To that extent Hugo became symbolic and *Gladiator* a satire. The rest was adventure, and perhaps more of the book derives from the unliterary excitement of imagining such a life than from a studious juxtaposition of incidents to a theme.[34]

Here Wylie identifies *The Gladiator* as a satire and reflects on the loneliness of the superhuman, indicating that some of the inspiration for the character and his powers came from what he describes as frustration with his own physical prowess and how machines humble humanity. Wylie has Danner explore some of the same thoughts.

> What would you do if you were the strongest man in the world, the strongest thing in the world, mightier than the machine? He made himself guess answers for that rhetorical query. "I would—I would have won the war. But I did not. I would run the universe single-handed. Literally single-handed. I would scorn the universe and turn it to my own ends. I would be a criminal. I would rip open banks and gut them. I would kill and destroy. I would be a secret, invisible blight. I would set out to stamp crime off the earth; I would be a super-detective, following and summarily punishing every criminal until no one dared to commit a felony. What would I do? What will I do?"[35]

It is probable that some elements of the character of Hugo Danner may have been based on American strongman and bodybuilder Bernarr Mac-Fadden (1868–1955). He was a well-known and controversial figure who built a publishing empire around physical fitness culture and pulp magazines. His outspoken views on sexuality (believing it to be a healthy activity rather than simply for procreation) and race (which were far less progressive) earned him notoriety, and he used that to promote bodybuilding and his various enterprises. His contribution to the idea of the superhero perhaps comes from the fact that it was his preference to be photographed lifting heavy weights with a look of serene, calm detachment rather than grimacing with the effort, suggesting superhuman power. Indeed, some of the images on the cover of later editions of *The Gladiator* bear a striking resemblance to MacFadden. A film version of the book came out in 1938, just months after Superman comics appeared on the newsstands, but the film was a very loose adaptation that turned the story into a comedy. Well-known comedian Joe E. Brown played the renamed Hugo Kipp, who wins some money and returns to college to play football and wrestle, rather improbably, but is given a super-serum which makes him excel, for a time.

Olaf Stapledon's novel *Odd John* (1935) is an often-overlooked precursor to the superhero, and many of the ideas that would be developed by later British comics creators as a critique of the superhero were fundamental to Stapledon's story. In the novel, a group of "super-normals" evolve and gradually become aware of each other's existence, mainly through telepathic means, which includes the ability to communicate across time. They are led by John Wainwright and the story is narrated by his human friend, who agrees to record the history of these superhumans, including the setting up of an isolated community on a remote island in the South Pacific. This narrator, a friend of John's family, traces his development as a child. His eyes are larger than they should be, and he appears much younger than he is. Indeed, as he uncovers more super-normals, it becomes clear that they are all extremely long-lived and several have remained undetected in human society for centuries. As with most of the super-normals, John's development is slow and strange. At five years old he still appears an infant and his growth appears to be stunted, but his leaps of intellectual and imaginative power quickly outstrip normal human capacity. He baffles university professors with his skills at advanced mathematics at a very young age and spends his early years honing his mental abilities, which include the ability to mentally manipulate matter. However, for all his amazing abilities, John does not seem very interested in saving humanity as a superhero might. Human concerns barely register with him, and his attention is very much focused on himself and the potential of the super-normal species. However, not all of the super-normals that he encounters are friends. Indeed, the story even has a super-villain in the form of a physically misshapen being that John meets on a trip to the Outer Hebrides. This being has a very powerful mind but is consumed by hate and terrifies John, who fears that this creature has psychically attacked him from the point of their first meeting.

John believes his kind to be the next evolutionary step and that the super-normals are poised to evolve yet further through a conscious act of will. He sets out to create the conditions in which they can flourish. Bringing together a team of fellow super-normals, he establishes a community on a remote island and develops fantastic technologies. However, in the course of doing this, John is faced with several moral and ethical dilemmas, but unlike a superhero he believes his duty to his own kind supersedes any obligation to normal humans, whom he regards as animals. In order to secure his island, he wipes out every man, woman, and child of the indigenous population, and his group also murder several people in order to protect their secrets.

At one point John says to the narrator, "Well, if we could wipe out your whole species, frankly, we would. For if your species discovers us, and realises at all what we are, it will certainly destroy us. And we know, you must remember, that Homo Sapiens has little more to contribute to the music of this planet, nothing in fact but vain repetition. It is time for finer instruments to take up the theme."[36] At the end of the novel, the humans learn of the super-normals' existence and plot to kill them, although John believes that his nemesis in the Outer Hebrides is engineering this plan, perhaps even taking mental control of the humans who attack the group. The super-normals seem to kill themselves at the close of the novel, though the ending is highly ambiguous, and it is suggested that John and his group transcend death and physical limits and perhaps travel to another dimension or time. This vision of the superhuman is the one conceived by Nietzsche—existing beyond good and evil. Stapleton's vision of superhumanity is compelling because he simultaneously captures the exotic appeal of beings so far in advance of humanity that they cannot help but inspire awe, while also portraying their inhumanity.

In this regard Stapledon was not alone, as similar themes were explored in Joseph Conrad's works and Ford Maddox Ford's *The Inheritors* (1901); H. G. Wells's *Food of the Gods* (1904); J. D. Beresford's *The Hampdenshire Wonder* (1911); and George Bernard Shaw's *Man and Superman* (1902), an apparent comedy of manners that is actually about natural selection and controlled breeding, and his *Back to Methuselah* (1923), which explores the ancient past and the far future, where humans are extremely long-lived. Stapledon's notions of the superhuman and future history are also explored in his later fiction, including *Last and First Men* (1930), *Star Maker* (1937), and *Sirius* (1944), and in time his ideas would be further explored by British comics writers such as Alan Moore, Grant Morrison, Warren Ellis, and Mark Millar. In this sense, science-fiction stories featuring superhuman characters not only influenced the first superhero characters of the 1930s but impacted them for decades to come. This came at a time when attitudes were changing rapidly. For many, the superbeings of science fiction were tied up in then-fashionable debates about eugenics, and as historian Richard Overy points out in *The Morbid Age* (2009), the notion of degeneration linked to unplanned breeding was carried over from public discourse about birth control and mental and physical illness into debates about art and culture.[37] America was seen by some as the source of pollution with its supposedly inferior art and decadent popular culture, but for others the interwar period saw a rise of something equally as poisonous from within. As historian Jan Morris observes, "Between the wars, almost for the first time, artistic intellectuals looked at the Empire speculatively in its decline, and dealt with it ironically."[38] However, as seen in this chapter and the next, the taint of irony was not limited to intellectuals but was perhaps first seen in the work of the producers of popular culture, or at the very least, they soon took up the theme with vigor.

Chapter Two

FALSE STARTS AND MINOR TRIUMPHS (1936–1949)

The influence of American comics was growing in the 1930s. The first reason was the increasing availability of the funnies, the comics sections that appeared in American newspapers. Leftover funny sections were shipped over and bundled into packets to be sold for two pence. This was a very cheap way for American comics to enter the British market, and they showcased superior American material, much to the delight of comics readers. Disney took advantage of this with a series of Mickey Mouse annuals for the British market, the first appearing in 1930. The success of these was such that Disney set up a studio in Britain and launched *Mickey Mouse Weekly* in 1936, the first British comic to use the expensive, full-color photogravure printing process. This was by far the most visually appealing and dynamic comic on the British newsstand.

As comics collector and historian Peter Hansen notes in an article on the comic, a decision rather surprisingly was taken "not to simply fill the comic with syndicated Disney strip material, but to recruit British artists and writers to produce new strips to run in the new comic. It was also decided to make the comic a mixture of strips like the popular *Film Fun* comic of the day. So in the summer of 1935, a small advert appeared in *The Daily Telegraph* (and perhaps other newspapers) inviting applicants with cartoon experience or with latent talent."[1] The comic was produced by Willbank Publications, based in London, right next to the British Disney headquarters. As Hansen says, printing the comic "was probably one of the earliest and most important jobs undertaken by Odhams Press at their new press in Watford."[2] The comic was a mixture of new British material and syndicated American strips from newspapers, and while this clearly worked and was hugely popular, there were some awkward indications of the hybrid nature of the comic, such as the use of slang and vernacular phrases that differed considerably between British and American strips. However, the success of this comic was a considerable turning point in Britain. This visually dynamic, full-color American-style comic looked very different compared to the British comics that it sat alongside on the newsstand, and British publishers would have to respond.

The success of *Mickey Mouse Weekly*, along with the popularity of the imported funnies sections, may well have been an influence on Thomas Volney Boardman's decision to launch the new titles *Wags* and *Okay Comics Weekly* in 1937.[3] *Wags* appeared in January 1937, running until November 1938, whereas *Okay Comics Weekly* appeared in October 1937 and ended in February 1938. These comics sprang from the relationship between Boardman and his partner, Joshua B. Powers, and were landmarks in the history of the relationship between the British and American (and Australian) comics industries. Boardman, whose early successes came with reprinting American science fiction and fantasy for the British market, was American by birth and came to Britain in the early 1930s. He worked for the Editors Press Service, where he was mainly absorbed in trying to sell syndicated American newspaper strips to British newspapers, although with great difficulty as American newspapers strips did not take off in Britain as they did elsewhere. Powers originally launched *Wags* as an Australian comic featuring American material in September 1936, and he and Boardman established the British version five months later. They commissioned the American Eisner-Iger studio run by Will Eisner and Jerry Iger to package American comics material for *Wags* and *Okay Comics Weekly*, which in Britain mainly sold through Woolworths, as did many of Boardman's later publications.

The Eisner-Iger shop was one of the most influential and productive comics studios in America. It played a huge role in establishing the American comic book industry in the 1930s and in growing the superhero genre. Will Eisner created covers for *Okay Comics Weekly*, and the contents included *Terry and the Pirates* by Milton Caniff and *Mutt and Jeff* by Bud Fisher. *Wags* also contained original comics, produced by the Eisner-Iger studio, such as Sheena, The Jungle Queen. Sheena was credited to W. Morgan Thomas, but that was a pseudonym for Eisner and Iger, who created a lot of the material for the studio and often adopted pseudonyms to disguise how small their staff actually was. Perhaps one of the most astounding things about *Wags* is that through the Eisner-Iger connection, some of the first published work of Jack Kirby and Bob Kane would be published in Britain. When *Wags* and *Okay Comics Weekly* were canceled, it appears that the printing plates were bought back by the Eisner-Iger studio, which went on to produce *Jumbo Comics*, reprinting the same material for the American market along with new stories. This was initially printed at tabloid size, the size used for the British market, but it quickly reverted to the standard American size. Even after *Okay Comics Weekly* and *Wags* failed, Boardman remained very interested in American comics, and as shall be discussed later, in 1940 the company entered into an arrangement with Quality Comics—which also had a close relationship with the Eisner-Iger studio and was publisher of Plastic Man and a host of other superheroes—to reprint its material in Britain.

In December 1937, DC Thomson responded to the increasing popularity of American comic books in Britain with the launch of *The Dandy*, which was followed by *The Beano* in 1938. By this point DC Thomson was in a very strong position, having consolidated its monopoly of Dundee's newspapers in the 1920s and dominated the story papers market with the success of the Big Five in the 1920s and 1930s. Given its leading position, DC Thomson was able to experiment in an effort to challenge its main rival, Amalgamated Press, and its *Comic Cuts* and *Illustrated Chips* comics, but DC Thomson was without a doubt also looking to take on *Mickey Mouse Weekly* and respond to the Boardman comics. Indeed, DC Thomson's approach demonstrated that it was looking at the American comics very closely and incorporating what was seen as the American style. The first stage came in the story papers themselves, which featured comic strips on the back covers, but in 1930 DC Thomson hit upon the idea of giving away small comic books inside their story papers. These miniature issues were called Midget Comics, and the first appeared in *The Wizard* in the 1930s, with more in *The Rover* in 1933 and 1935. These featured humorous characters like Nosey Parker and Stoney and Boney, two tramp characters (not unlike Weary Willie and Tired Tim from *Illustrated Chips*). These free comics were designed to pull readers from *Illustrated Chips* and *Comics Cuts*, and by 1937 DC Thomson was ready to challenge these comics more directly, developing *The Dandy* and *The Beano*.

The new DC Thomson comics were calculated to look very different from Amalgamated Press's comics. First, they were more compact, being half the size of the tabloid format of an Amalgamated Press comic, and they were longer, with twenty-eight pages. This felt like a much more substantial package, and for the same price (two pence) as the Amalgamated Press comics. Then there was the fact that DC Thomson privileged American-style visual storytelling on its covers, as opposed to the traditional Amalgamated Press–style of illustrations with blocks of text underneath. Instead, several strips had word balloons to give the stories the more immediate, almost cinematic appeal of American comics. The gamble worked, and *The Dandy* and *The Beano* became a double act that dominated British humor comics for decades. As Roger Sabin notes, "[*The Dandy* and *The Beano*] redefined the humour genre altogether. These comics introduced a new type of sharper, more knockabout japery, and a range of bizarre but loveable characters that made the old AP stable look decidedly dated."[4] However, DC Thomson hedged its bets, and both comics still contained traditional kinds of comics stories in the Amalgamated Press style, as well as in the story paper format, with pages of text containing spot illustrations. DC Thomson also covered several genres. While the Scottish publisher had experimented enough to make a considerable splash and undermine its competition, it was canny enough to still give readers what they expected and understood. The success of comics such as *The Dandy* and *The Beano* marked the end of the era of the boy's weeklies and the beginning of the dominance of comics. Although the boy's papers and Amalgamated Press's comics would persist for several years, they were no longer innovative or exciting, and the upsurge of comics readership in the postwar years would favor comics over story papers; furthermore, the emulation of American models would ultimately lead to the emergence of British superheroes. And then Superman arrived in Britain.

Triumph

Superman was first conceived as a character (a villain, in fact) for a story in a pulp magazine. Then it was offered to numerous newspapers as a comic strip before finally appearing in National Periodicals' *Action Comics* #1 in June 1938.[5] The success of Superman was nothing short of phenomenal, quickly reaching sales figures in excess of one million copies per issue, dwarfing sales of the then hugely popular *Life* magazine. This success ensured that the Superman stories were eventually reprinted around the world, and in Britain, Superman first appeared in Amalgamated Press's *Triumph* #772 on August 5, 1939, a little over a year after the character's debut and the first time Superman had been reprinted anywhere outside of America. Despite there being a considerable array of Superman covers on which to draw, Amalgamated Press produced its own cover images for *Triumph*, four in total (see Figure 6). These were drawn by British artist John "Jock"

60   False Starts and Minor Triumphs (1936–1949)

Fig. 6: *Triumph* #772, cover art by Jock McCail (Amalgamated Press, August 5, 1939). Superman ™ and © DC Comics.

McCail. However, rather than simply reprinting the Superman comic books as they had appeared in America, *Triumph* published Superman's origin from the syndicated newspaper strips.

This was one of the key moments in the history of superhero comics in Britain. Driven by the fact that *Mickey Mouse Weekly*, the Boardman comics, and the competition from DC Thomson pointed to the fact that British readers were eager for American comics, Amalgamated Press recognized that it needed to offer something new to readers, primarily to fight off the increasing dominance of the Dundee story papers. *Triumph* and its sister comic, *Champion*, had emerged in a period of intense competition between Amalgamated Press and DC Thomson, and by the time Superman

Fig. 7: Derickson Dene, in *Triumph*, by Nat Brand, aka Len Fullerton (Amalgamated Press, 1939).

appeared in 1939, Amalgamated Press was struggling to compete with its Scottish rival. Perhaps this is what prompted William B. Home-Gall, the editor of *Triumph*, to incorporate picture stories, and ultimately, Superman, which the magazine described as a "sensational new picture serial."[6] Superman had been a huge success in America, so this must have seemed like an ideal move. It may even have been a slightly desperate one, but given the popularity of American-style comics, it was also quite forward thinking. However, the first evidence of this new direction for *Triumph* pre-dated the appearance of Superman and appeared in early July 1939 with the first installment of Derickson Dene.

Derickson Dene was created by Len Fullerton, who used the name Nat Brand for his comic work. Fullerton, who is now best known as an illustrator of nature and wildlife, was born in Aberdeen and as a child was very much influenced by the illustrations in boy's weeklies. In his twenties he was fascinated by American newspaper strips, especially those by Alex Raymond, such as *Flash Gordon*. As comics historian Alan Clark notes, Fullerton was a "stylish adventure artist whose work emulated the American style of comic art."[7] It was perhaps this that landed him the job at *Triumph*. The introduction of Derickson Dene represented a change of policy for *Triumph* and was a landmark in British comics history, as now American-style picture stories were actually being commissioned rather than text with illustrations (see Figure 7). Indeed, Denis Gifford describes Derickson Dene as "the first British superhero in the American comic book style" (although the character is closer to a science hero than a superhero).[8] However, despite its importance, for a long time the fact that Fullerton was actually Brand was not apparent, and the reason why Fullerton chose the pseudonym Nat Brand is also a mystery, although it is possible that he thought it sounded more American than Len Fullerton, as Nat Brand does sounds like a hero from a Western story. It may also have been a pun on "natty," a colloquial term meaning "fashionable." The science hero Dene was an inventor who used his talents to combat fantastic villains, such as The Bat-Men, a gang of bank robbers working for a vampire. Dene also faced alien threats and monsters on distant planets. The character lasted less than a year, with his final appearance in *Triumph* #800 (February 17, 1940), but the series started a trend toward homegrown American-style characters and artwork that would have a huge effect on British comics. Importantly, this development was not a parody of American newspaper adventure strips but an earnest imitation of the style by an artist who admired it greatly.

Derickson Dene appeared just before the introduction of Superman, so it seems likely that it was commissioned at around the same time that the deal to reprint Superman was being worked on, pointing to a concerted effort to bring an America style into the publication. There were two series of Superman in *Triumph*, the first running from issues 772 to 792 in 1939, and the second series from issues 807 to 814 in 1940, amounting to twenty-one episodes in all. The choice of McCail for the cover art is intriguing. Born in Hartlepool in 1896, he had worked for a time at a shipyard before taking art classes. Around 1920 he went to work for DC Thomson, moving to Dundee and starting in the art department for *The Courier*, Thomson's daily newspaper. He was soon joined by his brother William, another comics artist. As Alan Clark notes in *The Dictionary of British Comics Artists, Writers, and Editors* (1998), "Around 1925 [McCail] moved to London where he became a freelance artist."[9] This was because both he and William were sacked from DC Thomson for trying to start up a union.[10] He went to work for Amalgamated Press in the early 1930s and established himself there, being tasked to do the Superman covers in the late 1930s. He was joined in London by his brother in 1940 and they both then worked for Amalgamated Press's competitor, Gerald Swan (discussed in more detail later in this chapter). Despite their skill and experience, both Jock and Bill were required to work very quickly, and this shows in a great deal of their output at this time. However, Jock McCail seems to have been given some time to work on the Superman covers for *Triumph*, as they represent some of his best work of the period. These covers clearly draw on the influence of the American Superman strips and comics, but interestingly, McCail did not simply copy an existing Superman image; rather, when Superman first appeared on the cover of *Triumph*, the image was rather startling (see Figure 6).

McCail's cover, which carried the first image of Superman to appear outside of the United States, shows Superman boldly leaping into space, the Earth far below, with the Moon and various planets in the background, at once demonstrating Superman's incredible powers while also indicating the science-fiction elements of his background (being the only survivor of the doomed planet Krypton). As normal for *Triumph*, the cover was printed in dark blue ink with an acidic yellow background. Superman's distinctive red and blue costume was therefore not on show in its full glory nor, due to the pose, the stylized "S" logo on his chest was not visible. Regardless, this was a very different cover from what readers of *Triumph*, or indeed any British weekly boy's paper, were used to. Superman seems to be leaping right out of the page in McCail's drawing, which was quite a change from the rather posed images of soldiers or cowboys that were more common on the cover of *Triumph*. Here Superman is dynamic and racing towards the reader, with the suggestion that this glamorous new American strip will be much more exciting than the usual fare.

However, McCail was very much an artist working in the British style and tradition, and like much of the work that appeared in boy's weekly adventure strips, his style had evolved to suit black and white printing on low quality paper and was therefore rather heavily rendered. This was Superman being translated into the British idiom. This is also clear on the cover of *Triumph* #775 (August 26, 1939), on which Superman throws a tree trunk (echoing two incidents in the Superman daily newspaper strips where he performs similar feats of strength), and the cover of *Triumph* #784 (October 28, 1939), which shows Superman tearing apart a steel bulkhead, lifted from a panel in a 1939 Superman newspaper strip called "Into the Steel Sanctum." McCail's covers are detailed and quite heavily rendered with lots of line work, especially compared to the interior artwork. However, by the time *Triumph* #788 appeared a few weeks later, Superman was being presented in a form more in keeping with the interior art, with more open line work and the exaggerated physique seen in the American comics. Indeed, the cover, which showed Superman lifting a car above his head, echoed the striking image from Superman's first appearance in *Action Comics* #1 as well as some panels from the newspaper serial. The character's first appearance in a British publication was therefore not as straightforward as reprinting the American comics just as they had appeared. The introduction of Superman was managed so that he appeared at once as something exotic and glamorous, a bold new kind of hero, while simultaneously presenting these strips in keeping with a British tradition. This approach was a difficult and intriguing negotiation of interests and styles. While not a parody of the American Superman, there was a certain doubling effect taking place, with a difference between how the American creators portrayed the character and how McCail did. This was also apparent in the way the material was presented.

Beyond the covers produced by McCail, the editors at *Triumph* made several other alterations. The fact that the daily newspaper strips were recut into a comic book is notable, as this was the first time that Superman's full origin story was published in comic book format anywhere in the world. That is ironic, because the American debut of Superman in *Action Comics* featured work that had been intended for newspaper strips and then was hastily recut to fit into a comic book format. In *Triumph*, the actual published newspaper strips were reshaped to fit into a British comic format (see Figures 8 and 9). In making these strips work for the British size, some alterations were required. At this time, the Superman newspaper strips were more well-known and widely distributed than the comics and were all written by Jerry Siegel. However, due to huge workloads and failing eyesight, Joe Shuster could not produce all the artwork, so it was largely done by Paul Cassidy and Wayne Boring, who worked out of the Siegel and Shuster studio (a small office in Cleveland).[11] The alterations made by *Triumph*'s editorial team to the material were not inconsiderable, with artists working for *Triumph*, and perhaps McCail, creating header illustrations to introduce the stories, some of which were inspired by panels in the original strips and comic book stories and redrawn by the British artists (see Figures 10 and 11).

These additions changed the look of the stories considerably but allowed the serialization of the longer American stories across several issues. In fact, this process was also used in America, where the daily Superman newspaper strips were reformatted to appear in early issues of the *Superman* comic book. These practices of re-cutting strips would become common strategies for dealing with the reprinting of American comics in British publications, but an even more invasive change appeared when the second series of Superman appeared in *Triumph*. Now the comic pages were radically altered with the inclusion of text underneath each panel to turn them into the traditional Amalgamated Press style (see Figures 12a and 12b). At first glance it is shocking to see the well-known Superman stories so altered for the British market, reworked with text under the panels, which seems like a retrograde step, destroying the narrative and making it look like an old British comic rather than a new American one. The result is not a parody in the sense that it is an attack on the meaning of the original story, but the result of the alterations is to create a simulation of the original that differs in important respects.

The reasons for these changes were largely about format and bound up in the expectations of British readers in relation to genre. The dynamic visual storytelling techniques copied by British creators from American comics was mostly used in the humor genre in British comics. From the long history of story papers, the adventure genre— of which Superman was clearly a part—was associated more with prose stories, or comics with text underneath panels, so that is what the editors at Amalgamated Press turned Superman into. With falling sales, the idea to import American comics and to produce "American style" material had not worked, so the

66   False Starts and Minor Triumphs (1936–1949)

Fig. 8: *Triumph* #772 (Amalgamated Press, August 5, 1939). Superman ™ and © DC Comics.

False Starts and Minor Triumphs (1936–1949) 67

Fig. 9: Superman origin from American daily newspaper strips (McClure Syndicate, 1939).
Superman ™ and © DC Comics

Fig. 10: Superman page from *Triumph* (1939). Superman ™ and © DC Comics.

False Starts and Minor Triumphs (1936–1949)   69

Fig. 11: Page from *Superman* #3 (National Periodicals, Winter 1939), originally published as a newspaper strip, "Superman and the Runaway" (McClure Syndicate, June to July, 1939). Superman ™ and © DC Comics.

70   False Starts and Minor Triumphs (1936–1949)

Fig. 12a: The second series of Superman in *Triumph* #807 (Amalgamated Press, 1940).
Superman ™ and © DC Comics.

False Starts and Minor Triumphs (1936–1949) 71

Fig. 12b: The second series of Superman in *Triumph* #807 (Amalgamated Press, 1940). Superman ™ and © DC Comics.

editors were trying anything they could to keep their titles going. In some respects, McCail's cover artwork and the adjustments made to the stories for publication in *Triumph* have become almost forgotten curios and historical footnotes, but they should be understood as central to the marketing and positioning of a very American hero in the well-established tradition of boy's adventure story papers. In a way, it might have made more sense for DC Thomson to have published Superman in one of The Big Five, but that was not to be. Rather, his placement in *Triumph* was a bold statement that Amalgamated Press was fighting back, but in the end it was falling sales and the paper restrictions brought about by the war that had the decisive say. *Triumph* and *Champion* were forced to merge, and soon afterward the combined title folded, Superman never having made another appearance in those pages, though he would later appear in Amalgamated Press's *Radio Fun*.

Part of the problem inhibiting the development of homegrown British superheroes was that the success of the boy's own adventure stories throughout the 1920s had established a certain style for such adventure series, and this style was hard to shake. These stories' supposedly improving narratives, bound up in ideals of masculinity, gentlemanly conduct, and imperialism (with the exception of Derickson Dene), resisted the encroachment from America, whereas the contrary strand in British comics, especially humor strips, which celebrated a raucous anti-authoritarianism, was much more receptive to influences from American cinema and comics. One example of an American-style humor strip was Ping the Elastic Man, who appeared in *The Beano* 1938–1940 (DC Thomson) and was drawn by Hugh McNeill. In some ways, this elastic hero anticipated the American superhero, Plastic Man, by Jack Cole, who first appeared in *Police Comics* #1 (August 1941), published by Quality Comics. Ping had similar powers, being able to stretch his body. He was not a crime fighter, however, although he did use his powers to escape harm in his numerous adventures, and to thwart many Axis plots during the war.

Similarly, DC Thomson's most famous "superpowered" character, Desperate Dan, was no superhero but rather drew on another American genre, the Western. Desperate Dan was created for *The Dandy* by Dudley D. Watkins. He had an impressive chin, reportedly modeled on the editor, Albert Barnes, and his stories were set in Cactusville, a curious amalgamation of the Old West and a typical British town. Dan's powers were incredible. He could rip a tree out of the ground and hurl it across a canyon, and at one point he lassoed the Moon and pulled it closer to the Earth. These fantastic feats of strength were not influenced by the Western, but rather by E. C. Segar's Popeye, who was also a superpowered character. In fact, comics historian Denis Gifford identified Popeye as the first superhero to appear in British comics (in *The Jolly Comic* [1937]) and argued that this led to Desperate Dan, whom he calls "the first British Superhero" (although Gifford plays a bit fast and loose with that designation).[12] Gifford adds that "[*The Beano* gave us a superheroine] in 1938, forty years ahead of [Britain's] Sex Equality Act. She was 'Pansy Potter, The Strongman's Daughter,' Britain's answer to Wonder Woman."[13]

Although there was much that was revolutionary in *The Dandy* and *The Beano*, Desperate Dan and Pansy Potter were not superheroes, and neither was Popeye, unless the definition of "superhero" is stretched to such a degree as to have no real meaning. More to the point, these comics perpetuated traditional Amalgamated Press–style stories, as well as the illustrated text stories that were found in story papers. The clash of the traditional with the modern and revolutionary was a trademark of *The Dandy* and *The Beano*, and there was a clear delineation in terms of the American, or more broadly speaking, foreign, influence. The adventure stories that the Amalgamated Press published were in the traditional story paper (text underneath illustration) style, and it was predominantly in the humor strips where innovation was found, with these strips making use of American-style storytelling techniques. With these new comics selling well and The Big Five continuing to dominate, DC Thomson were well-placed as Britain entered the war; however, the restrictions imposed by the conflict would have a profound effect on the British comics industry.

The War Years

With the outbreak of war, Britain's economy switched to military and military-related production, which meant restrictions on the availability of key resources, including paper. Throughout the war, publishers struggled to get paper but were restricted by quotas. This meant a government ban on additional publications, so that publishers could produce new titles only if they canceled an existing one, and also making it all but impossible for any new publishers to form. The search for paper became a constant worry for smaller publishers, and even the bigger outfits had to cut the number of pages in their publications. As Gifford notes,

> With shipping lines required for items considered more essential to the besieged British boy than Superman or spinach, the age of the superhero was

quickly superseded by the age of the evacuee.... Starved for our fix of Yankee funnies, we made do with our home grown heroes: Rockfist Rogan, R.A.F—not super, perhaps, but "jolly super" bashing the bosh without a blemish on his brylcreem. And Wilson the Wizard Wonderman, breaking the three-minute mile in barefeet and black longjohns. Super stuff, but not *super* stuff, if you see what I mean. Then suddenly it happened. Out of evil cometh, as ever, good. Out of the paper shortage came a new breed of comics, published and drawn by new men who owed nothing to the Great British tradition of sosses and mash [sausages and mashed potatoes, a working-class meal] at the Hotel de Posh, and everything to the Great American Tradition of hotdogs at Joe's Diner. Cashing in on our lust for super–strip action a rash of pseudo-Yankee comics erupted. Titles like *New Funnies* and *Thrill Comics* shoved staid old *Comic Cuts* from the corner shop counter, and the heroes came on like Flash Gordon conquering the Universe single-handed.[14]

The war footing of the economy meant a ban on American imports of comics. The reason was that all transatlantic shipping was now highly dangerous and everything shipped had to be of military value. Bullets were more valuable than comics, although some publishers managed to continue reprinting American comics using the printing plates, whose importation was allowed. The ban on American imports lasted long after the war ended, until the late 1950s, in fact, when British publishing had recovered to a prewar state. This continuation was meant to allow time for British publishers to reestablish themselves and to avoid being put out of business by American imports. As Gifford notes (and as shall be seen in the next chapter), this created an opportunity to fill a gap in the market that many British publishers exploited.

However, even though imports were banned, the war also saw thousands of American troops stationed in Britain, and they brought comics with them, so American comics were still available, albeit in a very limited way. Indeed, in the mid-to-late 1940s, Glasgow-based publisher Cartoon Art Productions was reprinting Superman, filling the gap created by the loss of *Triumph*. The American military presence brought with it American popular culture via the PX (Post Exchange), which operated as retail stores for American servicemen in their bases, and through the presence of the troops themselves, who brought over comics or received them from home, with some were even being issued directly by the military. Then there were the American newspaper strips, like Buck Rogers, Tarzan, and Flash Gordon, which outclassed most British newspaper strips in terms of style and narrative ambition. When American comics found themselves in the hands of British children, they were prized as glamorous products of an exotic culture, and the reprints of American material in Britain had a considerable impact on readers. As Peter Hunt notes in *Children's Literature: An Illustrated History* (1995), "Since the Second World War, the traditions of British and American children's literature have tended to converge, although the cultural colonization by the USA has been more visible. But for many years it was clear that the preoccupations of the two countries were different—possibly because of economic conditions, and the differing impact of the war."[15] American comics seemed so much more dynamic than British comics, and British publishers increasingly emulated their American counterparts. Two such publishers were Gerald Swan and A. Soloway.

Swan and Soloway

Gerald Swan Ltd was formed in 1948 by former barrow boy (a street hawker of fruits and vegetables), and later entrepreneur, Gerald G. Swan. He had a flair for business and an eye for what the reading public wanted, becoming a comics wholesaler when he saw the growth in popularity of imported American comics. Realizing that the outbreak of war was going to end the easy availability of these comics, he decided to produce his own American-style comics to fill the gap in the market. For most publishers, the onset of war and paper rationing was a crushing blow, but Swan had a reputation for being able to outmaneuver the competition. In this case, it was not only a matter of his forward-thinking publishing plans that demonstrated his skill but also the fact that he managed to find paper for publishing comics at a time when other publishers were shutting down comics publication due to the paper shortages. As Mike Ashley has said,

> With the declaration of war on September 3, 1939 the clamp came down on imports, and paper, ink and printing type—amongst a whole lot else—were rationed. For the next six years reading matter for entertainment (as opposed to propaganda) was at a premium. The war brought an end to many of Britain's popular magazines of the twenties and thirties and those that survived were shadows of their former selves. In order to continue operating publishers had to show considerable enterprise. One of the most enterprising[,] . . . Swan had taken note of the looming signs of war and during the late thirties had stockpiled paper in a large warehouse in Marylebone. When the restrictions came he was sitting pretty. He had established his publishing business

during the thirties with an emphasis on magazines and books for boys and girls, many of which are now collectors' items in themselves. He then expanded to cover gangster fiction, science fiction and weird fiction.[16]

Swan's stockpiling allowed him to corner the market for a time, putting out a prolific amount of low quality magazines and comics in all genres, often with very quick turnaround times. This gambit paid off, as did the fact that Swan managed to get these titles in print before rationing took hold. This meant that he was able to secure a paper quota for them that, for a while, enabled him to continue publishing once his surplus of paper was gone when other publishers were edged out the business, or at least had to cut back on the comics they produced. Denis Gifford notes that "[beginning] with *New Funnies* #1 in January 1940 . . . Swan built up a chain of threepenny comic books, un-English and pro-American in style."[17] Swan offered comics that looked like the bold American comics to which British readers were becoming accustomed. One of Swan's strategies was to explore genres that were associated with American comics but which were almost ignored in British comics. Naturally, that meant superheroes, but they also included supernatural horror stories.

Two Swan characters illustrate the company's strategy: The Bat and Dene Vernon. The Bat, who appeared in *Thrill Comics* (1940) and *Extra Fun* (1940), was described as a "Robin Hood on wings." He was armed with a gas gun, like the American Sandman, who also appeared in 1940, but the more obvious influence was Batman. The Bat was created by William A. Ward, and like Batman was uncompromising and ruthless when faced with criminals. The stories had clear gothic themes and imagery, drawn from horror films of the 1930s. Dene Vernon was a ghost investigator who, like The Bat, appeared in *Thrill Comics* #1 (April 1940). He was created by Jock McCail who, as noted above, went to work for Swan, along with his brother, William, in 1940. Dene Vernon was perhaps the first supernatural comic series in British comics, appearing from 1940 until 1946. Indeed, whereas the supernatural and the occult were common in American comics and Gerald Swan's line of publications, this was the kind of material that Amalgamated Press and DC Thomson would not touch. One of the best examples of Swan's horror comics was the series *Back from the Dead*, created by William McCail, who also drew The Phantom Raider, using the name Ron. Later, while working for Gerald Swan, both Jock and William McCail worked on Cast Iron Chris, a strongman character with superhuman levels of strength and invulnerability, but these were humor strips and had more in common with Popeye and Desperate Dan than Superman.

A. Soloway also started publishing comics in the early 1940s, probably inspired by the success of Gerald Swan. Their strategies were certainly similar, and they sought out the talents of Len Fullerton, who, as noted above, had worked for Amalgamated Press on *Triumph* during the late 1930s and early 1940s, creating the first American-style comics for a British publication. When paper rationing forced the merger of *Triumph* with *Champion*, Fullerton found himself out of work at Amalgamated Press. However, Soloway was launching some new comics and wanted to have an experienced creator of adventure stories in the American style, which suited Fullerton perfectly. For Soloway, he created Argo, who appeared in *All Star* from 1942 to 1945 and *Comic Adventures* in 1947; Crash Carew, who also appeared in *Comic Adventures*; Dandy McQueen, Dude of the Royal Mounted in *All Star*, *Comic Adventures*, and *Red Star Comic* from 1941 to 1948; and the jungle hero Halcon, who appeared in *All Fun Comic and Comic Capers* from 1942 to 1949. Like Derickson Dene, whom Fullerton had created for Amalgamated Press, Argo was a science hero, using a special electrically powered suit to "cleave his way through the ocean depths" in a series called "Argo under the Ocean." There was again something of an influence from *Flash Gordon*, particularly a story line in which Flash was altered so he could breathe underwater and investigate the mysterious undersea kingdoms of Mungo. Argo also encountered villains not unlike Ming the Merciless, such as Svang the Regent, who plotted the invasion of the land, just as Ming planned to conquer the Earth. Fullerton's other strip, "Crash Carew, Daredevil of the Stratosphere," bore an even closer relation to *Flash Gordon*, with spaceships, alien creatures, and plotlines modeled closely on Alex Raymond's work. The fast-paced action of Fullerton's pages and his energetic line work made his comics for Soloway some of the best that appeared in British publications of the time. However, since Soloway was a relatively small publisher, these comics received far less exposure than they deserved.

The fact that smaller publishers invested in the creation of American-style adventure comics during the war years shows that there was an ongoing appeal for these kinds of stories that the bigger publishers were not meeting. But given the margins and the fact that British readers were used to an anthology format, Soloway hedged its bets just as DC Thomson did, offering humor strips alongside adventure stories. Another way in which Soloway followed DC Thomson was in the creation of Halcon, Lord of The Crater Land, a jungle lord who wore a distinctive red waistcoat and fought Nazis and slave traders. The jungle hero was an established type in the boy's weeklies and comic strips, and Halcon naturally bore a close resemblance to Tarzan. However, DC Thomson had created two Tarzan knockoffs many years before, with Morgyn the Mighty and Strang the Terrible. Such jungle lords and strongmen were important precursors to superheroes in both America and Britain, and in some cases they were almost superheroes due to their incredible feats of strength; but then, in 1944, a real superhero landed in Dundee.

The Amazing Mr X

Upon seeing the success of Superman in America, and with *Triumph* reprinting this superhero's stories, Albert Barnes, editor of *The Dandy*, commissioned staff artist Jack Glass to try his hand at a superhero, and the result was The Amazing Mr X, who is Britain's first homegrown superhero. The series ran for fourteen installments between 1944 and 1945, in issues 272–286, and Jack Glass's work on the series very clearly shows the influence of the early Superman stories reprinted in *Triumph*. The Amazing Mr X stories extolled themes of social justice, with the hero standing up from the oppressed masses, just as in the first Superman stories. Also like Superman, The Amazing Mr X had an alter ego, but while Clark Kent was a reporter in Metropolis, Len Manners was a "private inquiry agent" based in a "large English town." Like Superman, he wears glasses as a disguise and on spotting trouble dons a costume. This consists of black tights, a black cloak and mask, and a white woollen jersey with a red X. By tensing his muscles and taking a deep breath, his loose frame is filled out with impressive muscles, enabling him to perform incredible feats. He is described as "a mysterious superman," but unlike his American equivalent, he does not have otherworldly origins. Instead, we are told that he has been "building up his strength and facilities" for some time. No other explanation is given, and like a true superhero, he seeks no reward for his actions. Indeed, we are told, "Mr X wanted no thanks or fuss." Indeed, The Amazing Mr X appeared and promptly disappeared without much fuss, and presumably any thanks, and was largely forgotten. As Grant Morrison observes,

> The great thing about Mr X was that his costume didn't fit properly, and that was kind of a template for all British superheroes. He didn't really have proper muscles; he had porridge muscles, the kind that people had from the days of rationing. And he has a white crappy suit with a huge "X" on it and a black cape, and that was it. That was our version of Superman. He could leap about eight feet in the air, maybe. He could lift a table, y'know. But that was enough to tackle crime in Britain![18]

However, some Amazing Mr X stories followed the themes of Superman comics very closely indeed, with the superhero rescuing trapped miners and capturing escaped criminals, just as Superman did, but there was also a distinctly British flavor. The Amazing Mr X pursued his enemies over rugged British landscapes, and the towns and cities in which he operated were distinctly British in character. He took on criminals who were stealing from the Royal Mail, necessitating a fight on a moving train, and visited Glasgow to solve a convoluted kidnapping, dealt with trouble at a shipyard, and even wrestled a stag at one point. This gave the stories a certain charm, but they were not quite the operatic and fantastic excess commonly found in American superhero comics. In one sense, this may have been something quite close to parody at work here, although if so, it is unknown whether this was intentional mockery of the American comics or of DC Thomson's rival, Amalgamated Press, which had reprinted Superman stories. Or it may have been that this was an attempt at a "straight" superhero story, but that the creators mixed it with a rather more down-to-earth British idiom and thereby produced stories that do not work as either adventure or humor.

Interestingly, several key elements usually found in superhero comics were missing. There was no cast of supporting characters, no love interest (a large part of the success of Superman was the relationship with the feisty Lois Lane), no fellow superheroes, and no recurring enemy. Indeed, The Amazing Mr X operated in an otherwise normal world in which he was the only unusual element (see Figure 13). There were no invading aliens or supervillains for him to fight. He did not even battle the Nazis. By 1944 there were some American comics available as reprints, and next to them this strip was singularly unimpressive. This was partly due to the format. The Amazing Mr X was created, rather perversely, using the traditional adventure strip format, although this was the same brand of perversity practiced by Amalgamated Press with Superman's second run in *Triumph*. Rather than mimic the dynamic American style that so obviously suited superhero stories, The Amazing Mr X strip is rendered in a rather straightforward way. The result was that the storytelling was not fluid and dynamic like American superhero comics, where action and fast, visually driven stories were crucial to their success. Glass was a talented artist, but he was no Will Eisner or Lou Fine, or Joe Shuster, Wayne Boring, or C. C. Beck for that matter, and the result is something of a strange hybrid between American and British comics.

However, there are clues that lend credence to the idea that The Amazing Mr X might not have actually been created in 1944. It is possible that the

Fig. 13: The Amazing Mr X in *The Dandy* #272 (DC Thomson, 1944). The Dandy © DC Thomson & Co Ltd.

series was actually made in 1939 (or shortly after) when the reprints of Superman were first appearing in *Triumph*. This would explain why The Amazing Mr X strips were so heavily influenced by the early Superman stories. By 1944 a vast range of superhero comics had been published, and they were more widely available in Britain through Len Miller and T. V. Boardman reprints, so it is odd that such a strip would be created in 1944, taking on board none of those influences. It is possible that upon learning that *Triumph* had given up on *Superman*, Barnes decided that he did not have to run The Amazing Mr X after all and shelved it. A few years later, the war effort had reduced the number of artists available in the DC Thomson offices to create new material, so perhaps this series was dusted off to fill space in the comic at a time when artists were at the front following the big push for D-Day in 1944. While not conclusive, this explains some of the things that seem oddly lacking in The Amazing Mr X and why there was not more of an effort to make something of this first homegrown superhero.

Soon afterward came several other British superheroes from smaller independent publishers, many of them making a much better attempt to copy the American style. These were more popular, but they never really overcame a key problem with all British superheroes: the fact that they lacked glamor. The superhero was supposed to soar between huge skyscrapers or charge through the noir urban sprawl and to embody the ideals of the American Dream and to challenge injustice. America's utopian idealism suited this genre and these characters, but the slow decline of the British Empire viewed from grimy tenement buildings was a rather less impressive backdrop for superhero narratives. There was always something a bit too down-to-earth about the British superheroes. There was a certain brand of idealism that British readers were attuned to accept, the plucky yet reserved heroism of Jack Harkaway, but the brigade of superpowered heroes who unselfconsciously wore underpants on top of tights while proudly waving the Stars and Stripes were not of that type. While The Amazing Mr X was not the most successful British superhero, he certainly set the tone for much of what was to follow, with homegrown superheroes struggling to mimic the tone of the American comics. But being too closely tied to the boy's own adventure genre, these stories sometimes seemed more like a parody of the superhero than a straight adventure story. Although other publishers who attempted to offer British superheroes would try to avoid some of those traps, this was sometimes quite tricky, but there was by now a new generation of comics creators coming through, many of whom had grown up on American reprints and early attempts to emulate the American style, who were eager to try their hand at British superheroes.

Gifford and Monkhouse

Denis Gifford and Bob Monkhouse were childhood friends who became comics creators before moving on to other careers. As well as being a comics creator, Gifford was a writer, collector, and a widely published historian of comics, film, and popular culture. Monkhouse was a very talented comics artist but later become a famous comedian and television personality, starring on *Celebrity Squares* and *The Golden Shot*. Gifford started early as a published comics creator with strips like "Pansy Potter" printed in *The Dandy* when he was just fourteen years old. He had a talent for humor that served him well throughout his career as a comics artist. However, he was also an avid reader of American superhero comics and created several crude homemade comics anthologies featuring American strips, a clear indication that even at a very young age he had early ambitions to be a comics publisher.

These homemade comics were somewhere between scrapbooks and tryouts for anthology titles of his devising. They were created in the mid-1940s and had titles like *Gee-Whiz* and *O'Boy American Comics* (a title he reworked for *Oh Boy! Comics* in 1948). These were likely prototypes for comics that Gifford wanted to produce for the British market and featured clippings of both British and American newspaper strips, including Batman, Donald Duck, Don Winslow, and many others, which were glued into a booklet, wrapped in handmade covers.[19] Some, such as *Gee-Whiz*, which had a cover featuring a rather rough image of Superman fighting a robot, experimented with a landscape format (something that Australian comics took up, and British comics reprinting American superhero material would return to in the 1970s). Besides *Gee-Whiz* and *O'Boy Comics*, the mock-ups he produced included *Giant Comics*; *Jumbo Comics*; *Merry Moments*: *Famous Fun*; *Mirror Comics*; *Mirror Special A1: Danger Comics*; *Overseas Comics* ("issued to members of Armed Forces"); *Stellar Comics* (which indicated that it was a "Monk House Publication"); *Surprise Comics*; *Swell*; *Well-Known Comics*; and many more.

The handwritten notes in the inside covers indicate Gifford's intention to establish a publishing empire under an imprint called ERA, and there are references to ERA Publishing Co, London SE26, which seems to have been an invented company, perhaps one that Gifford intended to set up to produce these comics. The postal code likely refers to Gifford's family's home address, where he was living at the time (aged eighteen). Gifford and Monkhouse drew covers and page headers for the various strips, and some of the pages were hand colored with watercolors, mainly using green, pink, and yellow. The newspaper strips Gifford had collected were black and white, but coloring made them look more like American comic books rather than newspaper strips. However, the limited color palate used suggests that Gifford knew that full-color printing was extremely unlikely to be done by British publishers, so he produced color samples using a limited number of colors, knowing that this was the outermost limit of what most British publishers could achieve. While Gifford's output may have been the flights of fancy of a young man, the industriousness that he applied throughout his career and over many ventures suggest otherwise and indicates that he was planning to get into the same kind of business as T. V. Boardman and was either using his early work as a way to figure out the practicalities of production and publishing—format, coloring, layout, branding, and so on—or creating sample publications for a publisher or investor to look at. Ultimately, these ambitions were frustrated, but Gifford and Monkhouse did work their way into the comics industry by other means.

In his autobiography, *Crying With Laughter* (1993), Monkhouse reveals that he was first published by *Mickey Mouse Weekly* when he was about twelve years old, having bombarded it with cartoons. He also recalls sending off samples to every publisher he could find.[20] His friendship and partnership with Gifford was a productive one, and both worked closely with Mick Anglo. Early contributions from Gifford were the superheroes Mr Muscle, who appeared in *Dynamic Comics* in 1945, which he produced, and Streamline, who first appeared in *Streamline Comics* in 1947, by Gifford and Monkhouse. *Dynamic Comics* was published by International Comics, based in Glasgow, and Gifford's Mr Muscle, who is identified as "Britain's Superman," gained superhuman abilities from a mysterious chemical compound. Created in 1944 when Gifford was just seventeen (and in the same year that The Amazing Mr X appeared in *The Dandy*, which also published Gifford's work), Mr Muscle was a rather weak effort. The character design is simple and the composition of the pages amateur. The figures are not drawn realistically but instead look like they are from a humor strip, yet this comic reads more like an attempt at a straight superhero story than an outright parody (see Figure 14). The story has Mr Muscle thwarting the plans of Japanese saboteurs, so it was likely influenced by the many American comics that adopted propaganda themes and imagery. Although they accepted this first story from him, the art editor at International Comics, John R. Lurner, wrote to Gifford in a letter dated August 10, 1945, that "I would also suggest that you drop the character Mr Muscle which I accepted in your previous

Fig. 14: Mr Muscle, Britain's Superman, by Denis Gifford, in *Dynamic Comics* (International Comics, 1945).

Fig. 15: Streamline, by Denis Gifford, in *Streamline* #1 (Cardal Publishing, 1947).

work. It is too near to the American 'Superman,' and a British Superman has already been tried here–in *The Dandy*, I believe, and dropped."[21] However, Gifford was not deterred in his efforts to create superheroes, and the next small publisher he worked with was Cardal, based in Manchester, who published the character Streamline.

The work in *Streamline Comics*, which was first published in 1947, showed that Gifford was improving as an artist, albeit slowly (see Figure 15). The tagline in *Streamline Comics* stated that the titular hero was "the speediest fighter in the world," and the character was every bit the American superhero. Keenan King was a scientist who had invented the mysterious "elixir X," which he injects into himself after witnessing a crime. This formula turns the scientist into a superhero. There is a strong influence from Joe Simon and Jack Kirby's *Captain America*, as Gifford acknowledged in an illustration he provided for *U.K. Comicdom* #0 (May 1970), a British fanzine edited by Phil Clarke and designed by Mike Higgs in which he stated that

Streamline is transformed into a superhero with "help from elixir X (and Captain America)."[22] However, the drawing is still quite crude, and things did not improve much when Bryan Berry took over the artwork.

The following year, Gifford approached publishers Martin and Reid Ltd, based on London, asking if they wanted to publish a Captain Marvel–type strip that he would produce. This was a good idea, as Captain Marvel reprints from L. Miller and Son were doing well, and as shall be seen in the next chapter, soon everyone was imitating Captain Marvel, so the business idea was sound. However, Martin and Reid were clearly not convinced that Gifford was the right person to do it. In their response, Boris Ashdon, writing for John Matthews in a letter of January 22, 1948, comes to the point: "We have already in our files a copy of your *Streamline Comics* for Cardal, and the work in this seems to be hurried and careless. You may be happier when working with a character of a humorous nature, giving you plenty of scope for smart gags and nutty characterisation."[23] In true Gifford style, he was undaunted, and indeed in 1949 he penned a twelve-thousand-word manuscript titled *How to Draw for the Comics*. This was a guide to creating comics, and there is evidence that he intended it to be published by Modern Fiction Ltd, a publisher of salacious pulp fiction (that also published Gifford's *Captain Might* comics in 1949), although it would appear that this book never saw print. Despite the fact that this was a how-to book from someone who was failing to find work in the industry, Gifford offers good advice, saying,

> Each panel of your strip must be interesting and gripping—it is no use to have a series of close-ups of character's faces talking to each other! . . . Each of your characters must be alive and animated. They must look full of life, even if they are merely standing around on-looking. The simple action of taking off a coat, for instance, must be made full of drama and action, otherwise your reader's interest will flag.[24]

Commenting on the differences between British and American comics, he adds, "Buy a few American Adventure strip comics, and compare the styles with those which appear in the British Comics. Decide for yourself which school of art you wish to follow in this line of comic work, for it is nigh impossible to draw in both techniques."[25] Gifford also takes the opportunity to criticize the British comics industry for not allowing creators to put bylines on their work and applauds American comics for allowing it.[26] Despite some setbacks, Gifford would go on to have a career in comics, working for Mick Anglo's studio in the 1950s and 1960s, but his lasting influence on comics would be as a historian producing a large number of invaluable reference works. He was also founder of the Association of Comics Enthusiasts (A.C.E.). Gifford and Monkhouse were therefore at the forefront of a new generation of postwar British comics creators who had grown up with American comics, and the floodgates were opening.

Cartoon Art Productions

Cartoon Art Productions was based at 141 Bath Street in Glasgow and was the same company that had previously been known as International Comics and Transatlantic Press, and which had produced *Dynamic Comics* in 1945, featuring Mr Muscle by Gifford. By 1946 the company had changed its name to Cartoon Art Productions and was sometimes referred to as CAP-toons. As Mike Higgs notes in *The Great British Fantasy Comic Book Heroes* (2009), Cartoon Art Productions "reprinted many American comic books, including some of the Magazine Enterprises stable, and Superman, along with a fair amount of original material too."[27] The location of such an operation in Glasgow was natural, as there was a significant American naval base nearby, and American comics often found their way into the hands of children on the west coast of Scotland.

In 1946 Cartoon Art Productions was ready to scale up its operation and produce more superhero comics. The company's main title was *Super-Duper Comics* (1946 to around 1950), an anthology featuring the usual mix of genres, comics, and text stories. The firm also had a very clever marketing strategy, putting a British price and an American price on the cover (three pence and five cents). The "cents" price label was designed to give readers the impression that this was an authentic American comic or that the company traded on both sides of the Atlantic (an ambition signaled by its earlier names, International Comics and Transatlantic Press), and this labeling was driven by the fact that these hard-to-find American comics were glamorous and prized by readers. In fact, distribution of the comics was limited to Britain and Northern Ireland, with no overseas distribution. Although a clever ploy, it would not have been worth attempting if Cartoon Art Productions did not have artwork that could pass as American. Fortunately, it had employed a young English artist called Dennis M. Reader, whose work was distinctly American in character. Indeed, Reader was a very gifted artist, so naturally the firm had him drawing as much as he could as quickly as he could, and much of its business seemed to be built upon his talents.

Dennis M. Reader was born in Peterborough in 1927 and like Gifford and Monkhouse, he was drawing his own comics while still at school. He was inspired to draw by his mother, who painted what Gifford refers to as "sensitive watercolours." At the age of fourteen, he was taken on as an apprentice by a local printer, with whom he stayed for six years. He balanced this experience with lessons from a retired art teacher. He found work with Swan in 1944, where his ability to create comics in the American style was instantly recognized. His first professional comics work was "Cat Girl," which appeared in Swan's *Topical Funnies* in 1944. As Gifford notes, "The possibilities of strip cartooning had hit Reader when he encountered the comic books published by the ex-barrow boy entrepreneur Gerald G. Swan ... but nobody Swan found echoed the true Yankee comic-book spirit until Reader submitted his four-page, 48-panel adventure of 'Cat Girl.' It was 1944 and Reader's sexy super-heroine was something never before seen in a British comic."[28]

This comic was close to what the Americans referred to as "Good Girl Art" (featuring well-drawn, sexy images of women). As Alan Clark notes, "Reader was one of the first British artists to emulate the American style of comic book and drawing," and Gifford concurs, noting that he was "one of the first British strip cartoonists specialising in super-heroes."[29] In fact, Len Fullterton was doing American-style comics six years earlier, but whereas Fullterton emphasized the high-adventure style of Flash Gordon, Reader added elements of film noir and influences from Milton Caniff's "Terry and the Pirates," *Superman*, and Will Eisner's *The Spirit*. These strips and many others were known to Reader from the bundles of remaindered funnies and the Boardman comics of the 1930s, as well, presumably, as *Triumph*'s short run of Superman stories. According to Gifford in *Super Duper Supermen* (1993), Reader was "a left-handed teenager in love with American comic books" who added an "M" (for Malcolm) to his name in order to sound more American, which, if true, is another link to Fullterton, who chose an American sounding pseudonym, Nat Brand, for his American-inspired work.[30]

Reader's work brought him to the attention of Cartoon Art Productions, and his style fit in exactly with what the Glasgow-based company was aiming to do. For them he produced a number of crime comics and many superheroes, including Powerman, G-Boy and Wonder Boy, Electro Girl, Phantom Maid, and Acromaid. As Gifford noted, the workload was intense and "meant late-night work for Reader, who hung on to his job at the local newspaper."[31] Gifford adds, "Consequently the polish on his style disappeared, but his creativity ran wild under pressure." This can be seen in one of Reader's best creations, Powerman, who appeared in *Super-Duper Comics* #3 (1946). The stories were set in America, but the hero, Kerry Lattimer, was a British crime reporter. In his first appearance, Lattimer is confronted by a ghost on Christmas Eve. It gives him a present, which turns out to be a copy of Dickens's *A Christmas Carol*, calling it "a seasonal present from the mists of time" (see Figure 16). When the book is opened, another ghost (the ghost of Christmas yet to come) appears and says, "On the dawn of Christmas Day you will become a crime fighting force endowed with superhuman gifts . . . be prepared! Fight evil and injustice . . . use this strength and wisdom to bring about good in this upset world." In the next panel, Powerman flies above the city. The caption says, "As Christmas Day dawned so dawned a new hero—Powerman." The final caption says, "Watch for action boys and gals! It'll smash out of the page with Powerman!"

In Reader's obituary, Gifford recorded that "despite being offered a staff job as an inker at DC Comics in New York [by the 1950s] Reader found himself drawn out. He gave up the comics and took charge of Perkins Engineering's art department, where he remained editor of their in-house magazine, Perkins Echo." Much later he produced a number of children's books, but in terms of comics output, Cartoon Art Productions had squeezed him dry. This, then, represented yet another similarity to Len Fullerton, who by the 1950s was also suffering from a similar type of fatigue with the constant deadlines and compromises on quality required by the comics industry. Fullerton moved to Dundee and joined William McCail's Mallard Studios in Glasgow. He produced work for the Dundee-based printer Valentines and Sons, which in the late 1940s started producing comics of its own. These were *Ace Comic* and *Super-Bumper Comic* (both single issues that appeared in 1948), but in time he started to produce postcards and calendars for Valentine, finding his true inspiration in drawing from nature rather than drawing adventure strips. So began a celebrated career as a naturalist. Although Fullerton was arguably one of the most important figures in the development of American-style comics in Britain, for many years his identity was not known, and there were only rumors of what had happened to Nat Brand, the mysterious Scotsman who had revolutionized British comics and then disappeared. In truth, he was hiding in plain sight and enjoying some distinction as an illustrator of nature, ironically having come to one of the great homes of comics in Britain, Dundee, to abandon his former career in favor of a life involved in conservation and painting.

While much of Cartoon Art Production's output was due to the industriousness of Reader, the firm had other talents, such as Crewe Davies,

Fig. 16: *Super-Duper Comics* #4, by Dennis M. Reader (Cartoon Art Productions of Glasgow, 1947).

who drew both Dane Jerrus, Agent One of the Interplanetary Solar Force, and Captain Magnet, who appeared in *Super-Duper* (1948–1950). Dane Jerrus, which was a mix of superheroics and science fiction, was stylistically the more adventurous of the two, drawn in a somewhat elastic style, with elements that seemed cartoony, as if it were a humor strip. The main character would often be contorted into strange poses, and Davies used this to give the pages dynamic compositions. In this he may have been influenced by reprints of the American Plastic Man comic, in which Jack Cole used the superpowers of the title character as a pretext to engage in some compositional playfulness. Plasticity of form was certainly on Davies's mind as in the *Super-Duper* annual he provided illustrations for a very unusual Dane Jerrus text story that included elements of comics storytelling, such as thought balloons and captions that accompanied the spot illustrations, making it something of a hybrid. It was in stories like this that a very productive tension between American-style storytelling and British traditions can be detected.

Then there were Speed Gale and Garry, who appeared in *Speed Gale* and *Super-Duper* in 1947 and were very much in the Batman and Robin mold and who, like Streamline, gained powers through a mysterious elixir. These stories were drawn by a Glasgow artist whose name is unknown, but they were carried off with some humor. There was something slightly risqué about these comics. In several stories, the superhero is tied up and tortured, writhing in pain in a rather suggestive fashion. In one story, Speed Gale pounced on the villain in what can only be described as a rather questionable tackle, apparently grabbing him between his legs from behind. Then there was the name of the sidekick. Some rather silly superhero names appear in comics, but there is something very tongue-in-cheek about the bathos of having a sidekick simply named Garry, as if he was so inconsequential that he did not even warrant a code name. There was certainly a strong element of parody at work here. Another oddity of Cartoon Art Productions was The Bat, by George McQueen. As Phil Clarke and Mike Higgs note in *The Great British Fantasy Comic Book Heroes* (2009), this Western-horror story was "cribbed panel by panel from Dick Ayer's *Ghost Rider* western/horror feature published by the US company, Magazine Enterprises."[32] The spirit of plagiarism that went all the way back to the chapbooks, unauthorized copies of Töpffer and penny dreadfuls, was evidently still alive and well.

Another key creator who worked between Glasgow and Dundee was Irish artist Paddy Brennan, who became a DC Thomson stalwart, although, according to Alan Clark, his first published work was for *The Magno Comics* (1946), a one-shot published in Glasgow for International Publications, the forerunner of Cartoon Art, for which he drew "Jeff Collins–Crime Reporter." Brennan then did *Marsman Comics* for Cartoon Art in 1948 before going on to do work for *Super-Duper*. The Marsman story may have been written by Dennis M. Reader, and while it ran for only one issue, it represents everything that was glorious about the output of the small publishers at this time.

The cover is unusually beautiful in its simplicity, but there is something not quite right about it. The angles of the buildings are all wrong, and the character is rather flat and leaps from right to left, creating a strange compositional tension, as the action would usually take place across the opposite axis. The effect is an eerie sense of stillness, as if the character is suspended, and the hint of art deco styling creates another tension, this time with the superhero iconography. The yellow circle for the price looks like

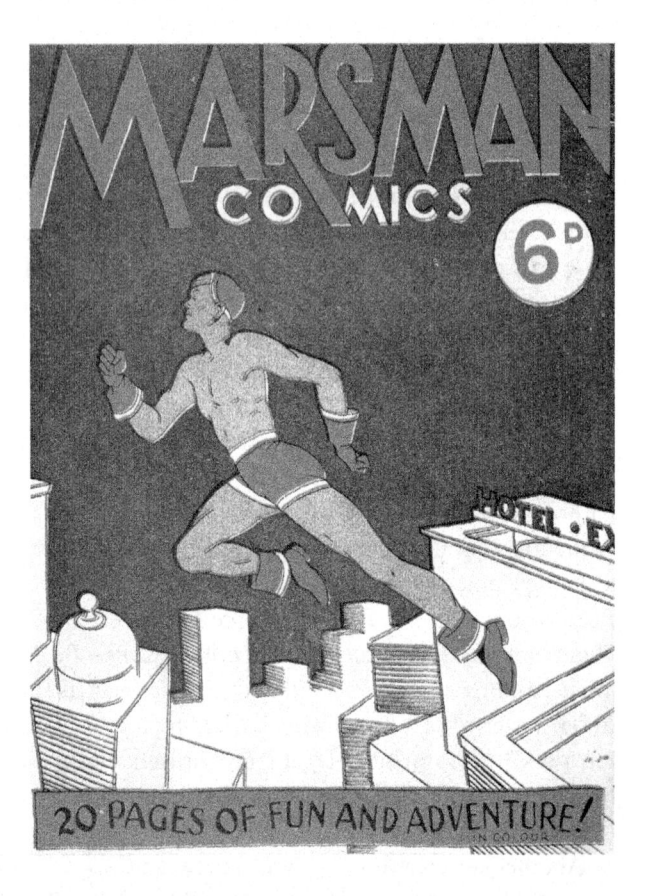

Fig. 17: *Marsman Comics*, by Paddy Brennan (Cartoon Art Productions of Glasgow, 1948).

it could represent the moon. And the colors should not work, but they do, with the dark blue background, acid yellow buildings, and red letters. Like everything else on this cover, they are wrong but seem to work (see Figure 17).

This is what makes comics produced by small publishers at this time so interesting. No such cover would have made it through the production line of editors and quality control in the American system, and the larger British publishers might have sent this back too, but there was an enormous amount of freedom and a sense of experimentation in the comics that emerged from smaller publishers. Often this meant that the quality was variable, often more amateur than professional, and sometimes downright bad, but sometimes this freedom would result in striking work. The interior artwork on *Marsman* was astounding and highly professional, and there is a clear influence from American comics, with a dramatic establishing panel showing Marsman flying over the city, and with wonderfully composed panels from shifting perspectives showing his first contact with humanity.

In the story, Marsman has come from Mars to make a close study of the Earth. He arrives at Bigburg USA to "make a report on Earth's social life and civilisation," but he is soon fighting crime. This was Brennan at his best. When he went to work for DC Thomson, he became one of their best staff artists and enjoyed a long career, but he was on a tighter leash. He took over many of the strips that Dudley D. Watkins had once done (such as "Jimmy and His Magic Patch," "The Shipwrecked Circus," and "Jack Flash") because he could emulate Watkins's style, which was a very valuable skill at DC Thomson. For *The Beano* he worked on "General Jumbo," and while this afforded a lot of scope for his imagination to run wild, it was within much tighter parameters than was possible with a small publisher like Cartoon Art Productions.[33]

Another innovative product that came out of Glasgow was "Quicksilver, The Wonderman of the West," by former DC Thomson and Swan employee William McCail. This Western superhero appeared in *The Round Up* (1948), which was published by the Children's Press in Glasgow and produced at McCail's Glasgow-based Mallard Studios. McCail had studios in both Dundee and Glasgow and was an instrumental figure in supporting freelance comics production in Scotland. *The Round Up* was an anthology of Western and humor strips, but Quicksilver was the lead strip and was featured on the cover. The character lived in a mountain cave in the Wild West and is the self-appointed guardian of nature. He has strength and invulnerability. Also, he can fly and can transfer this ability onto any animal with which he is in contact, resulting in a memorable sequence in which he flies a prize horse away from a gang of rustlers. When ambushed in his sleep by the head rustler, the bullets bounce off Quicksilver and he flies off with the villain, who then struggles and falls to his death in a stampede of horses. The hero says, "Justice has been done. I, Quicksilver, protector of the wild, am satisfied."

Ace Hart, the Atom Man, who starred in *Superthriller Comic* (1948–1950), was another superhero to come from Scotland. The title was initially published and printed by Foldes Press, which was based in Joppa, Edinburgh (later it was published by World Distributors Ltd, which was based in Manchester, England). One of the artists working on this comic was C. Purvis, but it is not clear how many he did or who else provided artwork for the series, although comics publisher and historian Terry Hooper attributes some stories to James Bleach, who later worked for Mick Anglo's studio drawing Marvelman comics. The character first appeared in *Superthriller Comic* #6 and was a scientist who had developed an elixir that allowed him to harness atomic power, giving him superhuman abilities. He operated out of his laboratory, which contained a miraculous computer of his own design that directed him to trouble, wherever it might be. Later, Ace Hart joined the Department of Space Defense and the stories began to be set in space, signaling the rise in popularity of science-fiction comics.

The series ran for eighty-two issues, and as Gifford notes, it underwent a change of name to "*Western Superthriller* in response to changing tastes among young readers."[34] The *Superthriller* series continued with a number of annuals that were released from 1957 through 1959 by World Distributors which featured Ace Hart text stories by Bryn Cullen with spot illustrations by Edgar Hodges. This was a rather retrograde step in some ways, but like Dane Jerrus, it showed that the story paper tradition of illustrated prose stories was still going strong well into the 1950s and beyond. Ace Hart and Quicksilver were excellent examples of a growing trend. Toward the end of the decade, several comics saw the superhero crossing over into other genres. There had always been a connection to crime and science fiction, and the superhero genre had always been a supergenre, drawing on many different influences, but rather than skewing toward humor and parody, these comics were a blend of distinct adventure genres, from the Western to science fiction, which was rare in American comics but not uncommon in British ones.

Dundee's DC Thomson, despite not having capitalized on The Amazing Mr X, still had a roster of superhero types, and every now and again they would try out a new one, such as Jack Flash, The Flying Boy, who appeared in *The Beano* #355 in 1949 and ran across several series throughout the 1950s. He was created by Dudley D. Watkins and was a boy from Mercury with wings on his feet, sent to Earth to experience an alien culture. Fred Sturrock took over on the art, then Paddy Brennan and subsequently Andy Hutton, with the final series in *The Beano* ending in 1958. As noted in *The History of The Beano* (2008), "This style of story signalled an acknowledgement of the popularity of the American comic strip."[35] DC Thomson staffers even produced mock-up version of an American-style Jack Flash comic using a Captain Marvel reprint comic by L. Miller and Son as a template. DC Thomson editor and historian Morris Heggie speculates that the ongoing rationing of paper probably stopped this plan from going forward.[36] A female version of the character, Jackie Flash, appeared in the girl's comic, *Mandy* #347, in 1973.

She could fly and deflect bullets with a gravity field, which was useful as she was pursed by the military who saw her as an invader rather than a harmless alien tourist. Jack Flash reappeared in *Nutty* in 1980.

The Falcon, by George Heath, appeared in Amalgamated Press's *Radio Fun* (1947–1960). He was not really a superhero but rather an adventurer accompanied by a female reporter, Wendy Dale, with something of the Superman and Lois/Flash Gordon and Dale Arden dynamic. There were elements of science fiction, such as when The Falcon and Dale are taken to another planet by the occupants of a UFO. Another flying man came in the form of Ray Spede The Rocket Man, who was the inventor of the "rocket ornithopter." He appeared in *Red Flash Comics* in 1947 and was a science hero and flying man of the type that had long been popular in the story papers. Indeed, the style of the artwork was a little old-fashioned, although he looked quite different just a couple of years later when he appeared in *Bob Comic Book* (1949), with stylized artwork and leopard print pants and a red superhero costume rather than science hero garb. In his later appearance, he fights a tiger with a spear in a jungle in a scene that could have been from the then-popular Tarzan film series. These comics were published by Philmar Ltd, which was based in London, and the character was created by C. Montford, who worked for Amalgamated Press before the war, which is perhaps why his first version of the character looks like the old flying men archetype from the story papers. The later version of the character was by Colin Merritt.[37]

Montford's origin story for Ray Spede was presented in a very strange format, mixing elements of the comic strip and the story paper. The strip has no word balloons, only captions, and at one point a substantial caption at the top of a page anticipates what is going to happen over the next several panels, revealing that the hero will rescue a young woman from certain death before the reader has the opportunity to read the panels depicting this. This is quite an odd story, even by the standards of British comics, but it showed the ongoing tension between text and images in the adventure genre, as seen in the second series of Superman in *Triumph* and The Amazing Mr X in *The Dandy*.

Scion, Paget, and Modern Fiction Ltd

Toward the end of the 1940s, comics emerged from several small publishers, such as Scion, a publisher of science-fiction paperbacks, and Paget, which published short novels but also dabbled in comics. Scion was established in 1948 by Binyimin Zeev Immanuel, who as Steve Holland notes, was "a Latvian student born in Riga in 1907, who had come to Britain in 1933 when Hitler rose to power, arriving with only £3 to his name."[38] After studying economics at University College, London, he became a teacher and then got into publishing, launching Scion Ltd along with his wife, Esther. Due to ongoing paper rationing, publishers could put out one-off issues but could rarely gain permission for a new series. As a consequence, Scion put out a range of "Big" comics (*Big Chuckle Comics, Big Shot Comics*, and so on) so that each issue looked like a one-off publication rather than a series. This proved to be a very successful strategy. Scion had a number of superhero types, such as Litening, who was featured in *Big Flame Wonder Comic* (1948), a one-shot by Ron Embleton, and Maskman, who appeared in *Big Game Comic* (also 1948).

Litening was an unusual superhero for a couple of reasons. First, he is referred to as the Son of the Gods, as he is granted superpowers by the pantheon of Greek gods after they witness a supposed act of heroism. Nothing too unusual there, but the heroic act they witness is him saving a cat from a stray dog. There is something (quite literally) pedestrian about Litening's origin. This is hardly superheroism on an epic scale; it seems to be too much of a rather everyday occurrence to warrant the grant of superpowers. This is yet another example of a parody of the high drama seen in American superhero comics. It is also unusual in that it was drawn by Ron Embleton, who went on to work on *Mickey Mouse Weekly*; for *Express Weekly* on "Wulf the Briton"; and for other comics such as *The Eagle, TV Century 21*, and *Look and Learn*. As Gifford observes, this was "a rare attempt at a superhero strip by Ron Embleton . . . who was much more at home turning out western strips."[39] Indeed, Embleton produced mostly Westerns for Scion, but this publisher ranged widely over a number of genres. In the 1950s, Scion would go into partnership with the King-Ganteaume studio and produce superhero comics like *Electroman* (discussed in the next chapter). Scion was based in London, but several of its early comics were printed in France, and it is possible that some of the artwork may have come through that country.

Paget Publications was also based in London, and like Scion it specialized in short pulp novels and salacious magazines, and for its comic line the firm used a trick similar to Scion's, giving each issue a slightly different name to avoid the restrictions on new series. Its main superhero character was Wonderman, also known as Captain Justice, who appeared in *Wonderman* monthly until 1951 (see Figure 18). The character was John Justice,

Fig. 18: Wonderman—The Atomic Marvel, by Mick Anglo, in *Wonderman* #4 (Paget, 1948).

Fig. 19: The Tornado, with art by Bob Monkhouse, in *Oh Boy! Comics* #2 (Paget, 1948).

"son of a world renowned scientist" and "a scientific product of his father's genius." As with many superheroes of the time, his powers are somehow "atomic" in nature, and like Batman, he acts up the role of wealthy playboy to hide the fact that he is a superhero. Many of the images in the comic seem to be lifted from Superman comics, and where Superman had an "S" on his chest, Wonderman has a "W." Some of the character dynamics were also the same, with Jan taking on a role similar to Lois Lane's. As Gifford observes, he even had "a familiar-sounding phrase, 'This looks like a job for Wonderman.'"[40] According to Gifford, this character was "the first of many superheroes created by Mick Anglo." The comic was a success for Paget and led to several more, including *Oh Boy! Comics* (1948), which introduced The Tornado, with art by Bob Monkhouse (who signed his work "Ramon") (see Figure 19). Around this time, Monkhouse rented a room in Anglo's Gower Street studios, which he used to create comics and to write comedy sketches for radio with his partner, Denis Goodwin.[41] *Oh Boy!* was another comic in which the British sense of humor was on show, and Monkhouse's comedic talents were put to good use. He took some delight in drawing the hero to look a little like himself and in including a number of dirty jokes. In the second issue, Monkhouse had The Tornado fight The Growth, "a mass of stinking glutinous fungi." Eagle-eyed (and dirty-minded) readers would have spotted the overt sexual allusions in the story.

While Monkhouse later became the face of family entertainment on British television as a stand-up comedian, he delighted in playing against this image with a brand of blue humor. His inventive wordplay and sharp wit were often best deployed through dirty jokes and sexual comedy, and he inserted them into his comics where possible. This would never have been allowed at DC Thomson or Amalgamated Press, where strict editorial control would have caught this "disreputable" material at a very early stage. The smaller publishers like Scion, Paget, and Cartoon Art Productions operated in a completely different way and with small profit margins, so there was less control and more opportunity for satire, parody, and subversion, especially given that they often dealt with less than reputable material, such as erotica, in other areas of their business, so such lewd imagery may have been actively encouraged. Monkhouse's work on The Tornado involved more than just some dirty jokes, though; this was the case of a British comics artist in full parody mode, undermining the conservatism and purity of the American superhero. He continued to parody the superhero concept in "Stuporman!," which featured a moronic character called Puttyhead who has "read so many comic books he thinks he is a superman" (see Figure 20). He continually finds himself in life-threatening situations, exacerbated by his belief in his invulnerability, but in the end he usually only has some bandages to show for it. This was an outright parody of the superhero, and some were concerned because they believed that such comics set a dangerous example to children.

Monkhouse was by now a very talented and professional artist, producing excellent comics artwork, and The Tornado is a fine example of this. The character was Steve Storm, a reporter for the fictional *London Tribune*, whose ancestors had been cursed by a band of murderers and thieves in the fifteenth-century town of Monkhouse. The villains were brought to justice by Stephen Storm, and upon his execution, the leader of the criminal gang curses his family to five hundred years of "crime and cruelty." The lifting of the curse at the end of the appointed time produces a superhero: The Tornado. Monkhouse was as enthusiastic a writer as he was an artist, and there is a lot of verbiage on the page, but he works this to his advantage. As Gifford says, "His excellent wordplay reaches heights hitherto unknown in British comics."[42] Once Monkhouse left comics to pursue a career in radio and television, other artists took over the work on The Tornado, including Anglo, Ron Embleton, and Hugh Stanley White. The latter's highly atmospheric artwork for The Tornado was extremely accomplished, but there was little in the way of parody. In any case, there could not have been much more from White, since following the 1951 merger of *Oh Boy!* and *Wonderman* (which lasted for only one issue), he got out of the comics business. White, like Monkhouse, had worked for *Mickey Mouse Weekly* and would work with Anglo again in later years, providing artwork for *Young Marvelman*.

As Monkhouse was leaving comics, his old school friend Gifford was creating another superhero, Captain Might, this time for Modern Fiction Ltd, which was, like Scion and Paget, based in London. Modern Fiction was another publisher of pulp fiction (mainly sexy crime stories). The company was owned by E. H. and I. L. Turvey and had begun as an importer of magazines before getting into publishing.[43] Captain Might, "The Nemesis of Crime," appeared in *Amazing Comics* (1949), which was another one-shot comic used to get around restrictions on producing a new series (see Figure 21). Like Gifford's work on *Streamline*, there was a clear influence from Joe Simon and Jack Kirby's *Captain America*, although this time it was all the stronger as Gifford's line work and composition had improved considerably (or, as he jokingly said, his ability to copy Simon's artwork was improving).[44]

Captain Might was Professor Alan English, a research scientist at Atomville, a secret village of atomic workers located "somewhere in England." An

Fig. 20: Stuporman!, by Bob Monkhouse, in *Oh Boy! Comics* (Paget, 1948).

Fig. 21: Captain Might—The Nemesis of Crime, by Denis Gifford, in *Amazing Comics*, 1949 (Modern Fiction Ltd, 1949).

accident in the laboratory results in a blinding flash, and the professor suddenly has superpowers. He says "Phew! That's odd—I feel amazing strength surging through me—must be due to the atomic radiation! I'm a superman—and that gives me an idea—I'll outdo those comic book heroes—as Captain Might!" Clearly, Professor English (or Gifford) was reading Captain America comics very closely. Like Captain America, Captain Might has a prominent white star on his chest, along with boots and gloves very much like Captain America's. In the story, Captain Might battles Marvo the Magician, who uses the guise of his theatrical magic show to kidnap the chief of Atomville, Professor Maxted. Marvo, complete with pointy devil's beard and a villain's moustache fit for twirling, makes the Professor disappear, then disappears himself. Following the clues, Captain Might bursts in to find the evil magician threatening the Professor with a red-hot poker. The gothic horror imagery recalls Simon and Kirby's Captain America from the early 1940s and the penny dreadfuls of the nineteenth century. Gifford was by now quite skilled at producing a sub-Kirby style that at least echoed the look of American comics but was, intentionally or not, still something of a parody of them.

By the end of the 1940s, the small publishers had a firm grip on the market for American-style superhero comics, but the bigger publishers were still competing in this area, though not always successfully. The next superhero to appear was Hugh McNeill's Thunderbolt Jaxon, published by Amalgamated Press. In the story, which was highly influenced by Captain Marvel (at that point being reprinted in Britain by L. Miller and Son), young Jack Jaxon dons the magic belt of Thor in order to be transformed into an adult hero in a flash of lightning. This series was originally intended for the Australian market as Amalgamated Press was suffering from the encroachment of American-style comics and American reprints and therefore sought new markets. This strategy was the brainchild of *Knockabout* editor Edward Holmes. Thunderbolt Jaxon therefore had his own title in an American comic book format in Australia, but in Britain the stories were serialized in the weekly *Comet*. However, the character was not particularly successful and lasted only six issues in Australia. There was a revival in *Knockout* in 1958, with art by Ian Kennedy, before the character was rebranded Johnny Samson in *Buster* in 1964. *Buster* reprinted the *Comet* material and then offered new stories, but this strip was not successful either, and the series came to an end in 1965. While Thunderbolt Jaxon was not particularly successful in his own right, he did point the way toward what was coming in the 1950s: an enormous number of superheroes who were essentially copies of the hugely successful Captain Marvel.

The late 1930s and the early 1940s had seen the first faltering attempts to reconcile the superhero genre with the expectations of British comics readers. The war years, with the deprivation that came with rationing and the pressures of the conflict, were lean ones for British comics in one sense, but they were also years of incredible inventiveness and ones in which the relationship between Britain and American popular culture were simultaneously very close and at a remove. American troops were stationed in Britain and brought their comics, films, animation, music, and slang with them, but the nature of war meant that access to this material was patchy, so British popular culture offered a simulation of it, as seen in many comics of the period. As the 1940s came to a close, the era of the British superhero was in full swing, with the ban on American imports still in effect, creating opportunities that British publishers exploited as best they could under the still-difficult postwar conditions. A British approach to superheroes was formed at this time and would persist for many decades, privileging satirical and parodic treatment of the genre and providing a somewhat subversive view of the superhero. The next decade would see a number of prominent British superheroes, including the popular Marvelman series, tackling the genre with a newfound confidence. However, the 1950s would also see a number of challenges, such as a wave of censorship and a backlash against "vulgar" American popular culture, along with a new threat to British superheroes and to British comics as whole: the ever-increasing number of reprints of American comics, and by the end of the 1950s, the lifting of the import ban, which changed the market considerably.

Chapter Three

FROM MARVELMEN TO POP ART (1950-1961)

The postwar years were difficult ones in Britain and across Europe. While the 1950s saw a huge growth in consumer culture and prosperity in America, Britain and much of Europe were still recovering from the devastation of the war, and the rationing of food and materials continued in Britain until 1954, almost a decade after the war's end. It took around the same time for the rationing of paper to end, and the publishing and newspaper industries were not fully returned to prewar levels until well into the 1950s. However, it was also a time of great expansion of comics, which was largely due to the postwar baby boom. By 1950 there were many more children of comics reading age than ever before. DC Thomson was selling two million copies of *The Beano* and *The Dandy* a week. Indeed, the company was selling every issue it could publish, and conservative estimates suggest that each copy sold may have been read by as many as five other people.

Comics were therefore one of the cornerstones of children's entertainment in the 1950s, and they were more lucrative than ever before, partly because they had fewer competitors at this time. Of course, children listened to the radio and went to the cinema, and pocket money and pay from paper rounds and weekend jobs and the like often went to sweets and toys as well as comics. But at a time before television sets were a common feature in British homes and video games had not yet been invented, the appeal of the comics was strong. This was the golden age of British comics, and the most popular genre was humor, but the superheroes still had a place, and there was still a strong desire for American comics.

However, accessibility was a problem. As detailed in the previous chapter, the start of the war in 1939 had brought about an import ban on American publications, which stayed in place well after the war was over and was lifted only in 1959. As a result, several smaller publishers produced pirate versions of American comics, designed to look like the real thing. Sometimes these comics contained original British material that passed itself off as American. Cartoon Art Productions in Glasgow was particularly good at doing this in the mid-to-late 1940s. Similar bans in Canada and Australia produced similar effects, with a range of homegrown comics appearing from small publishers to fill the gap left by American comics. However, some publishers took a different route and got around the ban by licensing American material and reprinting it for the British market. L. Miller and Son had been successful in this regard, striking a deal with Fawcett in 1942 to reprint its hugely popular Captain Marvel series of comics, including the various spinoff titles of the "Captain Marvel Family."

The desire for American comics was fueled by several factors. One was the "special relationship" between Britain and America, which had been immeasurably strengthened during the war years. In cultural terms, this closeness was expressed as fascination with and aspiration for glamorous American culture as seen in movies, magazines, and comics, even if in political terms the special relationship was moving into deep trouble. The Suez Crisis of 1956 stemmed in part from Prime Minister Anthony Eden's need to maintain international prestige in the face of a collapsing empire. Though he was clearly and repeatedly warned by President Eisenhower not to intervene, Eden's military action, along with the French, resulted in a humiliating defeat (resulting from international, and especially US, pressure to withdraw) and Eden's resignation. It was the effective end of the British Empire.[1]

The Suez Crisis was yet another signal that the old deference to empire and authority was waning. It became increasingly easy to detect a note of frustration in British art and popular culture. The cultural turn toward, and identification with, America was visible in British pop art, music, and the comics, which had long replicated the American style. Indeed, despite the difficulties associated with finding American comics, superheroes had very much entered the British popular consciousness and were even represented in prose stories in annuals and in novels. Two examples were the Human Bat novels written by Edward R. Home-Gall (1897–1974). Home-Gall was the son of *Triumph* editor William B. Home-Gall, one of the most prolific writers of boy's weeklies, and a contributor to many DC Thomson titles. In the 1950s, Edward R. Home-Gall wrote for *Lion* and *Tiger*, as well as text stories featuring "The Amazing Adventures of Mr X" under the pen name Edwin Dale. His two superhero novels, *The Human Bat* and *The Human Bat V the Robot Gangster* (both 1950) were published by Mark Goulden (an imprint of W. H. Allen) and advertised as "science fiction thrillers for all ages." For his character The Human Bat, Home-Gall drew upon a popular character type in British superhero comics and boy's weeklies—the winged hero. His character wore a bright red suit and had leathery, bat-like wings, looking very much like a brash and exciting American-style superhero.

One of the ways American comics continued to make their way into the country was through the PX stores on American military bases. Even though World War II was over, there continued to be a strong American military presence in Britain, as it was instrumental to Cold War military strategy. Or, as David Reynolds puts it in *Britannia Overruled: British Policy and World Power in the Twentieth Century* (1991), "Faced after 1945 by a Soviet Union deep in Eastern Europe, armed with vast conventional forces and, soon, nuclear weapons, Britain had little choice but to shelter under the nuclear umbrella of the USA. And as its economy and influence declined, it reluctantly sought incorporation into the European community."[2] In reaction, British culture leaned more toward America, seeking imaginative connections with its more glamorous, aspirational culture at a time when political and economic ties were straining. Critic Raymond Williams's book *Culture and Society* (1958) pointed to a new understanding of culture at the time, divorced from the view of the "Great Tradition" of literature held by F. R. Leavis, who thought that literature served as a buttress against encroaching Americanization.[3] Williams broadened the definition of culture to include popular and material culture and with that opened the door to the new field of cultural studies, which emerged over the next few decades. However, in the 1950s the Americanization of British culture was a very divisive topic.

Another means by which American comics came to Britain was via the unsold remainder copies that were often used as ballast in American ships, with piles offloaded at British ports (mainly Liverpool, Manchester, Belfast, and London). The comics that passed through the bases and trading ports made their way into the hands of eager British readers through newsdealers and secondhand bookstores located near the military bases and ports. Still, this was a matter of luck and happenstance and clearly could not substitute for a proper means of distribution. However, by the early 1950s there was an increasing range of American material available in the form of reprints. Albums like *The Ajax Adventure Annual* and *The Okay Adventure Annuals*, both published by Popular Press for T. V. Boardman and Company Ltd, would have a mixture of British prose stories and American reprints from the Quality Comics range, which was a continuation of a licensing agreement that T.V. Boardman had established with Quality Comics in 1940 (as discussed in the previous chapter). The 1952 *Ajax Adventure Annual* featured reprints of Plastic Man and Doll Man, some in full color, which was unusual, as British reprints of American material would usually be black and white. The 1955 *Okay Adventure Annual* featured a range of short stories originally published by Quality, but this time from the late 1930s and early 1940s.

These included historical adventure and crime stories, as well as "Hugh Hazzard and His Iron Man," which featured Bozo the Robot in a story by Wayne Reid, and "The Clock Strikes," by George Brenner, which featured the masked crime fighter, The Clock, perhaps the first masked hero in American comics, appearing in 1936. The 1956 *Okay Adventure Annual* reprinted two Plastic Man stories and one Doll Man story alongside several Western stories, all by Quality Comics and all originally published in 1951. The 1957 annual featured Blackhawks and Plastic Man, and the next year's contained The Flame. Both of these annuals contained the American Dennis the Menace (which is highly unusual, as the agreement between publishers regarding their identically named characters should have precluded this). These annuals also had striking covers and some interior artwork by the great British cover artist Denis McLoughlin. Resplendent as the covers were, the interior pages were mainly in black and white, with only the occasional page in color. Another way for American and American-style comics to reach Britain was via Australia. Like Britain, Australia had a ban on American imports, so Australian comics developed their own superheroes and licensing deals. Comics like *The Crimson Comet*, published by Action Comics, which was based in Sydney, showcased the talents of comics artists like John Dixon, who—like Len Fullerton, Dennis M. Reader, and Mick Anglo in Britain—did an excellent job of recreating the dynamics of American superhero comics. Through such publications, combined with the "pirates" or fake American comics, the licensed reprints by Miller, and imports from commonwealth countries like Australia, the availability of American and American-style comics was steadily improving in the early 1950s, but the situation was about to take a dramatic turn for the worse.

In the early 1950s, America went through a craze for a much more lurid and sensational brand of horror and crime comic than previously seen. Some of these, particularly those published by EC Comics, were of exceptionally good quality, were well written and drawn, and reached an adult readership. However, some were also quite violent and shocking. Some in America, such as Sterling North, and later, and more famously, Frederic Wertham, spoke out against such comics, arguing that they led to increased rates of juvenile delinquency.[4] This conclusion rested on little or no evidence, but the public outcry in America reached fever pitch and McCarthy-style hearings in the US Congress pushed the industry toward the adoption of a self-imposed code of censorship and control named the Comics Code. It is likely that the cynical aim of many of the publishers who pushed for the adoption of the code was to put EC Comics, a major competitor, out of business. The accusations leveled against the American comics industry were more or less repeated verbatim in Britain, with commentators and interest groups pushing for tighter controls on American comics. Despite the ban on imports, the comics were making it into Britain through indirect means and were being reprinted using the aforementioned licensing deals. Moreover, some British comics did pull off quite convincing copies of American comics, copies such as *The Bat Magazine* (1952), starring The Bat, written and drawn by George McQueen and featuring a supernatural hero. This character had nothing to do with William Ward's 1940s character, also called The Bat, but it had some passing similarities to Batman, including a symbol of a bat on his chest and small bat ears on his hood. The real influence, though, came from American horror comics, and McQueen did an excellent job of mirroring the surreal and nightmarish imagery seen in many American horror publications of the time.

When the crime and horror comics that were attracting such negative attention in America joined the piles of comics making their way across the Atlantic and being reprinted as British editions, a similar "moral panic" was sparked in Britain, echoing the concerns about the influence of penny dreadfuls in the nineteenth century (see Chapter One). This led to heated debate in the newspapers, questions in Parliament, and a campaign to ban the distribution of American crime and horror comics. This campaign involved religious figures such as the Archbishop of Canterbury, the Home Secretary, and the National Union of Teachers, as well as various parents groups. In response, the Children and Young Persons (Harmful Publications) Act was passed by Parliament in 1955. It prohibited

> any book, magazine or other like work which is of a kind likely to fall into the hands of children or young persons and consists wholly or mainly of stories told in pictures (with or without the addition of written matter), being stories portraying (a) the commission of crimes; or (b) acts of violence or cruelty; or (c) incidents of a repulsive or horrible nature; in such a way that the work as a whole would tend to corrupt a child or young person into whose hands it might fall.[5]

As Martin Barker demonstrates in *A Haunt of Fears: The Strange History of the British Horror Comics Campaign* (1984), the moral panic in Britain was driven by the unlikely coalition of conservative parents groups and the Communist Party, who were both opposed to the perceived encroachment of American popular culture, and therefore political ideas, into Britain.[6] While this campaign and the resulting Harmful Publications Act were directed at American horror and crime comics in the course of the heated debate, American comics in general came under suspicion. The import ban may have had an economic imperative, but the campaign and legislation had a moral one—or, rather, a political one disguised as a moral one—and soon almost all American comics carried the taint of suspicion.

The objections to American comics in Britain were borne out of a wider sense that American popular culture was crude and vulgar, much like the stereotypical "Yank." Moves to combat this influence actually predated the public outcry and resulting legislation. Indeed, the perhaps the most well-known British comic of the 1950s was *The Eagle*, which starred Dan Dare, who became an icon of British comics. It was born out of a desire to offer an alternative to American-style comics.[7] *The Eagle*, published by Hulton Press from 1950 to 1969, was founded by Marcus Morris, an Anglican vicar. It set new standards for British adventure comics, both in terms of storytelling and production, but its real aim to set a higher standard in terms of the message it portrayed. The intention was for it to be a wholesome and educational comic as well as an exciting one. With the artwork of Frank Hampson on Dan Dare and Morris's keen sense of design, the comic was an instant success. *The Eagle* was the most influential British comic of the period and had been formed with the overt intention of offering a supposedly wholesome alternative to American, and American-influenced, comics. In reality the comic, and particularly the Dan Dare strips, opposed supposedly vulgar American values by substituting an equally problematic nostalgic vision of British imperial greatness. They depicted the Great British Empire in space, fighting against an intractable enemy, the Mekon, along with Treen soldiers who obey his will unquestioningly. This was a time when science fiction was becoming more popular, and the huge success of *The Eagle* provoked imitation; in 1952 IPC launched *Lion* in a clear attempt to challenge *The Eagle*. Captain Condor was no match for Dan Dare, but *Lion*'s Robot Archie proved popular, and this mechanical hero would reappear over the years in both *Lion* (1952–1974) and *Vulcan* (1975–1976).

The early 1950s also saw the rise of girl's comics, and notably *The School Friend* and *Girl*. *School Friend* was originally published by Amalgamated Press as a girl's story paper, running from 1919 to 1929, at which point it was renamed *The Schoolgirl*. It remained under that title until 1940, when it was canceled due to the paper shortages brought on by wartime rationing and austerity. *The School Friend* reappeared in 1950, this time as a mix of comics and prose stories, as was common for the time. One of the comic strips was "The Silent Three," which featured three school friends who dressed in green robes and masks in order to solve mysteries at the school. This was very much in the traditional school story mold but was unusual in that it drew something from the adventure stories usually reserved for boy's comics and also because it was initially drawn by a female artist, Evelyn Flinders. The stories were written by Horace Boyten and Stewart Pride, and the strip ran for thirteen years. In 1951 the companion to *The Eagle*, named *Girl*, was launched, signaling an attempt to bolster the number of female comics readers. But it was, like *The Eagle*, somewhat constrained, and the stories tended to feature girl reporters or ballerinas rather than adventurers (with the possible exception of "Vicky and the Vengeance of the Incas"), and there were certainly no superheroines to be found. As with *The Eagle*, the aim was to divert readers from "unwholesome" American material.

While the early 1950s would be a difficult time for American and American-style comics, at the start of the decade the British superhero genre was a niche area of publishing but a relatively healthy one, although humor comics still dominated the market. It was natural, then, that parodies of the superhero would appear. One of the best examples of a humor character used to satirize the superhero genre came in the form of the Superstooge stories that appeared in several Gerald Swan albums from 1953 to 1956. Superstooge was the superhero version of a character Stoogie, created by Harry Banger, who had been appearing in Swan publications since 1940s (see Figure 22). Stoogie was a hapless buffoon with a huge nose and habit of getting himself into trouble. In the early 1950s, interest in superheroes was such that Stoogie went from being a normal humor character with no special powers to a superhero, wearing a parody of Superman's costume, with an "S" for Superstooge emblazoned on his chest. This was not the first superhero parody seen in Britain. That was Bob Monkhouse's Stuporman, who appeared in *Oh Boy!* in 1948. This tradition of parody superheroes in Britain's comics was a very popular one, and as shall be discussed in the next chapter, it included DC Thomson's Bananaman (1980–present), but the tradition was even stronger in America, where there were several superhero parodies, in animation especially, such as Mighty Mouse.

Perhaps the most notable American parody of superheroes was "Superduperman," by Harvey Kurtzman and Wally Wood, which appeared in *Mad* #4 (April–May 1953). It satirized the whole genre, but especially targeted

Fig. 22: *Slick Fun Album*, featuring Superstooge, by Harry Banger (Gerald Swan, 1956).

the most popular heroes of the time, Superman and Captain Marvel, and in particular the recently concluded court case between publishers DC Comics and Fawcett. It also made a strong impression on a young Alan Moore, who upon seeing "Superduperman" was inspired to do something similar with Marvelman, which he would have the chance to do many years later, in 1982, in *Warrior*. There he would revolutionize Marvelman; not, however, by using humor, but rather by employing realism and drama. It is possible that "Superduperman" had an influence on the development of Superstooge, but even if it not, they shared a strategy: undermining the superhero genre, and the figure of the superhero, through humor. This use of humor to parody the superhero was something that happened on a quite regular basis, particularly in the comics produced by the larger British publishers, but some smaller publishers continued to take superhero comics quite seriously, even if unintentional humor sometimes crept in between the straitlaced heroics. However, over time the humor and adventure genres started to come together, and some comics blended the two, sometimes using this as a means to offer a critique of the genre and at times of the pretentions of some American comics.

The (Continued) Rise of the Small Superhero Publishers

As detailed in the last chapter, several attempts were made to create homegrown British superheroes in the immediate postwar years, although these met with mixed success. Such efforts continued into the 1950s, with many small publishers releasing either one-off comics or short-lived runs of comics featuring superheroes. Often these were quite good facsimiles of American comics, but like the British superheroes of the mid- to late 1940s, they rarely captured the confident tone of American superheroes and were frequently a mix of adventure and humor. It may have been that for some British comics creators, the concept of the superhero was inherently easier to mock than to take seriously, or the humorous interjection may have been a more appealing approach to them because they were reacting to a deeper ambivalence about America.

The 1950s saw an increasing strain in British-American relations. It was, as Reynolds notes, "a period of extreme global instability when the Pax Americana was neither readily forthcoming nor perfectly tailored to British interests."[8] He also argues that Britain was trapped by illusions of grandeur, refusing to accept that the world had changed and victory in the war did not mean that the "greatness" of Britain could continue as it had in the past. International relationships had changed, the world economy had been turned upside down, and the British Empire was collapsing. Not keeping track with reality, British comics were increasingly conveying the politics of nostalgia. The relationship with America was therefore a complex one, mediated by some powerful political delusions about the equality of the British-American partnership.

However, as Reynolds says, "although increasingly unbalanced, the relationship [between Britain and America] did give the British unusual access to US policymaking and yielded results, such as the nuclear alliance, that were unique."[9] This delusion of being an equal partner with the United States was exacerbated in the 1950s when Europe started to recover and consolidate. Britain largely viewed itself as looking outward, across the Atlantic to its relationship with America, and it was painful for it to think of itself as no longer the center of the world, but rather clinging to the edge of Europe. This caused a tension between representation and reality, and as a result the Yanks as seen in British culture were glamorous and appealing on the one hand but also figures of fun on the other. The superhero offered the opportunity to exploit both attitudes towards America, synthesizing them into a satirical whole or playing them off against one another and using the humor to rebalance the imagined relationship between both countries as one of equals.

A good example of this conflicted attitude towards the superhero is seen in Captain Zenith, who was created by Mick Anglo and made one appearance in 1950 (see Figure 23). *Captain Zenith Comics* was published by London-based publisher Martin and Reid Ltd, which Gifford calls "one of the most prolific small publishers of the period."[10] The two-page story, which started on the cover (which was in color) and continued to the back page (black and white), has the title character responding to a cry for help and discovering that a man has been robbed of his priceless pearls. After receiving a description of the getaway car, he sets off running at superspeed. Not finding the car, he deduces that he must have been running too fast and has accidentally run past the car. The next day, reading about the crime in the newspaper, he discovers that the pearls were insured and quickly concludes that the seeming victim was actually the criminal (and therefore there was no getaway car, or at least the description was false). Confronting the criminal and his accomplice, Captain Zenith beats them into submission and announces to the reader, "One way or the other the law always wins."

Anglo's character design and artwork clearly evoke an American comic, although there are elements of the story that seem at odds with the genre. In some ways, the plot reads as a mockery of earnest American superheroics. The idea that the superhero might run past the getaway car due to his superspeed can be read as a knowing, playful mockery of the genre. Superheroes are often ridiculously overpowered in relation to the threats that they face (bank robbers and petty criminals), and the act of drawing attention to that in this story could be construed as a critique. However, it is just as likely that Anglo did not intend the story to be humorous, as he has to tell a complete story in just two pages, resulting in a rather truncated narrative. If this were an American comic book story, the narrative would be at least three times as long, and indeed it is short even for a British story. If it were longer, perhaps the narrative tension could have been maintained rather than being punctured by the image of the superhero defeated by his own powers. With just two pages, Anglo has to move quickly (at superspeed) and thus overtakes the drama, just as his character seems to overtake the getaway car, producing what appears to be unintentional comedy.

Fig. 23: *Captain Zenith*, by Mick Anglo (Martin and Reid Ltd, 1950).

But the slip is revealing. Also revealing is the fact that Anglo's style is very clearly influenced by early 1940s American comics, and most directly by Joe Simon and Jack Kirby's Captain America. This is evident from the title. (He is, after all, *Captain* Zenith, with a "Z" emblazoned on his chest, just as Captain America has an "A.") Another interesting point is made by Gifford, who argues that by the early 1950s, the concept of the superhero was so embedded in popular culture that there was no need to provide an origin for Captain Zenith or an explanation for his powers. The costume is enough to signify that he is a superhero, and all the other tropes of the genre, from superpowers to a secret identity, are assumed.

However, this is most likely a consequence of trying to fit into two pages a story that seems more suited to a newspaper strip like Batman or Dick Tracy. Another oddity is that the style makes it look more like a comic from the early 1940s rather than the ones being published in America in the 1950s. This time lag was a result of many factors, but mainly because many of the American comics to which Mick Anglo was likely exposed were quite old. Also, as pointed out by Gifford in *Super-Duper Supermen* (1991), Captain Zenith "arrived rather late in the super-hero field," long after the first flurry of British superheroes in the mid-1940s.[11] However, this was a time when American reprints and imports, especially those featuring Captain Marvel, published in America by Fawcett, were increasingly available in Britain, although the material being reprinted was years old. Indeed, Captain Marvel, drawn by C. C. Beck, was hugely popular in both America and Britain and had been reprinted by Miller for the British market since the 1940s, so British readers were well accustomed to this character and to his origin story. The next British superheroes to appear were strongly influenced by these comics, as well as by the old favorites, Superman and Batman.

Captain Marvel vs. the British Doppelgangers

The influence of Captain Marvel was clearly seen in *Electroman Comics*, published in 1951 by Scion and marked as a production of King-Ganteaume, a London-based studio that was set up by Americans Ken King and Malcolm Ganteaume to produce comics for small British publishers. The story goes that King and Ganteaume were former soldiers who used their severance pay to set up the studio. They worked with different publishers, including Scion and Miller, and produced six issues of *Electroman Comics* for Scion between 1951 and 1952. The covers stated that these comics were the "UK editions," but this assertion was meant to misleadingly give the impression that the superhero was an actual American, in the same way that Miller produced UK editions of Captain Marvel comics. This echoed the strategies of Cartoon Art Productions in Glasgow (discussed in the last chapter), which put American prices on the covers to create the impression that they were distributing an American product. Whereas Captain Zenith appeared in only two pages of a single comic, Electroman lasted for a bit longer, appearing in six comics, and there the appropriation of the American style was much more convincing (see Figure 24).

The first thing to note about Electroman is the character design, which mimics Captain Marvel very closely with a military-style tunic and short cape. Even the symbol displayed on his chest is similar, with two crossed lightning bolts rather than the single bolt displayed on Captain Marvel's chest. There is much in these comics that shows off King-Ganteaume's special ability to produce "fake" American comics. One cover shows Electroman fighting crooks in front of a New York City skyline, and one story opens in an American diner, with the artist doing a good job of communicating the idea that the scene is set in America, with signs for hamburgers, Coca-Cola, and Campbell's soup in the background and the prices in cents clearly displayed. But there were often slips in the script, and especially telling was the occasional use of British slang. Also, sometimes the artwork revealed its homegrown origin, for example, when it showed drivers sitting on the wrong side of the front seat. The debt to Captain Marvel is also revealed in the strange origin story. Whereas Captain Marvel is a young newsboy, Billy Batson, who is transformed into an adult hero by a mysterious wizard called Shazam, Electroman is an old man, also a newspaper seller, who is transformed from a criminal into a younger hero.

In the origin story, Dan Watkins (also known as Fingers for his safe-cracking abilities) is executed in the electric chair but does not die. In fact the shock "cures" him of his criminal proclivities. Later, when captured by a villain, he is electrocuted again, but this time he is transformed into a superhero. His altered molecular structure gives him powers of strength, invulnerability, and flight, which he can activate by coming into contact with electricity (typically by grabbing an electrical cable). Whereas Billy Batson merely had to utter the word "Shazam!" to trigger his transformation, Dan has to locate an electrical power source, but he usually does this in ingenious ways. His transformation is represented by a panel with an explosion, often with a sound effect (BAM! ZOWIE! or BOOM!), and in the next panel he is transformed, costume and all, into Electroman. In another nod to Captain Marvel, Dan/Electroman has a young accomplice, a would-be

Fig. 24: Electroman, in *Electroman Comics* (King-Ganteaume/Scion, 1951).

thief called Tim, whom he takes under his wing. This character is reminiscent of Billy Batson, and the artwork is a studied copy of C. C. Beck's style. It was one of the first British superhero comics for which the artwork was precisely modeled on the American style.

Another way in which Electroman mirrored American comics was that each of its stories was between five and nine pages long, and most were eight pages. This was the length of the typical American comic book story of the time. The artwork was professional and the page composition was dynamic. One of the first things that is apparent upon seeing these pages is that they have the same kind of pacing as an American comic. With about eight pages to thirteen pages in which to unfold a story, American comics were structured differently from British comics, which might have three to five pages (or in the case of Captain Zenith, just two). American stories would often open with a "splash page" or "splash panel," showcasing the action or establishing the scene. A page setting up the story would usually follow, and then the superhero would leap into action. British comics usually did not have the space to give to such preliminaries and relied on text to establish the scene and introduce the story before getting to the action, and doing so much more quickly than their American counterparts. The result was that British stories often felt more rushed and less satisfying. American comics also often took more care with the page composition and told the story much more visually. The best ones ensured that the page was balanced and the action foregrounded. C. C. Beck's Captain Marvel stories were particularly good in this regard. The artist of Electroman clearly studied American comics such as these with some attention, and the generous gutters (the spaces between panels) showed an influence of Superman, Captain Marvel, and several other American comics. The Electroman stories always open with a well-proportioned splash panel that takes up three-quarters of the page, and room is always given to the title, "Electroman," which looks convincingly American in its design and proportions. There are frequently panels that contain only text, and they advance the story; this is a feature that was seen in early Superman stories and Captain Marvel comics.

In the course of his six-issue run, Electroman tackled several villains. In his origin story, he confronts the thieves and murderers who framed him along with the crime boss, the monocled Baron Kotzbue, who also seems to be involved in espionage for a foreign power. He captures the Baron and delivers him to jail. In "The Treasure of El Chimborazo," Electroman once again meets the evil Baron Kotzbue, who is described as "the crookedest crook and the craftiest craftsman of skulduggery that you ever laid eyes on."

Electroman learns that the Baron is still in jail, but that his twin brother (who is himself called Baron Kotzbue) has kidnapped and plans to kill several archaeologists after they unwittingly lead him to an ancient hidden treasure in Ecuador. His plan to use these riches to become a dictator and rule all of South America is foiled when Electroman intervenes.

In a marked departure from most American superhero stories, not much attention is given to the protection of Electroman's secret identity. He openly transforms in front of several people, including a journalist. In another story "Electroman and the Million Dollar Robbery," he does battle with Porky Grogan and his gang of thieves. In the course of the story he again transforms, with the help of Tim, into Electroman in full view of witnesses before capturing the gang of criminals. In "The Great Electroman becomes a 3 Ring Circus," Electroman joins the circus to thwart the schemes of a murderous clown who is jealous because he does not have top billing at the circus. In "Electroman and the Great Train Robbery," the villain is Bugsy Norgo, the bug-eyed leader of a criminal gang. In an "imaginary story" called "Electroman and Tim meet Benjamin Franklin," Tim and Dan are drawn into a history book Tim is reading, where they meet a younger version of the American Founding Father when he is still postmaster of Philadelphia. When they are kidnapped by criminals, Dan rubs a cat to generate a static electric charge that transforms him into Electroman and allows him to defeat the criminals. In the end, all of this is revealed to be a dream; Tim has fallen asleep reading his history book and has imagined everything. This was a common trope in superhero comics, and it is well executed here.

Some elements of *Electroman* can be read as satirical, but then Captain Marvel was unusual among American superhero stories for having a sense of fun and playfulness, with Plastic Man being the other notable exception. This is an important point; rather than being an outright parody of the American superhero comics, Electroman was a successful imitation of a subset of American superhero comics that themselves parodied the genre, or were at least quite playful in tone. Indeed, given the imitations of these characters, Captain Marvel and Plastic Man seen to have been models of the superhero that made sense to British creators or were more palatable to readers. The only thing that separated Electroman stories from those in American comic books was that the artwork was black and white rather than color. As it was emulating artwork that was designed for color, it feels like color is missing. British comics, which were usually designed to be in black and white, often employed black ink and hatching to give the images some depth in the absence of color, but Electroman maintains the open feel of artwork waiting for color to be applied. For this reason, the stories look quite a lot like the black and white versions of American material that appeared in British reprints, thereby adding another degree of apparent authenticity.

The tactic of mimicking American comics was certainly about tapping into the appeal of American comics to British readers, but this should not obscure what was a likely ambition for Scion: to use this platform to break into the lucrative American market. To accomplish this goal, its strategy during the late 1940s had been to try out a wide variety of genres across a range of one-off comics. These included the Big Comics in 1948–1949, such as *Big Atlantis Comic*, *Big Castle Comic*, *Big Chuckle Comic*, and *Big Flame Comic* (which featured the superhero Litening), along with the Hero Comics in 1951–1952, namely *Adventure Hero*, *Daring Hero*, *Detective Hero*, *Sea Hero*, *Sky Hero*, and *Space Hero*. From humor to crime, science fiction, and superheroes, Scion was clearly experimenting with the market. The fact that the firm chose to develop Electroman as a series and as a title character demonstrated its confidence in the appeal of the superhero. Scion had good reason to trust in the character, as the Captain Marvel formula had proven hugely popular both in Britain and America, where the sales of Captain Marvel in America sometimes surpassed those of Superman. The threat to Superman's sales was treated so seriously by DC Comics that it sued Fawcett, the publisher of Captain Marvel, and eventually won the case, forcing Fawcett to cease publication of stories featuring the character.

Another British superhero modeled on Captain Marvel was Mr Apollo, who appeared in 1952 in *Dynamic Thrills*, published by Gerald G. Swan Ltd in what was the last comic the company produced. He was created by George Bunting and featured on the cover of *Dynamic Thrills* #7, which was drawn by Jock McCail (see Figure 25). Again, the costume was all but identical to Captain Marvel, albeit with a shooting star on his chest rather than a lightning bolt, and Mr Apollo's powers are described as "the strength of Hercules, plus the speed of Mercury," citing mythological figures in much the same way Captain Marvel did. The ability to instantly transform into the superhero was another key feature shared with Captain Marvel and Electroman, but this time the civilian identity was that of a schoolteacher, Jerry Gunn. His superpowers are explained (or, rather, not really explained) as being brought about by the power of Gunn's mind.

In contrast to Electroman, where the artist does a very good job of copying the American style, Mr Apollo is rather crudely drawn and expresses none of the compositional dynamism seen in Electroman. Nine- or

Fig. 25: Mr Apollo, in *Dynamic Thrills* (Gerald G. Swan Ltd, 1952).

twelve-panel grids are often employed, and there are no gutters between panels; rather, the panels are crammed together, which makes the pages look quite crowded. Whereas Electroman maintains the illusion of being an American strip with artwork that looked like it was designed with color in mind, Mr Apollo makes heavy use of black ink and is quite heavily rendered, which is much more in keeping with a British comics aesthetic. However, in contrast to the backgrounds, the images of Mr Apollo himself look stylistically different and are likely lifts from Captain Marvel comics, creating a rather distracting dissonance between the title character and his world. Moreover, the Mr Apollo story makes no attempt to appear as if it is set in America. It failed where Electroman succeeded. The story looked like a bad imitation of American comics, resulting in an uncomfortable hybrid of British and American styles.

One of the most interesting things about Mr Apollo occurs at the level of genre. The fact that Mr Apollo is a schoolteacher in his civilian guise establishes a link with the very popular school story genre in British boy's papers and comics. This association is strengthened when Toby, one of Mr Apollo's strangest opponents, makes an appearance in 1953's *Cute Fun Album*. Gifford notes that Toby is a "fat schoolboy who swallowed some of Professor Calitrope's atomic pills and expanded into a fat giant."[12] Arguably, this character is a version of the long-running British story paper character, Billy Bunter, an obnoxious schoolboy who cannot stop eating. In this sense, Mr Apollo was a strange collision between the superhero, the more heavily rendered style of illustrations from British adventure stories, and the then-popular school genre. Ultimately this does not work very well, and the fact that *Dynamic Thrills* was Swan's last comic perhaps provides the answer why. It may have been that this Swan song (if the pun can be forgiven) was something of a desperate move, made without a clear understanding of what the readership wanted, or perhaps was an attempt to bring two audiences together in this muddled effort. However, even though Swan was withdrawing from the publication of comics, the company continued to publish annuals, and Mr Apollo would appear in several, including *Slick Fun Album* (1952), *Funnies Album* (1953), and the aforementioned *Cute Fun Album* (1953), although no improvements are made in either the art or the pacing. Mr Apollo also made another appearance, in a different guise, in "The Amazing Adventures of Mr Atlas," which was published in *Funnies*. This was clearly a doctored Mr Apollo story that was repurposed to make it appear as if it was a new character, but this effort was futile, as it suffers from the same stylistic and compositional weaknesses as Mr Apollo.

The next British superhero to draw on Captain Marvel was Masterman, who appeared in twelve issues of *Masterman Comic* (1952–1953), published by Streamline. The artwork was provided by Joe Colquhoun (who would go on to have a distinguished career in British comics, including drawing the celebrated antiwar comic *Charley's War*, written by Pat Mills and published in *Battle* between 1978 and 1986). Masterman was another character who transformed from a child into an adult superhero (see Figure 26). Billy Fletcher is described as a "puny little runt" and is bullied by local children. When his father goes to Cairo on business, Billy tags along but is kidnapped and held hostage. Fleeing from his would-be killers, Billy finds a lost tomb and a strange ring. The ring was once possessed by Masterman, a long dead prince from Ancient Egypt who used the power in his special "ring of fate" to rule his people and bring justice to the land. This story element is more than a little reminiscent of Captain Marvel's origin (and Masterman is also the name of a superhero published by Fawcett in the 1940s, although he was, like Captain Marvel, the subject of a lawsuit from DC Comics and as a result appeared in only six issues). By reciting "O ring of fate I call upon you to help me fight for freedom and justice," Billy is transformed into the most powerful man on the world. His powers seem to be partly driven by willpower and imagination, which in a sense is reminiscent of Green Lantern's power ring.

Streamline Publications was even more explicit than Cartoon Art Productions and Scion, proudly proclaiming that *Masterman Comic* was an "American Comic." It is true that Streamline reprinted some American material (in the first issue, a 1950 Dick Briefer story called "Rattler Matt" that first appeared in Hillman's *Dead-Eye Western* #8 serves as the backup strip), but the Masterman comic was in no sense "American." As in the Electroman comics, some "errors," such as the misspelling of "tyres," gives the game away. However, this was no lazy Captain Marvel ripoff; rather, Masterman was well written, and very well drawn by Colquhoun (even though it is apparent that this is the work of a young man still learning his craft). The first issue, which presents the origin story, does not rush into a hasty introduction; it is well paced and establishes the character of Billy over fifteen pages. He is a bookish and privileged child who is bullied by local children, coddled by his mother, and is something of a disappointment to his father. When he is kidnapped, he uses courage and intelligence to escape his captors, and he is chosen by the spirit of Masterman as a worthy successor and is himself transformed into an adult hero. He receives the physical power to defeat his captors, and later his bullies.

Fig. 26: *Masterman Comic*, by Joe Colquhoun (Streamline, 1952).

The story is quite dark in comparison to typical comics of the time, yet there are moments of wit and visual humor. Also, just as Mr Apollo attempted to blend the superhero with the school story tradition, so does Masterman, but much more successfully. Billy Fletcher is right out of the school story tradition, and even without his powers he is an intelligent and resourceful character. This story succeeded where Mr Apollo failed in terms of blending the superhero and school story genres (although given the fact that Masterman only lasted six issues, that success has to be measured in artistic terms rather than financial ones). The key to this success was that Billy Fletcher was sufficiently developed as a character to allow the reader to empathize regarding his relationship to his parents and his struggles with the bullies. Another indicator of success was the delicate balancing act achieved in Colquhoun's style. Where in Mr Apollo British and American styles clash, Colquhoun achieves synthesis with his art for Masterman.

Figure 26 provides a perfect example. The first panel shows Billy and Lana, but he speaks directly to the reader in a word balloon that should perhaps be a thought bubble. This panel, along with the second one, is quite heavily rendered, with a lot of black ink and some suggestion of a horror story, but the third panel, which shows the transformation of Billy into Masterman, is quite different. The superhero is drawn in a much more open style—with linework that does not have a lot of shadow and crosshatching—and the smoke and flash of light dispel the dark rendering. In the next panel, where Masterman flies through the night, the two styles come together. The last two panels show the meeting of the Black Wizard and his followers, and the tropes of the horror genre are now much more in evidence, with the strange, undulating line work in the background adding to the surreal feeling. Oddly, the Black Wizard is dressed very much like an American superhero (his costume being that of a much more traditional superhero than Masterman's). Masterman was an amalgamation of the American and British superhero traditions and styles and one of the best examples of a British superhero from the 1950s.

Like Electroman's, Masterman's secret identity is not very secret at all. In the first story, Billy transforms into Masterman in front of the kidnappers and his father, then later in front of the bullies and a policeman. One of the things that set Masterman apart was that Colquhoun drew Billy in the act of transformation, showing him growing into the adult superhero. In Captain Marvel comics (as well as Electroman and Mr Apollo), a flash of light and a sound effect would obscure the actual transformation, but Masterman comics showed the change from Billy to the giant Masterman.

This was a small modification, but it made a difference. It was the equivalent of a cinematic special effect, adding a degree of drama and dynamism to the transformation and, crucially, allowing others to marvel at this change, and in particular, for villains and bullies to register horror and fear at Billy's metamorphosis. The panels that show Billy confronting the bullies are particularly significant, as they provide a humorous ending to the story, with the chief bully running away in terror and the policeman's hat flying off his head in surprise. Such occasional moments of comedy bring together the superhero genre with the humor genre and have a very British quality to them. The gag of the policemen's hat flying off his head could be straight out of a DC Thomson's humor story, which was another indication of the British tendency to undermine and parody the more serious American superhero genre

Another Captain Marvel copy came in the form of Captain Universe, who appeared in *Captain Universe* #1 (1954). It was created by Mick Anglo for the Arnold Book Company, which was based in London and represented part of Anglo's business model. His studio produced work for a number of publishers, and he would often reuse ideas and rework stories for different publishers, who would, naturally enough, be happy to receive work that competed with other material on the market. Science fiction was becoming increasingly popular in the atomic age of the 1950s, with stories of flying saucers in the newspapers and alien invasion a common theme in popular film. It was natural that science fiction and the superhero should come together; after all, they had been very closely associated from the start, and characters like Superman were science-fiction characters transposed to comics. Captain Universe appeared just as science fiction was becoming very popular in both America and Britain. Instead of receiving a magic word from a wizard, Captain Universe treated his body "electronically" and became receptive to electronic impulses that emanated from the furthest reaches of space, imbuing him with superhuman powers. His transformation from scientist Jim Logan (the surname being an anagram of Anglo) was triggered by a special word, but instead of "SHAZAM" he uttered the word "GALAP," which stood for "Galileo, master of the galaxies, Archimedes, master of physics, Leonardo da Vinci, master of invention, Aristotle, master of philosophy, and Pythagorus [sic], master of geometry." In his civilian guise as Jim Logan, he was a scientist for The Interplanetary Research Division of the United Nations, complete with herringbone jacket and a pipe, giving him the air of a detective as well as a scientist, associating him with Quatermass from the 1952 BBC television series, while as Captain

Universe he is a galactic policeman, thwarting invasions and keeping the peace. Like Marvelman, Electroman, and Masterman, this was excellent work, with Anglo combining the best elements of American and British superhero traditions.

Another superhero who received powers from the stars was Steve Samson, who appeared in 1953 from Sports Cartoons Ltd. He started off as a circus strongman with no superpowers but then became a space adventurer; then an encounter with the Masters of the Universe granted him superpowers. In the story "A Threat to the Capital," Samson is identified as the Guardian of the Galaxy, and he works for the world's security forces. A threat to cities all around the world is issued by a cabal of big businessmen who are opposed to world peace on the grounds that war is more profitable. Samson eventually locates them but is neutralized by their robot. After a great struggle, he uses his wits and strength to defeat the robot and then rounds up the villains. When the world is safe, he flies out to space to report to the Masters, and one, who is reminiscent of the wizard Shazam from *Captain Marvel*, tells him that through his efforts the Earth is "climbing in the regard of the other more advanced planets." The images of Samson in flight look very much like lifts from Superman comics, but overall the style is very British. It is rough, with lots of hatching, like the illustrations that were employed in story papers. Like many superhero stories of the time, it blended elements of science fiction, and the fact that the character started as a strongman shows that slippage between genres was not uncommon as the British superhero became all the more prominent.

The reason so many characters copied Captain Marvel was because he had already become a very popular character and his stories had been reprinted in Britain since 1945 by Miller. The success of these reprints led to these imitators, but the charge of imitation would itself bring the American comics to an end. In the 1940s, when sales of *Captain Marvel* were challenging those of *Superman*, DC Comics sued Fawcett, publisher of *Captain Marvel*, claiming plagiarism. If fact, there were many superheroes who were more directly copies of Superman, but Captain Marvel was the one that was most successful and so was in the firing line. The court case dragged on through the 1940s and into the 1950s. It came to a conclusion in 1953 when the court ruled in DC's favor, forcing Fawcett to cease publication of Captain Marvel. The result for Miller was that they soon ran out of material to reprint. However, rather than stopping to print a highly lucrative comic, Miller took steps to move the attention of its existing readership to a new, but not entirely unfamiliar, character: Marvelman.

Marvelman

Miller's strategy was a bold one, but given that there were so many Captain Marvel copies on the market, not a very surprising one by which Miller turned to Mick Anglo to create his own copy of Captain Marvel. Working out of his studio in Gower Street, Anglo and his team created material for a range of different publishers. They had been providing Miller with comic covers for some years, but the request that Len Miller delivered to Anglo at this point was of an altogether different order. He needed 250 comics pages per month. Meeting this was a daunting task, but Anglo's Studio could draw on a wide range of artists and he knew they could work quickly, so Anglo accepted the challenge. As he recalls,

> Preparing the transition from Marvel to Marvelman had its problems but was not too difficult. We never used elaborate blow-by-blow scripts for our artists. I credited artists with imagination and did not want to tie them rigidly to tight scripts.... I drew a standard depiction for all the main characters, including the villainous Gargunza created by my brother. The artists based their characters on my drawings, but each with his own individual stamp. However, any arbitrary deviation from the salient points of the characterisation, dress, and capabilities of Marvelman laid down in the original specifications was not tolerated.[13]

Anglo's methods worked well, and soon the Gower Studio was producing Marvelman stories at a high rate. Given the time pressures, there is no doubt that quality suffered at the outset, and so Marvelman was not the slick product that Captain Marvel had been. The shift from the artwork of Americans C. C. Beck and Mac Raboy to that produced by the Gower Studios was a stark one, but Anglo and Miller took care to carry the loyal readership along with them. Rather than end the very popular comic, cancel subscriptions, and wind down the Captain Marvel fan club, Miller made the decision to keep the numbering going and try to retain as many readers as possible. With issue #25, the title and character changed and the readers who were part of the British Captain Marvel fan club were automatically switched over to the Marvelman fan club (see Figure 27).

Anglo's reinvention of the character was skillfully handled, with the editor's pages introducing the character and asking for reader loyalty several weeks before the transition occurred. The key to the success of the title was that Anglo managed to retain all of the elements that made Captain Marvel

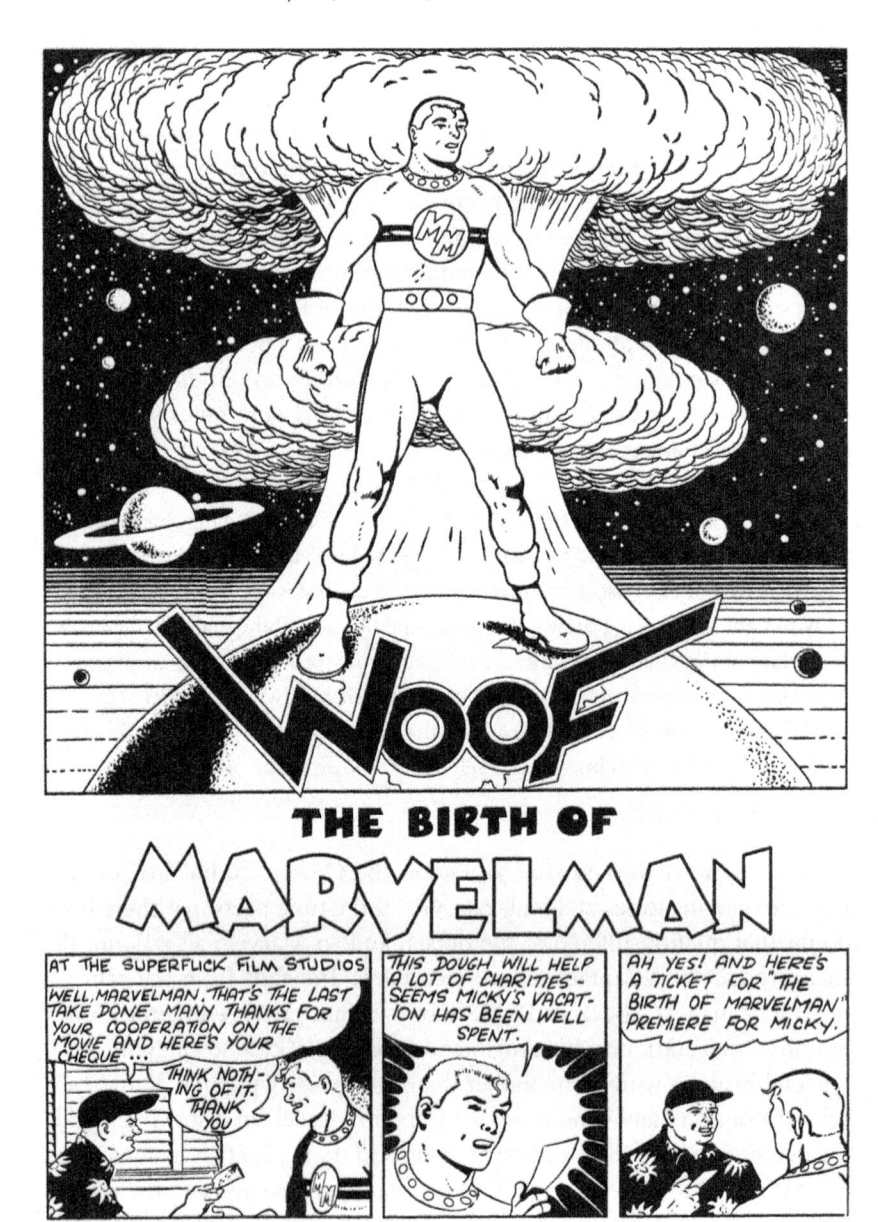

Fig. 27: *Marvelman* #65 (L. Miller and Son, 1954).

popular. This could not be just another Captain Marvel ripoff—it had to be *the* definitive Captain Marvel ripoff. As Phil Clarke and Mike Higgs note in *The Great British Fantasy Comic Book Heroes* (2009),

> Anglo came up with Marvelman to replace the Captain Marvel character, and Young Marvelman to replace Captain Marvel Jr. and made sure that they were as close to the original characters as possible in the hope that their readers wouldn't notice the sudden change of characters or wouldn't care. Marvelman was drawn as a blonde guy with a mainly blue costume to contrast with Captain Marvel's black hair and red costume. Young Marvelman had blonde hair and a red costume to be visually different from the black hair and blue costume of Captain Marvel Jr.... The readers did notice the change of course, but the characters were close enough to the original heroes to be accepted as a poor substitute and when British locations started to be used in some of the stories, readers adopted the new characters as "our heroes" [although] Miller still kept a "Yank" element in the comics to cover all tastes.[14]

Much would rest upon whether these characters would have the same appeal as the American ones, but as Clarke and Higgs suggest, while being less slick than the Captain Marvel stories may have been a problem initially, the move to make these distinct characters rather than simply clones of the American ones played an important part in building reader loyalty and identification with these heroes. The first Marvelman story dispenses with the origin in a caption box, which says,

> A recluse Astro-physicist discovers the key word to the Universe, one that can only be given to a Boy who is completely honest, studious, and of such integrity that he would only use it for the powers of good. He finds such a Boy in Micky Moran, a newspaper Copy Boy, and treats him with a special machine which enables him to use the secret. Just before the scientist dies he tells Micky the Key Word which is KIMOTA. Micky Moran remains as he was, but when he says the Key Word KIMOTA he becomes Marvelman, a Man of such strength and powers that he is invincible and indestructible.

The story then gets right to the action. In "Marvelman and the Atomic Bomber," the superhero is already well-known and is the "worst enemy" of a gang of terrorists. Learning Micky's secret, they incapacitate him. Specifically, they gag him so that he cannot say his special word, and they strap him to an atomic bomb that they have stolen and then drop Micky the Bomb on

Washington. When the bomb is falling its parachute deploys, ripping away the gag, and so he is able to transform and avert disaster. Several things about this story point to the fact that Marvelman is initially presented as an American hero. First, a caption in the first panel identifies the test site where the bomb is supposed to be exploded as being in Arizona and reveals that the terrorists will target Washington, DC. Second, the first panel showing Micky sees him on his way to the drugstore for a soda, using American vernacular to establish the setting. The "holy macaroni" exclamation in the next panel is intended to do the same thing. The key difference from Captain Marvel is that rather than the powers being magical in origin, Marvelman's powers derive from science. There is also a strong interest in atomic energy, with the first story showing Marvelman saving Washington from an atomic blast, and the cover to *Marvelman* #25 showing him tackling criminals who are working with a mad scientist to steal deadly radium. Finally, the manner of Micky's transformation also speaks to this interest. When he says his Key Word, namely KIMOTA ("atomic" spelled backwards, almost), his change is accompanied by a blast and a mushroom cloud (which makes the sound "woof," for reasons that are not clear).

The origin story for Marvelman, though suggested in the caption boxes that opened the stories, was not told in full for almost a year. It was revealed in *Marvelman* #65, forty weekly issues after the introduction of the character. "The Birth of Marvelman" opens with a large panel showing Marvelman just after a transformation from Micky Moran. He stands on top of the world, a mushroom cloud behind him and the sound effect "woof." The rest of the first page shows Marvelman at Superflick film studios receiving payment for his part in a Marvelman film. The American director and studio head (signified by baseball cap and Hawaiian shirt) gives him a ticket for the premiere, and the next page shows Micky in the movie theater, watching as the opening credits roll. The next panels make use of rounded edges in such a way as to suggest a slow track toward the cinema screen, and the effect puts the reader in Micky's perspective as a viewer, emulating a lap dissolve from the "reality" of the cinema into the fictional world of the film (albeit both are rendered in the same style of artwork). A voice-over introduces a scientist, Professor Guntag Barghelt, who has invented a process to create a superhuman and sets out to find a young boy virtuous enough to receive the "super" attribute. Luring him into a street fight, Barghelt is satisfied that Micky is tough and honorable and offers him a prize, whisking him away in a strange flying craft. Subjecting him to further tests, the Professor eventually puts Micky through the transformative process.

As Micky recovers, the Professor's former partner, the German scientist Herman Schwein, returns to extort the formula from the Professor. Returning to the lab, Micky finds the Professor wounded and that the villains have made off with the formula. Micky transforms into Marvelman and pursues Schwein and his henchmen but is too late to stop Schwein being killed in an explosion. With the action over and the secret of the formula upheld, Micky, now Marvelman, vows to fight evil "from now to eternity." Barghelt is shown ascending to the clouds, in a god-like image, and it is (rather bizarrely) explained that he "departs to some abode he has prepared on some asteroid in outer space, leaving Marvelman to use his powers . . . for good!" The tone here is very sarcastic, and the qualifications of "some" abode and "some" asteroid suggest a mocking attitude, as if the writer has abandoned the pretense of trying to have the story make sense. This narrative sticks quite closely to the origin as set out in the first Marvelman story, albeit with a key difference. Rather than dying, Barghelt is seen in robes, ascending to the heavens, which may be a visual symbol of his death, but the caption tells the reader something quite different, that he has retired to space.

This disjunction between text and image is strange and made all the more so when the framing device is considered. Everything that is being shown is supposedly part of the *Birth of Marvelman* film that Marvelman starred in and Micky is watching. This could be taken as an explanation of why the original origin story does not match with this retelling or why what is seen does not correspond to what is written, but that would be more credible had the story returned to the framing device as a commentary on it or offered Micky's perception of the film, but this does not happen.

Even more bizarre is that the film reveals the secret identity of Marvelman to any viewer. Perhaps the answer is that this story seems to owe a debt to a classic 1942 Superman story, "Superman-Matinee Idol," from *Superman* #19. This equally strange story has Clark Kent and Lois Lane go to the cinema and watch a Fleisher Brothers Superman animated short. This story was designed as marketing for the cartoons and is posited as an "imaginary story" (which is to say, not to be taken as an official part of Superman's continuity). The rationale for making this an imaginary story likely parallels the problem that arises in the Marvelman story—anyone watching the Superman cartoon or the Marvelman film would discover the secret identities of the superheroes. Indeed, in the Superman story, Clark resorts to knocking Lois's purse onto the floor to distract her when the on-screen Clark transforms into Superman, although he seems oblivious to the fact that a cinema full of people have just learned his secret, even if Lois misses it.

The reason for Anglo's referencing this Superman story is unknown, but it might be supposed that he wanted to give his origin story for Marvelman the air of a classic 1940s comic and to suggest that his relatively new hero, who was designed to mimic a superhero almost as old as Superman (Captain Marvel), had a similar lineage and importance, and that Marvelman was in the same league as Superman and Captain Marvel, which is to say, he warranted having cartoons and films made about him. Clearly, the storytelling here is much more sophisticated than in the early Marvelman stories, which were rushed and very rough. This comic is much more polished, but even then it does not look very much like a typical American comic for the early 1950s, but, rather, its reference points are comics from ten years previously (including, of course, *Whiz Comics* #2 from 1940, which introduced Captain Marvel).

Miller's strategy and his faith in Anglo were rewarded, as the series ran very successfully for nine years, from 1954 to 1963. For the first six years, all of the material was original; then, in the 1960s, the series went into reprints. Over the course of the six years, Anglo employed a wide range of talented artists at Gower Street. The two titles, *Marvelman* and *Young Marvelman*, were accompanied by *The Marvelman Family*, so there was a lot of work to be covered. The main artists involved in the Marvelman titles were Don Lawrence, Roy Parker, John Whitlock, Norman Light, and Frank Daniels, with George Parlett, Leo Rawlings, Charles Baker, and Stanley White working mainly on *Young Marvelman*. Other Marvelman artists included Maurice Saporito and Denis Gifford. Several of them were skilled artists, but Lawrence, Rawlings, and Gifford stand out for very different reasons.

Lawrence was one of the earliest artists to work on Marvelman besides Anglo, and his work for the series gave some small indication of the artist he would become. Lawrence is perhaps best known for his work on "The Rise and Fall of the Trigan Empire" in the British comics *Ranger* and *Look and Learn* (1965–1982). *Marvelman* was Lawrence's first professional comics work upon leaving art college (having failed his final exams), and the Gower Street studio was an important learning environment for the young artist. His work for *Marvelman* would be some of the best in the series, and he would become one of the most respected British comics creators of his generation, inspiring later comics artists, including Dave Gibbons and Brian Bolland. Gifford's time drawing Marvelman was less distinguished and noteworthy. His talents were best suited to humor strips rather than superheroes and adventure, and his Marvelman was later described by Anglo as a "stylised, spindly, wooden-faced puppet."[15] However, Gifford created several backup strips for Anglo's comics, including "Our Lad," which appeared in *Captain Miracle* (1961). This continued the long tradition of British comics anthologies that brought together adventure strips with humor ones. In America it was more common for a comic book to be of a certain genre, or to feature one character, whereas in Britain the anthology was the preferred format for publishers. They were intended to broaden the appeal of the comics and to maximize sales. Even in Anglo's comics intended to be in an American format, he often included humorous strips and backup stories, as well as puzzles and games, and while Gifford may not have been best suited to adventure strips, he certainly helped to bring diversity and humor to these publications.

Anglo's talent for reworking ideas was most famously put to the test by Miller's challenge to create a Captain Marvel substitute in Marvelman, but it did not end there. He also found an outlet in the Spanish market, for which he was approached to create a superhero. The result was *Super Hombre*, which appeared in 1958 and ran for sixty-eight issues. Rather than adapting Captain Marvel stories into Marvelman stories, this time he reworked Marvelman stories into Super Hombre. These comics were published in Spain by Editorial Ferma, which specialized in science fiction and spy novels but also published comics under the name Exclusavis Ferma. After Anglo had established the character, the comics was created by a Spanish team, with Juan Llarch writing the scripts and art done by Emilio Giralt Ferrando (also known as Giralt), an experienced Spanish artist who had drawn adventure strips since the 1940s. The story introduces Juanito Montaban, the brave young assistant to an Interpol inspector, Garcia Del. While pursuing a criminal, Juanito impresses a wise old man with his courage and is rewarded with the gift of a mysterious, glowing sun disc. Upon touching the disc, Juan is transformed into the older superhero, Super Hombre. This character was quite successful, but as ever, Anglo had yet another hand to play. When Top Sellers was looking to publish a new superhero title in 1965, Anglo sold them the translated and repurposed Super Hombre stories, this time using the name Miracleman. This comic ran for thirteen issues, and the hero was Johnny Chapman, again the young assistant to a rather ineffectual policeman called Inspector Stewart. As with so many superheroes of the time, a transformation into an adult superhero was triggered by a magic word, in this case "sundisc."

To complicate things further, Anglo set about publishing his own comics rather than simply providing content for other publishers. His comics were published under the imprint Anglo Features, and he produced a comic called *TV Features*, an anthology containing a mixture of superhero, Western, and historical stories, with some comedy strips. Another comic was *Captain Miracle*, which ran for nine issues from late 1960 to mid-1961. Here was another Captain Marvel–style hero. Some of the stories were actually reworked from Marvelman stories, and like Captain Marvel's "Marvel Family," which included Captain Marvel Jr. and Mary Marvel, and the Marvelman Family, which included Young Marvelman and Kid Marvelman, Captain Miracle had a young partner, Miracle Junior, who appeared in *TV Features*. In contrast to Marvelman, the powers are once again magical, deriving from a "magic eastern formula." To transform into superheroes, Captain Miracle and Miracle Junior shout the words "El-Karim," which sound eastern but are "miracle" backwards (sort of, using the Marvelman trick of substituting a K for a C).

One of the most remarkable stories in the short Captain Miracle run was called "Way Down South" (1961) in the third issue, which dealt head-on with the issue of racism and lynching in America's southern states (see Figure 28). It is an extraordinary story, and nothing like it could have been published in America at the time. It may even have been inspired by Harper Lee's *To Kill a Mockingbird* (1960). The story opens dramatically, with Captain Miracle and Miracle Junior racing to stop a young African American college student from being lynched by the Ku Klux Klan. The story then moves back in time, to African American students turning up to a southern university and meeting an angry crowd of white students. The caption says, "Federal law makes it illegal for any college or university to disbar coloured students, which of course, is exactly as it should be, but way down south racial discrimination is at its worst." Illustrating this, the next panel shows a white student standing on the college steps saying, "Bah! We don't want any coloured students attending *our* University" before throwing rocks at the African American students. As racist protests consume the town, a local lawyer speaks out, but he is no Atticus Finch, and when the Ku Klux Klan brutally attacks him, he stops sending letters to the press. Learning of discrimination there, Captain Miracle and Miracle Jr. race to the town. The next morning, a single African American student, John Custer, is brave enough to take a stand (and his surname is significant here), but he is attacked by white students. This time Captain Miracle and Miracle Jr. are on hand to assist, and they fight off the racists and escort John to his classes.

However, that night the Ku Klux Klan kidnaps John with the intention of lynching him. He is rescued by the superheroes, who chase off the Klan members. The next day they decide that the only way to root out the racists

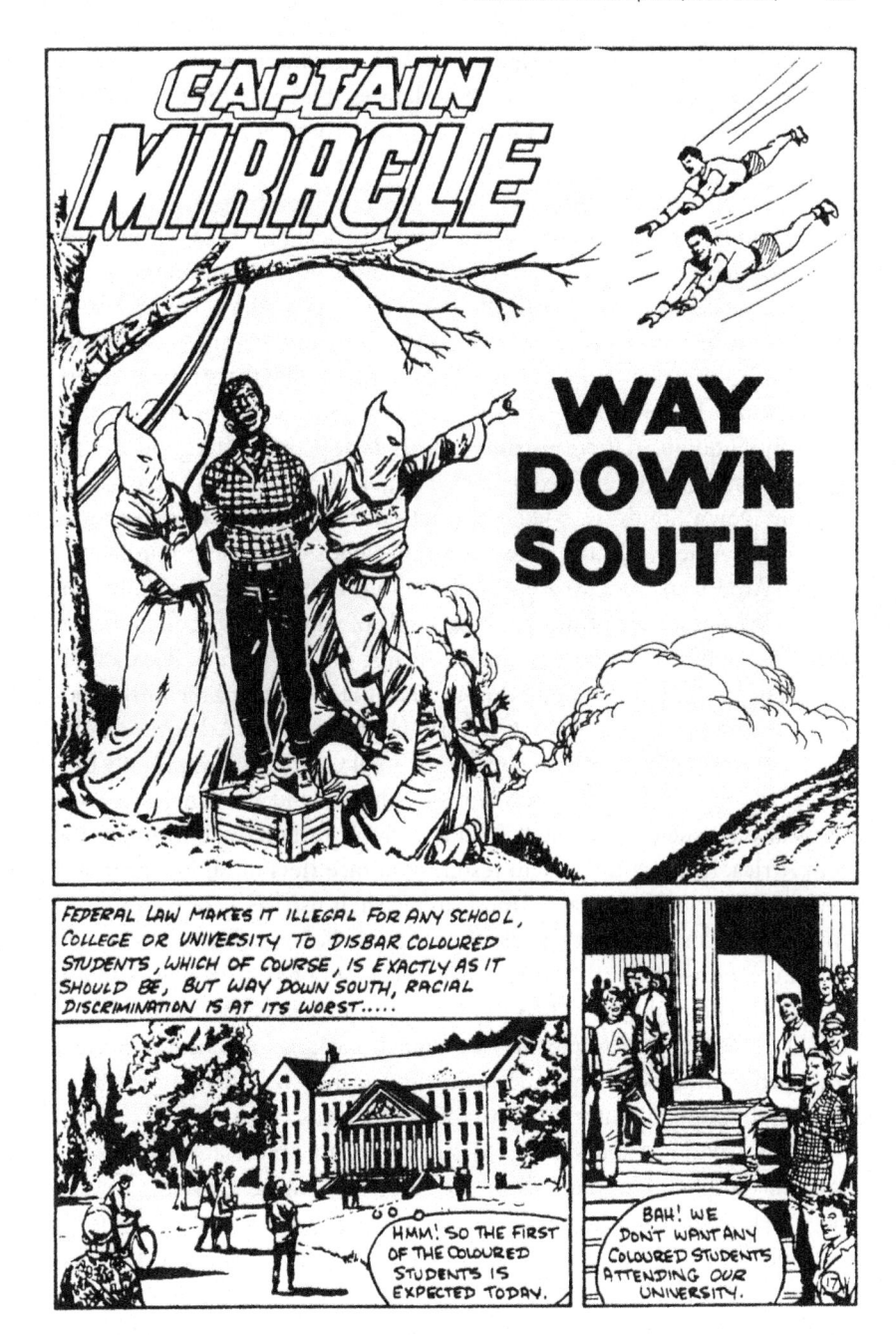

Fig. 28: *Captain Miracle* #3, by Mick Anglo (Anglo Features, 1961).

is to attend the university disguised as African American students, so in a rather regrettable turn, the two superheroes "blacken [their] faces with chemicals." The Ku Klux Klan burst into their room at night, saying "you defied us today, you monkeys." They abduct the two, only to be surprised to find that they are attempting to lynch two white superheroes. After shouting their magic word, the heroes transform and beat the racists, unhooding them to discover that they are respected leaders of the community. In the last panels a caption says, "With the resulting scandal, the Ku Klux Klan is forced to disband, and soon reason, good nature and common sense take over," as the university and its white students welcome the African American students. In the last panel Miracle Junior, in his civilian form, sums things up: "I quote . . . there are only two kinds of people—the good and the bad, and you'll find them mixed up everywhere."

"Way Down South" was likely a reaction to news reports about racial tensions in America in the 1950s and early 1960s. Increasing numbers of African American students were applying to previously all-white universities and colleges at this time, so these kinds of stories would often appear alongside high profile acts of defiance against racism, such as Rosa Parks's protest against segregation on buses in Alabama in 1955 and the Little Rock Nine's enrollment at Little Rock Central High School in Arkansas in 1957 despite protests and a barricade by the National Guard, which was only broken by the intervention of President Eisenhower and the army. However, it was also a time of increased racial tension in Britain, with immigration from Africa, India, and Pakistan resulting in race riots in rapidly changing communities.[16] In some ways, American racism is used as a cover to address British concerns about race at the time. Anglo's heart is clearly in the right place here, tackling an important social issue and presenting a view that is compassionate and just, but to modern eyes the sequence where the heroes black up in order to pass as African American is uncomfortably close to the white minstrel shows and racist humor that was a common feature throughout popular culture in both Britain and America.

It is clearly not Anglo's intent to mock African Americans in the same way, but the liberal credentials of the story are damaged by this feature. Nevertheless, the underlying sentiment of equality and social justice is remarkable for the time. It is all the more striking to see the racial situation in the American South portrayed from a liberal perspective in a comic that mimics American comics so well, especially as an American comic that dealt with such subject material would have been unthinkable at the time. It was not until much later in the 1960s that African American characters appeared in comics, and the first black superhero was Marvel's The Black Panther, who appeared in *Fantastic Four* #52 (July 1966). Prior to that, anyone of a race other than white was usually either a savage or a villain or, at best, an assistant or sidekick. Indeed, it was long thought to be the case that anything approaching a suggestion of racial equality would result in massive financial losses to the mainstream publishers, as it was feared that southern states would either return the books unsold or destroy them.[17] This is not to say that British comics were necessarily more progressive. There are countless examples of racial stereotypes in British comics, but it remains true that Anglo's "Way Down South" would not have been printed in America in 1961 and is a remarkable and surprising story.

By the late 1950s and early 1960s, the British superhero was embedded as a popular subgenre of British comics and was represented across other genres, with adventure, science-fiction, and humor comics crossing over into the superhero genre. The homegrown British superheroes had enjoyed a degree of success and popularity, and talented artists like Dennis M. Reader and Mick Anglo had specialized in superheroes. While the genre was represented in comics produced by the major publishers, there was a concentration of small publishers and studios that focused much of their efforts on superhero comics produced for the British market, and indeed, international markets like Spain, The Netherlands, and Australia were opening up to this material. But things were set to change.

At this time, the import ban on American material was coming to an end. The ban had, since the end of the war, never been particularly effective at stopping American comics coming into Britain, although it had limited their availability. Also, it did not stop American material from appearing in British comics. The moral panic of the 1950s may have been broadly focused on American comics, but the strongest arguments made against them focused on the horror genre, so superhero comics were less affected by this panic. When the import ban was lifted, there was a time of some uncertainty. It was not known whether American imports would suddenly flood the market or what this would mean for the homegrown "fake" American-style comics. The main barriers to American imports, now that the ban was lifted, were the cost of transporting the comics across the Atlantic and accessing the British distribution system, which primarily consisted of newsdealers and some national chains. In 1960 original American comics did in fact begin to be imported to Britain, but not in very significant numbers. In any case, the distribution network was somewhat unreliable, making it difficult to follow titles on a regular basis. One comics importer and distributor,

Alan Class, was wrestling with these issues in 1959 before finding a neat solution. He produced a series of black and white anthology titles that reprinted American comics.

The Class comics contained sixty-eight pages of superhero, science-fiction, and crime stories. Class had initially concentrated on importing and distributing old remainder American comics but found the shipping costs to be prohibitive. His masterstroke was to make a deal with an American syndication company, Syndicated Features Agency, granting him access to the stories published by Marvel, Charlton, Archie, and Fawcett, among others. He bought the orienting plates for the covers in order to reproduce them in color and then set about reprinting copies of the final printed pages in black and white. This cut costs considerably. Suddenly, British readers had reliable access to a lot of American material in a generously sized anthology. The only drawback was that there was no order or logic to what was reprinted, so there was no guarantee that a particular story line would be continued or that the same characters would appear in each issue, but this was not a huge problem, as most stories at this time were self-contained, and Class had access to a huge back catalogue of material. He also deliberately did not put dates on the comics, and he had a secondary market in midsummer resort towns. Rather than following the practices of most publishers, whose unsold comics were shredded to avoid bearing the costs of recovering and storing the stock, Class took care to collect unsold issues and made sure they were available at coastal resorts during the summer months. Class, in an interview conducted by Terry Hooper, noted that "beach and coastal resorts were thronged with thousands of holidaymakers with their children, who at certain times had to be kept quiet and happy, and what better way than to read a comic?"[18] The impact of the Class comics was considerable, as was his success, with the company publishing comics well into the 1980s.

The year 1959 was therefore a very important one for readers of superhero comics in Britain. The Alan Class reprints allowed greater access to American comics than ever before, and in a wider variety, too. The fact that Class comics did not reprint a great deal of DC Comics was compensated for by the availability of several annuals reprinting DC Comics stories, albeit mainly Superman. These factors produced two quite different consequences. First, many of the small publishers, whose business relied on providing American-style comics to a market largely deprived of the real thing, found themselves struggling. Second, it was theoretically possible that Class's syndication deal would enable him to publish a far larger volume of

American material than the small publishers, so bigger publishers started to take note. The small publishers were not such of a threat due to their size, but Class was tapping into a massive resource and publishing several titles in order to get the material into the eager hands of British readers. While the bigger publishers like DC Thomson and IPC could perhaps afford to ignore the smaller British publishers, the competition from American reprints that Class had created was harder to dismiss. This may be the reason why 1959, and the years immediately following it, saw an upsurge in the amount of superhero material comics from the bigger publishers.

Meanwhile, Back at the Fun Factory . . .

With the renewed interest in superheroes and science fiction at the end of the 1950s and the potential for competition from Alan Class comics, DC Thomson began running some stories that once again tried to capture that market with the introduction of Danger Man and Johnny Jett and the return of The Black Sapper. Danger Man appeared in *The Beano* for three series from 1959 to 1962, debuting in *The Beano* #885 on July 4, 1959, with artwork by Mike Darling. Danger Man's tale was a science fiction–inspired superhero story, with the title character having been kidnapped by aliens at the age of five when he is plucked from the Yorkshire moors and taken to Mars. He returns as an adult with an array of fantastic powers and a mission as an interplanetary ambassador of peace. Based at an artificial island and utilizing his Zoomer, an alien craft that can travel on land and sea and through the air, he sets about on his mission, and in time he adopts and trains two sidekicks, the orphaned Jet and Jane, aka the Danger Twins, whom he rescues from a shipwreck. However, the popularity of the twins was greater than that of the superhero himself, and third series, which started in 1961, was retitled "The Danger Twins."

Another DC Thomson superhero, created by Dudley D. Watkins, was Johnny Jett, who appeared in *New Hotspur* #1 (October 24, 1959). Described as a "super boy," he had been shipwrecked on Signal Island years before and adopted by a brilliant scientist, Samuel Holmes, who turns him into a superhero. When Johnny Jett is older, his adoptive father sends him to study at Manton College, armed with a range of powers and an energy belt. The return of The Black Sapper came in *The Beezer* of October 17, 1959, with artwork provided by Jack Glass, who had drawn the Sapper's original appearances in *The Rover* story paper thirty years earlier in 1929. Glass was an old hand at superhero stories, having also drawn The Amazing Mr X for

DC Thomson. The Black Sapper stories from *The Beezer* were quite visually inventive, albeit rather odd, especially as this story was given quite a high profile, indicated by the fact that it was presented in full color and that some of the pages make bold use of the color, sometimes in quite unusual and expressive ways. However, the artwork by Glass did not suit color. He was known for his heavily rendered style that made use of copious amounts of black ink. When bright primary colors are applied to it, the effect is jarring. Occasionally the use of color on this strip was effective, but only rarely, and if ever an artist's work was designed for black and white, it was Glass's. When the character was revised once again for *New Hotspur* in 1971, the art was provided by Terry Patrick, and the Sapper became a hero, joining forces with the authorities to repel an invasion.

It is conceivable that the resurrection of DC Thomson superheroes and the creation of new ones was a response to the success of the Alan Class reprints of American superhero stories. Other DC Thomson superheroes appeared in the 1960s, but they were in strange stories indeed, even by DC Thomson's standards. These included "The Purple Cloud," which was published in *The Dandy* in 1961 and featured Dandy Jim Brewster, a ranch owner who opposes the evil Purple Mask, a supervillain (who dresses somewhat like a superhero). The Purple Mask was "master of a mysterious purple cloud which sweeps across the cattle land of the USA, spreading chaos and destruction it its wake."[19] The cloud consumed metal and rendered unconscious anyone who was in contact with metal, while also turning them purple. The artwork was by Charlie Crigg and it shows an influence of Watkins, but the storytelling is hampered considerably by the odd choice to tell yet another superhero-inspired story in a style that takes nothing from the visually dynamic storytelling of American comics. There are no word balloons or thought bubbles, only captions that report speech and narration. This was a strange meeting between a Western, superhero, and science-fiction story and was therefore something of an oddity. An attempt was even made to recreate The Amazing Mr X in a text story in *The Dandy* annual (1962), with art by Watkins, although it played down the superhero aspects and portrayed the character as a strongman investigator. Again, the failure to adopt the visual conventions of American superhero comics by reverting to a text-based story made this a wasted opportunity, but DC Thomson's great rival, Amalgamated Press, which was by now known as Fleetway (and soon to be IPC), was also struggling with superheroes.

Fleetway/IPC

In 1959 Amalgamated Press, which dominated British comics for the last decade of the nineteenth century and the first three decades of the twentieth, was sold to the Mirror Group and renamed Fleetway (after Fleetway House, where Amalgamated Press has been based since 1912). In 1953 the long-running *Comic Cuts* and *Illustrated Chips* folded, both having run since 1890. By the late 1950s, *Film Fun*, *Radio Fun*, and *Knockout* were still in operation, but they were well past the peak of their success. As Fleetway closed down some old titles it invested heavily in others, and the war and adventure genres proved popular, so it moved away from humor strips. In an echo of the Superman run in *Triumph* twenty years before, *Radio Fun Weekly* started running Superman newspaper strips between 1959 and 1961, after which the strips transferred to *Buster* as part of a merger when *Radio Fun* closed, although the Superman strips quickly disappeared from *Buster*. However, *Radio Run*, which shortly before its merger was retitled *Radio Fun and Adventure*, featured another superhero, The Falcon, who was a winged adventurer. The Falcon had appeared in 1947 and ran until 1960, with artwork by George Heath. However, even the popularity of this series was not enough to save *Radio Fun*.

In 1958 another Fleetway title, *Knockout*, featured Thunderbolt Jaxon, a character based on Thor and Captain Marvel who was originally an Australian creation from 1949 but who appeared in the British comic *The Comet* in 1949, then in *Knockout* from 1958 to 1960, with Ian Kennedy providing the art when the character appeared on the cover of the 1960 *Knockout* annual. As Dave Gibbons, who later reinvented the character in a 2007 miniseries, notes, Thunderbolt Jaxon was somewhat emblematic of the problems with British superheroes. According to him, "Thunderbolt Jaxon was essentially Thor; he had the powers of Thor, but he didn't have Thor's hammer, he had his belt. And he was drawn in a Greek costume with a little mini-skirt—he was just ridiculous. It didn't really work as a superhero."[20]

Despite the cancellations, mergers, and uncertainty at Fleetway in the late 1950s, these were also exciting times for the company. A number of new titles were being developed, so many in fact that there were not enough British artists to take on the work. Therefore, Fleetway, like DC Thomson, contracted through art agencies to find overseas talent, and through these many Italian, Spanish, and South American artists gained work in the British comics industry. Few would actually move to Britain; a couple did, but the vast majority preferred to work at a distance and via the agencies. Fleetway had particular success with Spanish artists, and rather than hiring ones who could simply do a good imitation of a British style, Fleetway employed several artists whose work was distinctive and drew on European traditions, making some of their stories quite unlike anything else being published in Britain. The work of these artists initially appeared in *Knockout*, which offered "Kelly's Eye" by Solano Lopez in 1962, before being transferred to *Valiant* in 1962, which also featured "The Steel Claw" by Jesús Blasco.

The late 1950s and early 1960s were therefore very interesting times for British adventure comics. On the one hand, there was the huge success of *The Eagle*, with its implicit anti-American and pro-Imperialist values, and on the other there was an array of British superhero comics of varying quality that embraced American-style superheroics or else blended them with British traditions, such as the school story, to create a fascinating variant on the genre. The huge influence of Captain Marvel was evident in many comics, and the copies that appeared ranged from rather lazy ripoffs to lovingly produced and quite brilliant ripoffs. By the close of the decade, things had changed enormously in the industry. Going from a point where American comics were very hard to come by to their ready availability through a range of reprints, mainly through the Alan Class titles, the market was changing rapidly. The superhero genre had a healthy position within the mix of genres in British comics, but it was not as visible and dominant as it was in America. But the 1960s brought huge changes in America, notably with the launch of Marvel Comics in 1961. The comics created by Stan Lee, Jack Kirby, and Steve Ditko would bring about a great shift in the superhero genre in America, and the consequences of that were soon felt in Britain.

The changes in British comics, and particularly in representations of the superhero, were emblematic of wider changes in British culture and society. The swinging sixties were still on the horizon, but the seeds of social change were present in the 1950s. It was the era of the "angry young men"—writers such as John Osborne, Kingsley Amis, Harold Pinter, John Braine, Arnold Wesker, and Alan Sillitoe—whose novels and plays expressed discontentment and frustration. They were outsiders from the literary establishment and broke with convention. Their outlook was mirrored in British New Wave films like *Look Back in Anger* (1959) and *The Loneliness of the Long Distance Runner* (1962), by Tony Richardson, the former an adaptation of John Osborne's 1956 play and the latter an adaptation of Alan Sillitoe's 1959 short story. Commenting on this period and these plays and films, historian Ronald Hyam notes in *Britain's Declining Empire* (2006), "From this point onwards, deference to the Establishment, and indeed all establishments and hierarchies, would wither away. There was a new generation of protest, with criticism of foreign, imperial and nuclear arms policies better organised and more widespread than ever before."[21]

This disaffection was also reflected in art circles, where the so-called Independent Group was instrumental in founding what would become British pop art. This group of artists (known sometimes as IG) was founded in 1952 and consisted of painters, sculptors, photographers, architects, writers, and critics, including Eduardo Paolozzi, Richard Hamilton, Toni del Renzio, William Turnbull, Nigel Henderson, John McHale, Magda Cordell, and Lawrence Alloway. They were dedicated to challenging modernism and the dominant art practices by celebrating and examining popular culture.[22] Paolozzi's lecture at the 1952 meeting was about his collages, grouped together under the title *Bunk!*, which brought together imagery from popular culture (including advertising and comics) and was based on work he had produced in Paris in the late 1940s.

The best-known example of his work from this time is *I Was a Rich Man's Plaything* (1947), which has the word "pop" in a cloud of smoke emerging from a revolver and near the female figure's head, making it look like a word balloon (see Figure 29). Richard Hamilton's *Just what is it that makes today's homes so different, so appealing?* (1956) is another early British example of pop art, featuring a strongman carrying a lollipop and with a framed comic by Jack Kirby proudly displayed as art on the wall of the living room (see Figure 30). These two works embraced the imagery, conventions, and tropes of comics as a commentary on the relationship between popular culture and art, and between Britain and America. Their aim was to challenge the elitism of modern art and postwar austerity by offering images that were aspirational, playful, but also critical and challenging. They used the imagery of popular culture, often in ironic ways, employing parody, pastiche, and satire as a mode of critique. Had the British public rejected its own working-class culture and traditions for a simulacrum offered by television and American films, products, and comics? The question was provocative, and the work of the group culminated in the This is Tomorrow exhibition in 1956. Later, the British filmmaker Ken Russell made a film for the BBC about the group called *Pop Goes the Easel* (1962).

Several of the group used comics in their work, and Peter Blake produced a painting called *Children Reading Comics* in 1954 (and he continues to work on the themes of comics and childhood). There is an intriguing parallel between the work of the Independent Group and that of British

Fig. 29: Eduardo Paolozzi's *I Was a Rich Man's Plaything* (1947).

Fig. 30: Richard Hamilton's *Just What Is It That Makes Today's Homes So Different, So Appealing?* (1956).

comic artists of the same time period. It was not simply the case that the comic artists were all naïvely producing comic art and that then the artists of the Independent Group took American comic art and used it for political and social commentary. The comic artists were appropriating the style and themes of American comics and transforming them through parody, blending them with the humor genre, distorting and mutating them (as Dave Gibbons puts it) through a distorting lens. The pop artists were doing the same thing in a different way. The relationship between what British comics artists were doing with American material and what British pop artists were doing with similar material has not received any critical attention as yet, even though much has been written on the relationship between American pop artists and the comics they "appropriated."

The relationship between comics and the Independent Group and British pop art in general is less controversial, but it does point to the changes that were taking place throughout British art and cultural production in the 1950s and into the 1960s. In a sense, some of the best British comics creators were employing parody and copying American comics material in 1949 and the early 1950s in a way that is at least analogous to, and perhaps parallel with, the strategies employed by the British pop artists. As the 1950s gave way to the 1960s, a new attitude toward America emerged in Britain, with British film and music making inroads into the American market as never before. The direction of influence was starting to reverse as British art and popular culture found new confidence. It was here that the roots of the British Invasion of American music were formed as Britain moved from a period of postwar austerity to being a fashionable and dynamic society full of youthful protest and creative energy, which would be reflected in the comics.

Chapter Four

MERGERS AND MARVELS (1962–1980)

By the early 1960s, superheroes were once again dominant in American comics, partly because the Comics Code and the scrutiny of censors had put various genres and some publishers out of business. Horror and crime comics were all but gone, and a resurgence of superheroes in 1956 had seen the reinvention of characters like Green Lantern and The Flash. These were successful, alongside the ever popular Superman and Batman, and with Captain Marvel comics gone, DC Comics was in a very strong position. However, many of these comics had become rather staid. The challenge of reinventing the superhero for the 1960s was taken on by Stan Lee, an editor and writer with a grandiose style who harbored ambitions to write the Great American Novel. Given that DC editor Julius Schwartz had enjoyed great success with the Justice League of America (an updating of the 1940s Justice Society of America), the publisher of Marvel Comics, Martin Goodman, tasked Lee to put together a superhero team. The result was *The Fantastic Four* (1961). Much has been written about what happened next.[1] In short succession came Hulk, Spider-Man, Thor, Iron Man, X-Men, and several others. Jack Kirby produced most of the artwork, with Steve Ditko drawing Spider-Man.

The combination of Lee, Kirby, and Ditko was exactly what was needed to breathe new life into the genre. Marvel superheroes were down to earth, flawed, and argumentative. They fought each other, and the heroes sometimes had the qualities of villains. Lee's contribution was an operatic sense of drama and tragedy along with his incorporation of the horror and romance genres into the superhero genre more than ever before. Marvel superheroes were actually characters rather than costumes and a set of powers, but they would have come to nothing without the creative genius of Kirby and Ditko, who were producing truly innovative work. The Marvel revolution changed superhero comics profoundly and made DC Comics

149

look old-fashioned and stuffy in contrast. In Britain the early Marvel comics were reprinted by Alan Class, and although they were in black and white and mixed in with the superheroes from other publishers, the energy and vigor of these comics were unmistakable. Marvel had reinvented the superhero as a troubled character struggling with authority rather than simply embodying it. These were superhero comics that favored high drama but had a sense of fun rather than being the simple morality tales and parables of many superhero comics, the latter being especially associated with Superman stories, where the hero was an infallible moral guardian and idealized father figure or scout leader. Marvel superheroes were as likely to fight each other as a villain, and their powers often presented problems for them that crept into their private civilian lives, adding an element of soap opera tension to the superhero narrative that went far beyond the tired Superman/Clark Kent/Lois Lane love triangle. The next wave of British superhero and fantasy adventure characters would emulate these new models.

Fleetway/IPC

Just as the 1960s saw a rejuvenation of American popular culture and new liberal political aspirations, that decade also saw a new confidence in Britain, especially in popular culture, with music and television challenging the established order. It was also the golden age of British comics, which witnessed an anti-authoritarian zeal in the humor comics created by Leo Baxendale, Davey Law, Ken Reid, and others. It was a time of great upheavals. By 1959 Amalgamated Press had been taken over and renamed Fleetway Publications Ltd, which then took over Odhams in 1961. By 1963 the various publishing arms of Fleetway, which remained under separate management, became part of a larger parent company called International Publishing Corporation (IPC). This company underwent further reorganization throughout the 1960s, which led to several mergers of comics and cancellations of others, but in the early 1960s Fleetway/IPC controlled an enormous part of the British comics industry.

As many of the long-running Amalgamated Press titles had folded in the early 1950s, the roster of comics now running was a relatively new one (with the exception of *Radio Fun* and *Film Fun*, which themselves closed in 1961 and 1962, respectively). *Lion* had been running since 1952 as a response to *The Eagle*, and comics like *Buster* were designed to take on *The Dandy* and *The Beano*. *War Picture Library* had started in 1958 and was one of the first in the "pocket library" format comics. DC Thomson followed their example with the long-running *Commando* in 1961. The launch of *Valiant* in 1962 marked a significant return to superheroes for Fleetway with characters like The Steel Claw, Kelly, and Dolmann, who were joined in 1965 by The Spider and Adam Eterno in *Lion* and Janus Stark in *Smash!*, which was launched in 1966 by Odhams. Perhaps taking something from the Marvel comics being reprinted by Class, most of these characters would be antiheroes. However, there was something more to them. These were also tortured and flawed characters who owed something to the tradition of the penny dreadfuls.

Fleetway/IPC's adventure comics of the 1960s had a certain edge to them, and this was partly due to the editorial team of Ken Mennell, Jack Le Grand, and Sid Bicknell, who wanted to give *Valiant* a quite different identity from anything else on the newsstands. However, they had also been instructed to challenge *The Victor*, the DC Thomson comic that had been successfully launched in 1961. By creating Captain Hurricane, they were responding to the demand from Leonard Matthews, who headed up the juvenile publications section at Fleetway, that they include a war strip.[2] This stipulation being met, Mennell, Le Grand, and Bicknell made some of the other characters in the comic quite different from what had come before, largely because the company was employing a number of foreign artists through agencies. This was partly about workload, as so many British comics required artwork each week that it made sense to look to the cultures of foreign comics for talent, but it was also about costs, as it was often cheaper to hire foreign artists.

"The Steel Claw" scripts were initially written by Ken Bulmer, who is better known as a science-fiction writer, but were taken over by Tom Tully after the first three stories. Each weekly episode was just two pages long, and they often ended as a cliff-hanger. The artwork was by renowned Spanish artist Jesús Blasco, and later by a variety of Italian artists, including Massimo Belardinelli. In the story Louis Crandell, a lab assistant, loses his right hand in an accident and has it replaced by an artificial steel one. In a second accident, he receives a high voltage electrical shock that has the unexpected effect of making him invisible, except for his steel hand. From that point on, he is able to turn invisible upon receiving an electric shock. In these first stories, which draw on H. G. Wells's *The Invisible Man* (1897), Crandell is a villain, and Steve Holland describes the tone of these stories as "weird menace," but after a year he turns his powers to fighting crime (and it is explained that his accident had made him temporarily insane).[3]

This was another example of a British supervillain eventually becoming the hero, like The Black Sapper. In later stories Crandell even became a secret agent, and to help him in this role, his steel claw was equipped with a number of gadgets (the influence here was clearly from James Bond, notably the 1963 film *Dr. No*). In 1967, at the height of the Batman television series craze, the character became a traditional superhero type, but this change was short-lived, and before long he was a secret agent again.[4] Unusually for a British character, and perhaps because of the astounding artwork by Blasco, the strip was a worldwide success and was translated for a number of European countries, as well as for India and South America, which again showed the transnational nature of British comics of the time. Another demonstration of this came in Gadgetman and Gimmick Kid, who appeared in *Lion* in 1968 with art by Nevio Zeccara (see Figure 31). Stylistically, Zeccara drew on Jack Kirby's work from the 1940s and 1950s, and in this sense there was a connection to Gifford's less skillful imitations of early Kirby. Here was an Italian artist influenced by American comics being published in a British comic, yet again demonstrating the transnational nature of British superhero comics production. At this time, Fleetway's *Smash!* benefited from reprinting Batman strips on the cover, which helped sales considerably; however, for many, the Batman television series, despite being a huge hit, also confirmed the ridiculous and somewhat camp nature of the superhero genre, perhaps driving even more British creators to critique it.

"Kelly's Eye" was created by Solano Lopez, who had fled from Argentina after the politically sensitive science-fiction comic *El Eternauta* drew the attention of the government. Oesterheld, the writer of the series, was "disappeared," along with his whole family. Lopez worked from Spain, then London, on a number of British comics. "Kelly's Eye" first appeared in Fleetway's *Knockabout* before moving to *Valiant* when the two merged. The protagonist, Tim Kelly, was given a magical jewel called the Eye of Zoltec taken from a Mayan idol. Wearing the jewel around his neck, he is invulnerable to all harm. In later stories, the influence of *Doctor Who* is perceptible, with the story turning into a time travel adventure as Kelly teams up with Doctor Diamond.

Another IPC immortal time traveler was Adam Eterno, who appeared in *Thunder* in 1970, then in *Lion* from 1971 to 1974, before ending up in *Valiant* from 1974 to 1976. Eterno was born in 1549 and became the apprentice of an alchemist, Erasmus Hemlock, who had created an elixir that conferred immortality. Believing himself to be more worthy than his master, Eterno consumed the potion, becoming immortal, but was cursed for his betrayal, the result being that he was now vulnerable to weapons made of gold. Participating in many wars, by 1970—when the story began—Eterno was weary

Fig. 31: Gadgetman and Gimmick Kid, by Nevio Zeccara, in *Lion* (IPC, 1966).

and cynical, but an accident sent him back in time, and he seemed to travel somewhat randomly through years and centuries, fighting injustice and cruelty wherever he found it. The character was created by editors Chris Lowder and Jack Le Grand, and the series was written by Tom Tully with art by Tom Kerr. Like The Steel Claw, this strip was popular overseas, from France, Spain, and Portugal to Australia. Other popular Fleetway characters included Dolmann, who appeared in *Valiant* from 1966 into 1973, a puppeteer who controlled a band of miniature puppets, which he used to fight crime, and Janus Stark, an illusionist and escapologist in Victorian London whose bones were unusually flexible, allowing his body to bend like rubber, like the Fantastic Four's Mr Fantastic. This strip was drawn by Solano Lopez and was one of the most popular in *Smash!* and then *Valiant* when the two comics merged in 1971.

Perhaps the most popular and memorable Fleetway/IPC adventure character of the 1960s was The Spider, who appeared in *Lion* and was initially written by Ted Cowan and later by Jerry Siegel, co-creator of Superman. Siegel took over after the second story, having written to various comics publishers seeking work. He wrote to DC Thomson and Fleetway, and it was Fleetway that replied. Siegel had left DC Comics and brought his considerable expertise in writing superhero comics to "The Spider," which was drawn by Reg Bunn, one of the masters of the noir style in comics. The Spider was a master criminal who used technology and gadgets (like an evil James Bond) in his attempt to pull off the crime of the century. The character operated in New York from a Scottish castle that he had shipped across the Atlantic. He set about building an army of criminals, becoming a "king of crime."

The Spider had a sinister appearance, with pointed ears and arched eyebrows. He was a consummate supervillain and a type drawn straight out of the story papers. Bunn's atmospheric artwork was some of the best seen in British comics of the 1960s. When a criminal gang attempted to assassinate him, The Spider found the challenge of fighting villains to be appealing and so turned his talents to fighting crime. While the Spider was never really a superhero, he was yet another example of the villain being more interesting than the heroes, and like other Fleetway/IPC characters of this period, The Spider was very popular in overseas markets, including Germany, France, Spain, Italy, Turkey, and India. With the success of *Valiant*, *Lion*, and *Smash!* by the mid-1960s, Fleetway/IPC had responded to the new example set by Marvel, as seen by British readers in the pages of Alan Class comics when he reprinted Marvel stories. However, in 1966 there was a sudden shake-up as the Marvel license switched from Class to Odhams, giving Fleetway/IPC the opportunity to corner the market in superhero comics, with two arms of the company producing very different types of superhero comic. This created a unique situation but also planted the seeds of disaster.

Odhams and the Power Comics

Odhams had begun as a publisher of newspapers and books in the late nineteenth century, but in 1960 Cecil Harmsworth King proposed a merger between Odhams and Fleetway Publications Ltd (formerly Amalgamated Press). This may well have been closer to a takeover, and the changes, which came into effect in 1961 and continued through 1963, led to the formation of the Independent Publishing Corporation (IPC). Odhams still existed as a subsidiary within the larger company and became the publisher of a series of comics known as the Power Comics range, which included *Wham!*, *Pow!*, and *Smash!* This was a time when the increasing popularity of comics in America, especially Marvel Comics, started to be felt in Britain, with Odhams reprinting American material in *Pow!* in 1967. It was quickly followed by *Fantastic* (which launched on February 11, 1967) and, later, by *Terrific*. Some original content was produced by British creators based on American characters. The Power Comics imprint proved to be a successful mix of American adventure comics and British humor strips, which was something British readers had seen already in comics like *Marvelman*. Indeed, *Smash!* was a particularly interesting title, not only because it mixed humor and adventure genres, but also because it featured DC Comics newspaper strip material like Batman alongside Marvel comic book material, such as Daredevil. Furthermore, the American material was frequently recut, resized, edited, and recolored or printed in black and white.

The nature of these changes is fascinating and shows how British publishers frequently altered the pages in very odd ways, sometimes ruining the impact of pages and endangering the coherence of the stories. To fit the Marvel stories into four-page stories on the larger page size, the individual panels were often shuffled about to make them fit. British-sourced art was often inserted in and around the stories. This practice mirrored what had happened with Superman in *Triumph* during the late 1930s. The reworking of *Fantastic Four* #30 (1964) by Stan Lee and Jack Kirby in *Pow!* and *Wham!* #63 (March 30, 1968) is a typical example (see Figures 32 and 33). If comparisons are made between the original American comic and the British reprint, it immediately becomes clear that radical alterations have been

156   Mergers and Marvels (1962–1980)

Fig. 32: *Fantastic Four* #30, by Stan Lee and Jack Kirby (Marvel, 1964).

Mergers and Marvels (1962–1980) 157

Fig. 33: *Pow!* and *Wham!* #63 (Odhams, March 30, 1968).

made. In order to fit roughly two pages of the American comic into one taller and wider British page, the panels had to be reordered from two panels per tier in the original to three panels, and several of the panels were resized or squeezed. In some instances, two panels were compressed into one space and overlapped one another. In some cases, panels are cut out entirely. Even more bizarrely, in cases where this process has left blank spaces on the page, these have been filled with images of the characters doing things that have absolutely nothing to do with the story. The most striking example is a spot illustration that shows the Human Torch flying towards The Thing, in a composition that has clearly been cobbled together, although at this point in the story The Human Torch is looking for The Thing, who is unconscious and trapped inside a strange machine that is reverting him to human form. The cuts and insertions that have been made to accommodate the different formats have little consideration for the coherence of the story, continuity, or the composition of the page.

While Alan Class, who had been reprinting Marvel comics before Odhams, made some small changes, chiefly printing in black and white rather than color, Odham's editorial policy and format called for far more radical violations of the original pages. Where color was attempted, the results were equally strange. The 1969 *Fantastic* annual radically alters *The Uncanny X-Men* #24 with changes in costume color from panel to panel. Class had been able to reprint in better, more faithful dimensions and ironically, because his comics were a little wider than the American ones, his reprints of the American material from the printing plates was sometimes better than the American originals. When Odhams reprinted Marvel material in *Fantastic* and *Terrific*, they interfered with the pages a lot less as the proportions were closer to an American comic book. There were occasional changes, with the removal of a panel or two to create room for a header when a long story was split over two issues. In the main, however, changes were at a minimum, although the creator credits were removed in line with the editorial policies of British comics at the time.

The Power Comics often combined original British material with American stories, and while most of these comics were humor-based, there were some superhero characters, like Rubber Man in *Smash!* and Johnny Future in *Fantastic*. The latter started as a story called "The Missing Link," which was closely modeled on the Incredible Hulk, but after fifteen installments it became something quite different. The character was called Link, a creature that was found in the jungles of Africa by a scientific team searching for the missing link between apes and humans and was then brought to Britain, where it escapes and rampages across the country. When Link tries to hide in a nuclear power plant, he is caught up in an experiment involving a new kind of nuclear energy. The experiment goes awry due to an act of espionage, which results in an accident that releases massive amounts of radiation, causing Link to evolve rapidly and turn into a highly evolved superbeing with enormous strength and intelligence named Johnny Future. The story was written by Alf Wallace, who was managing editor of the Odhams group, with artwork by Spanish artist Luis Bermejo, who worked out of his Valencia studio in Spain for the agency Bardon Arts. As Steve Moore, comics writer and former Odhams employee, notes,

> In many ways, the story that began as *The Missing Link* was just that: a now-forgotten bridge between old-style British comics and the American superhero formula. . . . Wallace's influences are obvious . . . a little King Kong, a little Hulk, a fair amount of general Marvel Comics "superhero angst." The villains, however, and the way Johnny Future deals with them, are much more in the British style: not so much page after page of costumed punch-ups, but a more science-fiction approach where the conflicts are between heroes and villains of considerable or frankly impossible intelligence.[5]

Moreover, because this story was designed for the Odhams comics, it was conceived as a black and white strip, as opposed to the American material, designed for color but presented in the British comics in black and white. As a result of this and Bermejo's stylish artwork, Johnny Future was one of the best-looking strips in *Fantastic* (see Figure 34). The meeting of Jack Kirby's epic superhero style with Spanish and British comics, along with the occasional British humor strip, made *Fantastic* a truly odd publication, but it was all the better for that. Odhams made a splash with brightly colored covers on *Terrific* and *Fantastic*, and the latter proudly declared at the top of several covers that it was "Britain's brightest comic book." They also had full-page color pinups on the back cover, making these comics a very attractive package. They were almost pop art artifacts in their own right. In response to the Marvel heroes, DC Thomson offered Billy the Cat, a meek youngster named William Grange who dons a costume to fight crime. As Lew Stringer notes, "The parochial nature of the strip appealed to *The Beano*'s readers, and while Billy scurrying around on terraced rooftops may have lacked the spectacle of Spider-Man swinging around New York, it still looked cool."[6] However, the Missing Link/Johnny Future stories were some of the best and most overlooked British superhero comics of the 1960s.

160 Mergers and Marvels (1962–1980)

Fig. 34: Johnny Future, in *Fantastic*, by Luis Bermejo (Odhams, 1967).

By the late 1960s, there was a deluge of superhero material on the British newsstands. It was also a time when superhero stories appeared on television, from the Marvel animated series *The Marvel Superheroes* (1966) and *Spider-Man* (1967) to the British ITV series *The Champions* (1968), which aired on American television (on NBC, later in 1968). It was at this time, when Marvel Comics reprints and characters were at their most visible in Britain, that a number of comics briefly appeared on the newsstands and just as quickly disappeared, becoming all but forgotten. These were *Mark Tyme* and *The Purple Hood*, which appeared for two issues each in 1967 (see Figure 35). These comics were published by John Spencer (whose real name was Samuel Assael) and drawn by Michael Jay. The artwork by Jay was rather rushed in places, and at times the influence of Jack Kirby is overt, but these stories had the energy and charm of an amateur production and felt like a throwback to the comics being produced by small publishers of the mid-to-late 1940s. The production values of the comics were not very high, likely because these four issues were an experiment by Spencer to see if he could make money on comics, as—like Swan, Scion and Paget—he was more interested in pulp magazines and novels.

Strangely, it took Spencer much longer than those other publishers to try this out; his company was formed in 1947, but he waited twenty years to publish a comic, and when he did, he only published four issues and promptly retreated from the endeavor. Partly because his business was slowing down, he began to withdraw from publishing generally at this time. Spencer was not a publisher associated with high quality in any of his endeavors, and as Steve Holland points out, it printed notoriously bad pulp stories and had a reputation of being extremely tight with money, even cutting costs by eliminating entire sections of stories with little regard for continuity or narrative cohesion.[7] It is likely that Michael Jay was a young artist looking to break into comics, but very little else is known about him, and he seems to have produced nothing else. The first Purple Hood story says that the writer is Gerald Wood, but even less is known about him. One thing which is clear is that the creators of these comics were tapping into British popular culture and blending it with American superheroes. In spite of this, the time traveling of Mark Tyme would have been clearly reminiscent of the popular BBC science-fiction series *Doctor Who*, and *The Purple Hood* recalled some of the fantastic spy elements of James Bond (and its reputations for double entendres). However, this was 1967, not 1947, and these issues, while bound in attractive covers, would not have compared favorably with the polished pop art sensibility of the American

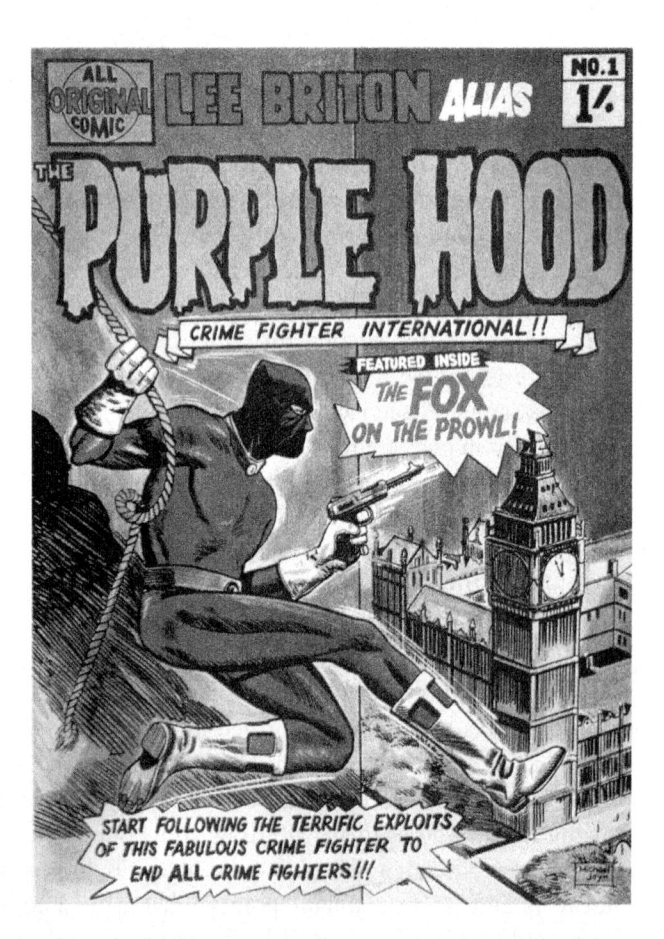

Fig. 35: *The Purple Hood* #1, by Michael Jay (Spencer, 1967).

material being reprinted by Odhams through their Power Comics line. In spite of this, however, by 1969 Odhams was in trouble.

In 1968 the weekly *Pow!* was canceled and the following year the company folded. The reasons for Odham's collapse were complex, but the situation was not aided by the economic crisis that swept Britain in 1968 and led to the devaluation of the pound. This caused problems for many small businesses, but in terms of comics publishers, Odhams and Power Comics were particularly vulnerable for several reasons. First, they had to cover the cost of the license from Marvel, which was not inexpensive, and in order to do so they had high cover prices. Their prices were much higher than those of other British comics publishers, and at 9d (nine pence), *Fantastic* and *Terrific* were three times as much as a DC Thomson comic (and the situation was not improved by the fact that DC Thomson had a policy of keeping its prices artificially low to hurt competitors). Second, Odhams published too many titles. When the economic crisis hit, it was clear that the company had overextended itself, and combined with a number of other factors, it could not bear the strain. Third, the purchase of Odhams by the IPC group had created an odd tension. Odhams was essentially the competition for comics like *Valiant* and *Lion*, which were published by a different part of the same company.

Corporate practice could certainly create odd situations like this but would not tolerate them for long, and in time, as IPC underwent internal reorganization, Odhams was folded up. Some of the comics it published, such as *Smash!*, were transferred to the parent company, IPC, whereas others simply ended. Indeed, when the Marvel superheroes were dropped from *Smash!*, there was some outcry from readers who complained, so in response the editors came up with Tri-Man in an attempt to satisfy them. This character appeared in late 1969 and some care was clearly taken to model him on the American example. Tri-Man was a young schoolboy named Johnny Small who suffered at the hands of the bullies at his school, much like Spider-Man's alter ego, Peter Parker. He gains his powers when subjected to a special ray invented by Professor Meek. This confers "triple powers" on Johnny, but they have to be recharged every twenty-four hours, recalling Green Lantern's power ring, which must be recharged through his lantern at regular intervals.

The problem was that while this was a very American plot element in one sense, the stories were of the very parochial sort often seen in British comics. A hypnotist would mesmerize the school bully and force him to rob the payroll at a builder's yard, Tri-Man would leap into action, and so on. In the meantime, the Fantastic Four would battle Galactus, the X-Men would fight the Sentinels, and Spider-Man would play a thrilling cat-and-mouse game with the Green Goblin. In comparison, characters like Tri-Man, try as they might, could never match the drama and scope of American comics. Tri-Man was not popular with readers and was soon dropped. At this time, Mick Anglo was reprinting DC Comics material in Top Sellers' *Super DC Comic*, with Gifford providing original several humor strips for the title, continuing the British tradition of mixing adventure genre material with humor material to cover as many bases as possible. Odhams had done that, too, but by this point Marvel reprints had a much stronger grip on the British market. With Odhams losing the license to reprint Marvel's material, it was unclear what would happen. Making the situation all the more confusing was the publication of the extraordinary *Pow!* annual for 1971, in what seems like a very strange death spasm from Odhams, or filler from IPC. In either case, the result was a book full of brand new superheroes who made this one appearance and were never heard of again.

Pow! Annual (1971)

The 1971 *Pow!* annual is a mysterious publication (see Figure 36). Published by Odhams in 1970 (annuals usually bore the date for the following year), the timing is significant. Odhams had published annuals featuring a mixture of Marvel reprints and homegrown humor strips in 1968, 1969, and 1970. These reflected the contents of the weekly comics, but the 1971 annual featured no Marvel stories or humor strips; instead, this annual contained all new stories with a new range of superheroes. These characters were created by Spanish artists, and they were never seen again. For a long time, the identities of the artists were not widely known, but when artwork from the annual appeared on an auction site, the identities of most of them became clear. While the rationale for commissioning these stories from a range of Spanish artists remains something of a mystery, it seems reasonable that, like Tri-Man, these characters were created to replace the Marvel superheroes that Odhams had lost the rights to reprint. Therefore, the fact that a 1970 annual was published is not much of a mystery. This would have been printed in 1969, and likely prepared in late 1968. That was before Odhams was forced to give up the expensive Marvel license in March 1969. The 1970 annual would therefore be the last to feature Marvel characters and was released as normal, despite the fact that the company was technically no longer operational. The fact that there was a 1971 annual is a little more mysterious, but it may well have been that the creation, printing, and distribution arrangements were already in place for the annuals being prepared in late 1969 and early 1970, having been put in motion well in advance of the company's closing. Indeed, it is not unusual for annuals to appear for a time after a weekly comic has come to an end (continuing after a company has collapsed is much rarer, although the fact that IPC had effectively taken the reins made this possible). Likely, these arrangements were honored with the support of IPC. In any case, by the time the 1971 annual was being prepared, Odhams no longer held the license for Marvel material, that having transferred to City Magazines, which featured Marvel reprints in *TV Century 21*.

Given the situation, with no Marvel material and no future for *Pow!*, the decision to make the 1971 annual an all-superhero publication is an

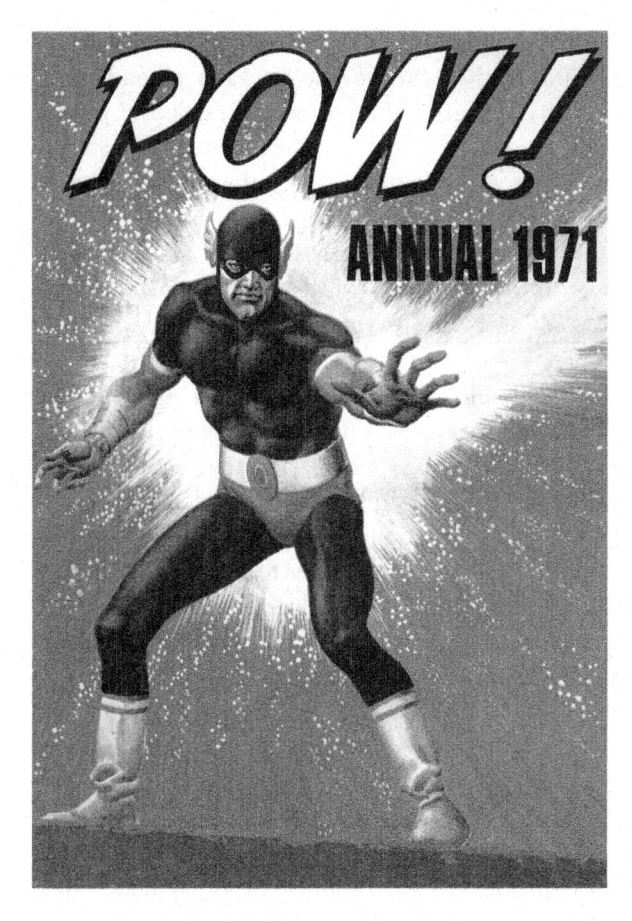

Fig. 36: *Pow!* annual (Odhams, 1971).

interesting one. Clearly, the popularity of superheroes at the time justified it, but where did this new material come from? One possibility is that in March 1969, when it was clear that new content would be required for this annual, the decision was taken to commission new work from Spanish artists, who were relatively inexpensive. It may have been that IPC, which had long experience with Spanish artists from *Valiant* and *Lion*, took charge and commissioned the artists through Selecciones Illustradas, a highly successful agency that provided Spanish artists with access to an international job market—to the British and American comics industries as well as the Europe continent, South Africa, Australia, and South America. The aim may have been to showcase the start of a proposed new line of IPC superheroes, or it may have been intended merely as filler—an opportunity to pull old ideas out of the filing cabinet.

Whatever the intention, the end result is intriguing. The cover of the annual is striking. It is certainly the best cover of the *Pow!* annuals and one of the most memorable annual covers from this period. The title is a bright appealing yellow, and the background is bright red. The cover is dominated by a single character, Magno, Man of Magnetism. His costume is clearly based on Cyclops from the X-Men, and his winged helmet recalls the DC Comics superhero, The Flash, and Marvel's Thor. His name and powers of magnetism are clear references to the popular X-Men villain Magneto. Magno is the first story in the book, and it is an origin story. University graduate Sandy Laker is returning to London and finds that his father is being extorted by a gang of criminals called the Maskmen. After a confrontation with the gang, Sandy is pursued at night in his car when he encounters a UFO. He crashes and is pulled from the wreck by a strange light that confers superpowers in him, making him a living magnet. He adopts a costume and the name Magno and foils the gang in the middle of a robbery, capturing its leader, The Mask, whom Magno hands over to the police The story ends with Magno vowing to continue to fight crime. The artwork for this story was provided by Spanish artist Miguel Quesada, who had previously worked in British comics on titles such as *Commando* for DC Thomson and *Look and Learn* for Fleetway/IPC. Quesada's style is very well suited to the superheroics in the story, and the expressive coloring works well, adding drama to his dynamic storytelling.

The next story is "Aquavenger," with art by Victor Ibanez, who had been working on British comics in the 1960s, primarily on *The Victor* for DC Thomson and *Pow!* for Odhams. The *Pow!* connection is key here, and it may have been through Ibanez that the other artists came to work on the annual. The story features the captain of a fishing boat, Bob Shane, whose encounter with the wizard Neptunius years before had given him the ability to transform into a superbeing. This transformation takes place when Shane says the name "Aquavenger," the magical name given to him by Neptunius. With a thunderclap and bolt of light comes an instant transformation, granting Shane the ability to breathe underwater, to swim faster than the fastest fish, and to exert incredible strength. This is another variation on the Captain Marvel formula, this time mixed with Marvel's Sub-Mariner and DC Comics' Aquaman and with Neptunius standing in for Shazam. In this story, which is again an origin story but this time told in flashback, Aquavenger battles with Captain Nemesis and foils his plan to plunder New York City. Like Magno, this was a full color story, and the color and art style work well, especially in the underwater sequences.

"Mr Tomorrow" tells of a master criminal who can see the future and read minds, but who has been sent back through time from the future as punishment for his crimes. Arriving in the present, the arch criminal—who is a cross between Superman's nemesis Lex Luther and Blofeld, the James Bond villain—proceeds to try taking over the world but is tricked by psychiatrist Phillip Mander, who convinces him to go without sleep, resulting in Mr Tomorrow's death in a plane crash. The art was by Matias Alonso, a highly experienced artist who also worked extensively in the British market, as well as the Spanish one. In Britain he worked for DC Thomson on *The Victor*, *Commando*, and *Bullet*, and he produced work for *Battle Picture Library*, *Air Ace Picture Library*, and *War Picture Library*, which were published by Amalgamated Press/Fleetway (later IPC). Demonstrating great versatility, he also produced artwork for DC Thomson's girl's comics such as *Judy*, *Diana*, *Debbie*, and *Emma*. The artwork here is colored with a red/purple wash rather than being in full color like the previous stories. This was also true of the next story, "The Hunter and the Hunted," also by Alonso, which is set in Chicago and centers around Chet Blair, who the reader is told was born a Sioux but has rejected that heritage in order to be "just another American lawyer." However, when he is caught up in the midst of a gun battle, the police suspect him of being involved in two deaths. Their racist attitudes towards him convince him that he will not get a fair hearing and he escapes. Returning to his apartment, he takes his Sioux weapons and clothes and searches the city using his tracking skills, becoming The Hunter. When he finally tracks down his quarry, he discovers that the "killer" is actually an undercover FBI agent, and working together they capture the criminals. Despite being offered a job as a crime fighter, Chet Blair refuses and returns to a quiet life as an ordinary person, although now with a renewed sense of pride in his Sioux heritage.

The next story in the annual is "Electro," with art by Jose Ortiz, who was a very well-known artist in his native Spain and in Britain, where he worked for *The Eagle* in the strips "Smokeman" and "UFO Agent" and later for Fleetway/IPC in *2000AD*, where he worked on high-profile strips such as "Judge Dredd" and "Rogue Trooper." He also was one of the Spanish artists who drew horror comics for Warren magazines in America in the 1970s. "Electro" is at the center of the book and is perhaps the best strip. The artwork from Ortiz is dynamic and the coloring is bold. What also makes the story stand out is the humor. On the surface it seems like a straightforward superhero story, with a power plant worker called Eddie being killed when a bolt of lightning strikes the turbine he is working on. He comes back to life and finds that he has a range of electromagnetic powers, including magnetism, elevation, flight, and the ability to fire bolts of energy. He is promptly recruited by the Super Security Bureau and given a costume and a code name: Electro. The ironic undercurrent is what makes the story stand out. At one point, the narration says that Eddie's "Electro-bolts fired from his finger-tips had lethal effect," but the image shows one of the bolts killing a fly, which rather undercuts the notion of their deadly power.

Also, in the recruiter's office Eddie is introduced to the other super-powered members of the Super Security force (who never show up in the story) by way of a range of posters on the wall. They identify the rest of the team as Miniman, Mr Whizz, Flame Man, and Iron Dog. Miniman seems to have the ability to shrink, like DC Comics' superhero, The Atom, or Marvel's Ant Man. Mr Whizz is clearly DC Comics' The Flash, or perhaps the more obscure Marvel character, The Whizzer, who appeared in the 1940s. Flame Man is clearly a reference to Marvel's The Human Torch, also from the 1940s, but was more famously the name of a member of Marvel's The Fantastic Four, who appeared in Odham's reprints of Marvel comics and would have been well-known to readers of *Pow!* Finally, there is Iron Dog, who is a robot dog. When the supervillain, The Great Dynamo, who looks a lot like the *Lion* villain/hero, The Spider, hears of Electro in the newspaper, he stages a robbery to draw out the new hero and quickly defeats him. Once Electro has recovered, the head of the Super Security Bureau tells Electro that "I wish I'd given the job to Miniman or the Iron Dog . . . they'd have copped Dynamo."

Of course, superhero comics are not always the place to find the most sophisticated dialogue, but there is something quite arch about how these lines are delivered, and the dissonance between the heroic images and the tone of the dialogue suggests that the writer and artist were smirking their way through this story. Humor comes to the fore again on the last page, when Electro tracks the villain down to his secret base and their whole conversation is held while Electro flies above the hideout and the villain is not seen, only heard, as indicated by speech balloons emanating from a window (see Figure 37). In the last panels, when Electro destroys the hideout by causing a flood, the Great Dynamo is found floating in a bathtub, which Electro promptly picks up and carries back to the authorities, complete with the villain, who shakes a fist at him and says, "You may have won this time Electro . . . but one of these days. . . ." Other points to note are that the story is set in the fictional Surf City, USA, which may have been inspired by the hit 1963 song "Surf City" written by Jan Berry and Brian Wilson (of The

Beach Boys) and recorded by Jan and Dean. The fact that the city is enduring a thunderstorm at the start of the story also creates a certain irony.

The fact that the head of the Secret Security Bureau has a costume waiting for Electro, hung up on the wall, suggests something about the ridiculous nature of superhero origin stories, as does the fact that when Eddie is next seen, he is no longer an ordinary power plant worker but a superhero living in a futuristic luxury penthouse suite, which does not seem to even remotely faze him. The deconstruction of the genre is very knowing and ironic, and if confirmation of the humorous and parodic undertone was needed, when Electro is defeated by The Great Dynamo, he is drained of all power and near death. The news anchor reports the situation by saying that "Electro's condition is said to be very run down." If comic pages could groan, this one surely would. But the humor works, partly because the artwork is so strong and plays it straight, allowing the writing to undermine the generic conventions. This is an important story because it brings together two strong traditions in British comics, the adventure/superhero story and the humor story, and more importantly, it sums up an attitude seen in many British comics, from *Captain Zenith* to *The Purple Hood*, that the superhero genre's seriousness needs to be punctured by humor and irony. If only the writing credits on the annual were known, it would be possible to acknowledge the achievement of the writer who summed up this attitude so perfectly.

The Esper Commandoes is the next story in the annual, featuring art by Enrique Badia Romero, a very well-known name in British comics. Romero worked on *Modesty Blaise* from 1970 to 1978 and then again from 1986 to 2001. He also worked on a science-fiction strip, "Axa," for the tabloid newspaper *The Sun* from 1978 to 1986. Alongside "Electro," this is the other standout story in the annual. Romero's style has the unmistakable quality, seen in *Modesty Blaise*, of being at once loose and fluid but also precise. The artwork is treated to the same red/purple wash as was Alonso's work, and in this case it slightly detracts from the overall effect, as Romero's powerful use of shadow works better in black and white, but there is no disguising his talent. As with "Electro," the script has several well-timed jokes that work perfectly with the images. Also, the variety of angles and shifts of perspective that Romero employs brings the story to life. The story and characters have the quality of a Marvel comic in that the Esper Commandoes are a mismatched band whose individuals have very different personalities and powers but who work well together, much like The Fantastic Four, The Avengers, or the X-Men. There are also clear similarities to the British television series

Fig. 37: "Electro," with art by Jose Ortiz, in *Pow!* annual (Odhams, 1971).

The Champions, which aired on ITV in 1969. It featured three UN special agents who acquire telepathic abilities and superhuman powers following a plane crash in the Himalayas. In the comic, foreign agents break into an atomic research facility and kidnap a top scientist. The Esper Commandoes parachute into the nation of Zornya and make their way to the castle headquarters of Zoltan Schweinzel, where they use their powers to defeat the Zornyan army and rescue the scientist.

"Marksman" is about a security agent with remarkable shooting skills. He guards a British secret base, and over the course of the story he manages to stop the theft of top-secret plans for a new type of rocket designed to guard the Earth against extraterrestrial threats. It is not known who did the artwork for "Marksman," but it is powerful and robust, and the action sequences are very effective. The character is similar in appearance to Marvel's The Punisher and has abilities similar to the supervillain, Bullseye, but they would not appear until 1974 and 1976 respectively. The artist for the next story, "The Phantom," was Eustaquio Segrelles, who mainly worked for the Spanish market and became well-known as a watercolor painter. The story revolves around a newspaper reporter, Jim McGuire, who is investigating robberies committed by a mysterious masked villain known as The Bat. The criminal targets the publisher of the newspaper and Jim's boss, Sir Jon Ryder, so he attends a costume party dressed as a masked man in a costume very similar to that of the pulp hero, The Shadow. Slipping away to investigate a possible robbery at a factory, Jim, wearing the costume, falls into some strange scientific equipment, then into a drum containing an unknown chemical. From that point on, Jim is possessed of superhuman strength and abilities, but only when he wears the costume. He captures The Bat, but finding out that he is a disgruntled employee of Ryder's, he decides not to turn him in. This does not make much sense, given the fact that throughout the story The Bat has acted more like a vicious criminal than a mere employee with a grudge, even laughing when he suspects that the fall that gives Jim his powers has actually killed him, but then narrative logic was never the strength of the superhero genre.

The penultimate strip in the annual is "Norstad of the Deep," drawn by Leopoldo Ortiz, the older brother of Jose Ortiz. Leopoldo Ortiz was very experienced in British comics, having been a very early contributor to DC Thomson's *Commando*, although most of his work was for Amalgamated Press/Fleetway on *Air Ace Picture Library* and *War Picture Library*, for which he had worked throughout the 1960s. "Norstad of the Deep" is the strangest strip in the annual and is not really a superhero story. It tells the tale of Norstad, a lizard creature that rules an undersea kingdom. He is a vicious and cruel king whose courtiers plan his downfall. After overthrowing Norstad, they banish him to a deep trench, "the valley of no return." He manages to survive but is discovered by a deep sea explorer in a bathysphere. Tuning into the same frequency that the explorer is using to communicate with his ship above the waves, Norstad becomes telepathically linked to the explorer and gains in strength and confidence through the link. This allows Norstad to regain his kingdom, and he plans a war with the other undersea kingdoms, but then, inexplicably, he decides that in order to retain the explorer's mental strength he will have to kill him, so he travels to the harbor town where the ship is docked and attacks. When the mental link is broken, Norstad's courage disappears and he is killed by the harbor police. The story makes as much sense as "The Phantom" (which is to say, not much), but the underwater sequences are particularly well-handled by Ortiz.

"The Time-Rider," with art by Victor Ibanez (who also drew "Aquavenger") is the last story in the annual. It is set in America, in Colorado to be precise, and moves between the present day and the Old West. The hero is Kash Pierce, a rancher and genius inventor who has built a flying robot horse and a time machine. Frustrated in his attempts to fight crime in the present, Kash travels back in time to make more of an impression. Narrowly avoiding an attack from Indians, whom he refers to as "screamin' apes," he sets his sights on wanted killer Buck Sawyer. After a failed attempt to capture the villain, Kash eventually delivers him to the local sheriff. Returning to the present, he finds that he has changed history. The history books record that Sawyer killed four men rather than ten and that legend records he was captured by a man with a flying horse. Like "Norstad of the Deep," this story seems designed to provide a bit of diversity to the annual. "Norstad of the Deep" offers a science-fiction element and recalls B-movie "creature features," while "The Time-Rider" seems designed to tap into the popularity of Western films, fiction, and comics.

Even though a lot more is now known about the 1971 *Pow!* annual, it remains an intriguing and mysterious publication. It may even be a glimpse of what might have been a new IPC range of superheroes. Perhaps this annual was designed to test out characters for a new comic, or perhaps they were designed to become part of *Smash!* or another IPC title, but for whatever reason, the decision was taken not to pursue these options. On the other hand, perhaps there never was an intention for there to be anything further so that this was always meant to be a one-off publication. The intentions of those who commissioned the annual remain unknown, and it is one of the more inexplicable outcomes of the demise of Odhams. Its collapse left Marvel without an outlet to publish its material in Britain. Although the Marvel license was picked up by City Magazines in 1970, its titles were in trouble, too. In 1971 IPC purchased City Magazines and its comic, *TV Century 21*, which since 1970 had included reprinted Marvel material. With IPC's purchase of *TV Century 21*, that title merged with *Valiant* and the Marvel reprints disappeared. There were no publishers who could readily take on the Marvel license, Marvel's financial burden having proven too much for so many other publishers. So Marvel decided to take matters into its own hands.

Marvel UK

In the early 1970s, Marvel Comics took the extraordinary step of setting up an arm of its business in Britain. The main remit of this subsidiary was to publish reprint material for the British market, but in time it would become much more ambitious. Odhams had enjoyed some considerable success with reprinting, but the collapse of the company in 1969 and then the move of the license *TV Century 21*, another Fleetway title that soon closed, left a gap in the market that Marvel decided to fill itself. Marvel UK's flagship title was *The Mighty World of Marvel*, which was launched on September 30, 1972. The first editor was Tony Isabella, a young American writer and editor who was based in America and oversaw what was being reprinted in this new British line. This title was the first job he was given when he was hired by Marvel, which suggests that the organization regarded it as something of an entry-level responsibility. *The Mighty World of Marvel* was followed by *Spider-Man Weekly*, which Isabella coordinated with Pippa Melling, who had been on staff at Odhams. After a while, however, it was decided that the editor should be based in Britain. So Isabella was replaced by Petra Skingley in 1973, and she adopted the male pseudonyms Peter L. Skingley and Peter Allan. New weeklies followed, including *The Avengers*, *The Complete Fantastic Four*, *The Superheroes*, and *The Titans*, the latter of which was presented in a landscape format allowing for two American-size pages per landscape-oriented page. However, this was not without its problems, as the pages were shrunk down, so the text was sometimes difficult to read.

Maureen Softly replaced Skingley as editor in late 1975, and she used her son's name, Matt Softly. Neil Tennant, who would later be famous as one-half of the pop group The Pet Shop Boys, was in charge for two years between 1975 and 1977 and has said of his time at Marvel UK that he was mainly responsible for changing things that looked too American or too adult for the young audience. He anglicized phrases and sometimes oversaw the retouching of certain panels, as some of the stories were sourced from Marvel's black and white magazine series, which was intended for an older audience and had some nudity.[8] However, the most important development for Marvel UK in 1976 was signaled by an advertisement on the back cover of *Mighty World of Marvel* #210 (October 6, 1976) that announced the launch of a new character, Captain Britain (see Figure 38). In fact, this was not the first Captain Britain, as IPC had created a character with the same name for a dummy comic in 1973. This was referred to internally as JNP55 to keep the project a secret, and artwork was produced by Eric Bradbury. The character could fly, was superstrong, had telepathic powers, and was born from the explosion of an underwater volcano. However, as the IPC version never saw print, Marvel UK was free to proceed with their Captain Britain.

Marvel UK launched *Captain Britain* toward the end of 1976. It featured new material starring this new superhero alongside reprints of *The Fantastic Four* and *Nick Fury, Agent of S.H.I.E.L.D.* However, while the new material was designed for the British market, it was not produced by British creators. Rather, Captain Britain was created by Chris Claremont, who had been born in London but moved to New York in his early years, and American artist Herbe Trimpe. Both worked for the American parent company and both were in Britain for a time, so the match of Claremont and Trimpe was a logical one. At the same time, another British character was being introduced to American readers. His name was Union Jack, who first appeared in *The Invaders* #7 (July 1976) and was created by Roy Thomas and Frank Robbins. To make sure the main office kept a close eye on things, the editor on *Captain Britain* was Larry Leiber, Stan Lee's brother. At first Trimpe was skeptical that a superhero in the American style would work in Britain, but Claremont felt that the time was right for something new. At this time, the comics of the 1940s and 1950s featuring British superheroes were all but forgotten, and the idea of a British superhero was deemed to be a somewhat radical one.

The first story introduces Captain Britain and his civilian counterpart, physicist Brian Braddock. When the atomic energy research station where Braddock works is attacked, he escapes capture by The Reaver, who wants to kidnap the scientists and fake their deaths. During Braddock's escape attempt, he crashes his motorbike and comes across the Siege Perilous, a mysterious gateway that allows him to contact otherworldly spirits who ask him

Fig. 38: Captain Britain advertisement on the back cover of *Mighty World of Marvel* #210 (Marvel UK, 1976).

to choose between an amulet and a sword. He chooses the amulet, a symbol of life and hope rather than the sword, a symbol of death, and in so doing he triggers cosmic forces that transform him into a superhero. Each episode, which was either seven or eight pages, was drawn in a typically American style, and the style associated with American Marvel comics at the time.

This is unsurprising, as Trimpe had been taught to be a comic book artist by Jack Kirby, who had created Marvel Comics a decade before with Steve Ditko and Stan Lee and whose style dominated Marvel's comics well into the 1970s. It was still imitated by a number of younger artists so that it became something akin to a house style for Marvel. The panels were big and the drama and action were heightened to a fever pitch. It was full color, although sometimes the last page would be left black and white, with an invitation to the reader to color it in (which was, rather bizarrely, offered as a bonus feature). Captain Britain was a rather odd strip. The costume seemed to evoke England specifically more than Britain, with the dominant red color of his costume suggesting the English flag's use of St. George's cross, but more than anything it was an amalgamation of American superheroes, from Daredevil's red costume and club to Captain America's patriotic use of the flag. And the story seems to have a rather generic superhero origin with some passing allusions to the British setting. There was not much in the way of culturally specific references, other than the Arthurian overtones, so it was rather off target. Upon taking over Captain Britain several years later, Alan Moore wrote a short (yet quite bitter) piece, "A Short History of Britain," chronicling the history of the character. It was published in *Marvel Superheroes* #389 (September 1982) and reflected upon the strip's American origins:

> Captain Britain always seemed like a good idea, and the mere thought of Britain—a nation previously known only for Vera Lynn and a series of fascinatingly demented murderers—producing its own superhero was indeed an exciting one. So exciting in fact that in 1976 Stan Lee decided to spare us any undue agitation by producing one for us. The Captain's earliest adventures, printed in what our primitive minds would later come to know as "color," were penciled by Herb Trimpe and inked by Fred Kida. The explosive, two-dimensional quality present in Trimpe's best work, while splendid when it came to delineating Lego-brick New York skyscrapers, looked a little out of place in a setting of dark British moorlands complete with standing stones.[9]

As Moore suggests, the fact that the character was conceived at the famous Marvel Bullpen in New York brought with it some problems.

Claremont and Trimpe knew Britain and had visited the country, but most of those involved in the production and planning of the comic had not. Indeed, as Lieber's editorial assistant, Bob Budiansky recalls,

> the reaction from Marvel's London office when Captain Britain was presented to them [was] decidedly cool, approaching frosty. We were told the British didn't like to be too showy about their patriotism; could we change his name? And that Union Jack plastered across his face mask—we British aren't into flag waiving like you Americans. Oh, and whatever you do, please keep the Royal Family out of it. Well, needless to say, when it came to creating British superheroes, the United States–based Marvel British Department knew better than anyone, so we ignored all that advice. By issue #38 of *Captain Britain* the Queen, herself was guest-starring.[10]

In his "A Short History of Britain" feature, Moore imagines the editorial pressures that Claremont seemed to be working under, saying that,

> Claremont . . . seems to have been a little constricted by corporate decisions concerning the character. For example, the Brian Braddock/Courtney Ross/Jacko Tenner triangle seemed to be little more than Peter Parker/Liz Allen and Flash Thompson, of Spider-Man fame played at the wrong speed. As for Captain Britain's character itself the general impression was of Captain America somehow tangled up with the origin story of the Mighty Thor. What we were in fact getting was an American superhero wrapped up in a Union Jack.[11]

Indeed, Claremont did clash with Lieber over the direction of the series and left after ten issues to be replaced by another American writer, Gary Friedrich. The artist also changed from Trimpe to John Buscema, then Ron Wilson; and subsequently Lieber took over much of the plotting, with writing by Jim Lawrence. This first series only ran for thirty-nine issues, but then Claremont paired Captain Britain with Spider-Man in the popular American title *Marvel Team-Up* (1978), with artwork by John Byrne. These stories were then reprinted in the British weekly Spider-Man comic, which was renamed *Super Spider-Man & Captain Britain* in 1977. However, things were changing at Marvel UK, and in 1978 the company launched a licensed title based on *Star Wars*, which drew on the American *Star Wars* film series, and reprinted old Marvel science-fiction stories. While this proved popular, overall sales were experiencing a downturn, and Nick Laing, who had taken over as editor in 1977, did not last long in that climate. In 1978 Dez Skinn took over, and while staying for less than two years, he made a considerable impression. Skinn had been handpicked by Stan Lee, who had visited Britain to discuss how to take the UK branch forward. Skinn followed Lee's example, presenting himself as a likeable character to the readers, giving the role of editor some personality the readers could connect with. He then set about rebranding the monthly magazine reprint titles to make them seem something closer to an original British publication. As he said,

> If sales were to be boosted, the first change was obvious, we needed to brand the monthlies as home-grown British titles. Because their content was so clearly American, they suffered by association with the much lower selling imports.... Plus they had no brand recognition to link them all together ... so I doodled up a house style that was both uniform and practical. In fact head honcho Stan Lee preferred the look so, much to his art department's probable disdain, he imposed the same design style on his US magazines. Suddenly Marvel US was following Marvel UK. That was a twist![12]

With sales boosted on the monthly magazines, Skinn launched *Doctor Who Weekly* in 1979, and that proved popular. He also launched a range of pocket-sized digests that sold well. Marvel UK was again doing good business, but Skinn believed that if it was to be sustained, Marvel UK would have to generate its own material. However, when that point had been reached before with Captain Britain, the parent company had kept tight control. Skinn resolved to make things different this time. He wanted to hire British artists and writers to produce new material and to take over Captain Britain, so he hatched a plan with British writer David Thorpe to bring the character back and go in a completely different direction than the American office's take on the character. As Thorpe said,

> I realised that we had to do more than import an American formula to make Captain Britain work. Comics like *2000AD*, at the time the most popular amongst the target readership in the UK, had a totally different flavour to American comics. They are more throwaway, humorous, self-aware and anarchic—they don't take themselves so seriously. Americans are generally prepared to be much more nationalistic than us and use their flag patriotically. Over here only fascists do that with the Union Jack. Captain Britain can never be an Anglicised Captain America. So I introduced a peculiarly British surreality, drawing on the tradition of Jonathan Swift, Lewis Carroll,

Charles Dickens, HG Wells, John Wyndham and Doctor Who, embodying eccentricities which I associated with the upper-class world that Brian Braddock comes from.[13]

Here in a nutshell is the argument that has occupied this book. The tension between American comics and British comics, between the world of New York comics publishing and much smaller British operations, and the considerable cultural and political differences of the two countries, are all captured by Thorpe's comments. While Thorpe's stories were successful in bringing Captain Britain back to a contemporary and relevant Britain, he was constrained in his ability to tackle real world problems. When Thorpe wrote a story that dramatized the conflict in Northern Ireland, it faced editorial censorship and artist Alan Davis refused to draw it. Frustrated by his inability to use the character to reflect contemporary concerns, Thorpe left the series. This was one instance where satire, a common feature of the British treatment of the superhero, faltered because this topic was too sensitive to approach in comics. Indeed, there was no more sensitive issue in British politics at the time than the conflict between the British establishment and Irish nationalists. By late 1980 Skinn had gone, too, to be replaced by Bernie Jaye (Benadette Jackowski), who made a huge contribution to the success of Marvel UK in the 1980s. She revived *The Mighty World of Marvel* and edited *The Daredevils* (the two of which later merged). *The Daredevils* saw Alan Moore take over the writing of Captain Britain from Thorpe and continue with artist Alan Davis in what would become a much celebrated run. It was infused with gothic horror and metafictional elements, notably the inclusion of a pantheon of characters from past British comics. (This, along with the run by Jamie Delano and Davis will be discussed in the next chapter.)

The other major original character to emerge from Marvel UK was Night Raven, created by editors Dez Skinn and Richard Burton, with stories by Steve Parkhouse and art by David Lloyd. The character was a Native American who fought crime in 1930s New York City and who first appeared in *Hulk Weekly* in 1979. In a throwback to old-style story papers, even some illustrated Night Raven text stories appeared in various Marvel UK magazines, which was appropriate given the fact that this comic was very much influenced by 1930s American pulp characters, namely The Shadow and The Spider. In later versions, the character became immortal and survives through to the present day, and like Captain Britain has become a recurring character in the Marvel Universe. The new material created by British comics creators at Marvel UK never seriously challenged the popularity of the American reprint material until Moore's run on Captain Britain, and the opportunities that Skinn and Jaye created had considerable long-terms effects, aiding the careers of artists such as David Lloyd, Alan Davis, Steve Dillon, and Dave Gibbons. Gibbons would go on, with Moore, to create *Watchmen*, one of the most celebrated superhero comics of all time. Along the way Gibbons also worked for Fleetway and DC Thomson.

Dave Gibbons at DC Thomson

In the mid-1970s, a young Dave Gibbons started working for DC Thomson. Within the space of ten years, he would be making a name for himself in American superhero comics and soon after would co-create (with Alan Moore) the groundbreaking *Watchmen* (1986), one of the most radical deconstructions of the superhero genre. But in the mid-1970s, Gibbons was a relative unknown just starting to make his way in the comics industry. He worked as a letterer at IPC and had re-lettered some American reprints. He engaged an agent in order to find freelance work and soon obtained employment on that basis for DC Thomson. Like many freelancers who worked through agents, Gibbons rarely dealt with DC Thomson directly and never actually came to Dundee at this time. As Jeremy Briggs notes in his article in *Spaceships Away* #36, Gibbons had started off as "a fan artist providing work for the fanzines and underground titles of the early 1970s.... However, his [first] regular British strip work before *2000AD* was for DC Thomson, for whom he freelanced on the weekly boy's anthology comics *Wizard* and *Hotspur*."[14] This work was published between 1974 and 1977 and ran the gamut of spine-chillers and war, heroics, and science-fiction stories.

Of these stories, a few were quite close to being superhero stories (e.g., "Jolly Roger" and "Hammerhand"), and one, "Spring-Heeled Jackson," was DC Thomson's version of the Victorian urban legend and star of penny dreadfuls. Spring-Heeled Jack certainly came close to a superhero story (see Figure 39). He first appeared in Victorian folklore and popular culture following reports of a demonic, ghost-like figure who roamed London and manifested a range of strange abilities, including the ability to leap over walls and buildings. This creature was first reported in 1837, and sightings were claimed all over the country throughout the rest of the century. It was suspected that the initial instances were either pranks or common assaults that were elaborated upon and sensationalized by the press. However, the descriptions of a being with a helmet and cloak who could breathe blue flame caught the public imagination.

Mergers and Marvels (1962–1980) 181

Fig. 39: Spring-Heeled Jackson, by Dave Gibbons, in *Hotspur* #941 (DC Thomson, 1977). The Hotspur © DC Thomson & Co Ltd.

Penny dreadfuls and serial stories featuring the creature appeared from around 1863 to the turn of the century. The DC Thomson version appeared in *Hotspur* #941 (October 1977), running intermittently until *Hotspur* #950 (December 1977). This was Gibbons's last issue, but Gibbons's work on this character continued to appear for several years and would also continue to appear in *Hotspur* annuals for many years. As Briggs notes, "In Victorian London, John Jackson is a bespectacled police clerk by day, much put upon by Sergeant Drew, but by night he hunts the capital's criminals as the hatted and eye-masked Spring-Heeled Jack."[15] The strip was also notable because there is evidence in it of the style Gibbons would later perfect in *Watchmen*. Some of the composition and figure work is much more dynamic than usually found in DC Thomson comics, which are usually more economical with their storytelling. As Gibbons gained in skill and confidence during his time working on *The Hotspur* and *The Wizard*, a more refined style came to the fore, as well as more superhero-oriented dynamism. This training was put to good use in Gibbons's later career in superhero comics, but less well-known is the 1975 comic *Powerman* that he did with Brian Bolland. It was written by Donne Avenell and Norman Worker and although published in Britain, it was designed exclusively for the Nigerian market.

The idea came about when a Nigerian businessman noticed that comics were popular in his country but that they were all foreign reprints featuring white characters. With no Nigerian comic book industry or artists to employ, he commissioned Bardon Press Features to produce the comic, and Bardon employed Gibbons and Bolland for the job. The comic, which ran for two years and featured Powerman, an African superhero, was Bolland's first published work, and he and Gibbons took turns doing stories. The series was later reprinted in South Africa without permission from the publisher. By 1988 Gibbons and Bolland were big names, and the comic was reprinted by Eclipse for the American market under the heading "Gibbons and Bolland—The Jungle Years." The title was changed to *Power Comics* and the character was renamed Power Bolt as there was already a Marvel hero called Power Man. The stories were quite basic, and Powerman was essentially an African Captain Marvel. He fought dinosaurs and robots, but part of the goal of the comic was also to combat illiteracy and help with English-language skills. Gibbons had risen through the ranks from fanzine contributor to letterer and ghost artist and then gained work in mainstream British comics published by DC Thomson and IPC, all before becoming a pioneer of Nigerian superhero comics. He was then headhunted by American publishers and became one of the best-known and most respected artists in the field, which was no small feat.

At this time, DC Thomson was also expanding the number of superhero stories it published, beginning with the introduction of King Cobra in 1976. He appeared in *The Hotspur* #852 and was Bill King, a reporter whose scientist father had been killed by criminals. He inherits a high-tech suit that looks like snake and was invented by his father. At the pull of a hidden cord, the suit instantly covers Bill's street clothes. The suit confers a number of abilities on him, allowing him to fly (or at least to glide), to climb walls, and administer electric shocks. It is also bulletproof, which proves to be very useful as he embarks on a quest for revenge and vows to fight all criminals. The character was created by Ron Smith, and King Cobra proved to be popular, appearing on several covers, and in annuals. However, at this time DC Thomson also started to target different readers with superhero-type stories.

A notable example was "Supercats" (1974–1978), which was originally known as "The Fabulous Four," at once referencing the Fantastic Four and The Beatles. The Supercats were a team of female space adventurers, three of whom had superpowers: Fauna, who had chameleon powers of disguise; Electra, who had electrical powers; and Hercula, who was superstrong. They were led by Helen Millar, the captain of their spaceship, The Lynx (see Figure 40). The artwork was by Spanish artist Romero, who also provided art for the 1971 *Pow!* annual. The series appeared in *Diana* annuals from 1974 to 1977 and ran in *Spellbound* from 1976 to 1978, then in *Debbie* from early 1978 till it ended in April of the same year. In 1977 DC Thomson also ran a series called "Supergirl" in the girl's comic *The Bunty*. The lead character was a schoolgirl who was injured in a car accident and becames a government agent, equipped with robotic legs and a sophisticated artificial eye. This turned her into a version of the Bionic Woman, who was featured in the then–very popular television series starring Lindsay Wagner, a spin-off from the *Six Million Dollar Man*, starring Lee Majors. These stories were science-fiction oriented with superhero characters that tapped into the resurgence of interest in both genres, as also seen in film, television, and animation. This attunement is one of the key features of British comics, with their weekly anthology format that made them very responsive to trends in popular culture and current events. This was also one of the strengths of *2000AD*.

Fig. 40: Supercats, by Romero, in *Spellbound* #56 (DC Thomson, 1977). Spellbound © DC Thomson & Co Ltd.

The Galaxies' Greatest Comic

The late 1970s saw the beginnings of the independent comics scene, supported by the development of comics marts and more organized fandom. The launch of *2000AD* in 1977 was a turning point as the science-fiction genre became more dystopian and influenced by punk. Dan Dare may have appeared in *2000AD* for a time, but fantasies of a British Empire in space was no longer the ideology underpinning the stories, and far from being cautious of vulgar American culture, *2000AD* embraced American popular culture references, but under the guiding hands of Pat Mills and John Wagner the reference points were usually the cynical films of the 1970s that revealed problems in America rather than the utopian conservatism bound up in most American superhero comics. The anthology *2000AD* was a science-fiction collection showcasing Judge Dredd, a fascistic future lawman, created by writers Mills and Wagner and artists Mike McMahon and Carlos Ezquerra. They had worked for DC Thomson and Fleetway but wanted to pursue more controversial themes than were usually permissible.[16] The result was a trio of comics, *Battle*, *Action*, and *2000AD*, which were tough and violent and inspired by American popular culture, notably Hollywood films: *Battle* had "The Rat Pack," modeled on *The Dirty Dozen* (1967); *Action* featured Hookjaw, a murderous great white shark inspired by *Jaws* (1975); and Judge Dredd was a science-fiction version of *Dirty Harry* (1971).

This made Fleetway an even stronger competitor to DC Thomson, although the strategy was not without some controversy, which was mainly centered on *Action*, which was accused of contributing to juvenile delinquency and was canceled amid calls for it to be banned. *2000AD*, learning its lesson from the fate of *Action*, was tempered by the fact that it was a science-fiction comic and the stories were more fantastic. It became one of the great success stories of contemporary British comics. In its long history (far outliving *Action* and *Battle*), *2000AD* nurtured the talents of Alan Moore, Neil Gaiman, Grant Morrison, Mark Millar, Garth Ennis, Dave Gibbons, Steve Dillon, and Simon Bisley, among countless others. The comic even had a sister publication for a time, titled *Tornado*, with a superhero for an editor, The Big E, who was portrayed by Dave Gibbons. *Tornado*, however, was created to mop up unfinished stories from *Starlord* and *Action*, so it did not last very long before being merged with *2000AD*. Despite the economic and social crises of early 1980s Britain, the mood of impending danger and unrest was accompanied by a burst of creativity in art and literature, which seemed full of oppositional energy. British comics shared something of the politics and complexity seen in contemporaneous cultural forms, and the tensions of the times created a generation of outspoken writers and artists who used comics as a forum for political debate. The parody and imitation of American films was one of the means by which *2000AD* addressed the relationship between British and American culture. A number of innovative anthology titles emerged at this time, alongside a slowly growing underground, supported by the opening of specialist comic shops such as Forbidden Planet. This spirit was infectious, and soon the independent comics scene grew, with edgier stories of the sort seen in *2000AD*, many of them subverting superheroes.

Independent Comics

The British independent comics of the 1970s and 1980s were cheaply produced and had very small print runs, but often expressed an enormous amount of passion, along with some skill. Some of these comics offered superhero stories, and some dealt with violent and sexual themes that mainstream publishers would not approach for several years. One independent creator producing work of this kind was Dave Hornsby, whose comic *The Mighty Apocalypse* ran for four issues, first appearing in 1977 and finishing in early 1978. It saw the superhero, Apocalypse, fighting his arch nemesis, Warlord, for control of an alien planet, and later, the Earth. The influence of American superhero comics is strong here, and particularly Marvel comics. *The Mighty Apocalypse* starts on an alien planet that is attacked by a villain called Warlord, who acts like a supervillain similar to Darkseid and whose costume is like that of a superhero. Demanding the immediate surrender of the planet's armed forces, Warlord is tricked by the planet's leader, Macros, who has his army launch an attack on Warlord's ship while he has his top scientist finalize Project Apocalypse, which involves turning a volunteer into a superhuman in order to combat the threat. However, Warlord launches a rocket and destroys the laboratory where the transformation is underway, and while Macros and the Professor survive, the volunteer is apparently killed.

The desperate attempts to save his life are successful, but the resulting brain damage causes Apocalypse to have a split personality and to be psychotic. He is consumed with hatred for Warlord and his attack on Warlord's warship forces the villain to teleport his ship away with Apocalypse on board. In the final issue, they materialize in an unknown sector of space and just happen to be orbiting Earth, which Warlord immediately decides to claim for himself. In its damaged state, however, Warlord's ship cannot survive the attack from the "primitive rockets" fired by American forces. The ship crashes in New York with the force on an atomic bomb (which apparently kills "hundreds" of people). Apocalypse and Warlord fight, but when more rockets are launched at them, Warlord avoids death by teleporting away at the last second, leaving Apocalypse, who is killed in the explosion. And there the story ends. The back cover has a poster showing the battered Warlord launching his attack on humanity. This kind of cynical storytelling—where the superhero is as psychotic as the supervillain and the stories end in the defeat of the "hero," and often in death—was becoming increasingly popular in the 1970s, and would become a hallmark of the revisionist work of the 1980s. Hornsby was clearly very young at the time of writing these stories, and the last issue was delayed because he was taking his "O" Level exams (exams at the end of high school, in American terms), which would put him at around sixteen at the time of creating the book. Hornsby notes,

Apocalypse started off purely as something for me and my school friends. I wasn't aware of any other "fanzines" or part of any scene—I literally just had a handful of school friends that collected comics like me. As a result of starting my own fanzine though, I did become aware of what else was going on and met up with some of the other guys in Hertfordshire—like Mike Gibas from *Super Adventure Stories* and Mike Harris from Dwellers of the Unknown in Rickmansworth. We even "teamed up" a little for some joint projects and provided illustrations for each other's zines. . . . I was 16 when I drew the first issue so should really have been putting all that effort into my O levels. My Dad had a photocopier at work so I asked him to run off a few copies for my friends and eagerly awaited him coming home from work with them. After a week or so of "forgetting them" he finally returned with 200 copies that he'd had professionally printed. Although I was pretty thrilled, I quickly realised I didn't have that many friends. Once I'd given away copies to anybody that wanted them (and quite a few that didn't) I still had loads left. I managed to talk a local newsagent into putting a couple on his shelf. They kept selling out and, as a result, I made some great new (local) comic friends. I plucked up the courage to ask Dark They Were and Golden Eyed, London's biggest comic shop (pre–Forbidden Planet) if they'd be so kind to sell some.[17]

The influences of Captain America, the Silver Surfer, and especially Jim Starlin's cosmic heroes Adam Warlock and Captain Marvel, are clear. Hornsby recounts, "I was a pretty dyed-in-the-wool Marvel fan at the time and didn't come across Jack Kirby's *Fourth World* stuff until later when numerous people mentioned the Apokolips connection and assumed I'd been a fan."[18] While the writing and art display some rough edges, there is also a great deal of wit and a deconstruction of superhero tropes that is playful and parodic, in keeping with the tradition of British superheroes (see Figure 41).

As Hornsby notes, there was a group of young independent comics creators around Hertfordshire at the time, but there was nothing organized. Third Kind Magazines, however, was based there, too, and published *Super Adventure Stories*, which appeared in 1978. Michael-Jan Gibas was the publisher, wrote many of the stories, and provided some of the art. Like *The Mighty Apocalypse*, this comic offered cosmic superhero stories of the sort that were popular in American comics of the late 1960s and the 1970s. They were quite similar to the work that Grant Morrison was doing in *Near Myths*, another independent comic, which was this time produced in Edinburgh and featuring early work by Bryan Talbot. The superhero story in *Super Adventure Stories* was called D-Riders and was written by Clive Boyd with illustration by Michael-Jan Gibas. As Terry Hooper notes,

> [*The Mighty Apocalypse* and *Super Adventure Stories*] comics obviously had their Marvel/DC influences to a degree but Underground Comix were also, I'm guessing, an influence. [*Super Adventure Stories* had] nudity and very definitely not Comics Code Authority approved language [and in "Sons of the Phoenix, written by Michael-Jan Gibas with art by Stephen O'Leary] there are some good story twists. And here's a kicker of a next issue tag line: "Some of you . . . are going to die!" These guys were well ahead of Moore, Ellis and Morrison.[19]

Another Third Kind character was Omicron. As Hopper says, he was a biker called Jason Harris "who was out on his motorbike, got involved in a UFO incident, grabbed an alien suit and became [a superhuman]." There were elements of Captain Britain's origin, as well as Magno's from the 1971 *Pow!* annual. As Hooper records, the character was created by Gibas and artist Andrew Dyrdzinski, who drew the story, and the scripts were provided by Stephen O'Leary. So it is clear that the members of this very creative team were sharing the duties, sometimes acting as writers, sometimes as artists, and in the spirit of collective working together to produce as much material as possible with limited resources and time. Another notable character to appear in *Super Adventure Stories* was The Red Dragon, who was

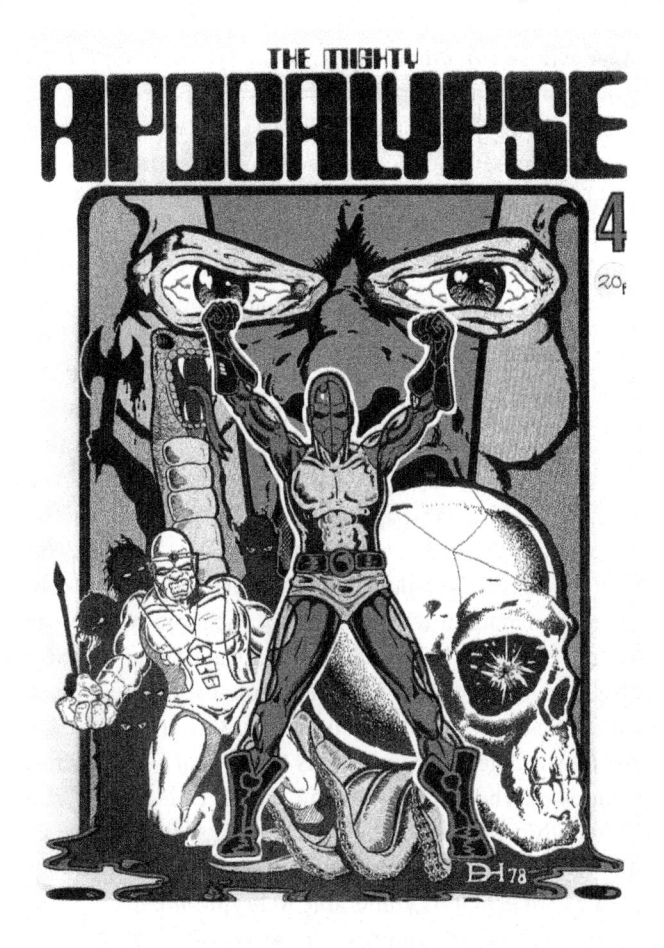

Fig. 41: *The Mighty Apocalypse*, by David Hornsby (1977).

created by Jonathan "Jonny" Kurzman. The influence of Neal Adams is obvious, as is the skill with which the story was produced. As Hooper recalls, "The story was an epic one, ending in a full issue story in *Super Adventure Stories # 5*."

It is worthwhile noting that comics publisher and blogger Terry Hooper's appreciation of these comics is one of the main factors that have kept them from slipping beyond obscurity and being completely forgotten. As he says, "These creators were true inspirations because they took superheroes and put a British slant on them, made them grittier than any US company did."[20] As Hooper suggests, these comics pointed the way to what was to come over the next few years, with British creators challenging the conventions of the superhero genre in increasingly overt ways. Another parody of American superhero comics came in 1979 from British comics artist and historian Lew Stringer, whose Brickman strips were a spoof of superhero comics in general and Batman in particular. Brickman was Loose Brayne, and he battled against crime in Guffon City. This strip started in a fanzine called *After Image* and expanded over the years across several publications.

In 2005 a collection was published that brought the old strips together with new "fan" art by some of the top creative talents in the industry, along with an introduction by no less than Alan Moore. The series is a perfect example of the British attitude toward superheroes, and if the British superhero genre has rubbed shoulders with the humor genre over the years, then Stringer collides them together in a way that recalls Harry Banger's Superstooge and Bob Monkhouse's Stuporman. However, perhaps the best-known and well-loved British superhero parody, in Britain anyway, is Bananaman. Created in 1980 and initially appearing in *Nutty* before moving to *The Dandy* and *The Beano*, Bananaman also appeared in a successful animated television series on the BBC (1983–1986) (see Figure 42). The character was created by Steve Bright and Dave Donaldson, and the original stories were drawn by John Geering. Bananaman was Eric Wimp, a schoolboy who was sent from the Moon in a rocket as a baby (echoing the origin of Superman). As a banana resembles the shape of the crescent moon, eating them gives him superpowers, which he uses to fight villains such as General Blight. He has a hideaway at the North Pole, like Superman's Fortress of Solitude, and is accompanied by a sidekick who is a talking crow, simply called "crow." His allies include Chief O'Reilly, who resembles Commissioner Jim Gordon as portrayed in the 1960s Batman television series, and he has a vulnerability to moldy bananas, just as Superman is vulnerable to kryptonite.

However, perhaps the most significant thing in terms of the current argument is that here is yet another example of a British superhero drawn from Captain Marvel, or indeed, Marvelman, as when he eats a banana, schoolboy Eric is transformed into an adult superhero. The power of satire and parody as deployed through British humor comics is fully in evidence here. The animated series took this British superhero to a much wider audience than the comics alone would have, and this character is still going strong. To this day most British people, if asked to name a British superhero, would likely say "Bananaman."

In the early 1980s, British comics were under real pressure from American imports and reprints, and the shape of the market was changing. The humor genre remained strong, and science fiction was increasingly popular due to the huge international success of the *Star Wars* films and related merchandise and tie-ins, including comics, but the war genre, sports comics,

Mergers and Marvels (1962–1980)   191

Fig. 42: The first appearance of Bananaman in *Nutty*, by John Geering (DC Thomson, 1980). Nutty © DC Thomson & Co Ltd.

and girl's comics were losing readers. There was also strong competition from other media, with computer games making a particular impact on the leisure time of younger readers. There was, on the other hand, a steadily growing older readership, but readership in that demographic was growing slower than the younger reader demographic was falling. The result was that the market for British comics started to contract, and it would continue to do so over the next several decades. This meant that smaller publishers fell away and repeated attempts to launch new comics would fail. However, as seen in this chapter, and discussed further in the next, there were the beginnings of a small but vibrant independent comics scene, in part growing out of the fanzines and the comics marts, and a new generation of creators started to come through. Some of them emerged from independent and underground comics and others through mainstream publications, but several had a foot in each camp. The success of *2000AD* and Marvel UK created opportunities, and there was increased visibility of British comics creators in America and the beginnings of the British Invasion that would take off in the 1980s. And Dez Skinn was starting to think about his own company and anthology title. As the 1980s dawned, the stage was set for a major resurgence of the British superhero. As Dave Gibbons has observed, the influx of British creators into American comics in the 1980s "wasn't so much an invasion but an infiltration, followed by an invitation, followed by an infatuation. Then possibly an insubordination!"[21]

Chapter Five

REVISIONISM AND THE BRITISH INVASION (1981–1993)

The start of the 1980s saw British comics in relatively fine health, at least in creative terms. While overall sales figures were falling due to competition from other forms of entertainment, mainly television and video games, *2000AD* was entering a period of enormous creative vitality, with some of the best work in British comics' history appearing at this time. In 1982 writer Alan Moore started writing Captain Britain for Marvel UK, and a new comic, *Warrior*, appeared to challenge *2000AD*. It was conceived by former Marvel UK editor Dez Skinn and featured *Marvelman* and *V for Vendetta*, written by Alan Moore with artwork by Garry Leach and David Lloyd, respectively. Skinn's philosophy was simple—to give creators a lot more creative freedom than was normal at the time, especially with regard to political and graphic content, mirroring the moves toward more adult content in mainstream American comics, such as Frank Miller's *Daredevil* (1979–1983). The creative partnerships that matured as a result of *2000AD* and *Warrior* and the attention they brought to British comics resulted in an increasing number of British comics creators finding work in American comics. And the re-workings of the superhero genre in Captain Britain, via *Marvelman* and *V for Vendetta*, meant that there was something akin to a branch of the revisionist trend operating out of Britain. This ultimately led to *Watchmen*, by Moore and Dave Gibbons, who took the British attitude towards superheroes to a worldwide readership. This chapter will trace the development of the revisionist trend in British comics and examine it as a continuation and refocusing of the satirical reaction to the superhero genre that has been in evidence in British comics for decades. It will also examine the so-called British Invasion of American comics and its aftermath.

Moore's Captain Britain

As discussed in the previous chapter, Marvel UK had enjoyed considerable success in the 1970's, and the American office had overseen the development of Captain Britain for this British market. There were, however, several problems with the office's approach. The character was given a new direction by British writer David Thorpe, but he left over a disagreement about how political his stories could be (see previous chapter). At this point, Alan Moore joined Alan Davis to produce a memorable run. Moore had been fascinated with comics as a child, copying pictures from British comics, but at the age of seven he encountered some American comics for the first time. They were a revelation. He continued reading comics through his teens, including Charlton Comics, upon which *Watchmen* was later based. In the early 1980s, Moore wrote stories appearing in *Star Wars* and *Doctor Who* for Marvel UK, and in 1982 he took over writing Captain Britain for Marvel UK in *Daredevils* and *Mighty World of Marvel*. Moore's Captain Britain was very different from what had come before and became a testing ground for many of the ideas he would develop later. Moore's celebrated run of Captain Britain opened with the introduction of The Fury, a creature designed to kill superheroes who had massacred every superbeing in its dimension. It kills Captain Britain's companions and then murders him, although Merlin brings him back to life and returns him to his own dimension. However, when The Fury's parallel world is destroyed, he manages to survive and follows Captain Britain across dimensions.

In the meantime, Captain Britain tries to put his life back together, meeting up with his sister Betsy (later to become Psylocke of the X-Men) and battles the villain Slaymaster in a Forbidden Planet comic shop in London. Moore's strategy was to put the character back into a realistic, relatable world before whisking him off to other dimensions. In his travels, he finds himself in a fascistic Britain that resembles the world of *V for Vendetta* run by Mad Jim Jaspers, a villain with reality-warping powers, who looks like Oswald Mosley, the British fascist leader of the 1930s. In the stories that preceded Moore's run, Captain Britain had traveled in fantasy worlds and been through massive upheavals and transformations (see Figure 43). Now Moore grounded the stories in the everyday and the particular before taking the hero back across a range of parallel realities. Eventually, he defeats The Fury with the help of Captain UK, a female version of Captain Britain from another dimension.

The Fury is one of the key characters of Moore's run, if the creature could be said to be a character. More correctly, the violence that it embodies and enacts sets the tone for these stories. It cannot be reasoned with, and it kills without remorse. When it first encounters Captain Britain, it murders his companions and then pursues him relentlessly until it kills him. When his friend Jackdaw is murdered, Captain Britain is filled with hatred, launching himself at The Fury, who bats him away. The narration states, simply and directly, that all of Captain Britain's power and rage "isn't enough." As Captain Britain struggles to comprehend how the creature could have broken his arm, Jim Jaspers appears (in a large flying teapot no less) and explains how he created The Fury in a parallel dimension in order to remove the competition. He raised support for the extermination of the superhumans through his role as a politician, campaigning on the slogan, "If they were honest they wouldn't wear masks." As Captain Britain flees The Fury and Jaspers, he finds himself in a graveyard of fallen British superheroes who have been exterminated as part of this superhero holocaust. The headstones reveal alternate names for the British heroes who have been killed, including alternate versions of Robot Archie, Kelly and Marvelman, as well as General Jumbo, Steel Claw, and The Spider, here renamed Android Andy, Tom Rosetta, Miracleman, Colonel Tusker, Iron Tallon, and the Arachnid.

The level of violence seen here does not match what Moore would unleash in Marvelman, but the same tone is in evidence, and Captain Britain feels the same desperate helplessness in the face of extreme violence that Marvelman experiences. That was still at this point a novel approach. The idea of flawed superheroes was still relatively new, but to see such despair was shocking. One of the keys to this is the fact that Moore was mixing the superhero genre with another genre, this one with close associations to the British literary tradition: the Gothic. Moore incorporated themes of loss, despair, and the uncanny.[1] Making the superhero both physically and psychologically vulnerable was an important aspect of this strategy. The associations with Gothic also link back to the influence of the penny dreadfuls on comics, and in many ways Moore's innovation, blending the superhero genre with gothic tropes and conventions, is very much in keeping with a longer tradition of influence from the gothic literature on British serial publications. Another important aspect of the text that linked back to the penny dreadfuls was the inclusion of political commentary. The story offers a vision of a warped, violent, and repressive fascist Britain. It represented a critique of Britain under the rule of the conservative Tory party, led by Prime Minister Margaret Thatcher. Moore would offer a much richer and sustained critique of British politics of the 1980s in *V for Vendetta*, but

Fig. 43: Captain Britain, art by Alan Davis, in *Marvel Super-Heroes* #387 (Marvel UK, 1982).

similar ideas are to be found here. When Moore left Captain Britain, Jamie Delano took over. Moore then developed *Marvelman* and *V for Vendetta* for the short-lived but hugely influential *Warrior*. In both these stories, Moore continued to explore gothic themes and imagery.

Warrior—Marvelman and *V for Vendetta*

A short time after leaving Marvel UK, Dez Skinn formed his own company, Quality Communications, and published *Warrior*. Skinn ensured that quality was at the forefront of the endeavor, as indicated in the name of the company, and did so by transplanting the creative team that he had fostered over the previous years, including Alan Moore, David Lloyd, and Steve Dillon. The fact that this comic was designed to challenge *2000AD* is underscored by the fact that the comic tackled genres that *2000AD* largely stayed away from, namely superheroes, horror, and comedy but included the key genre that *2000AD* traded in—science fiction. Indeed, *2000AD* could be said to have had an editorial policy against superhero comics in that it was well-known that the editor, Pat Mills, and John Wagner, the co-creator and writer of Judge Dredd, did not like superheroes. Like *2000AD*, the stories in *Warrior* would have a political subtext, many of them responding to the Tory government of Margaret Thatcher. The revisionist treatment of the superhero in Moore's *Marvelman* and *V for Vendetta* was therefore politically loaded, and Moore's critique of the superhero was very much an attack on American imperialism, particularly how it was manifested in the "special relationship" between Britain and America and Thatcher and Reagan.[2] Liberal sentiment was very much against this relationship, and the superhero became an emblem of it in Moore's comics. Indeed, Marvelman was in a sense about the American influence on Britain, both politically and culturally. In some ways, the story was an allegory for what had happened to British comics due to the influence of the American style and genres, which was in turn a metaphor for how that lopsided relationship had shaped British politics and identity in the postwar years.

V for Vendetta, on the other hand, reveled in its Britishness (or perhaps Englishness) and featured a protagonist who could have very easily been pulled from the pages of the penny dreadfuls and story papers of the late nineteenth and early twentieth centuries. *Marvelman* and *V for Vendetta*, together with Moore's *Captain Britain*, mirrored the beginning of a revisionist trend in American superhero comics, however, while most American revisionist texts, such as those produced by Frank Miller, from *Daredevil* to *The*

Dark Knight Returns (1986), emphasized the right-wing characteristics of the superhero, challenging formerly liberal conceptions of these characters in favor of a much more brutal "realism," the British revisionist trend, spearheaded by Alan Moore, proceeded from a rather more left-wing sensibility. These comics critiqued the performance of power and the cultural imperialism, embodied in the superhero, seeing them as grotesque extensions of American foreign policy. The revisionist trend on both sides of the Atlantic was therefore deeply politicized, albeit in very different ways.

In addition, one of the key features of the British revisionist texts was their reaffirmation of the existence of a British superhero tradition, in defiance of the dominant American tradition. *Marvelman*, with art by Garry Leach and Alan Davis, prefigures much of what Moore would later do with *Watchmen*, although it is much darker in tone. Originally, Marvelman stories were produced in Britain in the 1950s by Mick Anglo to fill the gap left by the disappearance of Captain Marvel, the American character who was the subject of lengthy legal wranglings between DC Comics and Fawcett Publications (see Chapter Three). Moore's take on Marvelman was, like his work on Captain Britain, full of gothic tropes, which was itself an aspect of the essential Britishness of Moore's approach, embedding the text in a series of references to the gothic literary tradition and, to a certain extent, the penny dreadfuls that fed on them. Moore's Marvelman was unsure of himself, and the violence he faced was excessive. In Marvelmen stories, he was surrounded by death and forces that challenged his very understanding of reality.

At the start of the story, Micky Moran has lost his memory and has no knowledge of his powers or his former life as a superhero. He dreams of flying and of a violent death at the heart of a nuclear explosion. Caught up in a terrorist raid on a nuclear power plant and facing death, he rediscovers his secret word and is transformed into Marvelman for the first time in decades. He struggles to reconcile his forgotten former life with his current one. His girlfriend Liz laughs at his ridiculous stories of superheroic adventures, based as they are on the rather silly 1950s Marvelman stories. When they encounter Kid Marvelman, his former sidekick, the tone changes considerably. Kid Marvelman has been in his superhero form for decades, having survived the nuclear explosion that killed Young Marvelman and robbed Marvelman of his powers and memory. In the intervening time, Kid Marvelman has become a powerful businessman, but Marvelman recognizes that he has been driven mad by his double life and is now an inhuman killer, completely divorced from humanity. In the violent and desperate battle that ensues, innocent bystanders are killed. This was unlike anything seen before in superhero comics, and the most shocking aspect of the violence was that the superhero could barely comprehend it, much less fight back. Here Moore placed Marvelman in an equivalent position to a real person faced with violence, experiencing terror in the face of it (see Figure 44). His superpowers are no guarantee of victory, or that he can save himself, or rescue the civilians caught up in the battle. This was a superhero conflict with consequences. It ends only when Kid Marvelman accidentally says his special word, transforming him back to his human form: an innocent child. Believing him to have burned out his powers Marvelman spares his life, but there is no happy ending or resolution to be had, and indeed, Marvelman's decision to show mercy at this point will have terrible consequences later in the series.

Over the course of the rest of Moore's run, Marvelman learns that he is the product of an experiment by Dr Gargunza, a scientist working for the government, who was tasked with uncovering the secrets of a crashed alien spaceship found in Britain in the 1950s. Gargunza discovers the secret of the alien technology that allowed the craft's pilot to shift between bodies. The alien has an implant in his head, and when a trigger word is spoken, the alien's real body is replaced by a perfect superpowered cloned version of itself, which is suspended in a pocket dimension with the consciousness of the alien shifting between the two bodies as part of the transfer. Gargunza applies this technology to his test subjects and creates four super beings: Marvelman, Young Marvelan, Kid Marvelman, and Miraclewoman. One day while in the laboratory's cafeteria, he comes across a copy of an L. Miller and Son British reprint of an American Captain Marvel story left by one of the workers and decides to create a computer-generated illusion that feeds his subjects the fantasy that they are living as superheroes. This repositions all the 1950s stories (or most of them) as fantasies, created in order to control the superbeings. Gargunza also sexually abuses his young test subjects, adding another level of cynicism and horror to Moore's reinterpretation.

Moore's revised origin foregrounds a science-fiction explanation rather than the magical fantasy of the Captain Marvel comics. It extended the changes made by Mick Anglo in the Marvelman comics from the 1950s, where a pseudoscientific process rather than magic seems to be behind Micky Moran's transformation. Over the course of Moore's story, Marvelman kills Gargunza and once again faces Kid Marvelman, who devastates London, killing thousands of innocents in imagery that recalls a vision of Hell, with victims tied together with barbed wire, a vicar impaled on a

Fig. 44: Marvelman, by Alan Moore and Garry Leach, in *Warrior* #1 (Quality Communications, 1982).

spike, and a young mother with her arms torn off. The extreme, repugnant violence, drawn in excruciating detail by John Totleben, is one of the most effective examples of a superbeing's potential for evil. At one point in the conflict Marvelman, the supposed hero, picks up a car containing a family, and in his desperation throws it at his enemy, killing the occupants. When Kid Marvelman again reverts to his innocent childhood form, Marvelman kills his former sidekick and friend in a scene that is truly harrowing. Not even *Watchmen* would deliver such a hard-hitting indictment of the superhero concept. By the end of Moore's run, Marvelman has become hardened, a brutal killer and god-like creature. Moore's critique was leveled at authority and abuses of power. The commentary was all the more powerful because it centered around a British superhero who had been an imitation of an American character and was now employing explicitly political themes and extreme violence to undermine the superhero concept. All the frustration and anger that Moore saw in Britain, from a defeated Left and a generation that rejected the nuclear arms race but felt largely powerless to resist, was focused through this comic.

When *Warrior* came to a close, the American publisher Eclipse continued the story, which it had been reprinting for the American market, with Moore suggesting Neil Gaiman as his successor. Gaiman took a very different approach, exploring the effect of having a God on Earth. Miracleman (as he was now known in America due to pressure from Marvel Comics) took over world governance and brought about a golden age. However, Miracleman's shift to Godhood increasingly divorces him from human concerns, much like *Watchmen*'s Dr Manhattan. In these stories, Gaiman explores this strange unsettling utopia, as well as the connections between comics, pop art, and surrealism, with a resurrected Andy Warhol (who had died three years previously) appearing as a character, making a link back to the rise of pop art and British superhero comics of the 1950s (as discussed in Chapter Three) and other pop art–inspired comics such as *Paradax* (see below). This was a quite different way of engaging with the relationship between British superhero comics, politics, and art. Where Moore stories had become increasingly nightmarish, Gaiman's captured a sense of wonder at this new society ruled over by supergods but was equally cynical about the potential abuse of power. As the story went on, Gaiman increasingly focused on the human perspective, and the superbeings became distant and aloof.

A character with an altogether more human perspective was V from Moore and David Lloyd's dystopian tale of a near-future fascist Britain terrorized by a mysterious freedom fighter. This brooding story initially appeared alongside Moore's *Marvelman* and was originally in black and white and like *Marvelman* was incomplete at the time when *Warrior* ceased publication. Moore's rising stardom in American comics, however, especially with his acclaimed *Watchmen*, ensured that *V for Vendetta* was reprinted by DC Comics, allowing Moore and Lloyd to complete the story. The American comic was colored and was collected as a book in the wake of the graphic novel boom of the mid-1980s. *V for Vendetta* emerged from a number of sources. In his early 1920s, Moore had submitted a proposal for a character called The Doll to DC Thomson. The idea was rejected, and Moore later admitted that expecting that publisher to publish a story about a transsexual terrorist was perhaps unrealistic. When *Warrior* launched, editor Dez Skinn paired Moore with Lloyd and asked for a dark, mysterious strip, capturing the edgy tone that for which *Warrior* was striving. Lloyd had previously worked on *Night Raven* for Marvel UK, a dark thriller set in the 1930s. Asked to do another 1930s mystery, Lloyd resisted, wanting a chance to do something more contemporary. Moore turned back to his idea for The Doll, and things slowly came together. From initial character designs that were quite conventionally superheroic emerged the idea to blend a range of influences that would make this a uniquely British series. In an article called "Behind the Painted Smile," Moore recounts that his inspiration came from

> Orwell. Huxley. Thomas Disch. Judge Dredd. Harlan Ellison's "'Repent, Harlequin!' Said the Ticktockman," "Catman" and "The Prowler in the City at the Edge of the World" by the same author. Vincent Price's Dr. Phibes and Theatre of Blood. David Bowie. The Shadow. Night Raven. Batman. Fahrenheit 451. The writings of the New Worlds school of science fiction. Max Ernst's painting "Europe After the Rains." Thomas Pynchon. The atmosphere of British Second World War films. The Prisoner. Robin Hood. Dick Turpin.[3]

When Lloyd suggested that the character be modeled on Guy Fawkes, V was born. Fawkes was a Catholic soldier who was executed for his part in the Gunpowder Plot of November 5, 1605, when a small group planned to blow up the English Houses of Parliament in order to destroy Protestant rule. He was a character who was embedded in British history and whose effigy was the subject of annual burnings on Guy Fawkes night, a ritual observed by children who in all likelihood did not understand the political dimension of the act.

V for Vendetta was a platform for Moore's political views. He showed a society on the verge of collapse and divided by the inequalities that were associated with the government of Conservative Prime Minister Margaret Thatcher.[4] Moore's vision of this world was very much influenced by George Orwell's *Nineteen Eighty-Four* (1949), but it also drew on postwar British comics. The artwork was influenced by the British noir style of filmmaker Graham Greene and the social realism of Tony Richardson. The main character, V, is an anarchist, reflecting Moore's politics. He is never clearly identified, although it is clear that he has been a victim of the fascist government's repressive policies towards dissidents, minorities, and homosexuals.

Escaping from a concentration camp where cruel experiments have been performed, V disguises himself in a Guy Fawkes costume, clearly identifying himself as a terrorist, rebel, and martyr. The story opens with V rescuing a young woman, Evey Hammond, from the police, who intend to assault her following her arrest for prostitution. He takes her to a rooftop and blows up the Houses of Parliament. She is then taken to his hideout, the Shadow Gallery, and becomes his unwilling accomplice in his war against those who have tortured him. A police detective, Eric Finch, investigates V but has little luck in discovering his identity, as V is systematically murdering everyone who might identify him. Evey becomes disenchanted with V's methods and after an argument he abandons her. Sometime later he kidnaps her, subjects her to an ordeal modeled on his own torture experience, and shows her how she can free herself from fear and oppression. V continues his war on the government as Finch slowly closes in. Upon finding V's hideout, Finch shoots and mortally wounds V. As he dies, he passes his legacy on to Evey, who adopts his costume and sends his body in an underground train full of explosives to destroy Downing Street. Evey announces that with the government gone, people must now choose what comes next. Finch stumbles out into the now chaotic streets, leaving London behind. With the once-repressive mechanisms of state control now destroyed, or at least temporarily disrupted, the future is left unclear, but at least there is now an opportunity for the people to choose a different future.

The appearance of Marvelman and V in *Warrior* was an important turning point for British superhero comics. Whereas most had brought the superhero into dialogue with the more dominant humor genre, producing a parody of the American superhero, *Marvelman* and *V for Vendetta* were quite different. Moore's voice dominated the narration, with his prose style matching the portentous, apocalyptic tone of the story. Even when the ridiculousness of the 1950s source material for *Marvelman* is taken into account, it is not a parody. Similarly, *V for Vendetta* does not parody the superhero genre as such. It is, however, indebted to folklore and the mystery men stories of the penny dreadfuls and pulp fiction of the late Victorian period, mixed with imagery by Lloyd that looks distinctly old-fashioned by recalling the "kitchen sink" social realism of much British literature, art, and filmmaking of the 1950s and 1960s. Moore and Lloyd's innovation is to contrast the social realism of the world presented in *V* with the Romanticism of the character of V himself. He is not the typical "angry young man" from a working-class background who dominates kitchen sink dramas, but is rather a sober, analytical, yet passionate revolutionary. His anger is tempered by his cultured and intellectual manner, and while he is certainly a killer and may be a madman, he is also an appealing voice for a generation oppressed by conservatism and the politics of selfishness.

The target of the satire in both *V for Vendetta* and *Marvelman* is therefore the nostalgic longing for the 1950s seen in British politics and popular culture of the 1970s and 1980s. *Marvelman* offers a violent deconstruction of the British Marvelman superhero comics of the 1950s, while *V for Vendetta* uses the look and style of 1950s British literature, drama and film as the backdrop for a story of resistance to right-wing values and oppression by the state. The conception of British power in relation to the political and cultural landscape of the 1950s is therefore very important to both stories. This was a decade that was seen, somewhat nostalgically from the viewpoint of the 1980s, as a time of morality, social cohesion, and family values in the aftermath of the war and before the "decadence" of the 1960s. In fact, it was the Suez crisis of 1956, in which Britain and France backed an invasion of Egypt by Israel, which was a military disaster and that many historians view as the end of Britain as a major world power.[5] Prime Minister Margaret Thatcher, with her robust foreign policy and belief in individualism and the free market, appealed to this nostalgia for the power Britain wielded before the collapse of empire and the humiliation of Suez, and in the face of an economic crisis that was driving Britain into a closer relationship with Europe.[6] In response Thatcher sought to emphasize cultural and military ties with America and fostered a close relationship with President Ronald Reagan. Moore found Thatcher's polices and views were anathema to Moore, who felt that her government was pushing Britain towards being a neo-fascist state. As Moore said in his 1988 introduction to the collected edition of *V for Vendetta*, "I am thinking of taking my family and getting out of this country soon, sometime over the next couple of years. It's cold and it's mean-spirited and I don't like it here anymore."[7]

Marvelman and *V for Vendetta* were therefore pointed attacks on Thatcher's Britain, which was seen as corrupt, violent, and divisive. This was seen in *Marvelman*'s depiction of the grim state of 1980s Britain, the threat from terrorism (which echoed the ongoing struggle between the British government and the Irish Republican Army), and the fact that Kid Marvelman, the alpha predator of humanity, disguises himself as a businessman and arch capitalist. He is a satire on Thatcher's fierce individualism, seeing himself as far above humans as humans are above insects. Marvelman's world is dark, cold, and violent and is a reflection of the unrest and callousness of Thatcher's Britain. At the end of Moore's run, in his last issue, *Miracleman* #16 (Eclipse, 1989) outlines his plan for restructuring the world economy, meeting with Prime Minister Margaret Thatcher and her government. Miracleman humiliates the prime minister, who realizes that her authority is now meaningless in the face of a superhuman god. It is not just the British Empire that has been superseded, but all human authority. It was a prophetic issue: less than a year later, Thatcher would be deposed as leader.

Marvelman and *V for Vendetta* had showcased all of Moore's talents, his tight plotting, his keen sense for characterization, his ability to sustain tension and suspense over a long and dense narrative, and his powers as a satirist. When he won the Eagle Award—granted by fans voting for best comic of the year—two years in a row (1982 and 1983), he came to the attention of American publishers. With a fan following in Britain and an increasing reputation in America, Moore found himself the darling of the comics world for a time. He became renowned in the industry for his elaborate scripts and his ability to deconstruct generic clichés. When he was recruited by DC Comics in 1983, Moore was given the ailing *Swamp Thing* title. Here his fascination with the arcane and the political was evident in his reinvention of the comic as gothic horror meets ecological parable. In these stories Moore introduced John Constantine, later to get his own title, *Hellblazer*, a vehicle for Moore's interest in the occult. These comics later became the backbone of DC's Vertigo line of comics for "mature readers." In 1985 Moore collaborated with Dave Gibbons on the Superman Annual, producing a story called "For the Man who has Everything." The following year he wrote the last original continuity Superman story, "Whatever Happened to the Man of Tomorrow?," with art by Curt Swan, before the series was revamped by John Byrne. These series paved the way to *Watchmen* in 1986, co-created with Gibbons. This groundbreaking series was hugely successful and is widely celebrated by critics as one of the best superhero comics ever made.

Who Watches . . . ?

Watchmen (1986), by Moore and Gibbons, is one of the most influential superhero comics of all time. Its satirical deconstruction of the superhero came at exactly the right time, driving the so-called graphic novel boom of the mid-1980s. It became the standard against which superhero comics are judged, but rarely equal. The success of *Watchmen* was phenomenal. In its wake, DC Comics reprinted and completed *V for Vendetta*, which was then recolored, and like *Watchmen*, collected as a graphic novel, the format that would redefine the fortunes of the medium in the following years. *Watchmen* is an insightful homage to the superhero genre as well as a deconstruction of its clichés, forms, and influences. Originally published as a twelve-issue series beginning in September 1986, *Watchmen* was collected as a book in 1987. The origin of *Watchmen* was DC Comics' purchase of the rights for characters previously published by the defunct Charlton Comics, characters Moore had known and loved as a child. In addition, the character of Nite Owl was also based on Night Owl, a character that Gibbons had created years earlier in his youth and in his drawings fought a villain called H-Bomb, which—given the nature of Dr Manhattan's powers—seems eerily prescient.

When the idea was first being pitched, Moore produced a treatment outlining how he would perform the same alchemy with the Charlton characters as he had with *Swamp Thing*. As the proposal was a radical departure from the established characters (making them murderers, psychopaths, and rapists), Moore was given the go-ahead to create new characters based on the Charlton heroes, as DC wanted to retain some of the Charlton characters for use in the DC Universe. Beginning with the murder of Edward Blake, a masked vigilante and government operative also known as The Comedian, the story follows the unhinged vigilante Rorschach (aka Walter Kovacs) as he investigates his hunch that there is a "mask killer" targeting superheroes. This investigation brings him into contact with his retired former teammates, Dan Dreiberg (Nite Owl), Laurie Juspeczyk (Silk Spectre), Jon Osterman (Dr Manhattan), and Adrian Veidt (Ozymandias). In terms of the story, Moore broke with the conventions of the superhero genre from the outset, eschewing the adventure genre for a murder mystery structure and slowly unveiling clues to the identity of the "villain," if such a thing could be said to exist in the morally complex and compromised world presented in *Watchmen*. Indeed, like *V for Vendetta*, *Watchmen* plays with the idea of the superhero genre. Although there are superheroes in the story, the narrative structure and pacing defies the conventions of the genre. This is a story in which the genre and the form are somewhat at odds with one another, but the artwork and writing so perfectly complement each other that these disjunctions are disguised. They are, however, slowly revealed over the course of the narrative as the reader's expectations are challenged and subverted, and an underlying unity, the presence of incomprehensible synchronicity, replaces human certainties. There are forces beyond human understanding at work in this world, and they do not wear spandex or capes.

Watchmen was ambitious, with a complex narrative structure and a disciplined adherence to a nine-panel grid format, broken occasionally for dramatic effect. The extensive flashback structure and the interpolation of a pirate comic as a commentary on the story adds to the complexity of the narrative. It gains power through its literary treatment of time and memory, its recurrent symbolism, and the ingenuity with which Moore weaves together all the disparate elements with exacting precision, which is matched by Gibbons's artwork. All of these elements invoke the image of the universe as a mechanism driven by synchronicity and patterns. In this sense, the comic is not just a deconstruction of a particular genre but of the medium and form of comics themselves. Themes of determinism, fate, and free will move from the cosmic scale down to the subatomic, moving through the intermediate stage of everyday human affairs. The only real superbeing, Dr Manhattan, adopts a relativist view, seeing no difference between past, present, and future or between life and death. Rorschach's view represents the polar opposite, with a black and white Objectivist moral stance drawn from Steve Ditko's Randian character, The Question.

While the formal elements of *Watchmen* have received much attention, at its heart the story is a morality tale, disguised as a murder mystery, disguised as a superhero story. Ultimately it reveals that the smallest moments matter, that events reverberate through time and memory with devastating consequences. Moore's scripts were unusually dense for a comic script, full of extraneous detail and description, as is his habit, but he was not prescriptive about the artwork, allowing for a very fluid collaboration with Gibbons. The format of the comics was equally bold, with distinctive covers and no letters page or adverts; instead, Moore used the extra pages to present supplementary material such as text stories that were related to the main narrative. Moore also consciously decided not to use an external narrative voice in captions or to use thought bubbles, forcing himself and Gibbons to tell the story primarily through dialogue and images, leaving character's motivations and thoughts ambiguous. The result was a comic that seemed, in terms of both story and artwork, to be much more sophisticated than most superhero comics of the time, but for all its innovation, the tone of *Watchmen* was very much drawn from the long tradition of satirical approaches to the superhero seen in British comics since the 1940s. That included the questioning of heroic values and the presentation of villains as protagonists, and indeed the title of the series was drawn from the Roman author Juvenal's *Satires*, giving some indication of the satirical undercurrent of the work.

Paradax

In 1985 Eclipse Comics published *Strange Days* #3, which introduced Paradax, a character created in 1984 by artist Brendan McCarthy, with scripts by writer Peter Milligan. The character then appeared in his own title published by Vortex in 1987, which presented stories created in 1986. Paradax was Al Cooper, formerly a New York cabbie and now "the world's greatest superhero," having found a book left on the back seat of the cab out from which, when opened, sprung a suit that bestowed superpowers. The suit, which was bright yellow, recalled the costume of the Flash's nemesis, Professor Zoom, and gave Paradax the power to move through solid objects. The short-lived series made a considerable impression on readers due to Milligan's sharp scripts and McCarthy's striking concept design and artwork, which combined something of a European flavor with American superhero comics, containing echoes of Jack Kirby, Steve Ditko, and Moebius. McCarthy also identifies the influence of Carmine Infantino's work on 1960s American comic, *The Flash*, which he refers to as "super-stylish," noting that his aim with *Paradax* was to "recreate that flavour, which had a breezy feel to it."[8] This was a conscious attempt to shake off the supposed "grim and gritty" ethos of revisionist superhero stories that were common at the time. The character was, as his creators observe, "a man of his time: the avaricious 'loadsa money' eighties. He was a normal, working-class guy trying to hitch a ride on the gravy train that so many others were riding."[9] In this sense, Paradax was responding to the same political and cultural condition as *Marvelman* and *V for Vendetta*, but in a very different way. *Paradax* was playful and fun in a way that Moore's violent, brooding stories could never be. As noted in *The Best of Milligan and McCarthy* (2013), "In an era of long and bloated 'concept album' comics, where more pages meant more importance, *Paradax* was more of a short, sharp, throwaway pop single. The type you danced to. The type you had sex to."[10]

If Moore's Marvelman was influenced by William Blake and the ethos of Thatcherism, then Paradax's main point of reference was pop art and surrealism (like Gaiman's later Miracleman stories). Indeed, the series was dedicated to "Andy Warhol—artist of the highest order," and in the story Paradax appears on a chat show hosted by Warhol. As noted above, Paradax is motivated by celebrity, money and sex, and in this respect he was very much the precursor of *Zenith* and *Kick-ass*, which drew a lot from the attitude and style that Milligan and McCarthy established. The stories were surreal parodies of the superhero genre that in some ways reacted against the so-called serious and political work that was associated with the revisionist trend in superhero comics that dominated the early-to- mid-1980s and was exemplified by the work of Frank Miller and Alan Moore. That is not to say that there was not a political edge to Paradax, but rather than it was deployed through satirical means rather than by attempting to make the world of the superhero realistic. Indeed, as McCarthy notes,

> There was there was no new thought on superheroes at that time in British comics other than Alan Moore's revamped *Marvelman*. But to my mind, it was a continuation of the Steve Englehart and Don McGregor school of overwrought "serious" purple-po-faced comics that I really disliked. *Paradax* was a reaction to that. *Marvelman* bored me (not the original, but Moore's new take) and *Paradax* was a new paradigm for the superhero. Punk iconoclasm played a big role. I wanted the *Paradax* strip to be a like a pop single. *Paradax* is the far more significant piece of thought on superheroes, and was wholly original at the time. Morrison's "media brat with manager" in *Zenith* was lifted off *Paradax* wholesale.[11]

Paradax was, as McCarthy argues, a significant advance on the idea of the superhero, and although the character was an American and the stories were set in America, the humor and sensibility drew very much on a British surrealist tradition that included Monty Python and a host of other influences. As Milligan and McCarthy note,

> Growing up in the sixties and then being teenagers in the seventies, we soaked up loads of British culture—from the weirdness of the Beatles

psychedelic music to the stylised "glam" of performers like Bolan, Bowie and Roxy music... We were both products of art schools so many ideas from paintings made their way into our comics, like Surrealism, Dada, Pop, and conceptual art. We felt we were fine artists doing comics and seeing what we could get away with, bending the rules of what was possible.[12]

Here was another link to the surrealist mode of British pop art seen in The Independent Group's work in the mid-1950s, which played with the intersection of British and American popular culture and offered a critique of elitist values. In this sense, Paradax very clearly paved the way for Morrison and Yeowell's *Zenith* (for which McCarthy produced the character designs). Like Paradax, Zenith is something of a brat, obsessed with fashion and style rather than traditional superheroics, and there are also aspects of the Dada-inspired weirdness that would later become a feature of Morrison's *Doom Patrol*. However, despite having a huge influence on several comics creators and well-known characters, *Paradax* has been somewhat overlooked as one of the key British superhero comics of the 1980s.

Zenith

Zenith appeared in 1987 and was a deconstruction of superhero comics, referencing the occult, the poetry of William Blake, the Cthulhu mythos of H. P. Lovecraft, popular fashion and music, and a host of other eclectic sources (see Figure 45). It was also about the influence of American comics on British comics, carried off with irony and precision and with stylish artwork by Steve Yeowell. From the very beginning, *Zenith* paid homage to the history of British comics, and Morrison openly admitted, albeit playfully, to plagiarism with *Zenith*, referring to it as a "hip-hop" comic that sampled and re-edited old material, presenting it as a new, elaborate intertextual weave of references, with Morrison and Yeowell experimenting with manga style decompressed storytelling techniques.[13] This was *Marvelman* meets *Paradax*, but it was also something quite different and unique. If this was plagiarism, it was arguably in the tradition seen in the old penny dreadfuls, but this was also a postmodern paratext engaging in a complex dialogue with the all but forgotten superheroes of British comics history.

Zenith himself, like Paradax, was a brash young man seeking fame and fortune rather than superhero status. The character was an avatar of sorts for Morrison, who also wore a leather jacket and was working on a bad boy of Brit-comics image. *Zenith* comprised four chapters, or "phases" as Morrison

Fig. 45: *Zenith*, by Grant Morrison and Steve Yeowell (Fleetway, 1987). 2000 AD is a registered trademark. Zenith copyright 2016 Rebellion A/S. All rights reserved. Reproduced with permission. www.2000ADonline.com.

called them, and represented *2000AD*'s first attempt at a superhero story, although Morrison broke with many of the traditions of both American superhero comics and British adventure comics. Zenith represents petty and arrogant human values, and he is unable and unwilling to comprehend the powers that threaten and control him. In Morrison's view, he is what normal people would be with superpowers, not a psychotic vigilante as Miller and Moore suggest, but a spoiled rock star with a massive ego.

As Morrison noted in an interview for *Amazing Heroes Magazine*, "I am sure if I had superpowers I'd be a super-villain.... I'd like to be able to walk through walls just to get into other people's homes. Straight away I'd be a super-villain. I'd steal all sorts of money and set myself up in luxury. That's why it's easier to sympathize with these people. I don't understand why anybody would want to be a super-hero and defend the law."[14] The first phase of *Zenith*, "Tygers"—drawing its title from a poem by William Blake—contemplates the theme of the superhuman as the next evolutionary step. The main action of the story involves the battle against a resurrected Nazi superhuman, Masterman, who has been possessed by the spirit of an interdimensional Dark God, a creature known as a Lloigor, or a "many-angled one" (a creature straight out of Lovecraft's weird fiction). This character takes his name from several sources, chiefly the Nazi villain in the 1970s Marvel comic *The Invaders*, the Fawcett superhero who appeared at the same time as Captain Marvel in the late 1930s, the Kid Eternity villain from the 1940s, and the postwar British superhero Masterman (see Chapter Three).

The second phase, "The Hollow Land," explores Zenith's origins and has him confronting Dr Michael Peyne, the creator of superhumans and a power-crazed industrialist, Wallace Scott (a thinly veiled caricature of Richard Branson), who are attempting to take over the world. Underneath the deliberately clichéd James Bond–style plot, there is a thoughtfully staged psychological drama, a kind of Oedipal conflict, in which Zenith has to battle his father; the cyborg Warhead; and the father of the superhumans, Dr Peyne. The third phase, "War in Heaven," reveals the intricate structure of the larger story. It plays with the idea of superhero "universes," a common trope in American comics, and further develops the theme of the villains as interdimensional Dark Gods who attempt to take over the universe and have to be stopped by a coalition of superheroes from various alternate realities (who are actually heroes from various British adventure comics). Ultimately, the superheroes defeat the Lloigor with very little help from Zenith, but only by destroying entire universes in order to do so. The fourth phase, "Fear of Flying" brings the story full circle. Here, in the aftermath of the war in the third phase, Zenith finds that his former allies are planning to take over the world.

The seven superhumans created by Dr Peyne are Peter St John (Mandala), Ruby Fox (Voltage), Siadwel Rhys (The Red Dragon), David Cambridge (Lux), Penelope Moon (Spook), and White Heat and Dr Beat (Zenith's parent's, whose real names are never revealed). Their creator, Dr Peyne, instills within them the belief that they are humanity's evolutionary successors, and he envisages a world ruled by pure beings, superseding humanity and the corrupt world that condemned to death Maximan—the first British superhuman created by Dr. Peyne during World War II to defeat the Nazi superhuman, both of whom were killed when the Americans dropped an atomic bomb on Berlin in the opening installment of *Zenith*. This scenario echoes the evolutionary war prophesized in *The Coming Race* (1871), the plan discussed by the scientist and Hugo Danner in *The Gladiator* (1930), and the plans hatched by the supernormals in *Odd John* (1935). Indeed, Ruby Fox owns a copy of *The Coming Race*, and at one point Peter St John confronts her, waving a copy of the book at her and asking, "Is this what you want us to be?" There are several other literary reference points, and Peyne claims that he was inspired in his work by the poetry of William Blake, in particular "The Tyger." He says,

> During that fragile spring of '45, when our planet woke at last from a nightmare of war, I continued with my researches into superhumanity. There was a new optimism in the air, a sense of infinite possibility. I knew it could not last. The signs were clear; shadows cast back by the light of a terrible future. Mankind would be destroyed. We had fulfilled our evolutionary purpose and must now make way for the coming race, the children of the quantum era. I re-read Blake's poem "The Tyger"—that evocation of the power and terror of raw creation—and I saw my purpose clearly articulated. I would create "Tygers." I knew then how gods must feel.[15]

Rejecting their role as "Task Force UK" and refusing to help the Americans in Vietnam, Peyne's seven superhumans form a group called Cloud 9 founded on 1960s idealism. Then, in the late 1960s and early 1970s, most of the group are either killed or mysteriously disappear. Dr Beat and White Heat are killed by CIA agents known as Shadowmen, humans with psychic abilities who are trained to kill superhumans, but not before Zenith is born and placed in hiding. The surviving superhumans, St John, Ruby Fox, and Siadwel Rhys, become ill and apparently lose their powers. All three, however, regain their powers when threatened by the resurrected Masterman, fighting in the streets of London in a sequence that recalls the epic battles in Moore's *Marvelman*. However, although Zenith tries to put up a fight he is ultimately not up to the job, and it is only the intervention of Peter St John that saves the day. Like *Paradax*, *Zenith* was mocking superhero traditions as well as the violent revisionist deconstructions of them, but whereas Paradax was surreal and playful, *Zenith* achieved a dramatic edge as well as providing a tongue-in-cheek parody of the genre.

In the second phase, "The Hollow Land," Morrison explores Zenith's origins in more depth. He meets Dr Payne, who says to Zenith, "We have reached the gates of paradise and stand on the threshold of the age of Homo Novus, the New Man.... You are our purest dreams made flesh. Everything that is splendid and noble about our species, is refined and embodied in yours! And you are evolution's perfect child." Of course, there is a level of irony at work here, as Zenith is far from perfect, The ironic biblical connotations are evident also when Zenith meets Dr Peyne for the first time, which is presented as an allusion to Michelangelo's famous painting from the ceiling of the Sistine Chapel, "The Creation of Adam." The symbolism could not be more overt, but there is also some ambiguity. Is Peyne meeting God for the first time in the form of Zenith, "evolution's perfect child," or is Zenith meeting God in the shape of Peyne, his father/creator figure? The text leaves this unresolved, as Zenith is located in the lower position, reaching up, as Adam reaches up to God. This is affirmed by the fact that Peyne's finger is extended so as to impart the spark of life, but Peyne is on the right and Zenith is on the left, reversing the positions in Michelangelo's painting. Such details adds a level of subtext and playful ambiguity to the story. The story then turns into a version of the Oedipus myth, with Zenith fighting and killing his father (who lived on after his apparent death in the 1960s as a cyborg, Warhead, who is controlled by Peyne). Zenith is also tricked into having sex with a clone of his mother as part of Peyne's plan to create a new generation of superhumans. At the same time, St John is haunted by nightmarish visions of a destroyed world orbiting a black sun and fears that it is a vision of the future.

Phase Three, "War in Heaven," raises the stakes, opening in a devastated alternative universe, Alternative 666, which represents a world populated by versions of DC Thomson's superheroes. Here Dark Gods, or the Lloigor, as they are more commonly known, have possessed superhuman bodies and slaughtered almost the entire human population, leaving it a ruin. Prince Mamba (King Cobra) records his thoughts about the destruction of his world, and there is even a cameo by Korky the Cat (who appears as a stuffed doll on the wreckage). Tiger Tom and Tammy (Billy the Cat and Katie) are wounded and die in each other's arms, Johnny Quick (Billy Whizz) is incinerated, while The Amazing Mr X is now the murderous and psychotic Mr Why, possessed by the Lloigor. General Jumbo is apparently raped and murdered, while Black Bob is cruelly thrown against a wall and killed. Leading the battle is Hotspur from Alternate 257, a religious zealot and Prince Hal rolled into one. The name of this character is a reference to DC Thomson's story paper (then comic) *The Hotspur*. Desperate Dan becomes Big Ben, a Soviet depressive who is wracked with guilt and insecurity after his world is destroyed. The fact that he is a Soviet hero is possibly a jibe at DC Thomson's former history of antiunion policies.

The war against the Lloiger draws in a vast array of superheroes from British comics besides the ones from DC Thomson, including Thunderbolt

Jaxon, Len Fullerton's Argo, Electroman, Ace Hart, Mr Apollo, Dennis M. Reader's Electrogirl, The Falcon from *Radio Fun*, Masterman by Joe Colquhoun, Anglo's Captain Miracle and Miracleman, The Steel Claw, The Amazing Three (Tanya, The Blue Wizard, and Oakman) from IPC's *Jackpot*, and Gifford's Streamline (who is revealed to be a traitor, working for the Lloigor). The roster of British superheroes that Morrison and Yeowell bring together is impressive. (The above is not a remotely comprehensive list.) Traveling to another alternate Earth, Axis Mundi, Zenith, and Peter St John, along with Ruby Fox, David Cambridge, and Penelope Moon, join an army that is being assembled to fight the Lloigor. It is led by an alternative Maximan, one who in his reality survived the Berlin A-Bomb. Archie, the robot hero from *Lion*, becomes an LSD-addled anarchist. The stage is set for an epic battle between parallel worlds, which can be read as a parody of DC Comics' *Crisis on Infinite Earths* series from 1985.

Over the course of the story, Maximan reveals the Lloigor's plan to ascend to Godhood, achieving total mastery of the universe through an alignment of the omnihedron (the structure created by all parallel universes coexisting). In order to do this, the Lloigor have invaded and destroyed two parallel Earths, Alternative 666 and Alternative 257, apparently to remove imperfections in the omnihedron's structure. However, Masterman is lying. He is one of the Lloigor, and it is discovered that the destruction of these worlds has created the conditions under which the Lloigor can now ascend. The battle is won when the rest of the superhumans arrive and destroy the alternative universe Maximan inhabits, thus ruining the Lloigor's plans. At the end of the third phase, St John, Ruby Fox, and Zenith are accompanied to their home universe by David Cambridge; Penelope Moon; and two other superhumans from an alternative universe, DJ Chill and Domino. This sets the stage for what is to come in the fourth phase, "Fear of Flying," in which many of the surviving superhumans move to eradicate humanity, with only Zenith, Robot Archie, and Peter St John to oppose them. As David Cambridge says, "It's time to start playing God games."

The references to Olaf Stapledon's *Odd John* (1935) and Edward Bulwer-Lytton's *The Coming Race* (1871) in Phase Four are pronounced. Told in flashback from the perspective of Peyne, who has witnessed the end of the world and is now aged backwards by the Lloigor, it becomes clear that Zenith and St John are helpless to avert the apocalypse. As Peyne says in his autobiography, "Seizing the Fire" (another reference to Blake's poem, "The Tyger"), which becomes more and more incoherent as he reverts to a child, "I have loosed the tygers upon the world. I have swept away the old order.

I have cast down the cities of men. And laid the foundation stones of the New Jerusalem." St John's prophesy has come to pass, the world is dead and the sun is black. The Lloigor have turned the cities of the world into grotesque semiorganic structures. Peyne describes the transformed London as the New Jerusalem, but it is clear that it is literally hell on Earth. The "people" that now populate the cities have huge hands where their heads should be and clap when the Lloigor fly overhead, otherwise their hands remain clasped as though in prayer. Peyne's narration reveals that at some point near the start of the war and shortly after America was destroyed, the two sides meet and David tries to convince St John and Zenith to join him. They refuse and escape by traveling into the near future, only to find that the superhumans have implemented their plan and that the world is devastated. The sun is black and humanity has been wiped out. At this point, David Cambridge delivers a startling revelation about the true origin of the Lloigor, revealing to Peyne that by creating superhumans, he himself has brought about the apocalypse.

In a twist that mirrors Blake's epic unfinished poem, *The Four Zoas*, it emerges that the former heroes are, were, and always have been the villains—the superhumans are the Lloigor. Zenith, Archie, and St. John are killed and Dr Peyne is forced to age backwards, becoming a boy, then a fetus before disappearing, as all the while the world is reshaped by the Lloigor, who have become monstrous Cthulhu-type creatures, becoming one with the universe, imposing their will on all of existence. Zenith and St John's final confrontation with the Lloigor takes place in London, near the Houses of Parliament. The battle is short. Ruby Fox tells St John, "This is Heaven and you've been cast out" and drops him from a great height, impaling him on the raised fist of the statue of Maximan. Zenith is killed by his young son who, it turns out, is Iok Sotot, the Lloigor who possessed Masterman in Phase One. Victorious, the Lloigor leave Earth, expanding to become one with everything until they fill the whole universe.

However, as they are about to grow beyond the universe and truly become gods, they become aware of a barrier and something beyond, a hand. The "shot" pans out until we can see that the universe that they have become one with is in fact a miniature universe, a construct that had appeared earlier in the series and which St John had psychically trapped them in at the start of Phase Four. As he holds this miniature universe containing his enemies, St John contemplates his victory and quotes yet another poem by Blake, "The Auguries of Innocence": "to see a world in a grain of sand, and a heaven in a wild flower. Hold infinity in the palm of your hand, and eternity in an hour." Phase Four ends with St John using his powers to win the general election, so The Plan to control humanity lives on in another form. The ending is a direct reference to the poetry of William Blake and the structure of his mythology. The Four Zoas (meaning "beasts") was Blake's attempt to contain his elaborate mythological system, and shows the forces of rebellion becoming the forces of conformity, then reverting in an endless cycle. It should be noted that Morrison writes four phases of Zenith, echoing Blake's schema. Zenith may have started *Zenith* with references to "The Tyger," one of Blake's most famous and accessible poems, but it ends intertwined with some of his most challenging and obscure work. This is significant, as the story initially drew on influences such as *Marvelman* and *Paradax*, but this simplicity was only a disguise for something much more complex.

Despite being arguably the equal of *Watchmen* and *The Dark Knight Returns*, *Zenith* suffered a number of setbacks. It was not collected as a single book until 2014, so it never appeared as a complete graphic novel during the 1980s, when other reputations were being forged. Although the first three phases were collected in separate volumes by Titan Books, it was never reprinted in America in a form that led to widespread exposure. It was, however, reprinted by Quality Communications, which had the license to reprint *2000AD* material in the United States. But it resized the comics pages, cutting them up and coloring them, which destroyed Yeowell's work. Ironically, the pages of a British comic being colored and recut to fit the American format was an inversion of the practice of American comics being recut and having the color removed for reprinting in British comics like *Pow!* (see Chapter Four). It was just as destructive in the opposite direction. However, Zenith was a sharp satire of British politics and the relationship of the American comics industry to the British one, but it was also, to a certain extent, a parody of the high-mindedness of Alan Moore's approach to superhero revisionism. Moore's works seem very bleak, but Morrison's tactic is to continually undermine serious or dramatic moments with a twist of humor or irony. *Zenith* reincorporated the spirit of parody into the British superhero and in so doing became perhaps one of the very best examples of this subgenre.

Following the success of *Watchmen*, *The Dark Knight Returns*, and *Zenith*, a whole new generation of independent comics creators were inspired to generate superheroes set free of the comics code. In Britain the comic marts of Bath and Bristol were home to David A. Johnson's *Blue Saviour*, and in Scotland, *Atomic Comics* (1986) featured Captain Scotland, by Tony Foster, Michael Duncan, Eggy Harding, and Craig Conlan. The year 1987 saw the release of A. O. Potter's *Alpha Omega Collection*.[16] It was something of a throwback to the amateur comics being produced by the small publishers in the 1940s and 1950s, mixed with a rather poor imitation of Marvel comics of the early 1980s. *Sunrise* (1987), produced by Harrier Comics, featured a superhero called Sunrise. It was written by Bill W. Ryard with artwork by Lou Manna. Like Potter's work, it was very rough and amateur, looking extremely old-fashioned, and in the second issue the quality was considerably worse. More professional was the backup story, "Abraxas," by Grant Morrison and Tony O'Donnell, a science-fiction fantasy tale that they had created earlier and had intended as a European-style graphic album before publishing with Harrier.

Super Satire Gets Vicious

In 1987, the same year *Zenith* appeared, Pat Mills and Kevin O'Neill created *Marshal Law*, a biting satire on American superheroes that was in part motivated by the revisionist tradition and the centrality of British creators to it. Mills had created *Action* and *2000AD* in the 1970s and was partly responsible for the creation of Judge Dredd. Kevin O'Neill had produced brilliant work for *2000AD*, notably in "Nemesis the Warlock," but he was one of the British artists for whom the British invasion did not work out very well. His work on *Tales of the Green Lantern Corps* Annual #2, written by Alan Moore for DC Comics, was famously censured by the Comics Code Authority because the style, with his trademark scratchy ugliness, was deemed too frightening for young readers.[17] Likewise, as Moore, Morrison, and Gaiman were capitalizing on the American markets' fascination with British writers, Mills missed out, perhaps because he was not amenable to American superhero stories, or when he did take them on, as in *Marshal Law*, his vicious satire left little to the imagination—it was very clear that he hated the imperialist, authoritarian nature of superheroes. Readers found Moore's take on superheroes in *Marvelman* and *Watchmen* to be downbeat, perhaps even cynical, but that was taken as an antidote to decades of patriotic super do-gooding. *Marshal Law*, on the other hand, was no antidote; it was pure poison. O'Neill's artwork perfectly channeled and materialized Mills's visceral hatred of superheroes. It was published by Epic Comics, an imprint of Marvel that produced work for "mature readers" (see Figure 46).

The story of *Marshal Law* was set in the near future world of San Futuro (rebuilt from the ruins of San Francisco after a devastating earthquake) and introduced the Jesus League of America, led by the superhero The Public

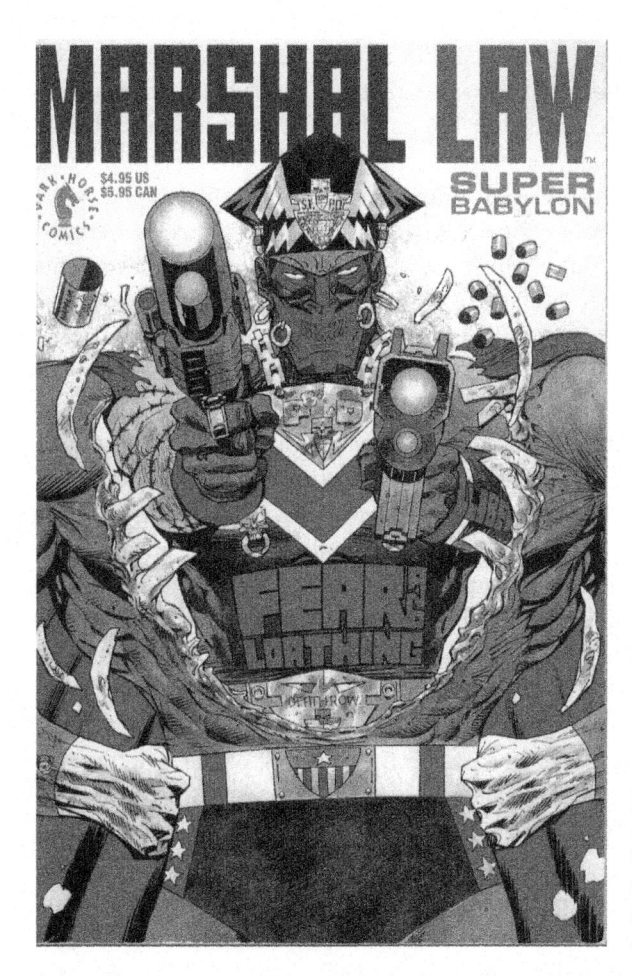

Fig. 46: *Marshal Law: Super Babylon*, by Pat Mills and Kevin O'Neill (Dark Horse, 1992). Courtesy of Pat Mills, co-creator.

Spirit, modeled on Superman, whose costume boasted an eagle on his chest with a white cross. These superheroes were Christian, moralistic and pure, at least on the surface. Inspired by their example, Joe Gilmore joins the American army and becomes a supersoldier, genetically engineered for combat in The Zone, which is a brutal conflict imagined as a futuristic Vietnam War. Traumatized by his time in The Zone, Gilmore returns to San Futuro to become a lawman taking on the persona of Marshal Law, a "superhero hunter" with a special remit to arrest or kill rogue superheroes. Dressed in fetish gear, this S&M version of Judge Dredd takes special delight in inflicting pain on superheroes. The plot of the first story sees him tracking down the Sleepman, who targets women dressed as the superheroine Celeste. When Marshal Law's girlfriend is raped and murdered by the

Sleepman, he is hell-bent on revenge but initially believes the villain to be The Public Spirit. In the end, it transpires that it is The Public Spirit's illegitimate son who is the Sleepman, but The Public Spirit is also revealed to be a murderer and psychopath. As Marshal Law says in the closing pages, "I'm a hero hunter. I hunt heroes. Haven't found any yet."

There were several other, shorter Marshal Law stories, such as *Marshal Law Takes Manhattan* (1989), which parodied Marvel comics characters and was, ironically, published by Epic (a branch of Marvel), and *The Kingdom of the Blind* (1990), which parodied Batman and was published by Apocalypse Comics, a British company formed by Mills, O'Neill, John Wagner, and Alan Grant, which also produced a weekly comic called *Toxic!* which ran for thirty-one issues and featured Marshal Law as the lead character. In addition to Marshal Law, *Toxic!* contained another superhero series, *Brats Bizarre*, by Mills and Tony Skinner, with art by Duke Mighten. This team of "super-kind" was created by a genetic engineering program designed to cure autism but which accidentally generates the Brats Bizarre, amoral pleasure seekers rebelling against a strict religious upbringing. After Apocalypse collapsed in 1992, Marshal Law found a home at another American publisher, Dark Horse Comics, and Brats Bizarre was continued by Epic. Without the stylized art of Mighten, however, much of the appeal was gone. *Marshal Law* and *Brats Bizarre* took the British satire of the superhero to new extremes and were unmatched in this regard until Garth Ennis and Darick Robertson released *The Boys* in 2006 (see next chapter).

In 1988, *2000AD* gained a sister comic, *Crisis*, which was intended for an older readership and had more explicitly political themes. One of the headline stories was "The New Statesmen," by writer John Smith, with art by Jim Baikie, also with Sean Phillips and Duncan Fegredo. It was promoted as a "political superhero series" and was later reprinted as a limited series for the American market in 1989. The story was set in 2047 America, with Britain now the fifty-first state. This world has been transformed by genetic engineering, which produces superhumans (or Optimen), who act as soldiers and weapons but also serve as political representatives for each state. The political message is quite blunt, but the satire is effective. With corporate and government corruption being beyond the ability of the Optimen to challenge, they end up as pawns of political power, or worse, the best practitioners of this corruption. The story offered one of the most overt examples of the superhero being used for satirical effect in British comics, showing them literally as weapons that have replaced the democratic process. The idea that superheroes could represent the special relationship between

Britain and America has rarely been tackled so directly, and the theme of the dangers of genetic engineering and the corporate commodification of humanity is influenced to a degree by Aldous Huxley's novel *Brave New World* (1932), as well as films like *Bladerunner* (1982). However, despite this, the satire did not have the savagery of *Marshal Law* or the artistic consistency and invention of *Watchmen*, and therefore it suffers somewhat in comparison, despite being a provocative comic in its own right.

In 1989 the London-based publisher Atomeka Press launched a new title, *A1*, featuring the best talent working in comics at the time. Edited by Dave Elliot and Garry Leach, the editorial statement in the first issue notes that the comic was "originally devised as a comics forum where creators could experiment on practical projects, indulge in unlikely creative combinations and generally have fun."[18] The first issue opened with a story called "Ghostdance," by Alan Moore with art by Garry Leach, featuring characters from *Marvelman*. Another story, "Survivor," was written by Dave Gibbons, with art by Ted McKeever (one of those "unlikely creative combinations" that was echoed in the comic with another story written by McKeever and drawn by Gibbons). "Survivor" was told from the (literal) viewpoint of a superhero very clearly based on Superman, but with a dark, twisted version of the character having no emotions or empathy; as he says repeatedly, "I feel nothing."

His powers and alien heritage mark him apart from humanity, and his career as a superhero has been an elaborate performance that he can no longer maintain. He fantasizes about wiping out humanity, wondering if his vast intellect and the prospect of eternity alone as an immortal being would drive him mad. Fearing what he might do, he plots his own death, manipulating the character clearly meant to recall Lex Luthor into trying to kill him with a mineral that is supposed to represent kryptonite. The exposure to radiation kills the villain, but rather than killing the superhero, it makes him mortal so he can finally feel. Whereas Moore and Swan's *Whatever Happened to the Man of Tomorrow* was a homage to the absurdity of 1950s and 1960s Superman comics combined with the deconstructive approach of *Watchmen*, here Superman is imagined as an amoral, inhuman being, somewhat like Dr Manhattan, but the satire is darker. Whereas Dr Manhattan has no human feelings, or is in the process of losing touch with them, the superbeing of "Survivor" contemplates murdering every human being just to alleviate his boredom. This was another pointed indictment of the superhero concept at a time when such critiques had become extremely fashionable.

One of the best-known dark superhero stories of the period was *Arkham Asylum* (1989), by Grant Morrison and with stunning painted artwork from Dave McKean. Following the success of *Zenith*, Morrison had come to the attention of American publishers, chiefly DC Comics, that were looking for the next Alan Moore. Morrison would eventually contribute to DC's new Vertigo line of adult comics; however, his early work with DC saw him revamping second-rate superhero comics such as *Animal Man* and *Doom Patrol*. In *Animal Man*, the story became a platform for his animal rights views, and it ultimately twisted in on itself in a postmodern reconstruction of the comics form itself. Likewise, *Doom Patrol* became a surreal rumination on madness, dada, disability, and art that quickly caught the attention of readers and soon came under the Vertigo banner.

However, Morrison achieved international success with his strange vision of Batman's world in *Arkham Asylum* (1989). This graphic novel was a huge success when it was published, selling five hundred thousand copies. It held the record as the biggest-selling graphic novel for a long time. Its success was partly driven by the interest in more sophisticated comics following *Watchmen* and *The Dark Knight Returns* and the fact that the Tim Burton *Batman* film that came out in the same year, the fiftieth anniversary of Batman. Also, this was an original graphic novel (not previously serialized in comic form), so sales were boosted by that factor alone. The treatment of the relationship between Batman and The Joker was controversial, suggesting their interdependency rather than their opposition and presenting Batman as troubled and fearful as he descends into the hypnotic and dream-like world of the Asylum, confronting his greatest fear: that he in fact belongs there. Morrison has said that *Arkham Asylum* was his reaction to the grim and gritty realistic trend in 1980s superhero comics. The story is disorienting, maddening, and surreal, which is natural enough given that his primary influences were Lewis Carroll, Jan Svankmajer, Lovecraft via Jung, and Freud. Morrison once described the comic as "Pilgrim's Progress in a Batmobile."[19] The satirical elements derive from the inversions that take place throughout, and the palpable fear that Batman experiences on his decent through the psychodrama. This was diametrically opposed to the stoical Batman seen in Frank Miller's work. Morrison has Batman as Christ, enduring the passion, and driven to the point of madness.

In the late 1980s, Karen Berger, the groundbreaking editor who headed Vertigo, the DC Comics line of comics for "mature readers," was in the process of establishing its brand of quality writing and superior artwork by head-hunting British talent. Gaiman, like Moore before him, was offered the choice of a defunct character to recreate. He opted for The Sandman. The result was one of the most successful and celebrated American comics of the 1980s and 1990; however, the character began life in a rather different form than he became. The Sandman was originally a character who appeared in the late 1930s as a crime fighter/man of mystery (like The Shadow) with a gasmask and gas gun. He was reworked in the 1940s as a more generic superhero (complete with sidekick). The Sandman was later recreated in the mid-1970s by Joe Simon and Jack Kirby as an immortal being who exits in the "dream stream," where, in the guise of a superhero, he protects dreamers (usually children) from nightmares.

It was this character whom Gaiman would later choose to recreate; however, the character was still active in DC comics in the 1980s (and continues to be), so Berger allowed Gaiman to take the name and create an entirely new character (just as Moore had been allowed to do with *Watchmen*). The series ran from 1989 to 1996, telling the story of Morpheus, also known as Dream, an immortal being who escapes imprisonment and proceeds to put his domain, The Dreaming, back in order after his long absence. The story started more or less within the DC Universe but soon established its own distinct world, and it became clear that Gaiman had an ambitious story in mind, one which was about the very nature of stories. In this sense, *The Sandman* was an elaborate work of metafiction, self-consciously revealing the devices and tools of storytelling. Several themes are key to *The Sandman* (imprisonment, torment, responsibility, sacrifice, imagination, memory, and storytelling), and these are embedded within a range of references, many of them classical, including Greek myths; ancient history; folktales; Norse mythology; and literature, especially of the Renaissance. This makes *The Sandman* a highly intertextual narrative that draws freely from a huge number of sources. The series won eighteen Eisner awards, two Bram Stoker awards for best illustrated narrative, and an Angouleme International Comics Festival prize. In 1991, "A Midsummer Night's Dream" (*The Sandman* #19) won the World Fantasy Award for best short fiction. As seen on the back covers of many of the collections of *The Sandman*, Gaiman has often drawn high praise from other notable writers.

The move into American comics made by the likes of Moore, Morrison, and Gaiman brought with it a huge degree of critical and commercial success and access to a much bigger readership and fan base, but it also meant that the best British creators were no longer working in British comics. However, the attention focused on the British scene was considerable and American publishers were eager to draw from this talent pool, so there were moves to reconstruct the ailing British comics industry to facilitate this borrowing and take advantage of new opportunities. Throughout the 1980s, Marvel UK had been relying more heavily than before on licensed material, although some very good work had been produced within this constraint, including memorable runs by Simon Furman on *Transformers* and by Morrison on *Zoids*. Some titles, like *The Knights of Pengradon, Dragon's Claws*, and *Death's Head* appeared at the end of the 1980s, during a period when Marvel UK was expanding and seeking to break into the American market, exploiting the attention that British comics creators had been receiving in America. *The Knights of Pendragon* (1990–1993) was a superhero series starring Captain Britain that drew on British folklore and mythology and had some crossover with the popular American series *Excalibur*, which was a spinoff from the hugely successful *X-Men* comics. The comic also had a strong conservationist message, backed that up by the comics being printed on environmentally friendly paper. The series was critically acclaimed at first but later became a substandard superhero comic and soon ended. *The Knights of Pendragon*, like *Dragon's Claws* and *Death's Head*, was published in the American format and had some early success, but the British market was not big enough to sustain a sales base from which to build upon, and they struggled.

However, there was still confidence that Marvel UK could break the American market, and so in 1992 Paul Neary, who had been an artist for Marvel UK in its early years, then editor-in-chief when Dez Skinn departed, and then a successful artist for American Marvel Comics, returned as editor-in-chief. John Freeman became group editor of the superhero comics range at Marvel UK, and he and Neary set about creating a new line of titles, including *Havoc* and *Meltdown*, which reprinted American stories (as well as Marvel/Epic's translation of *Akira*, the popular science fiction manga), and the anthology *Overkill*, which published original British material that was a mixture of science fiction and superheroes and was very much in competition with *2000AD*. *Overkill* featured new characters like Motormouth and Killpower, Dark Angel, Genetix, Warheads, and Digitek, plus guest appearances from Spider-Man and Wolverine, establishing these new characters within the wider Marvel Universe continuity.

In response to a feeling that the American format titles were hard to spot on British newsstands, where they were surrounded by larger British comics, *Overkill* retained the British format although there were American-sized reprints for the overseas market. Indeed, the American comics and penetration into the American market was key to the business plan. In effect, the British title was secondary to the push to capture American readers. Despite some very popular characters, the success of this strategy, and of *Overkill*, was short-lived. Like the entire British comics boom of the early 1990s, they were eventually pulled under by the collapse of the speculator market in 1993, which threatened the entire comics industry and in particular threatened to bring down the American Marvel Comics. In such desperate circumstances, support for the Marvel UK line was one of the first things to be cut, which was a huge blow to Neary and Freeman, who had developed an ambitious relaunch of the Marvel UK titles. In 1995 Marvel UK was taken over by Panini UK, which continued reprinting American Marvel comics for the British market. For a time they put out some original British material alongside the reprints, but there was no possibility of continuing with the work Neary and Freeman had started, and the use of original material was gradually phased out and their titles became reprint only, though some of the characters from the 1990s Marvel UK line do occasionally still appear in Marvel comics (notably in the 2014 *Revolutionary War* miniseries that reunited many of these characters and their creators).

One of the most memorable publications featuring British superheroes in the early 1990s was *The 2000AD Action Special*, published in 1992 and featured reworkings of old IPC characters such as the Steel Claw, Kelly, The Spider, Mytek the Mighty, and Cursitor Doom. This came about because the editors of Fleetway's *2000AD* mistakenly believed that they had inherited the copyright to all IPC comics and set about reworking them for a contemporary readership. The revised Steel Claw, written by Peter Hogan, had striking painted artwork by Sean Phillips and was perhaps the best strip in the special, although there was a host of talent on display, including John Tomlinson and Jim Baikie's "Cursitor Doom," Alan McKenzie and Brett Ewing's "Kelly's Eye" (which continued in *2000AD* for a time), "Mytek the Mighty" by Si Spencer and Shaky Kane, and "Dr Sin" by John Smith and John Burns. Perhaps the most notorious strip was Mark Millar's "The Spider," with art by John Higgins and David Hine, which turned the king of crooks into an animalistic serial killer and cannibal. This was not well received by fans of "The Spider." The special also contained a history of British comics by Lew Stringer, which explained the nature of British adventure strips before *2000AD* to a generation of readers who were unlikely to have heard of these long-forgotten characters. Like the 1971 *Pow!* annual (see Chapter Four), *The 2000AD Action Special* is an intriguing glimpse of what might have been if the copyright to the characters had indeed belonged to Fleetway, which might have used this special as a springboard to reintroduce these characters.

Superhumor

The late 1980s and early 1990s saw a huge resurgence in the popularity of superheroes, boosted by *Watchmen* and *The Dark Knight Returns* and the 1989 Batman film. As a consequence there were an increasing number of parodies of the genre, and naturally, given the long tradition of parodying the superhero genre in Britain, British comics and creators led the way in mocking superheroes. In 1988 Dave Gibbons, Alan Moore's collaborator on *Watchmen*, worked with Lew Stringer on a quite different superhero narrative for the British humor comic *Oink!*, where they produced the one-page strip "The Superhero's Day Off," which appeared in issue 49 and showed a Superman-style character tackling normal everyday activities, like shopping and walking the dog, although in typical *Oink!* fashion, the most challenging activity is a trip to the toilet.

Similarly crude was *How to Be a Superhero* (1990), published by Penguin Books and written by Mark Leigh and Mike Lepine, with illustrations by up-and-coming British artist Steve Dillon. It was a brilliant parody of the superhero genre and self-help books that punctured the absurdities of the genre with rude yet insightful humor directed at an adult audience. When suggesting names for a superhero team, Leigh and Lepine offered "Challengers of the Fucking Impossible," "The Cretins," and "All Star Spanking Squad." One of the highlights of the book is the section, "What really happened vs How the comic portrayed it," which shows the superheroes as cowardly, pretentious, and incompetent. "The Superhero's Day off" and *How to Be a Superhero* are perfect examples of the British attitude towards the superhero genre, bringing superheroes back down to earth and stripping away their pretensions and nobility to reveal petty and fallible human beings underneath the costumes and posturing (see Figures 47 and 48). These texts took all of the observations about the genre revealed in *Watchman*, *Marvelman*, and *Zenith*, and indeed the long tradition of parody and satire of the superhero in British comics, and presented it in a new way for members of a savvy adult readership who were highly aware of comics history.

In a way similar to *How to Be a Superhero*, the six-part series *1963* (1993), by Alan Moore for Image, relied a good deal on the reader's knowledge of early 1960s Marvel comics and the mythos surrounding their creation. After being outside of mainstream comics for a few years, Moore had returned to superheroes, working for Image, a company founded on the principle of creator's rights and ownership of the characters by popular artists who had

Fig. 47: "The Superhero's Day Off," in *Oink!* #49, by Lew Stringer and Dave Gibbons (Fleetway, 1988). Art by Dave Gibbons.

228   Revisionism and the British Invasion (1981–1993)

WHAT REALLY HAPPENED

HOW THE COMIC PORTRAYED IT

Fig. 48: *How to Be a Superhero*, written by Mark Leigh and Mike Lepine, with illustrations by Steve Dillon (Penguin Books, 1990).

previously worked for Marvel. It was headed by two of the most successful artists in recent comics history, Jim Lee and Rob Liefeld. Image was hugely successful, with top-selling titles like *Spawn* (Todd McFarlane), *WildC.A.T.S* (Jim Lee), *Youngblood* (Liefeld), and *Gen 13* (Lee and J. Scott Campbell). In 1993 Moore published *1963* with Image, a parody of the 1960s Marvel comics created by Stan Lee, Jack Kirby, and Steve Ditko. This miniseries, published on the occasion of Marvel's thirtieth anniversary, was co-created with Steve Bissette, Rick Veitch, and John Totleben. *1963* was somewhere between an affectionate parody and a savage indictment of Marvel comics. *Mystery Incorporated* was *The Fantastic Four*, *The Fury* was somewhere between Spider-Man and The Question (two Ditko characters), while *Tales of the Uncanny* was *The X-Men* and *The Avengers*. *Tales from Beyond* was *Tales of Suspense* and *Dr Strange*, *Horus* was *Thor*, and *The Tomorrow Syndicate* reflected the increasingly trippy cosmic comics Marvel was publishing in the late 1960s and early 1970s.

The artwork was a brilliant recreation of the styles of Kirby and Ditko, which made the satire all the more effective. The comic was also printed on relatively poor quality paper, which completed the illusion that these were in fact old comics. This was Moore reacting against two trends, the "grim and gritty" approach that had gripped the comics industry since his own *Watchmen* and Miller's *The Dark Knight Returns* and the early 1990s vogue for foil-embossed or hologram covers and high production values that had driven the so-called speculator boom, which burst in 1993, the same year this comic came out. It was also an opportunity for Moore to return to the kind of metafictional play he had indulged in throughout *Watchmen*, particularly with "The Tales of the Black Freighter" pirate story within it. *1963*'s parody of Marvel extended to Moore referring to himself as "Affable Al" in the Sixty Three Sweatshop editorials, which recalled the jovial tone of Stan "The Man" Lee's Marvel Bullpen. Moore also took great delight in his parodies of comics advertisements from the 1960s. However, these elements were not just parody; there was also a pointed satire about the exploitative nature of the comics industry, and several jokes came at the expense of Stan Lee, particularly when Affable Al reminded readers to buy his new book, "How I Created Everything All By Myself and Why I Am Great." The series was never completed, as it ended with the characters flung forward in time, finding themselves trapped in the contemporary world of comics. There was supposed to be an annual, drawn by Jim Lee, that would conclude the story, but it never appeared. Lee took some time off from comics (nearly a year), and by the time he returned, the legal issues at the then-changing Image Comics meant that the project became unworkable. However, *1963* set the stage for the reworkings of comics history that Moore would return to repeatedly over the next few years, expanding greatly on what he had already done in *Watchmen*.

The rise of such overt parodies of the superhero genre was evidence of its huge popularity and cultural penetration. By the late 1980s and the early 1990s, the success of the superhero genre in comics, film, and television was such that parodies like those discussed here could arise. Popularity leads to widespread familiarity with the unique tropes and conventions of a genre, which leads to the possibility of successful parody, as parody does not work without recognition. But as with the examples of parody of the superhero that have been in evidence in Britain since at least the 1940s, the target was not simply the conventions of the genre, as odd as they might be, but also the differences in attitudes towards power and heroism between Britain and America.

By the mid-1990s, the British comics scene and creators had a huge influence on American comics, and the rise of a second wave of the British Invasion showed that this was not a one-time phenomenon. At the same time, the British comics industry was in disarray, finding it almost impossible to capitalize on this success. The 1980s had been a hugely inventive time for British superhero comics, and British creators had come to dominate the market. It was also a time when the balance between parody and satire in British superhero comics shifted toward satire, especially in the work of Alan Moore, Pat Mills, Brendan McCarthy, and John Smith. Morrison's work retained a strong element of parody, but it parodied the seriousness of the satirical comics created by Moore (which was undoubtedly one of the causes of the long-standing friction between them). As the 1980s came to a close and a second generation of the British Invasion came to the fore in the 1990s, the relationship between British and American comics would continue to be mediated through satire and parody, but it would also move much more into the mainstream.

Chapter Six

CONTEMPORARY BRITISH SUPERHEROES (1994–PRESENT)

The mid-1990s was a strange time for British comics. In the aftermath of the huge international success of *Watchmen*, *Arkham Asylum*, and *The Sandman*, British creators were some of the most influential in the field and British artists were in great demand. With the so-called British Invasion a largely undisputed critical and commercial success, the American comics industry, which had long seemed an unassailable edifice to outsiders now opened up. Therefore, it became increasingly common for British creators to remain based in Britain while producing material for the American market. For a time, it seemed like DC Comics' Vertigo imprint was an arm of the British comics industry operating out of a mainstream American publisher. The success of the so-called adult comics boom and the rise of graphic novels in the public consciousness had been partly built around the work of British creators, and bookstores now had graphic novel sections, as did the big record chains such as Virgin, and the rise of more speciality shops like Forbidden Planet made comics and graphic novels much easier to come by in Britain. However, the comic shops were still dominated by American comics and related merchandise, and increasingly by manga and anime, the phenomena from Japan that Western readers were just discovering. Indeed, the increased popularity of comics and the changing demographics of readership did not translate into success for the British comics industry as a whole. Several new British comics had appeared in the late 1980s and early 1990s to cater to the older readership that the rise of graphic novels had identified, but they all failed. *2000AD* was still there, but most of the other comics that had sprung up found themselves in trouble. Even the ambitious relaunch of Marvel UK had faltered. British comics felt like a surefire investment that had gone badly wrong somehow.

The mid-1990s also saw those who had been at the forefront of the first British Invasion taking very different paths. Alan Moore seemed to be perpetually unhappy with the comics industry, but he repeatedly produced new and innovative work that was critically acclaimed, although much of his output suffered from endless comparison to *Watchmen*. He had sparked renewed interest in the superhero genre when he was trying to have the last word on it, so while fans wanted more *Watchmen*, he delivered increasingly experimental work that challenged taboos about the representation of sex and violence. On the other hand, Neil Gaiman actually left comics. He completed *The Sandman* at the height of its popularity and left the stage, turning his attention to fantasy novels, where he was enormously successful. At this time, Grant Morrison was going from strength to strength in comics, producing his magnum opus, *The Invisibles*, and a number of other critically acclaimed works. He also increasingly worked for Marvel and DC on high profile projects like the hugely successful *JLA* (1997). This chapter will trace the development of British comics and creators from the mid-1990s to the present, with an emphasis on the continuing influence of the first wave of the British Invasion (discussed in the previous chapter) and the rise of the second wave, as well as other developments, including the rise of the British small press and independently produced titles.

In political terms, Britain was changing fast. The landslide victory of Tony Blair's New Labour in the 1997 general election saw the first Labour government since 1979. This promised to give an enormous boost to the creative sectors. The repressive Tory government was gone and Prime Minister Blair courted pop musicians, writers, and artists in a deliberate attempt to echo the creative confidence felt in the nation following the 1964 election of Labour prime minister Harold Wilson, who embraced the idea of Swinging London and was photographed with The Beatles.[1]

For Blair it was Oasis and The Spice Girls, which perhaps should have given some warning of what was to come. For all the talk of the rebirth of "Cool Britannia," Blair was essentially a Thatcherite, and his aggressive foreign policies led to a series of unpopular military engagements. Furthermore, in the aftermath of 9/11 Blair's model was not Wilson, or even Churchill; rather, he aimed to reaffirm the bonds of the "special relationship" as it had existed in the time of Reagan and Thatcher. The rise of an international terrorist threat was addressed with familiar Cold War rhetoric, and the close alliance between the Republican president George Bush Jr. and the Labour leader felt like a betrayal to many on the Left in Britain. New Labour's strategy was lurching from the political Left to the center ground, cutting ties with the trade unions, and from there Blair pushed a Thatcherite economic model and gave unqualified support to Bush's hawkish government, leading Britain into joint participation in a series of potentially illegal actions and wars, justified by little else than Blair's considerable oratory skills.[2] Readers of *Zenith* might have been forgiven for a sense of unease. In the last phase, released in 1992, it is suggested that Peter St John has engineered the death by heart attack of Labour leader John Smith. St John, who does not look unlike Tony Blair, is then swept to power and becomes prime minister. In reality, John Smith did die of a heart attack, but in 1994, well after *Zenith* was published, and his death led directly to the ascendancy of Tony Blair, first to leadership of the Labour Party, then to prime minister. When Morrison talks about fiction shaping reality, sometimes it pays to simply take him at his word.

Morrison's *The Invisibles*, which began in 1994 and ran till 2000, followed a band of anarchist terrorists fighting against the forces of order and conformity. Their rebellion is one that calls for a new consciousness and begins with the rescue and recruitment of Dane McGowan (otherwise known as Jack Frost), a foul-mouthed youth from Liverpool who may be on his way to becoming the next Buddha. When Dane is incarcerated for criminal damage and assault, he finds himself facing indoctrination and torture by followers of the Outer Church who are attempting to enslave humanity. Dane is liberated by a cell of Invisibles, which consists of King Mob, an occult assassin and a surrogate for Morrison himself; Ragged Robin, a girl from the future who reads a book called *The Invisibles* and comes back in time to make it a reality; Lord Fanny, a Brazilian transvestite shaman; and Boy, an expert in martial arts. While this only superficially works as a superhero story and is closer to science fiction in many respects, the characters have occult powers of time travel and healing that operate like superpowers.

The story starts with the premise that all conspiracy theories are true, tapping into the popularity of *The X-Files* television series at the time, but by the end, Morrison's true message had revealed itself. The great conspiracy is actually the illusion called reality, which is an experience generated by our perceptions. Morrison argues that we find ourselves trapped in a world that is a fictional construct of our own making. We are framed and controlled by the cages we call "personalities," and we have forgotten the essential truth of all being: that we create the world. Religion, morality, or social institutions are the framework of our obedience, and the Invisibles are determined to bring about the next stage of human evolution by breaking free of these restraints. Morrison's vision, informed by his view of magic, which he practices, is that all art has transformative potential and that art, narrative, and magic are all sides of the same thing. It was his intention that *The Invisibles* be both an entertaining and provocative narrative and an instruction manual on bringing transformative power into the lives of its readers by showing them that they could exercise the power of their imaginations. The argument is that everyone has superhuman potential and the ability to transcend limitations. In this sense, the comic works as a superhero story, albeit a very strange one in which the real superhero is the reader. Reportedly, the Wachowski brothers, who created the film *The Matrix* (1999), were inspired by *The Invisibles* and had copies of the trade paperback collections on set. However, whereas the film shows that reality is a computer-generated fantasy from which humans can break free, *The Invisibles* draws on linguistics, psychology, philosophy, and esoteric belief systems to argue that the constraints applied to us are not those of a villainous race of machines but of a much older form of technology—language.

A more obviously superhero-inspired story from Morrison at around the same time and dealing with similar themes was *Flex Mentallo* (1996), with art by Morrison's fellow Glaswegian, Frank Quitely. This is one of the best examples of the superhero story as metafiction, with the title character, who began life in *Doom Patrol*, being a parody of the Charles Atlas bodybuilding advertisements that used to appear in comics. The four-issue series comprises a number of parallel plots. In one, Wally Sage, a young musician who is in the process of committing suicide, talks on the phone to someone about his past love of comics and how he created comics as a child that starred a character he invented, Flex Mentallo. At the same time, another narrative plays out: the superhero Flex Mentallo tries to solve a mystery involving the return of his old colleague, The Fact, a character based on Ditko's The Question, who also inspired *Watchmen*'s Rorschach.

The two narratives interweave and blend, and Flex ultimately finds Wally, who, near death, is plagued by apocalyptic visions of superheroes returning to earth. It is revealed that superheroes from a dying parallel world have survived the end of their Universe by becoming fictional in ours. When Flex confronts the villain, The Man in the Moon, he is revealed to be Wally's adolescent self—the being that he must transcend or incorporate into his adult life in order to overcome his situation. In effect, the younger Wally has created the means of defeating his own doubts and insecurities in the form of Flex. He, along with other aspects of his personality—The Hoaxer, the Detective, and The Fact—lead Wally to a key realization and the recovery of a secret he knew as a child but has forgotten as an adult: our imaginations shape our reality. He is told that "we made comics because we knew. Somehow we knew something was missing and we tried to fill the gap with stories about gods and superheroes . . . comics are just crude attempts to remember the truth about reality." This "truth" is the same gnosis argued for in *The Invisibles*, the potential of the imagination to overcome all constraints. When Wally finally unlocks the secret to his empowered self, the solution in his crossword puzzle looks like it is going to be "Shazam," thereby invoking the long British tradition of invoking Captain Marvel. At the last second, however, it is revealed that the word is actually "Shaman." At this point, Wally is struck by a bolt of lightning (another Captain Marvel reference) that reduces him to blue lines (a reference to the production of comic art, as comic artists would usually draw the artwork with blue pencil before it was inked).

The ending is ambiguous, but it would appear that all the superheroes of the parallel universe have crossed over into Wally's reality through his act of using fiction to change his consciousness. *Flex Mentallo* was just as invested in comics history as *Zenith*—although incorporating more elements of metafiction, surrealism, and the carnivalesque. It revealed the superhero genre as a mode of psychodrama, much as Morison had done in *Arkham Asylum*. It was also a return to the mode of parody and satire that was absent in *Arkham Asylum* and *The Invisibles*. *Flex Mentallo* has the same playful spirit found in *Zenith* and is similarly knowing with regard to British comics history, adding a bubblegum pop aesthetic that Morrison would later refer to as "future-pop." Importantly, the key theme is that the superhero is a form of psychic self-help therapy, and a young British boy dreams his superhero self into existence. Initially, the dream was to protect himself from his terrifying upbringing, with the shadow of nuclear war and his father's activism resulting in fear and anxiety, and then he dreamed again, later in life, when as a frustrated artist Wally contemplates suicide.

The fact that Flex is an old-fashioned superhero strongman type from the late 1940s and early 50s, and that Quitely's style evokes American comics of the 1950s and 1960s, makes this comic a parody of the British "American style" comics that emerged from small British publishers in the postwar years. The fact that both Morrison and Quitely are from Glasgow makes an even closer association with Cartoon Art Productions, and the fake stamps and British prices on the covers of *Flex Mentallo* add to these associations. It also evokes a time when American comics were rare in Britain and were prized artifacts of a remote, alien, yet glamorous world—America, which was encountered more readily through fiction than real experience. These appropriations of American popular culture and their juxtaposition with British cultural references is one of the most powerful yet often overlooked aspects of this story. Wally Sage, the young British schoolboy who reads American superhero comics and creates his own heroes is part of a tradition that goes back to Len Fullerton, Bob Monkhouse, Denis Gifford, Dennis M. Reader, Mick Anglo, Dave Gibbons, Dave Hornsby, and through to Frank Quitely and a host of others. They dreamed of creating American superheroes but distorted them into a commentary and critique on the American tradition.

The success of British comics creators and the opening up of the American market to them led DC Thomson to explore new directions. In 1995 they developed a secret project to create a comic for older readers that would challenge *2000AD*. Tony Luke's "Renga Media" led this development and *Renga!* was the title of the dummy comic that was produced to show its potential. ("Renga" means "collaborative poetry" in Japanese, suggesting a mix of many different creative elements and styles.) Luke had previously worked with Alan Grant on *The Dominator*, the first British manga series, and some of the sensibility *of The Dominator* is evident in the dummy comic that was produced for DC Thomson's consideration. It declared on the cover that it would feature "all-Brit action in yer face." The cover was provided by Glenn Farby and scripts were by Alan Grant and Paul Cornell. Of most interest was "The Thunderhawks" story by Alan Mitchel and Les Spink, which brought together various DC Thomson superheroes.

This whole project ultimately came to nothing, and the existence of this plan only came to light in 2015, twenty years after it was first conceived.[3] However, two years after the dummy comic was produced, Grant Morrison submitted a script to DC Thomson for something that was obliquely referred to as Project X. It involved another script for Thunderhawks, a group bringing together DC Thomson's superheroes, which suggests that the plan to produce a comic for older readers continued long after the *Renga!* project was abandoned. Morrison's script features William Grange (aka Billy the Cat) and his cousin Katie, a schoolgirl, whose superhero costume is described as a "fetish Catgirl outfit with pumped up breasts and thigh boots." Other heroes include Captain Hornet, described as "a self-made, working class superhero," as well as Brass Neck and King Cobra.

The story opens with what is referred to as "Akira style disaster imagery" when the huge robot Smasher attacks London. As the robot destroys the capital city, the Thunderhawks bicker, with much of the attention being focused on Katie and her revealing costume. Billy spends much of the early part of the script stealing glances at his cousin and wishing that they were not related. When Katie says "I wish we just had our old costumes," Billy replies, "Don't be daft, Katie, think of it like the sort of clothes you'd go clubbing in . . . anyway, we have to move with the times to compete with the American superheroes. It's all about image these days." This is arguably a reference to Image comics and their brand of hypersexualized superhero comics such as *Gen 13*, which was extremely popular at the time. When King Cobra appears, he also seems to be sexually obsessed with Katie. The Smasher turns out to be a time machine designed to make raids on the past but which has lost its pilot. As they attack the rampaging robot, the Thunderhawks rescue civilians. However, even the people whom Katie rescues (described as "Dad's, young men and coppers") stare at her lustfully. Needless to say, and in spite of Morrison's fame, DC Thomson did not accept this proposed script, though it would have been a startling and noteworthy development had it been possible to make this work somehow. The script reads like a parody of the Image comics of the time, with a joke at the expense of DC Thomson's tame characters who had changed little since the 1950s. There were similarities to *The Invisibles*, too, but the tone was a little too aggressive and the parody too perverse to work for DC Thomson.

If Morrison was exploring future-pop, then Moore was moving in the opposite direction. In 1997 Moore agreed to write Rob Liefeld's *Supreme*, published by Image, which had started as a vicious but substandard satire of Superman. Moore took over on the understanding that he could rework it completely. In his hands, it became an homage to Silver Age Superman comics but with a twist, in the same way that his "Whatever Happened to the Man of Tomorrow" and *1963* had challenged nostalgia for these old comics and the supposed innocence they represented. Moore's *Supreme* journeyed through past styles, and like *1963*, it even included pages that were printed on lesser quality yellowed paper in order to recreate the look and feel of old comics, foregrounding not only comics history but their materiality and publishing history. In 1999, following this success with Image, Moore was invited to publish his own line of comics through Jim Lee's studio, Wildstorm. Moore's line was called ABC, which stood for America's Best Comics, and he was promised complete creative control and ownership of any new characters he created. This allowed him to continue his project of reworking characters from the past, but increasingly he found himself drawn to archetypes that pre-dated superheroes, such as Tarzan, Doc Savage, and Flash Gordon. ABC published several series, including *Tom Strong*, *Top 10*, *Tomorrow Stories*, and *Promethea*, all of which were quite successful;

however, perhaps the most important series was *The League of Extraordinary Gentlemen*.

The League of Extraordinary Gentlemen, with artwork by Kevin O'Neill, saw Moore doing what he has done time and again, reinventing preexisting characters, this time taking various literary and pulp heroes of the Victorian era and weaving them into one shared continuity. The edgy artwork by O'Neill matched this period in much the same way that Eddie Campbell's artwork captured the feel of Victorian popular culture, and especially the penny dreadfuls and police magazines in *From Hell*. In creating a Justice League of Victorian England, Moore turned to the immediate precursors of comics, Victorian popular fiction, penny dreadfuls, and nineteenth-century serials (see Chapter One). The comic features Mina Murray from Bram Stoker's *Dracula* (1897); Allan Quatermain, from H. Rider Haggard's *King Soloman's Mines* (1885); Hawley Griffin, otherwise known as the Invisible Man, from H. G. Wells's 1897 story of the same name; Henry Jekyll/Edward Hyde from Robert Louis Stevenson's *The Strange Case of Dr Jekyll and Mr Hyde* (1886); and Jules Verne's enigmatic Captain Nemo, from *20,000 Leagues Under the Sea* (1870). Also featured over the course of the series are characters from Arthur Conan Doyle's Sherlock Holmes stories, Fu Manchu, the Martians from Wells's *The War of the Worlds* (1898), and characters from Edwin Lester Linden Arnold's *Gullivar of Mars* (1905). In addition, in later stories there were James Bond and even Hugo Hercules, one of the earliest superhumans in comic strips, as well as a host of other cameos.

The first volume tells the story of the League being gathered together to protect the British Empire against a plot by Fu Manchu to create a deadly airship. The second volume takes a more apocalyptic stance, being set during the Martian invasion envisaged by Wells in *The War of the Worlds*. As in *1963*, Moore used advertisements not only to create a sense of the time period in which the series is set, but also in an attempt to embed the reader in the wider ethos and material life of these original texts to show how the values expressed in these advertisements, which are usually patronizing and misogynistic, permeated the culture. The mode here was not parody, but as with much of Moore's work, it was satirical in its implications. The idea of characters from lots of different texts sharing the same world was not innovative in itself, but the level of detail Moore brought to this world, and the compelling interconnections he made between the narratives, created the sense that these characters were somehow more authentic than the versions encountered in the novels and stories, and that the original characters were in fact watered-down versions of this reality made for public consumption.

In a sense, Moore's comic suggests that the source novels are simulations of a reality portrayed through his text, which is a provocative claim for an adaptation.

Alongside *The League of Extraordinary Gentlemen*, the other important work to emerge from the ABC line was *Promethea*, with artwork by J. H. Williams III. Promethea is a version of Wonder Woman and a female version of the mythological Greek god, Prometheus, a benefactor of humanity. The series served as a vehicle for Moore's interest in magic and was a critique of sexism and materialism. Fortunately, like *The League of Extraordinary Gentlemen*, the series survived the collapse of ABC following Moore's refusal to work for DC Comics, which had taken over Wildstorm. Promethea tells the story of a young woman, Sophie, who is a college student researching the myth of Promethea, who then finds out that she is to be the next incarnation of this living myth, a being who has attained immortality by existing as a story. Her role, which she struggles to accept, is to bring about the Apocalypse, an event that is defined as a mass redefinition of consciousness, somewhat similar to the emergence of the Supercontext at the end of *The Invisibles*. Moore used the comic didactically to address philosophical problems using the methodology of the kabbalah. These problems involved some of the same ideas that Moore had explored in *From Hell* but here made more accessible in the form of a superhero story.

British Superheroes Reborn

The Marvel UK experiment of the early 1990s had failed, having been caught up in the speculator bubble that nearly brought down the parent company, and the same fate befell a number of titles and independent publishers. One such small company was CM Comics, which was one of the leaders in a revival of independent comics in Britain, many of them influenced by *Watchmen* and *Zenith*. This small publisher was similar to the kind that had appeared in Britain in the 1940s, such as Swan, Scion, and Cartoon Art Productions, and was launched by Southampton-based creator and editor Chris Morgan (later known as Chris Ryan), who produced, among other titles, *Brit Force*, which featured a British superhero team. In some ways, this series was comparable to *The Mighty Apocalypse* from twenty years earlier. As Ryan recalls, *Brit Force* was his attempt to capitalize on the popularity of comics like *The X-Men,* and his company was one of the first British independent comics publishers to attempt to break into the professional comics distribution network dominated by Diamond and

Capital Comics. While his CM Comics line met with some initial success, the larger publishers ultimately did not tolerate the encroachment on sales from smaller publishers.

> *Brit Force* was [sold in Britain] through Virgin Megastore and Hamleys toy shop in London . . . as well as all of the small comic book stores around the country. It went well which prompted me to look for distribution in America and I got it. *The Brit Force* comic was handled through two of the largest distribution companies, Diamond Comics and Capital City. At the time in the UK no other comic company was doing what I was doing. Because Brit Force sold well. . . . I took on some of the best freelancers around the UK. My home at Maybush in Southampton became a veritable comicbook factory. Twelve different titles a month at our peak, most of which I wrote but could never have drawn them all. We had *Alley Cat, Wild Card, Stray Dogs, Death Heart, The Monoverse, Brit Force, Lionheart* [and] *Stonehenge.* . . . Looking back I was being over ambitious far too early. Which meant I was over-stretched. When the bubble burst I had no protection. . . . Basically what happened was that the major distributors also handled the big comic book publishers like Marvel and DC Comics. The big boys were getting fed up of sharing their spots with the small independents. . . . They pushed Diamond and Capital to raise the limits of issues needed to be ordered by the American stores . . . to something ridiculous. I didn't meet that criteria, along with many other companies, and they dropped the CM Comics range.[4]

The series was revived in 2009 by Andrew Radbourne, one of the contributors to the first series, and the revival was published through Moonface Press. However, it suffered from the same problem as the original series. Both attempted to do relatively "straight" versions of hyperbolic, American-style superhero action with little sense of critical distance, parody, or satire. The resulting comics seemed like rather substandard versions of American comics, adopting their clichés and conventions but having little of their style and offering little in the way of political commentary. Still, *Brit Force* was an ambitious attempt to take on American publishers at their own game, although ultimately it also served to underscore the weakness of British comics publishers in comparison to their American counterparts (see Figure 49).

A more successful independent comic, and perhaps the most self-referential British superhero comic since *Zenith*, was *Jack Staff*, by Paul Grist, which appeared in 2000. The comic was initially published in black and

Contemporary British Superheroes (1994–present)   241

Fig. 49: *Brit Force* #6, art by Russ Leach (CM Comics, 1994).

white by Grist's Dancing Elephant Press and the character of Jack Staff was loosely based on Marvel's Union Jack, who appeared in *The Invaders* series in the mid-1970s and had appeared in several stories since then, notably a Captain America story from 1981 by John Byrne that saw Union Jack battling Baron Blood, a Nazi vampire. *Jack Staff* incorporated many elements of Union Jack and some elements from early Captain Britain (such as the staff), which is unsurprising as the story had emerged from a Union Jack story pitch that Grist had delivered to Marvel but had been rejected. Jack Staff is a crime fighter and adventurer who has been active since the Victorian era. He is long-lived and able to channel energy, which he most often does through his staff. He fought in World War II with a team called The Freedom Fighters, who are modeled on The Invaders, and then worked with a group called Unit D, which was inspired by *Doctor Who*'s Unit, and also The Bureau for Paranormal Research and Defence from Mike Mignola's *Hellboy*.

At some point in the early 1980s, Jack Staff fought the superhuman Hurricane, who was based on Captain Hurricane from IPC's *Valiant* in a parody of DC Comics' *The Death of Superman* storyline (1992). In the aftermath of the battle Jack Staff goes missing for fifteen years, or more accurately, he retires from superheroics and takes work as a builder. The story opens with him working on a building site and encountering a tenacious reporter, Becky Burdock (an equivalent of Lois Lane), who is investigating the disappearance of Jack Staff. Like *Zenith*, the series is full of cameos from alternate versions of British superheroes. Apart from Captain Hurricane, there is Tom Tom the Robot Man, who is a version of Robot Archie, and there are also versions of The Spider, The Steel Claw, and various other IPC superheroes of the 1960s. There is also a character based on DC Thomson's General Jumbo, a boy who can remotely control an army of toys, and the Freedom Fighters group that Jack Staff is a member of in the 1940s includes Sgt States, a version of Captain America. In the flashback to World War II, the British home guard consists of characters from the well-loved 1970s British television comic series, *Dad's Army*. The series is full of very specific British cultural references and is carried off with a very British sensibility, foregrounding dark humor, irony, and parody. As Grist said,

> The one thing that British comics have never really done is superheroes, which is kind of funny really when you consider that many of the most highly respected writers and artists working for American comics (by which I mean superhero comics) come from the British Isles. That's not to say that British comics have not had their share of unusual characters with distinctive abilities. We've had giant robots, men with metal claws who could turn invisible, indestructible adventurers and the like. But they've always been a bit more down to earth than their colonial cousins. . . . We just don't do superheroes. Here's my attempt at correcting the cultural imbalance.[5]

Of course, on the evidence of this book one would have to disagree with Grist's general point that British comics have "never really done superheroes," but the underlying meaning of his point is correct. British comics have never really done superheroes the way that American comics do them. British superheroes parody American superheroes and change them to meet British expectations, often turning them into "unusual characters," as Grist puts it, rather than superheroes as such. The approach that Grist takes with Jack Staff is in some ways the whole of the British approach to superheroes in a microcosm, and perhaps more so than any other comic, his exemplifies the spirit of the British Superhero. The series was picked up by American publisher Image in 2004, and the work from that point has been in color.

In 2005 Wildstorm released *Albion*, a six-issue series that was plotted by Alan Moore and written by his daughter, Leah Moore, and her husband, John Reppion, with art by Shane Oakley and George Freeman and covers by Dave Gibbons. This series reintroduced some classic British superheroes and villains from the Odhams and IPC stable of the 1960s and 1970s, primarily from *Lion*, *Valiant*, and *Smash!* The story has Bad Penny (the daughter of Dolmann, whose name is a reference to penny dreadfuls) joining forces with Danny, a comics collector and son of Cursitor Doom, who embark on a journey to discover what has happened to all the British superbeings who have disappeared or been largely forgotten. In fact, most of the superbeings have been arrested by the British government and held at a remote Scottish castle that serves as an asylum and prison. As Penny and Danny come closer to discovering their location, they join forces with Robot Archie and Charlie Peace. It is revealed that the prisoners are in the process of being prepared for rendition to America, where they will presumably be experimented upon and dissected by shadowy government forces. Once again the superhero genre is employed as a means to satirize the unequal relationship between British and American governments, and the story offers parallels to real world political controversies, such as government-supported illegal rendition of terrorist suspects, who were held without due process and tortured.

Some of the best parts of the story involve flashbacks that are rendered in the style of old British comics, such as Penny's childhood memories which are drawn to resemble Dennis the Menace and Bash Street Kids strips. Also, at another point the artists mimic the style and appearance of a Janus Stark strip. *Albion* led to a spinoff series, *Thunderbolt Jaxon*, written by Dave Gibbons and drawn by John Higgins, the colorist of *Watchmen*. Their take on the character's origin, which Gibbons had always felt was rather confused, was to return to Norse mythology, making the mix of Thor and Captain Marvel more explicit. *Albion* benefited greatly from Alan Moore's plotting, in which he drew on his extensive knowledge of British comics history. The result is extremely satisfying if the reader is aware of the comics being referenced and the long-forgotten characters coming back to life. While *Zenith* and *Jack Staff* do similar things, they also stand on its own terms, whereas

Albion is a little too reliant on possessing background information and is therefore perhaps less satisfying for a general reader.

The Second Wave

By the mid-1990s, ten years on from the first wave of the British Invasion, the huge success of Moore, Gaiman, Morrison, Gibbons, Bolland, and McKean, as well as Delano, Milligan, and a host of British creators, had paved the way for more British comic creators to enter the previously impenetrable American comics industry. There grew a perception that British writers were edgier than American ones, who seemed permanently enthralled by the mythology of the superhero. The ironic distance achieved by the first wave came to be seen as the prerequisite for British success in America, but a new generation of upcoming writers, spearheaded by Garth Ennis, Warren Ellis, and Mark Millar and artists such as Bryan Hitch and Steve Dillon, found great success through somewhat different strategies. However, this success did not extend to the British comics industry itself. The British Invasion had led to increased visibility for British comics and creators and a rise in independently produced superhero material, of which *Jack Staff* was probably the best. Comics like this were picked up by American publishers due to the increased visibility of British material, but a second wave was also forming, and that would have a quite different character from the first.

The output of the first wave of the British Invasion was dominated by comics that subverted the superhero genre and drew upon literary and esoteric sources, notably Romantic poetry and the occult. This Brit invasion was also very much a "lit invasion," with the writers offering postmodern deconstructions of the medium and the superhero genre using the tools of literature. Their appropriation of superheroes did not come from an ideological connection to the values the genre represented but instead stemmed from a deeply cynical attitude to power, having been raised in a country partially colonized by American popular culture and used as an outpost of American military might. The political alliance between Britain and America in the 1970s and 1980s was one of mutual convenience, but it was not one of equals. The superhero was therefore a problematic figure for the many British creators, and their work employed various means to deflate the myth. Those belonging to the second wave of British creators were equally cynical about America, power, and superheroes, but their approach was different. Garth Ennis and Steve Dillon offered homage to two American genres, the Western and the road movie, and blended them with horror and conspiracy theories in *Preacher*, whereas Warren Ellis brought the British science-fiction tradition into his work.

Mark Millar revolutionized the American superhero by talking it back to its essence, but with a contemporary twist of sex and extreme violence. His update of The Avengers, titled *The Ultimates*, with artwork by Bryan Hitch, drew very heavily on Marvel comics from the 1940s and 1960s and made the superhero iconic and patriotic once again. Similarly, *Kick-Ass*, by Millar and American artist John Romita Jr. captured the appeal of early Spider-Man comics, with their protagonist's faltering attempts at learning how to be a superhero. The kinds of comics Ellis and Millar were writing for American publishers with artist Bryan Hitch became known as "widescreen comics." This term was first applied to Ellis's *The Authority*, with art by Hitch, and also to Millar's and Hitch's work on *The Ultimates*. Many of these comics had crowded, dynamic splash pages and double-page spreads and often employed rectangular panels against a black background, mimicking the widescreen ratio of the cinema screen and alluding to the experience of being in the cinema. There was also a degree of narrative decompression that saw fight scenes being spread out over many pages in a way usually associated with manga. Spectacle and action were privileged in these comics, and the cinematic qualities of Hitch's style contributed to the effect.

These comics also had great influence on the style of superhero films that would come to dominate cinema screens in the early twenty-first century. The irony was that for decades, American comics had been thought of as more visually dynamic than British comics, but now British artists were producing some of the most dynamic and exciting superhero material available. These second-wave comics were not reliant on literary or esoteric references or clever metafiction, or even necessarily parody or satire; rather, they were exceptionally well-crafted adventure stories with a political edge. In some ways, if the writers of the first British Invasion were deconstructing the superhero, then the second-wave writers were reconstructing the superhero in a different form. However, as noted above, despite the greatly increased influence and visibility of British creators, all was not well in the British comics industry. The opportunities in America meant that there was a significant brain drain effect, and that more British creators started to use *2000AD* as a training ground or stepping-stone to the American market. The relationship between British creators and American comics would take yet another turn in the wake of 9/11, when in political and military terms, the relationship between Britain and America became "special" once again, prompting new anxieties about the superhero as an icon of American power and an emblem of the close ties between Britain and America, which were again being explored through the superhero genre.

Another comic that is often compared to *The Authority* is *Cla$$war*, a six-part series issued by British publisher Com.x (2002–2004) and written by British creative team Rob Williams and Trevor Hairsine (with American artist Travel Foreman replacing Hairsine from the fourth issue). The series starts with a member of a superhuman black-ops team rebelling against the American government and kidnapping the president. The rogue superhero brands the word *liar* on the president's forehead using heat vision. As Williams said,

> *Cla$$war* was influenced by my love of people like Noam Chomsky—I was reading his *Class Warfare* when I came up with the idea for the series—and Bill Hicks, my fascination with Nixon and American politics in general. I spend half my time reading books on subjects like the CIA, biographies of people like Martin Luther King. For some reason I'm captivated by US history over the past 50 years. . . . I also love intelligent superhero comics—a legacy from my dysfunctional youth and the effect Alan Moore's *Captain Britain* and *Marvelman* had on me in the early eighties. So I figured I'd combine the two.[6]

The publication of the first issue of *Cla$$war* was delayed by the events of September 11, 2001, which made its critiques of military adventurism and the corrupt leadership of the United States highly controversial. This was a time of swelling patriotism in America, and like *The Authority* and *The Ultimates*, this series satirized American foreign policy using the superhero as a metaphor for the American military. Whereas *The Authority* and *The Ultimates* walked a fine line between celebrating the superhero as a symbol of power and satirizing such representations, *Cla$$war* was much more overt in its subversive attack on authority. In this sense, there was something of the spirit of Mills and O'Neill's *Marshal Law* embedded in *Cla$$war*.

Garth Ennis came from Northern Ireland and drew much of his inspiration from the British comics of his childhood, notably *Battle* and *Action*. Ennis started in American comics with *Hellblazer* for DC in 1991, following a celebrated run by Jamie Delano. Ennis and Dillon produced a popular run of *The Punisher* (2004), but Ennis demonstrated his distaste for superheroes in *The Pro* (2002), with art by Amanda Conner, and in the series *The Boys* (2006), with artist Darick Robertson. *The Pro* was a one-shot published by Image telling the story of a single mother and prostitute who is given superpowers by an alien who makes a wager that anyone can become a superhero. Joining the League of Honor (which is based on The Justice League), she finds herself surrounded by pious do gooders, whom she offends with her lifestyle, profanity, and extreme violence. In the end, she sacrifices herself to save the city from a nuclear bomb, but she leaves her mark on the superheroes, who end up swearing and acting violently like her. As the superbeings engage in yet another pointless battle, the closing narration tells the reader, "Her kid grew up. Not a bad idea, when you think about it."

The critique of the superhero genre is blunt; Ennis argues that it is an immature power fantasy that perpetuates cartoonish notions of good and evil. As with *Marshal Law*, there was a strong element of both satire and parody and a critique of the vogue for "realistic" superhero comics like *The Ultimates*. *The Pro* points to the conservatism and commercialization that is bound up in these representations. *The Boys* makes a similar point, although rather than superheroes being idealized children and do gooders, they are corrupt murderers and rapists who act like celebrities and flout the law. *The Boys* follows a team of CIA-funded agents whose job it is to monitor and regulate superheroes and, if necessary, to kill them. The series was initially published by Wildstorm, by then a subsidiary of DC Comics, but was canceled after the sixth issue, reportedly because DC felt uncomfortable with the vicious antisuperhero sentiment. The series moved to the smaller publisher Dynamite with its seventh issue. The attitude of the series is summed up on the very first page, which shows a superhero's head being crushed by a boot. The gruesome image recalls the famous line from Orwell's *Nineteen Eighty-Four*, "If you want a picture of the future imagine a boot stamping on a human face—for ever," but in this instance the oppression of the superhero has met its match in the extreme violence of the human characters, led by Butcher, whose wife was raped and murdered by a superbeing. The image offered here is of a superhuman face being stamped down by a boot and signifies the human capacity for violence that not even the most powerful superheroes can match.

The Boys features twisted versions of characters drawn from the British comics of Ennis's childhood, such as Dennis the Menace (Butcher) and Oor Wullie (Wee Hughie) from DC Thomson comics. It is not difficult to read this as a critique of the dominance of American superhero comics over the British comics industry, and in this regard *The Boys* is aligned with Mills and O'Neill's *Marshal Law* in terms of its vicious satire of the superhero genre. Ennis summed up his feelings about the superhero in a 2012 interview with *SciFi Now* magazine, saying,

> I find most superhero stories completely meaningless . . . which is not to say I don't think there's potential for the genre—Alan Moore and Warren Ellis have both done interesting work with the notion of what it might be like to be and think beyond human, see *Miracleman*, *Watchmen* and *Supergod*. But so long as the industry is geared towards fulfilling audience demand—ie, for the same brightly coloured characters doing the same thing forever—you're never going to see any real growth. The stories can't end, so they'll never mean anything.[7]

Ennis's stories always drive towards definite endings and are usually about the consequences of violence and the use of power. As in *Marshal Law*, the superheroes encountered in *The Boys* make the world a far worse place, and they inspire even greater violence from the humans. For Mills and Ennis, superheroes are primarily an expression of privilege, corruption, and the abuse of power and stand for imperialism and monarchical or feudal rule.

Warren Ellis, an English writer, followed quickly behind Ennis, first working for the British magazine *Deadline* in 1990, then for *2000AD*. His first notable work was "Lazarus Churchyard," which appeared in the short-lived *Blast!* Ellis found success in America when he began work for Wildstorm on *DV8*, a spinoff from the then very successful *Gen-13*. Later he then took over on *Stormwatch*, turning a formulaic superhero comic into one of the best-paced, best-written superhero comics of the mid-1990s. With *Transmetropolitan* (1997), a creator-owned comic that was part of DC's ill-fated Helix imprint, Ellis garnered a huge fan following and critical acclaim. When Helix collapsed, *Transmetropolitan* survived and was transplanted to Vertigo. In 1999 Ellis teamed up with British artist Bryan Hitch to launch *The Authority*, a spinoff from *Stormwatch*, turning up the intensity of action and violence.

It was *Planetary*, however, with art by John Cassady, in which Ellis really interrogated the history of the superhero genre. *Planetary* was published between 1999 and 2009 by Wildstorm and featured a group of superpowered beings who regard themselves as "Archaeologists of the Impossible," investigating the secret history of the world. This team consists of Elijah Snow, who has lost his memory, and his companions Jakita Wagner and The Drummer, who combat the forces of repression in order to "keep the world strange." These forces include The Four, an evil version of The Fantastic Four who use alien technology and other discoveries to benefit themselves rather than the world. In one issue, it is revealed that The Four killed a version of the infant Superman as well as alternate versions of Wonder Woman and The Green Lantern, robbing the world of these inspirational protectors. Ellis and Cassady explore the crossover between the superhero, gothic literature, science fiction, and various other genres. Like Moore's *The League of Extraordinary Gentlemen*, the series explores the prehistory of the superhero genre, and like Morrison's *The Invisibles*, it reflects an interest in human evolution through the reframing of consciousness and interaction with technology.

Similar transhumanist themes were found in *Freakangels*, which Ellis wrote between 2008 and 2011, with art by Paul Duffield. This was released as a web comic which was then collected as a series of graphic novels published by Avatar Press. The plot focuses on twelve twenty-three-year-old psychics living in Whitechapel six years after civilization in Great Britain is destroyed. They are like the psychic children of John Wyndam's *The Midwich Cuckoos* (1957) or the supernormals encountered in Stapledon's *Odd John* (1935). They set up a community and establish a form of government while exploring the limits of their powers, eventually coming to realize that they are immortal. The emphasis on environmental disaster also establishes a connection to a British science-fiction tradition that includes Wyndham's *The Day of the Triffids* (1951) and *The Crysalids* (1955), J. G. Ballard's *The Drowned World* (1962), and John Christopher's *The Death of Grass* (1956). Ellis is therefore a writer very much in the British science-fiction tradition, and *Freakangels* combines this with contemporary steampunk and an influence from manga and anime. Similar influences are seen in *Ignition City* (2010), also from Avatar Press, which brought together science fiction and the science hero tradition from comics and newspaper strips, recalling early science heroes like Derickson Dene.

In *Supergod* (2009), Ellis returns to themes that dominated his runs on *Stormwatch*, *The Authority*, and *Planetary*: the potential for a superhuman arms race that would dwarf the Cold War. As he said in an essay on the Avatar website,

> *Supergod* is the story of what an actual superhuman arms race might be like. It's a simple thing to imagine. Humans have been fashioning their own gods with their own hands since the dawn of our time on Earth. We can't help ourselves. Fertility figures brazen idols, vast chalk etchings, carvings, myths and legends, science fiction writers generating science fiction religions from whole cloth. It's not such a great leapt to conceive of the builders of nuclear weapons and particle accelerators turning their attention to the oldest of human pursuits. Dress it up as superhuman defence, as discovering the limits of the human body, as trans-humanism and post-humanism.[8]

The British supergod is a huge, triple-headed mutation of three astronauts exposed to a space fungus. This draws on the origin of the Fantastic Four (just as Ellis had done in *Planetary*) but mainly recalls the British science-fiction film *The Quatermass Xperiment* (1955), which saw three British astronauts being sent into space and encountering an alien being. When the rocket returns, only one astronaut emerges, and he has been infected with alien spores and is hunted through the streets of London. The American superhuman is derived from *The Six Million Dollar Man*, the popular 1970s television series whose title character was designed to combat the Russian superbeing, a cyborg constructed from the body of a dead cosmonaut. The Chinese superbeing creates a huge Cthulhu-type creature from human bodies, and the Iraqi and Iranian superbeings are based on Dr Manhattan from *Watchmen*, as one can perceive time and the other can unzip matter, killing everything in its presence. All of them are drawn into conflict and several of them travel to the epicenter of this apocalypse to confront Krisna, the Indian supergod who has killed 90 percent of the Indian population and has started terraforming the environment to remove pollutants, all in order to save the country. The conflict results in the apparent death of all the supergods with the exception of the British one, who reigns supreme at the end, infecting the entire planet with its fungal spores. This is perhaps the bleakest of Ellis's visions of the superhero, with beings who are completely oblivious to humanity or operate beyond conventional morality. This comic, like *Freakangels*, brings the superhero narrative together with the British science-fiction tradition and Ellis's interest in trans- and posthumanism.

Scottish writer Mark Millar, who claims to have been inspired to become a comic writer after meeting Alan Moore in his youth, began his career at *2000AD* in 1990 and frequently collaborated with fellow Glaswegian Grant Morrison. Millar started working for DC in 1994, taking on the now ailing *Swamp Thing* series, but it was only in 2000 when he replaced Ellis on *The Authority* that he reached a substantial mainstream audience. Millar's hugely successful *The Ultimates* (2002), with Bryan Hitch, delivered the same kind of high intensity widescreen action that Hitch had popularized with Ellis in *The Authority*. Millar continued in this vein with *Wanted* (2003), a violent story about a world ruled by supervillains that was adapted into a Hollywood film in 2008. Millar's runs on *The Authority* and *The Ultimates* were in some ways a response to the attacks of September 11, 2001, reflecting the reawakening of patriotic feeling in America and a huge resurgence of popular propaganda, much of it reactionary and right wing, at least initially.

America found a new enemy, Al Qaeda, and an archnemesis, Osama Bin Laden. This was seized upon by President George Bush Jr. to develop a foreign policy that continually placed the new War on Terror in the context of World War II. There was a strong propaganda reason for this: the War on Terror did not have the same clear-cut moral and political narrative that characterized the so-called Good War. Comics like *The Ultimates* and *The Authority* reflected the Bush doctrine with their emphasis on preemptive strikes with overwhelming force, and the superhero became a metaphor for this approach.

Millar's work was both an expression of this line of attack and a critique, with the superheroes positioned as weapons or a strike force. Millar's real target, though, was the media and how it can be manipulated to mislead the public. This clearly references the circumstances that led American and Britain into a second Gulf War in the wake of 9/11, with politicians and the media exploiting the tragedy of 9/11 to justify war in the Middle East. From this point, Millar became a virtual one-man comics script factory, with an impressive output of hit stories illustrated by some of the best artists in the business. Following on from *The Ultimates* he wrote *Civil War*, with art by Steve McNiven, which pitched the heroes of the Marvel universe against one another in an epic battle concerning government regulation of superheroes, continuing the critique of the media and the manipulation of public opinion seen in *The Ultimates*.

The *Civil War* miniseries was just one part of a massive crossover event that ran over 2006–2007 and through all the Marvel titles. This series divided the heroes of the Marvel Universe into two camps following an incident in which a group of young superhumans caused the deaths of hundreds of innocent people. The resulting political debate broke out into civil war between the superheroes, with Iron Man representing the military-industrial complex and coming down on the side of the government and Captain America, representing libertarian values, opposing government regulation. The *Civil War* was a sharp satire of the post 9/11 Bush doctrine, homeland security measures, and the Patriot Act as well as the power of the media, but as always with Millar it was also a pretext for some thrilling superhero action, culminating in the death of Captain America at the hands of an assassin. These comics had tremendous influence on the tone and style of the hugely successful Marvel movies, although most of Millar's political critique is stripped out of them, and neither he nor Hitch have received much recognition for the films. Indeed, the movies *The Avengers* (2012) and *Captain America: Civil War* (2016) were largely based on Millar's stories, but it is unlikely that many of the millions of viewers of these films would know that they are based on the work of a Scottish comics writer.

Millar's considerable success is evidenced by his MillarWorld publishing venture and the fact that many of his stories have been optioned for film and television, some of them before the comics have even been finished, as was the case with *Kick-Ass*. The story is reminiscent of early 1960s Marvel comics, especially *Spider-Man*, as it focuses on the struggles of young Dave Lizewski to become a superhero and on his troubled family and romantic relationships. It also has an enormous amount of extreme violence, and like the 1980s revisionist comics, it tackled the question "what would superheroes be like in the real world?" but in a different way. This is Millar's answer for the internet generation—they would be obsessed with hits on social media and celebrity status. The comic, like earlier Marvel comics, is also very cynical about the virtue of the superhero. The 2010 *Kick-Ass* film is somewhat different in tone as the superhero concept is confirmed rather than desecrated. One notable example is the character of Big Daddy, portrayed by Nick Cage as a heroic vigilante in the film but in the comic is a deluded comics collector who finances his fantasy of being a superhero by selling his comics collection and acting out a life as an adventurous superhero as a means of engaging with his young daughter. He dies begging for his life, his fantasy of being a supervigilante collapsing when he encounters real violence from the gangsters he has taken on. The comic worked because there are elements taken from *Watchmen*, *Zenith*, and *Marshal Law* along with Spider-Man and The Punisher while it also draws on the long tradition of downbeat British superhero comics. Conversely, the film celebrates heroism, and the transcendent violence of the superhero, as redemptive qualities.

Superior (2010–2012) was a remarkable return to an old British superhero comic tradition—the homage to Captain Marvel. Published by Icon, an imprint of Marvel Comics, and with artwork by Leinil Francis Yu, the story revolves around twelve-year-old Simon Pooni who is confined to a wheelchair with multiple sclerosis. Simon is visited by Ormon (an anagram of moron), a mysterious "space monkey" who grants his greatest wish, to become Superior, a comic book superhero who has featured in a long-running comics series and movie franchise (much like the *Superman* films of the 1970s and 1980s). Simon is transformed into an adult hero, and Ormon says that he will return in a week to explain his "gift." As Simon explores his powers with his best friend, his parents believe him to have run away or to have been abducted. After a week of saving lives and making the world a better place, Simon learns that Ormon is a demon who has given him his greatest wish in order to take it away and force him to sell his soul to regain the power. To force his hand, Ormon transforms Simon's tormentor, the school bully, into a superpowered killer and himself into a huge supermonster. Simon has little choice but to sell his soul to stop the carnage, but in doing so, Ormon is tricked out of ever collecting on the debt (as Superior is immortal). This story blends the Superman mythos, Captain Marvel, the 1988 film *Big*, starring Tom Hanks, and Christopher Marlowe's *Dr Faustus* (1604), with an affectionate homage to the Superman films starring Christopher Reeve and directed by Richard Donner. (The graphic novel collection is dedicated to both of them.) The story is all the more poignant as like Simon, Christopher Reeve was confined to a wheelchair after a riding accident in 1995 and died in 2004. The story is full of the same exciting set pieces that Millar excels at in other works, but it has a bit more heart than many of his stories, which are usually much more violent and cynical.

In 2000 Grant Morrison completed work on his magnum opus, *The Invisibles*, which he had begun in 1994. It was a striking reevaluation of the potential of the superhero narrative, which he followed with *The Filth* (2002–2003), a collaboration with Chris Weston that offered a disturbing picture of mental degeneration, with a collage of influences, from science fiction and horror to superhero comics. At the same time as Morrison had been working on *The Invisibles* and *The Filth*, he had also been working in mainstream comics, primarily for DC and later for Marvel. Whereas Morrison's association with DC characters had been a long one, his work for Marvel began in the mid-1990s with *The Skrull Kill Krew*, which he co-wrote with Mark Millar. In 2000 he wrote *Marvel Boy*, a six-issue series with art by J. G. Jones.

Marvel Boy set the tone for Morrison's take on Marvel. It started in medias res, dropping a new character into the Marvel Universe and freely referencing Marvel continuity and lore. It seemed as if a new perspective on the Marvel Universe came into being in this series, seen through the eyes of Noh-Varr, a young Kree soldier from another dimension who is stranded on Earth when his ship is shot down by Doctor Midas, a villain obsessed with using cosmic rays to acquire superpowers. Noh-Varr's companions are killed in the crash, and he is taken captive by Midas. Breaking free, he evades S.H.I.E.L.D., fights Hexus the living corporation, and eventually kills Midas with the assistance of his psychotic daughter, Oubliette. Captured by S.H.I.E.L.D. and imprisoned in The Cube, its jail for supervillains, Noh-Varr vows to conquer Earth for the Kree Empire. This series was innovative for many reasons, including its dark tone, which was possible because it came out under the new, adult-oriented Marvel Knights banner, but also because it additionally attempted to recapture some of the innovative work Kirby was engaged in toward the end of his career, including the manic atmosphere of those comics, where Kirby's experimental impulses often overrode narrative logic. Morrison noted the ambitions he had for the series in an interview with Warren Ellis.

> *Marvel Boy*'s visual style becomes more like MTV and adverts; from #3 on its filled with all kinds of new techniques; rapid cuts, strobed lenticular panels, distressed layouts, 64 panel grids, whatever. We've only started to experiment but already *Marvel Boy* looks like nothing else around. Some of the stuff J.G. is doing is like an update of the whole Steranko Pop Art approach to the comics page. Instead of Orson Welles, op art and spy movies, J.G.'s using digital editing effects, percussive rhythms, cutting the action closer and harder, illuminated by the frantic glow of the image-crazed hallucination of 21st century media culture and all that. Comics do not need to be like films. They do not need to look like storyboards. . . . I wanted to go back and explore some of the possibilities of comics as music. I'm doing Marvel Boy and whatever else in a Utopian 21st century spirit—I'll aim the comics at a wide, media-literate mainstream audience and slowly but surely help generate that audience. . . . I'll continue to act as if being a comic book writer is the same as being a pop star. I'll continue to learn from stuff I think breaks new ground. If at the moment I think comics aren't being sexy enough or FuturePop enough or incendiary enough, I'll attempt to fill the gap with the sort of thing I want to read.[9]

As Morrison suggests, the series is brash, quick moving, and full of ideas and over-the-top characters, driven forward by plotting that has much more punch than it does narrative cohesion. The same future-pop spirit is evident in Morrison's *New X-Men* (2001–2004). The early issues had art by Frank Quitely, and the partnership of the two once again worked perfectly. The first three-issue storyline, "E is for Extinction" (issues 114–116) offered a startlingly off-kilter take on *The X-Men*. Gone was the angst and melodrama of the series; instead, in Morrison's hands these characters became, like pop stars—effortlessly cool and media savvy. What Morrison was doing was trying to recapture some of the anarchic spirit of Marvel Comics in the 1960s, combining that with a new future-pop sensibility for the twenty-first century. The tone of this series, and the revelations that Morrison built toward over the course of it, were controversial. These included the destruction of Genosha, the apparent death of Magneto, and the fact that the mutant Xorn, a Chinese mutant with a star of a brain, was actually Magneto. Indeed, when Morrison left the series, it soon reverted to its original title and several of his plot lines were reversed, including the Xorn/Magneto revelation. This reveals that while Morrison's brand of future-pop worked well within a limited series, it did not entirely fit with the aims and objectives of the larger Marvel Universe, perhaps because there were few writers working for Marvel who could follow him or match his radical ideas.

When the next successful run on X-Men came along in the form of Joss Whedon and John Cassaday's *Astonishing X-Men*, this point was proved. Their run, while very well crafted and popular, was not as daring as Morrison's, and if anything, harked back to the days of Chris Claremont and John Byrne's run on the series in the 1980s. Solid storytelling and characterization were the focus rather than experiments with tone and narrative. Marvel soon parted ways with Morrison after he announced that he would take on a major role in the reworking of the DC Universe, signing an exclusive contract with Marvel's oldest rival. His move back to DC also set the stage for some groundbreaking reinventions of its characters, namely, his acclaimed twelve-issue series, *All-Star Superman* (2005–2008); *Seven Soldiers of Victory* (2005–2006); *52* (2006–2007), with Geoff Johns, Greg Rucka, and Mark Waid; *Final Crisis* (2009); *Batman and Robin* (2010); and runs on the revamped *Action Comics* and *Batman Incorporated* (2012).

Morrison and Quitely's *All-Star Superman*, often hailed as one of the best Superman stories, distills the essence of Superman and recaptures the spirit of the character. This marked a significant turning point for Morrison, who, rather than revising or satirizing the superhero, actually celebrates the concept. As he notes in his semiautobiography/semihistory of comics, *Supergods: Our World in the Age of the Superhero* (2011), the superhero is the best idea about itself that humanity has conceived—the superhero is an idea to combat the atomic bomb. He explored the same idea—that superheroes can rescue us from ourselves—in *Flex Mentallo*. In *All Star Superman*, however, the focus is not on metafictional play or on revealing the absurdities of the genre; rather, it is an unselfconscious celebration of the joy of superhero comics and the dignity and moral courage of the superhero. Another celebration of the mythic power of the superhero came in 2009, when Gaiman returned to comics with "Whatever Happened to the Caped Crusader?," which, like Moore's "Whatever Happened to the Man of Tomorrow?" presented the "last" story of Batman before the events of *Final Crisis*. In the story, Batman has been killed and various villains tell how they did it, but all these stories are incompatible, leaving us to ponder the power and resonance of the Batman mythos and the mystery at its heart. There is an echo of the conclusion to Gaiman's *The Sandman*, titled "The Wake," in which friends and foes attend the funeral of Morpheus. This strange but touching Batman story pulls at the same heartstrings and engages in the same kind of metafictional play, regressing Batman to the core elements of a folktale. It also continued in the tradition whereby the British Invasion writers imported literary references into superhero comics; the story itself is modeled on Geoffrey Chaucer's fourteenth-century *Canterbury Tales*.

Another example of returning characters to their essence was the reinvention of Captain Britain undertaken in 2005. The character had a regular, but not major place in the Marvel Universe in his early years, although his visibility was increased considerably when his creator, Chris Claremont, made him the leader of the team Excalibur in the comic of that name. *Excalibur* had art by Alan Davis, who had been closely associated with Captain Britain since his defining run on the British series in the early 1980s. Starting in 1988, *Excalibur* ran for ten years, ending in 1998, but it returned as *New Excalibur* in 2005, written by British writer Paul Cornell with art by Canadian artist Leonard Kirk. It then became *Captain Britain and MI:13*, which ran from 2008 to 2009. Cornell's relaunch of *Excalibur* and Captain Britain were notable in that he returned to some of the earlier British Captain Britain comics, bringing the Black Knight into the team as well as Union Jack. As Cornell says in the introduction to the first collected edition of the series, he wanted to return some dignity to the character and to reemphasize the magical elements, which he notes were largely indebted to Captain Marvel. One of the ways he did this was by returning to the spirit of the stories written by Thorpe and Moore in the early 1980s.

Cornell and Kirk's stories featured many British cultural references, just like Thorpe's and Moore's versions, and combined exactly what a reader would expect from a contemporary Marvel superhero comic, with some dark humor and satire in the best British superhero tradition. After very promising early sales, boosted by the crossover with the "Secret Invasion" storyline that ran across all Marvel comics in summer 2008, and despite a nomination for a Hugo award and press attention when Prime Minister Gordon Brown appeared in one story, the series was canceled with issue 15. However, in 2015 a new Captain Britain arose as part of the "Secret Wars" summer event in a series called *Captain Britain and the Mighty Defenders*, written by British writer Al Ewing with art by Alan Davis. This new Captain Britain was Dr Faiza Hussain, the burka-wearing Muslim hero who is also a National Health Service doctor and appeared in Cornell's run. In Ewing's and Davis' story, she is the Captain Britain of Battleworld in an alternate universe. Ewing, who has also written for *2000AD*, features alternate versions of Judge Dredd and Judge Anderson, blending *2000AD* characters with Marvel ones, playfully reflecting the intertwined history of British and American comics.

The Standard, which began in 2008 and ran until 2014, was an independently produced superhero comic written by Glaswegian John Lees and drawn by Canadian Jon Rector, later joined by Will Robson. The story follows two superheroes from different generations, both taking up the mantle of The Standard. While the first Standard was the world's greatest superhero, the second is a shallow celebrity, obsessed with fame rather than a heroic mission. This story line is somewhat influenced by *Paradax* and *Zenith*; it expands on the idea that the modern world has become too cynical for heroism, but the story is also driven by a number of references to superhero history, much like Ellis's *Planetary*. The origin story of the first Standard is based on several famous superhero origin stories, most notably The Flash. When a meteor collies with his laboratory, scientist Gilbert Graham is transformed into a superhuman by the mixing of chemicals and material from the meteor. Upon his retirement many years later, his former sidekick, Alex Thomas (aka Fabu-Lad), takes up the role of The Standard, but it soon becomes clear that he has not really learned the lessons of what it takes to be a superhero (see Figure 50). He acts out heroic adventures for his reality television show, looking a lot like a Marvel superhero of the early 1990s, as if he has leapt out of the pages of Jim Lee's *X-Men*. The villain, the Corpse, looks like a Todd MacFarlane character, such as Spawn. The story is a commentary on changing values in superhero comics from the moralistic adventures of the 1930s and 1940s to later comics of the 1980s and 1990s, which emphasized style over substance. It does not, however, have the vicious edge that characterizes other satires of the genre, such as *Marshal Law* or *The Boys*. As Lees says,

> *The Standard* [is] my love-letter to the superhero genre, an ode to a genre that has given me countless hours of entertainment across multiple mediums since I was a small child. When you consider that some of the most influential stories by some of the most iconic of American superheroes have been written by Brits, the modern American superhero could be seen as a kind of symbiotic melding of British and American sensibilities.... I think it's interesting to see how often British superhero comics adopt the aesthetic of their American counterparts, be it in pastiche or parody. There could be

something to say in that about the Americanisation of British pop culture in a wider sense.[10]

Other comics to emerge from the British independent and small press include *Sugar Glider*, created by writer Daniel Clifford and artist Gary Bainbridge in 2009 and set in Newcastle upon Tyne. It tells the story of Susie Sullivan, a young girl who is having trouble finding her place in the world and is about to drop out of college when she discovers a high-tech gliding suit. Susie uses the suit to embark on a series of adventures and finds that she has some aptitude for life as a superhero; she finds herself in trouble, however, when it becomes clear that the suit is one of those used by MI5's new Vigilance superagents. As Bainbridge has said, "The book as a whole is a modern and hopefully fresh interpretation of the superhero genre. It's a nod to the influence of the Marvel Silver Age, Ditko, Kirby et al, while also maintaining some sensibilities and DIY ethos of the British small press."[11] It is also very much in the tradition of adventurers in winged suits that goes back to the early twentieth century in British comics and remained popular in the 1930s and through to the 1950s like The Winged Man and *Radio Fun*'s The Falcon. Then there are comics like *The Atomic Society of Justice*, by John and Rob Miller, and *The United*, by Jonny Pickering, which features a British superhero team. *Spandex!* (2012), by Martin Eden, features an all-gay superhero team based in Brighton. As Eden notes,

> After a few years of working with other indie creators, I decided to launch my own title, which was a superhero soap opera called *The O Men*. Kind of a cross between *Watchmen* and *EastEnders* (in tone—I'm not saying it was as good as *Watchmen*). The comic did okay and had a nice little following, but after 30 issues, I felt the urge to do something new. In the meantime, some background characters were starting to grab my attention. So I got thinking about creating a comic about a gay superhero team and how unique that would be.[12]

Other notable comics to emerge from the small press include the ingenious *Paradox Girl* (2014), by Cayti Elle Bourquin and Yishan Li, published by Hana Comics, which has a character who travels through time, allowing several versions of herself to coexist simultaneously. It is a brilliant meeting of American and manga styles drawn by a British-Chinese artist working in Edinburgh and collaborating with an American writer. The considerable rise in the number of comics-related events, from marts, to conventions,

Fig. 50: *The Standard*, by John Lees and Jon Rector (ComixTribe, 2008).

and conferences, has given a huge boost to the small press and independent comics, and some of this activity has been centered on one of the great seats of British comics: Dundee.

Dundee—One City, Many Comics

The resurgence of comics in Dundee, beyond the publications of DC Thomson, stems from several factors, including the rise of Comics Studies courses at the University of Dundee, which runs its own comics imprint, UniVerse, which publishes work by the students. One example is *Cosmic*, by Scottish comics creator Letty Wilson and American writer Erin Keepers, a story about a hybrid alien/human girl caught up in a battle for the Earth. This story was initially created as part of the University's Comics Studies Masters, where the two met and collaborated, and later expanded and published, first through the UniVerse imprint, then through Panels Comics, a company set up by former students from the course. In 2015 Wilson released a science-fiction superhero comic, *Meteor*, released through Panels Comics (see Figure 51). Wilson's style is a striking mix of influences and, in keeping with the traditions of British comics, is strange and parodic, presenting an unusual take on familiar themes.

Other publications to emerge from UniVerse include a collection called *Alpha: The British Superhero* (2016), featuring reworkings of The Amazing Mr X and a title featuring the superhero Alpha, who is a pastiche and parody of the British superhero tradition written by the current author, and featuring work by artists Phillip Vaughan, Norrie Millar, Rossi Gifford, Rebecca Horner, Elliot Balson, Jillian Fleck, Helen Robinson, and Yannis Giagias. There is also a poster by Dave Gibbons, showing Alpha meeting his Tornado alter-ego, The Big E. The character of Alpha is imagined as the first British superhero, appearing before The Amazing Mr X (see Figures 52 and 53). His civilian guise is Nat Fullerton, a blending of Len Fullerton's real name and his pseudonym, Nat Brand. He works as a comics artist at the McCail art studios in Dundee, and his early adventures are rendered by Norrie Millar in a style reminiscent of Glass's work on "The Amazing Mr X" from *The Dandy* in 1944, and in the Amalgamated Press style, with text underneath the images. In "Pop Goes the Art World," drawn by Letty Wilson, Alpha investigates the mysterious disappearance of British pop art artworks by the Independent Group in 1956 (see Figure 54). A mock Alpha cover by Elliot Balson echoes a 1950s Electroman cover, and like the story illustrated by Wilson, it echoes the "fake" American comics being produced in Britain in the 1940s and 1950s (see Chapter Two). Another story drawn by Balson mimics the style of 1980s British superhero stories like *Marvelman* and *Zenith*, while those by Vaughan and Gifford are more contemporary versions. *Alpha: The British Superhero* is written to dramatize some of the ideas that have been formed over the course of researching this book (see Figure 55).

In 2012, comics in Dundee and Britain in general were dealt a blow when DC Thomson announced that their longest-running comic, *The Dandy*, would cease publication in print and move over to an online version. The aim was to create a "best of" version of the comic that drew on the comic's long history and returned some of the diversity to the title. It appeared in 2013. A key part of the strategy was the development of *Retroactive*, a strip that features numerous DC Thomson superheroes, including a team led by The Amazing Mr X (see Figure 56). As the publicity said,

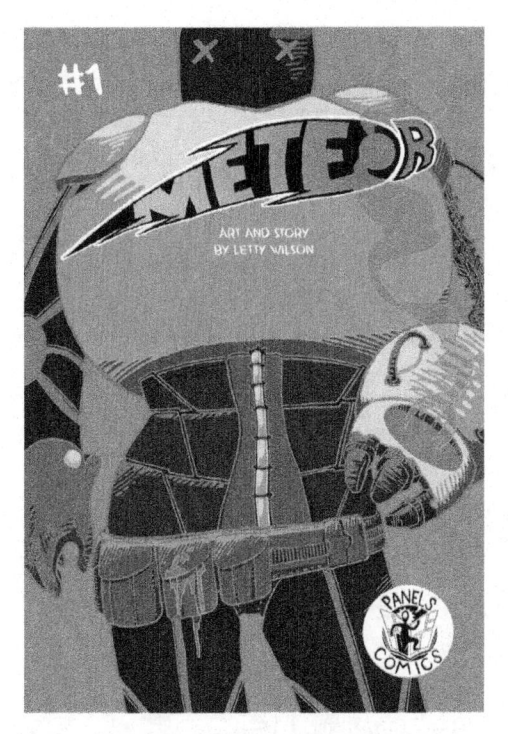

Fig. 51: *Meteor*, by Letty Wilson (Panels Comics, 2015).

Fig. 52: *Alpha*, written by Chris Murray, with art by Phillip Vaughan (UniVerse, 2016).

262 Contemporary British Superheroes (1994–present)

A LONE ENEMY PLANE, AND A MYSTERY CLOSE TO HOME

A NAZI PLANE WEAVES BETWEEN THE FLAK AND SPOTLIGHTS OF DUNDEE'S WARTIME DEFENCES.

IN HIS OFFICE AT MACCAIL'S ART STUDIO NAT FULLERTON HEARS THE BATTLE RAGING OVERHEAD AND BURSTS INTO ACTION, AS ALPHA!

THE SUPER-NORMAL ALPHA MAKES SHORT WORK OF THE ENEMY PLANE, SENDING IT SPIRALLING TOWARDS THE GROUND BELOW.

ALPHA HELPS THE SOLDIERS PULL THE PILOT FROM THE WRECKAGE AND IS SHOCKED TO FIND THAT IT IS NONE OTHER THAN RUDOLPH HESS OF NAZI HIGH COMMAND!

A QUICK SEARCH OF HESS REVEALS THAT HE IS CARRYING SEVERAL LETTERS IN A STRANGE CODE. ONE IS ADDRESSED TO A MYSTERIOUS FIGURE WHO LIVES NEARBY.

FULLERTON TAKES THE SHORT TRAIN JOURNEY TO HOSPITALFIELD HOUSE, AN EERIE PLACE THAT WAS ONCE A HOSPITAL FOR PLAGUE VICTIMS.

THERE HE MEETS DR. OCULUS, AN OLD MAGICIAN WITH AN ODD TATTOO ON HIS FOREHEAD.

WHEN FULLERTON MENTIONS THE LETTER, DR. OCULUS'S DEMEANOUR CHANGES AND HE USES MAGICAL POWERS TO HYPNOTIZE FULLERTON.

FULLERTON AWAKENS THE NEXT MORNING WITH NO MEMORY OF WHAT HAPPENED. HE IS ONCE AGAIN AT HIS DESK AT MACCAIL STUDIOS.

Fig. 53: "The Amazing Alpha," by Chris Murray and Norrie Millar (UniVerse, 2016).

Fig. 54: "Pop Goes the Art World," by Chris Murray and Letty Wilson (UniVerse, 2016).

Fig. 55: "Alpha vs Doc Holiday and his Goons," by Chris Murray and Elliot Balson (UniVerse, 2016).

The line-up is Valda, from *Mandy*; The Amazing Mr X, a wartime character from *The Dandy*, and rookies called Cobra, Hornet and Kat, who are mentored by King Cobra, from *Hotspur*; Captain Hornet, from *Hornet*; and Katie the Cat, Billy the Cat's cousin and former sidekick from *The Beano*. The team was created by Peter Flint, Codename Warlord, from *The Warlord* comic. William Grange, the civilian alter ego of Billy the Cat, has appeared in the story as a police chief inspector.[13]

This was another version of the long dormant Thunderhawks project. The plan was taken forward by writer and editor Dan McGachey, whose initial story treatment was very promising, drawing the various DC Thomson heroes into a shared universe. The concept work and character designs that were developed realized his vision and marked out a new direction for DC Thomson comics. It looked set to appeal to a slightly older demographic and to reintroduce these British superheroes to a teenage market, but in the end these ideas were watered down and the final version reflected little of this ambition. The *Digital Dandy* suffered from too little development time, and the project ultimately failed. However, the idea to relaunch DC Thomson's rich stable of superheroes was a good one whose time is hopefully yet to come. It almost came to pass when *Strip* appeared, also in 2013. This was a short-lived anthology comics produced by Bosnia-based Print Media, owned by Ivo Milicevric, who had grown up in the former Yugoslavia with reprints of British comics such as *Lion* and *Valiant*. One of the centerpieces to *Strip* was the reworking of the old DC Thomson character, King Cobra, produced under license and written by John Freeman, former editor at Marvel UK, with art by Wamberto Nicomendes. Despite pitching this at an older readership than the *Digital Dandy*, *Strip* was not a success either. However, with the huge popularity of superhero films, DC Thomson's *The Beano* has often featured Dennis the Menace in a superhero costume, as Supermenace, or the Prank Knight, and Bananaman (the Man of Peel) is still being published and remains popular.

In 2013 Scottish publisher Diamondsteel, based in Dundee, released *Saltire*, a graphic novel series about Scotland's immortal guardian. It was written by John Ferguson, and the company is jointly run with his wife, Clare Ferguson. They worked with a team of young comics creators: Gary Welsh, Tone Julskjaer, and Claire Roe, who were from Duncan of Jordanstone College of Art and Design in Dundee, most of whom had taken a course on creating comics run by lecturer Phillip Vaughan. As Ferguson says, politics was central to his vision of the character,

Fig. 56: The Amazing Mr X, redesigned for the *Digital Dandy* (DC Thomson, 2012). © DC Thomson & Co Ltd.

A Scottish superhero represents something that an imperialist hero can't. The story of the underdog, the quest for freedom and liberation. UK and US comics have a status quo where everything is right with the world when capitalism reigns and the illusion of democracy is in place, this is what the heroes protect and represent. Most of the British superheroes I'm aware of over the years have been very upper class "our empire's better than your empire" type stuff, but *Zenith* and *Miracleman* had their merits being a lot more irreverent and satirical. American comic books are always better because they never have an issue with embarrassment like the British do. They are happy to dress in bright spandex and a codpiece and stand on the top of a building without the slightest hint of irony. When they don't work we all point and laugh but when it does they create cultural icons that are embraced the world over, and that has to be admired, in fact applauded.[14]

On the topic of the relationship between Scottish history and the American superhero tradition, he adds,

> I see superheroes as modern mythology, created by the new world to fill the void of legend and folklore which the old world took for granted in their storytelling and tradition. A country that is only a hundred and fifty years old lacks the cultural heritage to be able to revere embellished historical figures as their legends. So they make their own, from scratch, taking the best elements of every heroic myth from Greece to Rome, from Persia to Egypt, and adding in a fair dose of science fiction for good measure. It's brilliant. *Saltire* tries to take the best of both new and old. The history, folklore and tradition of an ancient country, and adding in the modern dynamic element of the otherworldly, unachievable superhero. I think what makes [Saltire] different is that ancient heroes and modern superheroes are all champions of the empire, where Saltire is protecting the people of a small nation of varying cultures, languages and beliefs.[15]

Saltire is particularly interesting because it emerged at a time when Scotland was questioning its relationship to what many Scots saw as an imperial oppressor: England. The superhero featured in this comic was an emblem for an independent Scotland and a powerful aspirational figure in the context of the historic national referendum on Scottish independence (see Figure 57). However, the series also showed the flexibility of the superhero concept once more. The superhero can be molded to fit any political situation and lends itself to intertextual allusions. An example is seen in the artwork produced by Vaughan, which echoes the advertisement that announced the launch of Captain Britain and offers a wry commentary on nationalist superheroes, and especially on Captain Britain, who purports to represent the entire country but is really more of an English hero.

Another superhero comic being written in Dundee is *Death Sentence*, by writer Monty Nero, with artwork by Mike Dowling in the first series and Martin Simmons in the second. In the story, which was first published in 2013, a number of young people gain superpowers through a sexually transmitted disease, the G+ virus, that is fatal within six months. The characters Verity, a graphic designer, and Weasel, a self-absorbed rock star, find themselves on the run from the government and brought together in a battle against Monty, a media personality turned psychotic supervillain, leading to a climax that recalls *Akira* and *Zenith*. This story is reminiscent of the best Vertigo comics from the early 1990s and easily takes its place among the best works of twenty-first-century superhero stories, including Morrison's *All-Star Superman*, Ellis's *Planetary*, and Millar's *Kick-Ass*. It is another sharp satire of current politics and the relationship between the individual

Contemporary British Superheroes (1994–present) 267

Fig. 57: Saltire, by Phillip Vaughan. Saltire created by John Ferguson (Diamondsteel Comics, 2015).

and authority, and it proves that the British superhero comic is still very adaptable for the purposes of satire.

Satire was also a key component of the seven-part series *America's Got Powers* (2012–2013), published by Image and written by British radio and television personality Jonathan Ross, one of Britain's biggest comics collectors and the husband of Jane Goldman, the screenwriter of the films *Kick-Ass* and *X-Men: First Class*. Ross teamed up with top British comics artist Bryan Hitch to produce a superhero comic that on one level appears to be a straightforward satire of reality television shows like *America's Got Talent* and a superpowered version of *The Hunger Games*. As the story unfolds, however, it becomes a lot more interesting. Like Ellis's *Freakangels*, it contains elements of *The Midwich Cuckoos* by John Wyndham, with a mysterious alien object landing in San Francisco and making every pregnant women in a five-mile radius give birth to superpowered children. Seventeen years later, as these superbeings mature, a gladiatorial competition is televised, with the superbeings pitched against one another, ostensibly in order to entertain the home audience, but in reality the aim is to control the superbeings. The story features several caricatures of American politicians, notably Sarah Palin, who intend to use the superbeings for their own ends. Hitch's artwork is once again dynamic, giving the story a cinematic quality. Like Millar's *The Ultimates* and *Civil War*, the satire is directed not only against power and the government but also the media.

Mark Millar's *Jupiter's Legacy* (2013), with art by Frank Quietly, and *Starlight* (2014), with art by Goran Parlov, both return to some earlier reference points. *Jupiter's Legacy* certainly has elements of *Watchmen* and *Zenith*, but the idea of superhumans finding a remote island that grants them powers then taking over the world is reminiscent of Stapledon's *Odd John* (1935), in which the supernormals retreat to a Caribbean island to hone their powers. There is also the artwork from Frank Quietly that, like his earlier work, combines influences from the British, American, French, and Japanese comics traditions. This is contemporary comic art at its very best, and Millar's writing is also at its best here with a story that is less hyperbolic than some of his other work. Likewise, *Starlight* is a welcome change of pace from Millar's "widescreen comics" and recalls the science-fiction newspaper strips of the 1920s and 1930s, particularly Flash Gordon and Buck Rogers, but also the British science-fiction comics of the 1950s like Dan Dare. In terms of satirical content, *Jupiter's Legacy* makes reference to the global economic crisis of 2007 and 2008. The protagonist, Sheldon Sampson (The Utopian), is driven to seek superhuman powers after he loses his wealth and influence following the Wall Street Crash of the 1929. When he is betrayed by his fellow superhumans decades later, it is because he refuses to allow them to take away political and economic power from humanity in the wake of the economic crisis. Once again Millar uses the superhero genre as a means to satirize real world political issues.

In 2014 Marvel produced a miniseries of comics under the Revolutionary War banner which featured the heroes of Marvel UK who had been defunct since 1994, such as Death's Head, Dark Angel, Motor Mouth and Killpower, the Warheads, and Super-soldiers. They are joined by Captain Britain, Union Jack, the Knights of Pendragon, and Pete Wisdom to battle the forces of the old Marvel villain Mephisto. This series was published on the twentieth anniversary of the cancellation of the Marvel UK comics, and many of the creators who had started at Marvel UK returned to write and draw the series, including Alan Cowsill, Andy Lanning, Kieron Gillen, Rob Williams, Glen Dorkin, Richard Elson, Deitrich Smith, Brent Anderson, Ronan Cliquet de Oliveiro, Nick Roche, and Gary Erskine, most of whom had gone on to work for the parent company.

The story picks up twenty years after the final battle with Mys-tech. It is discovered that former hero Killpower has been subverted and has become a villain. There are numerous references to the fact that the American intelligence agency S.H.I.E.L.D. has taken over Britain's MI:13, making the British junior partners in the war against superhuman threats in a satire of the real world asymmetrical political and military alliance between the two countries. At the same time the story alludes to the similarly asymmetrical relationship between the former Marvel UK and its dominant parent company that, when it was in financial difficulty, quickly shut down the British operation. As in *Jupiter's Legacy*, "Revolutionary War" contains several references to the global financial crisis, which is often attributed to the collapse of American lenders who had overextended on subprime mortgages, which in turn had enormous financial consequences for banks all around the world, causing a huge economic downturn in Britain and elsewhere. The recurring theme of the series is the difficulties that arise from inherited debts. As Dark Angel struggles under the weight of her father's debt to Mephisto that bought her superpowers, she refers to herself as a superhero for the age of austerity, and when she delivers a wounded friend to a local hospital, she is told that economic cuts means that the hospital will be closed down soon. Once again, the British superhero story is a site of satirical intervention in current events, commenting on the relationship between Britain and America both in the world of the comics and in the real world.

Pax Americana (2014), by Grant Morrison and Frank Quitely, is a comic about the effects of violence and leading violent lives. It is a subversion of the Charlton heroes via *Watchmen*, but its mode of satire is not that of parody; rather, it takes an important theme and filters it through the distorting lens of the superhero genre. The ingenious structure is designed to be read in multiple directions, and its references to *Watchmen* are at once overt and subtle, presenting images of a bloodstained flag that recall the iconic smiley face from *Watchmen* or having Captain Atom discuss his powers in a way that, like Dr Manhattan, reveals that they are a metaphor for the process of reading comics. Indeed, Captain Atom is reading a comic in the story, fascinated by its form, and he may even be reshaping reality to match the form of the comic. On a deeper level, however, what Morrison and Quitley achieve is a compression and refocusing of all the ideas in *Watchmen*, and several others besides, twisting it into a Möbius strip. As Morrison said in an interview with *Comic Heroes* magazine,

> We thought it would be appropriate to re-think and update the kind of in-your-face self-reflecting narrative techniques used by Alan Moore and Dave Gibbons and to apply them to a whole new story which asks what if *Watchmen* had been conceived now, in the contemporary political landscape and with the Charlton characters themselves, rather than analogues? So the cover has a close-up on a burning peace flag and a Delmore Schwartz quote—"Time is the school in which we learn, time is the fire in which we burn"—and it all blossoms from there. [These stories] are designed to be told over and over again. If you were an Aboriginal kid or a tribal shaman, that's what you'd do, you'd participate in the recycling of old stories, the "revamping" of characters and scenarios, the explaining away of plot holes. Some do the job with more skill than others, but if you work with Marvel, DC or other companies' pulp fiction characters, you're basically repainting pictures of the ancestors on cave walls.[16]

Pax Americana represents Morrison and Quitely at the height of their powers. The simple act of equating a Möbius strip with a superhero domino mask has enormous symbolic implications, reflecting the cyclical nature of the superhero genre and recursive nature of comics form.

In October 2015, Grain Media released *SuperBob*, an independent British film directed by Jon Drever and starring Brett Goldstein as the titular former postman turned superhero. The story follows Bob on his day off as he tries to prepare for a date, and it is told in a documentary form. His boss at the Ministry of Defense, played by Catherine Tate, is attempting to engineer an alliance with various world powers, and notably an American senator, who are envious of Britain's status as the only state with a superbeing. The style is influenced by the BBC television series *The Office* (2001–2003) and the film *Shaun of the Dead* (2004), and it is a parody of the superhero films that have proved extremely popular in the early years of the twenty-first century. As the director notes,

> I love superhero films. I love the escapism and the brashness of them. They're cool. But the reason we don't really have a superhero culture in the UK, at least, not in the same way the US does, is because our collective psyche isn't brash and cool. If Iron Man was British he couldn't stand up in front of a bunch of reporters and whip off his designer shades, look them in the eye and say "I'm Iron Man." No. He'd say "Erm, yes, sorry, about the whole 'Iron Bloke' thing, well, sorry, but that was me. *I know!* It sounds so crazy, but, yes, it was me. Sorry about that."[17]

However, for Drever the film was primarily a satire on the British civil service and bureaucracy, as he says, "The kernel of *SuperBob* came from asking myself a question 'what if a superhero actually existed in the real world, and what if he was British?' Now that question instantly creates a funny answer. Make him a lonely postman from Peckham and the story naturally evolves from there. So, perhaps we are subverting American culture, but that wasn't the principal aim. If anything, I think *SuperBob* holds a mirror up to British culture"[18] (see Figure 38). Drever also notes that during the process of writing the film, he interviewed a contact at the Foreign Office who confirmed that if a British superhero existed, then he would instantly become a political pawn. "Oh hello Iran, an earthquake you say? OK, we'll send Bob just as soon as you've signed that nuclear non-proliferation document we've been waiting on."[19]

The film offers a critique of the media and government spin that is blunt but echoes the message in Millar's *The Ultimates*. Given the bombastic nature of most superhero films, *SuperBob* is refreshingly restrained and quiet, and very British. A very well-observed piece of comedy occurs when Bob twice hangs up his phone abruptly to emphasize dramatic decision making and is immediately called back, the other caller believing that the signal has been interrupted. This is a reference to the fact that in American films and television shows, characters often hang up the telephone without saying goodbye, which looks and sounds very strange to British viewers.

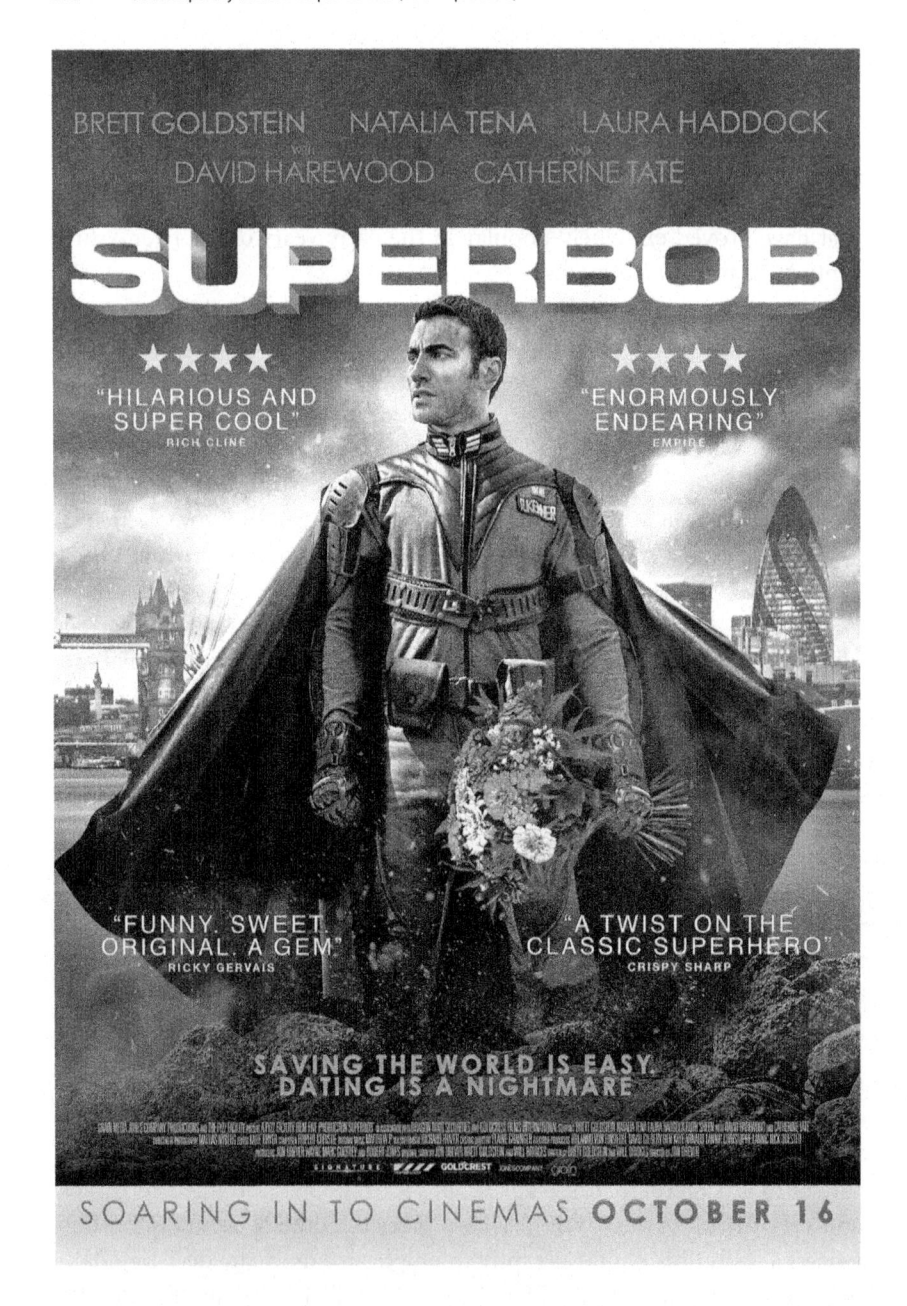

272   Contemporary British Superheroes (1994–present)

Fig. 58: *SuperBob*, directed by Jon Drever (Grain Media, 2015).

This is a subtle but effective way to parody cultural differences, either real or imagined, between Britain and America. As Drever notes, "Growing up the comics that I read incessantly were *The Beano*, *Whizzer and Chips* and *Buster*. When I was a bit older I got into Spider-Man and Batman. But I never connected to Spider-Man the way I connected to Dennis the Menace, Roger the Dodger or The Bash Street Kids. I think you can probably see that in *SuperBob*. It's a *Beano* film more than it's a Spider-Man film."[20] The film draws something from various British superhero comics since the 1980s, from *Zenith* and *Jack Staff* to *How to Be a Superhero*, and while the writers and director may not be familiar with the long tradition of British superheroes going back to the 1930s, *SuperBob* certainly is consistent with the conventions of this countertradition within British comics.

This chapter has looked at the state of contemporary British comics and the place of the superhero within them, and it has charted the continued rise of British creators working for American comics, and how their treatment of the superhero differs from, or converges with, American treatments of the superhero, or indeed, representations of the superhero more widely in, for example, in films, games, television, and other comics traditions. It is clear that the role of British creators within the industry and their influence upon the genre is considerable. The British superhero is still being employed by creators to comment upon the state of the British comics industry and its complicated relationship to American comics and to the political ties and tensions between the two countries.

CONCLUSION

The British superhero has had a considerable impact on comics. Despite the fact that the British comics industry has declined over the last several decades and reprints of American superhero material or licensed toy or television characters dominate the newsstands and comic shops, British writers like Grant Morrison, Alan Moore, Warren Ellis, and Mark Millar are extremely successful and influential worldwide, and artists such as Frank Quitely and Bryan Hitch have come to define the look of contemporary superhero comics. Added to this, the British independent comics scene is very healthy, and superhero narratives have an important place within the very diverse output from small publishers. Moreover, given Britain's relatively small size, it is quite common for the "superstar" talent to rub shoulders with the largely unknown and underappreciated talent from the independent presses. Larger national events, like Thoughtbubble in Leeds—one of the biggest comics conventions in the United Kingdom and always featuring an impressive lineup of international creators and top British talent—reveal the strength of independent publishing and the close community of British creators. Given this, it is arguable that British comics remain a powerful force, though not in the way they once were, and that the fascination with the figure of the superhero remains strong. As this book has demonstrated, that has been due to the close connections between the comics cultures of Britain and America and the political relationship between the two countries, for both of which the superhero has long been a metaphor. British creators have consistently offered a different interpretation of the superhero and have used the genre as a vehicle for parody and satire that has addressed this relationship.

This book has shown that the British superhero has a long and complex history, even though many have now faded into obscurity. These characters have had an impact, and British creators continue to take the superhero in new directions. Alan Moore, Grant Morrison, Warren Ellis, Garth Ennis, and Mark Millar have produced celebrated deconstructions of the superhero, but this is only one part of a lesser-known history of British appropriation and subversion of the superhero. The aim of this book has been to establish these connections and to revise the understanding of the history of the British superhero, pushing it back much further. It has also revealed the political subtexts at work in these narratives and the ever-shifting balance between parody and satire in British comics and comics produced for international markets by British creators. This has also been a study of the changing industrial and social context of British publishing and the market forces that have shaped British comics.

A key element of this argument has been the complex relationship that has emerged between American and British comics industries and the impact which it had upon readers, creators, and publishers. This relationship was not only considered in terms of the so-called British Invasion of American comics in the 1980s and its considerable aftermath that is still being felt. Rather, this argument was extended to an examination of the transnational nature of comics and, in particular, the close connections between the American and British markets that existed in the nineteenth century, were developed in the early twentieth century, and continue to grow. An important aspect of these connections was the shared language and commercial partnerships, but in the mid-twentieth century the relationship increasingly became about the popularity of products of American popular culture in the British market and the perceived glamor of American films, comics, and other forms of mass culture and Britain's changing economic and political conditions in the postwar world. These were times when the British and American comics industries developed in quite different ways, although with notable points of crossover. As reprints of American material began to slowly take over, edging out British comics in the later part of the twentieth century, some publishers embraced this trend while others attempted to create British comics and characters that mimicked American ones. Others substantially reworked American comics to fit into the format of British comics, resulting in some very interesting hybrid texts.

The generation of comics creators who emerged in Britain in the late 1970s and early 1980s were very much a product of the complex relationship between British and American comics just as much as they are influenced by the difficult relationship between the two countries. Many of their works from this time dramatize these tensions. A common trope was the resurrection of characters from past British comics in an affirmation that America's comics culture, though dominant, was not singular. This is often posited as a mode of defiance to the attitudes prevalent in American comics, and in the late 1980s and the 1990s the attitude of some works, such as *Marshal Law*, moved from resistance to outright hostility, and a certain amount of that persists to this day, as seen in *The Boys* and numerous other comics that satirize the superhero and current events, including American foreign policy and Britain's subordinate role in legitimizing it. The first wave of the so-called British Invasion made significant inroads to the American comics market, and some even made their careers by redefining the superhero and subverting that figure. The next generation of British comics creators followed in these footsteps and some went even further, savagely critiquing the superheroes or else celebrating the excess of these figures and helping to reshape the them into a dominant cultural icon currently enjoying unprecedented success across media, and in particular computer games, television, and films.

At each point in this analysis, there has been an emphasis on the relationship between the genre and its political concerns, and the contention has been that the superhero is an inherently political figure and that the genre is primed to communicate politically loaded imagery and themes. The American superhero is a powerful icon of the so-called American Dream, and more specifically, the patriotic narratives found in superhero comics have been shown to respond to American foreign policy, mostly in support of its political narrative and ideology but sometimes reacting against it.[1] The British superhero has been shown to be a politically complex figure, at times in sympathy with the rhetorical strategies appearing in American superhero comics, as well as with British attitudes towards America, and other times clearly in opposition to the rhetoric of the special relationship and the tacit Anglo-American pact that was forged during World War II, perpetuating throughout the Cold War and beyond, and carrying on into the present. The range of modes of representation found in British superhero comics, from reverence to parody, illuminates the complexity of British feelings toward America, its foreign policy, and the dominance of its culture, as well as positioning the superhero as a figure that can be appropriated and reshaped as a tool of resistance to American political and military authority. In recent years, several texts have emerged from British creators that celebrate the superhero and no longer employ overt satire and parody to mutate and distort this figure and the genre, but rather celebrate them.

The fact that so many British creators have been successful in creating superhero comics not only for the British market but for the American one points to the extent to which American comics penetrated into British comics culture from the 1930s onwards. This also demonstrates that by the early to mid-1980s there was an appetite for the subversive reworking of the superhero genre that these British creators responded to and specialized in. Notably they expressed their somewhat cynical attitude towards America and the bombastic representations of the American Dream, with which superheroes were very closely associated. After all, Superman, the (supposedly) archetypal superhero, fights for "Truth, justice and the American way," as if these ideas are synonymous. Not everyone agrees.

The subversions of the superhero struck a chord with many American as well as British readers, and in fact, with readers worldwide who recognized the challenge to the politics of the superhero that were embedded in the likes of *Paradax*, *Marvelman*, *Watchmen*, *Zenith*, *Arkham Asylum*, *Flex Mentallo*, *The Authority*, *The Boys*, *Kick-Ass*, and a host of others. But just as British creators could tear down the superhero, they could also build them back up, for example, in Morrison and Quitely's *All-Star Superman*, which is perhaps the definitive Superman story. Indeed, the fact that the key film in Marvel's hugely successful superhero blockbuster film series, *The Avengers*, was based on comics created by a British creative team (Mark Millar and Bryan Hitch) demonstrates just how deeply British comics creators have infiltrated the once alien and remote world of American mainstream comics. Indeed, Grant Morrison has been instrumental in directing the shape of the DC Universe in recent years, and some of the best new and emerging talent shaping the American comics industry is still British. However, despite the success of several high profile British creators, the fact remains that the British comics industry has been in terminal decline for several decades, and the majority of British talent is to be found in either American companies, or in independent comics.

One of the points noted in this book's later chapters is the strength of the British independent small press and the recent rise of the support network around them, from Thoughtbubble in Leeds to Glasgow Comic Con, The Lakes Festival in Kendal, and Dundee's Comics Expo and D-Con, to name but a few (and with more emerging all the time). Within the small press, there is a continuing fascination with superheroes. Comics like John Lee's *The Standard* and John Ferguson's *Saltire* testify to the fact that creating superhero narratives, or subverting and deconstructing them, remains popular with aspiring British creators. Some of these more recent works are even finding new and thought-provoking ways to critique the superhero and the newfound mainstream respectability of the genre. A notable success has been *Death Sentence*, by Monty Nero, a self-published title that was picked up by Titan, a major British publisher. This led to work in mainstream American comics for the writer, who has now written Hulk and X-Men annuals for Marvel and has also worked for Vertigo.

Other creators, like Dan McDaid, Alex Ronald, and James Devlin, represent a generation which creates for American publishers whom they deal with at a distance and in some cases have never actually met; the Internet allows the delivery of their artwork and scripts to American publishers without the creators ever setting foot in the headquarters of their publishers. The Internet's elimination of the need for travel has brought about a revolution in how we communicate and work. In creative industries like comics, it has also opened up opportunities that did not exist until very recently. Many non-American creators now choose not to relocate to America when they start work in American superhero comics. Some might argue that it matters little, as American popular culture reaches so far and American foreign policy so influences British politics that Britain is effectively the American military base envisaged by George Orwell in *Nineteen Eighty-Four*, or Airstrip One as he termed it.

The cultural and political imperialism of America and its influence on Britain is something that has been depicted in detail in this book, from the American comics that made their way into the hands of British readers through American military bases and personnel in the 1940s and 1950s, to the "special relationship" of Britain and America throughout the Cold War, to the generation of creators who grew up in the shadow of Trident and resisted the totalizing logic of the patriotic All-American superhero, to the renewed vows of the Anglo-American pact post-9/11.[2] However, America is not the world, and Britain is not America. The perspective of the British media is not identical with the perspective of America, so the act of creating American superheroes from a distance, removed from the inwardness of America media, still carries with it the potential for ironic commentary and subversion, of an overt or subtle nature, depending on the creator. In any case, it is clear that there remain a large number of British creators whose careers are very much tied to American publishers and the superhero genre.

With a thriving independent scene and several British high-profile creators in American mainstream comics, it may seem strange that the mainstream British comics industry is all but gone, with only a few holdouts, such as *2000AD* and DC Thomson's *The Beano*, along with some newer titles such as *The Phoenix*. There are complex reasons for this situation, but the key ones relate to the career paths that are open and the existing patterns of readership. Regarding British comics talent, there has been a brain drain effect resulting from the British Invasion; however, the writers and artists do not actually have to leave Britain anymore due to changes in technology that make working at distance from publishers feasible. For this reason, many British creators choose to work for the more high profile publishers, who offer better page rates, and they tend to be American publishers. In terms of readership, the factors are more complex. There are now far fewer readers for comics, but interest in superhero films, television, and merchandise is huge. The market and culture has shifted considerably over the decades. There are lots of other media and forms of entertainment that now compete with comics: computer games in the 1970s and 1980s, now, in addition, the Internet and social media. There was also a huge shift in tastes in the West in the early 1990s, with increasing numbers of readers drawn to manga and anime. In some ways, both American and British adventure comics became unfashionable as Japanese imports dominated, and the influence of its style of storytelling grew. Again, this was not to the benefit of the superhero, at least at the time.

That said, the market for comics and graphic novels aimed at an older market remains strong and is actually growing, but superheroes are a small part of that expansion; there is much more emphasis on autobiography and art comics. Another issue was the widespread availability of American comics and other forms of comics, including manga and a much wider range of comics that came with the increase in the number of dedicated comic shops in Britain throughout the late 1980s and 1990s. Shops like Forbidden Planet catered to a generation hungry for the next *Watchmen* and keen to see reprints of superhero material that had long been unavailable. These shops, however, also lured many readers away from superheroes and British comics by exposing them to a world of comics. Taken together, these factors changed the market and contributed to the slow demise of British comics industry. There are still several children's comics on the newsstands, but these are mainly licensed properties with sales driven by free gifts, games, and competitions. There is little story content and still less that is produced in Britain. Panini UK keeps some titles alive, like *Spider-Man* and *Mighty World of Marvel*, but these are American-sized reprint titles bundling together several issues worth of stories with no original content. These are the inheritors of the Alan Class comics of the 1950s and 1960s and the Marvel UK reprints of the 1960s and 1970s, but the exciting times when Marvel UK produced its own content seem very distant.

The distribution of comics has also changed considerably. Whereas imports and reprints of American material would once have taken a long time to reach British newsstands, the time frame is much shorter. Moreover, comics are now being consumed digitally, taking newsstands, and even specialized comics shops, out of the equation. This has perhaps removed what once made American comics seem so special: their glamor and rarity. If there is hope for a revival it may lie in the digital domain, with its power to reach far more readers than the number of those who would visit a newsstand or a comic shop. And aside from the increased availability of new content, the Internet holds the potential to make available stories from the all but forgotten past, reintroducing readers to a lost legacy of British superheroes. The development of digital- and tablet-based applications offers the opportunity for relatively cheap re-dissemination of the comics discussed in this book, so perhaps some of the old British superheroes might be rediscovered by a new generation of readers. They should. There is great merit in many of these stories, and they should be enjoyed again. Marvel's 2010 release of several Marvelman stories of L. Miller and Son from the 1950s was a rare treat in this regard.

Finally, there is a slowly growing body of criticism and scholarship about British comics, and there has been a rejuvenation of Comics Studies in Britain, some of it picking up from where the likes of Denis Gifford and Alan Clark left off. Indeed, there is still a lot of work being done outside of academia, by collectors, amateur historians, and bloggers such as Peter Hansen, Lew Stringer, Morris Heggie, Steve Holland, Mike Higgs, and Phil Clarke. The long-planned development of national archives and galleries dedicated to comics will hopefully enter a new phase soon, and the growth of comics scholarship will make possible yet more research on British comics and establish yet more scholarly resources. Such developments, if supported, will deepen the appreciation for and knowledge of the British comics industry and the writers, artists, and publishers who have worked within it. British superheroes are a relatively small but very important section of British comics production, but is one that challenges preconceptions about the figure of the superhero. As has been shown, the British superheroes still have much to reveal about the political and cultural relationship between the two countries, past and present, and will no doubt continue to do so into the foreseeable future.

NOTES

Introduction

1. Shane Denson, Christina Meyer, and Daniel Stein, eds., *Transnational Perspectives on Graphic Narratives: Comics at the Crossroads* (London: Bloomsbury, 2013), 5.

2. Dave Gibbons, interviewed by Ricky Serrano Denis and Cletus Jacobs, "Dave Gibbons at DC Thomson" (exhibition, University of Dundee, Dundee, Scotland, June 15, 2015).

3. Chris Murray, "Signals from Airstrip One: The British Invasion of American Mainstream Comics" in *The Rise of the American Comics Artist: Creators and their Contexts*, ed. Paul Williams and James Lyon (Jackson: University Press of Mississippi, 2010).

4. Jeffrey Richards, Introduction to *Spaghetti Westerns: Cowboys and Europeans from Karl May to Sergio Leone*, by Christopher Frayling, rev. paperback ed. (London: I. B. Tauris, 2006), vi.

5. Ronald Hyam, *Britain's Declining Empire: The Road to Decolonisation, 1918–1968* (New York: Cambridge University Press, 2006), 27.

6. Churchill made this claim about the "special relationship" in a speech in Missouri on March 5, 1946, but the sentiment was not a new one; close diplomatic and military ties between Britain and America went back to the nineteenth century. It was also in evidence throughout World War I, World War II, and the Cold War and reemphasized through the close relationship between Prime Minister Margaret Thatcher and President Ronald Reagan in the 1980s and Prime Minister Tony Blair and President George W. Bush in the aftermath of the events of September 11, 2001, at the start of the twenty-first century.

7. Richard H. Pells, *Not Like Us: How Europeans Loved, Hated, and Transformed American Culture since World War II* (New York: Basic Books, 1997), 2.

8. Hyam, *Britain's Declining Empire*, 28–29.

9. Letter, Jerry DeFuccio to Denis Gifford, November 22, 1957, Denis Gifford Archive, British Film Institute, London (hereafter BFI).

10. Denis Gifford, "From Beau Ogleby to Bristow: The International Strip in Great Britain," (address, Incontro Sul Fumetto [Conference on Comic Strips], Bologna, Italy, Children's Book Fair, Denis Gifford Archive, BFI, 1977).

11. Hyam, *Britain's Declining Empire*, 130–31.

12. Martin Barker, *A Haunt of Fears: The Strange History of the British Horror Comics Campaign* (1984; repr., Jackson: University Press of Mississippi, 1992).

13. Peter Coogan, *Superhero: The Secret Origin of a Genre* (Austin, TX: MonkeyBrain Press, 2006), 30.

14. Richard Reynolds, *Superheroes: A Modern Mythology* (1992; repr., Jackson: University Press of Mississippi, 1994), 41.

15. It must be noted that for too long the superhero genre has foregrounded powerful white men as the heroes, ignored or demonized other races, and posited women as sex objects. Likewise, the comics industry in both Britain and America has marginalized the role of women and nonwhite creators, and there have been few women or nonwhite editors and publishers. These aspects of the industry support the belief that superhero comics, and the industry in general, has been, and to a certain extend remains, an exclusive club.

16. Richard Reynolds, "Masked Heroes," in *The Superhero Reader*, ed. Kent Worcester, Jeet Heer, and Charles Hatfield (Jackson: University Press of Mississippi, 2013), 106–7).

17. Joseph Campbell, *The Hero with a Thousand Faces*, 3rd ed. (Novato, CA: New World Library, 2008), 23.

18. Robert Jewett and John Shelton Lawrence, *The Myth of the American Superhero* (Grand Rapids, MI: Eerdmans, 2002).

19. Chris Murray, *Champions of the Oppressed: Superhero Comics, Popular Culture, and Propaganda in America During World War Two* (Cresskill, NJ: Hampton Press, 2011), 253–57.

20. Margaret A. Rose, *Parody: Ancient, Modern, and Post-modern* (Cambridge: Cambridge University Press, 1993), 20.

21. Linda Hutcheon, *A Theory of Parody: The Teachings of Twentieth Century Art Forms*, (1985; Urbana: University of Illinois Press, 2000), 32.

22. Ibid., xii.

23. John Fiske, *Understanding Popular Culture*, rev. 2nd ed. (London: Routledge, 2010), 92.

24. Gibbons, interviewed by Ricky Serrano Denis and Cletus Jacobs.

Chapter One

1. Robert William Henderson, *Ball, Bat, and Bishop: The Origin of Ball Games* (1947; Champaign: University of Illinois Press, 2001), 153.

2. Roger Sabin, "Ally Sloper: The First Comics Superstar?," in *Image and Narrative* (2003), at http://www.imageandnarrative.be/inarchive/graphicnovel/rogersabin.htm.

3. Charlie Chaplin, "Exclusive: The Chaplin Story," interview conducted by Victor Thompson, *Daily Herald* (London), 9–16 September 9–16, 1957.

4. Paul Ferris, *The House of Northcliffe: The Harmsworths of Fleet Street* (Letchworth, UK: Garden City Press Ltd, 1971).

5. Robert Harvey, *Children of the Yellow Kid: The Evolution of the American Comic Strip* (Seattle: Frye Art Museum, 1998).

6. David Kunzle in *The History of the Comic Strip*, vol. 1: *The Early Comic Strip* (Berkeley: University of California, 1973), 157–96.

7. E. S. Turner, *Boys Will Be Boys*, new rev. ed. (London: Michael Joseph, 1975), 17.

8. Ibid., 18.

9. Ibid., 18–19.

10. Peter Haining, *Sweeney Todd: The True Story of the Demon Barber of Fleet Street*, rev. ed. (London: Robson Books, 2007), 110–17.

11. Gibbons, interviewed by Ricky Serrano Denis and Cletus Jacobs.

12. Joseph Bristow, *Empire Boys: Adventures in a Man's World* (London: Harper Collins Academic, 1991), 11–19.

13. Turner, *Boys*, 9–10.

14. Thomas Wright, "On a Possible Popular Culture," *Contemporary Review* 40 (1881): 36.

15. Kevin Carpenter, Introduction, *Penny Dreadfuls and Comics* (London: Victoria and Albert Museum, 1983), 5.

16. Edward Salmon, *Juvenile Literature As It Is* (1888), chapter 8, cited in Kevin Carpenter's Introduction to *Penny Dreadfuls*, 1983), 5.

17. Turner, *Boys*, 10.

18. Bristow, *Empire Boys*, 13.

19. Patrick Dunae, "Penny Dreadful: Late Nineteenth-Century Boy's Literature and Crime," *Victorian Studies*, #2 (1979): 133–50.

20. Stefan Dziemianowicz, ed., *Penny Dreadfuls: Sensational Tales of Terror* (New York: Fall River Press, 2014), xii.

21. Bristow, *Empire Boys*, 38–48.

22. Kelly Boyd, *Manliness and the Boy's Story Paper in Britain: A Cultural History, 1855–1940* (Basingstoke, UK: Palgrave Macmillan, 2003), 58–67.

23. Dziemianowicz, ed., *Penny Dreadfuls*, xii.

24. Boyd, *Manliness*, 1–2.

25. Ibid., 2.

26. George Orwell, "Boy's Weeklies" (1939), in Sonia Orwell and Ian Angus, eds., *The Collected Essays, Journalism, and Letters of George Orwell*, vol. 1: *An Age Like This, 1920–1940* (London: Secker and Warburg, 1968).

27. Arnold Freeman, *Boy Life and Labour: The Manufacture of Inefficiency*, rev. ed. (New York: Garland, 1980), 144.

28. Orwell, "Boy's Weeklies," 460–85.

29. Christopher Riches, ed., *The History of the Beano* (Dundee, Scotland: DC Thomson and Waverley Books, 2008), 18–19.

30. *The Wonder* actually started out as *The Penny Wonder* in 1912 before being renamed in 1913. The following year it became *The Halfpenny Wonder*, and later in 1914 it changed again, to *The Funny Wonder*.

31. Peter Haining, *The Classic Era of American Pulp Magazines* (London: Prion Books, 2000).

32. Julian C. Chambliss and William L Svitavsky, "The Origin of the Superhero: Culture, Race and Identity in US Popular Culture, 1890–1940," in *Ages of Heroes, Eras of Men: Superheroes and the American Experience*, ed. Julian C. Chambliss, William L. Svitavsky, and Thomas Donaldson (Newcastle upon Tyne, UK: Cambridge Scholars, 2013), 7.

33. Edward Bulwer-Lytton, *The Coming Race* (1871; London: Hesperus Press, 2007), 129.

34. Philip Wylie, introduction to *The Gladiator* (1930), in *The Book League Monthly* 3, no. 5 (March 1930).

35. Philip Wylie, *The Gladiator* (1930; Lincoln: University of Nebraska Press, 2004), 232.

36. Olaf Stapleton, *Odd John*, rev. ed. (1935; London: Gollancz, 2012), 160.

37. Richard Overy, *The Morbid Age: Britain and the Crisis of Civilisation, 1919–1939* (London: Penguin Books, 2009), 107–36; Jan Morris, *Farewell the Trumpets: An Imperial Retreat*, vol. 3, Pax Britannica Trilogy (London: Faber and Faber, 1978), 364.

38. Morris, *Farewell the Trumpets*, vol. 3, 364.

Chapter Two

1. Peter Hansen, "Mickey Mouse Weekly, or How WE Brits turned an American Icon into a staple of British Comicdom!," *Crikey!*, #8 (Manchester, UK: Sequential Media, 2008), 31.
2. Ibid., 33.
3. Denis Gifford, *Happy Days: One Hundred Years of Comics* (1975; London: Bloomsbury Books, 1988), 94.
4. Roger Sabin, *Adult Comics: An Introduction* (London: Routledge, 1993), 23.
5. Les Daniels, *Superman: The Complete History* (London: Titan Books, 1998), 10–31.
6. Advertisement in *Triumph*, #771, July 29, 1939, announcing the appearance of Superman in the following week's issue.
7. Alan Clark, *The Dictionary of British Comics Artists, Writers, and Editors* (London: The British Library, 1998), 23.
8. Denis Gifford, *The Encyclopaedia of Comic Characters* (Harlow: Longman Group UK, 1987), 62.
9. Clark, *Dictionary of British Comics Artists*, 97.
10. Terry Hooper, Introduction, in his reprint of William McCail's *Back from the Dead* (1940; repr., Bristol, UK: Swan, 2010), n.p.
11. James Vance, "A Job for Superman," in *Superman: The Dailies, 1939–1940*, ed. Peter Poplaski, Dave Schreiner, and Christopher Couch (New York: DC Comics, 1999).
12. Denis Gifford "Pow! Splat! Bop! Make Way for Another Superman," in *TV Times*, June 8, 1978. NB: Written as *The Incredible Hulk* television series aired on UK TV, 2.
13. Ibid., 3.
14. Ibid.
15. Peter Hunt, *Children's Literature: An Illustrated History* (Oxford: Oxford University Press, 1995), 252.
16. Mike Ashley, "Weird Tales—English Style," at http://www.sfcovers.net/Magazines/GGS/index.htm.
17. Denis Gifford, obituary for Dennis M. Reader, *The Independent*, June 7, 1995, also at http://www.independent.co.uk/news/people/obituary-dennis-m-reader-1585282.html.
18. Grant Morrison, interviewed by Chris Murray, in *Studies in Comics* 4, no. 2 (Bristol, UK: Intellect, 2013), 221.
19. These are held in the Gifford Collection at the British Film Institute.
20. Bob Monkhouse, *Crying with Laughter* (1993; repr., London: Arrow Books, 1994), 49.
21. John R. Lurner, letter to Denis Gifford, August 10, 1945, Gifford Archive, BFI.
22. *U.K. Comicdom*, #0 (May 1970), a British fanzine edited by Phil Clarke and designed by Mike Higgs.
23. Boris Ashdon, letter to Denis Gifford, January 22, 1948, Gifford Archive, BFI.
24. Denis Gifford, *How to Draw for the Comics*, unpublished MS, Gifford Archive, BFI, 31.
25. Ibid., 32
26. Ibid.
27. Mike Higgs and Phil Clarke, eds., *The Great British Fantasy Comic Book Heroes* (Redditch, UK: Ugly Duckling Press, 2009), 10.
28. Gifford, obituary for Dennis M. Reader.
29. Clark, *Dictionary of British Comics Artists, Writers, and Editors*, 141–42.
30. Denis Gifford, *Super-Duper Supermen* (London: Greenwood, 1993), n.p.
31. Gifford, obituary for Dennis M. Reader.

32. Higgs and Clarke, *Great British Fantasy Comic Book Heroes*, 10.
33. Clark, *Dictionary of British Comics Artists, Writers, and Editors*, 25.
34. Gifford, *Super-Duper Supermen*.
35. Riches, ed., *History of the Beano*, 100.
36. Ibid., 101.
37. Higgs and Clarke, *Great British Fantasy Comic Book Heroes*, 11.
38. Steve Holland, *The Mushroom Jungle: A History of Postwar Paperback Publishing* (Westbury, UK: Zeon Books, 1993), 40.
39. Gifford, *Super-Duper Supermen*.
40. Ibid.
41. Monkhouse, *Crying with Laughter*, 84.
42. Gifford, *Super-Duper Supermen*.
43. Holland, *Mushroom Jungle*, 31.
44. Cartoon by Denis Gifford, in Higgs and Clarke, *Great British Fantasy Comic Book Heroes*.

Chapter Three

1. Hyam, *Britain's Declining Empire*, 226–40.
2. David Reynolds, *Britannia Overruled: British Policy and World Power in the Twentieth Century*, 2nd ed. (Harlow, UK: Pearson Education, 2000), 305.
3. Peter Mandler, "Two Cultures—One—Or Many?," in *The British Isles since 1945*, ed. Kathleen Burk (Oxford: Oxford University Press, 2003), 128.
4. Bradford W. Wright, *Comic Book Nation: The Transformation of Youth Culture in America* (Baltimore: Johns Hopkins University Press, 2001), 154–79.
5. www.legislation.gov.uk/ukpga/Eliz2/3-4/28
6. Barker, *A Haunt of Fears*.
7. James Chapman, *British Comics: A Cultural History* (London: Reaktion Books, 2011), 45–75.
8. Reynolds, *Britannia Overruled*, 311.
9. Ibid., 313.
10. Gifford, *Super-Duper Supermen*.
11. Ibid.
12. Ibid.
13. Mick Anglo, *Nostalgia: Spotlight on the Fifties* (London: Jupiter Books, 1977), 118.
14. Higgs and Clarke, *Great British Fantasy Comic Book Heroes*, 12.
15. Anglo, *Nostalgia*, 119.
16. Mark Donnelly, *Sixties Britain: Culture, Society, and Politics* (Harlow, UK: Pearson Education, 2005), 111–15.
17. Gerard Jones and Will Jacobs, *The Comic Book Heroes* (Rocklin, CA: Prima Publishing, 1997), 71.
18. Alan Class, interviewed by Terry Hooper, in *The Amazing World of Alan Class*, ed. Terry Hooper (Bristol, UK: Black Tower Comics Group, 2011), n.p.
19. Christopher Riches, ed., *The Art and History of The Dandy* (Dundee, Scotland: DC Thomson and Waverley Books, 2012), 277.
20. Gibbons, interviewed by Ricky Serrano Denis and Cletus Jacobs.
21. Hyam, *Britain's Declining Empire*, 240.
22. See Anne Massey, *The Independent Group: Modernism and Mass Culture in Britain, 1945–59* (Manchester, UK: Manchester University Press, 1995), and David Robbins, ed., *The*

Independent Group: Postwar Britain and the Aesthetics of Plenty (Cambridge, MA: MIT Press, 1990).

Chapter Four

1. See Les Daniels, *Marvel: Five Fabulous Decades of the World's Finest Comics* (London: Virgin Books, 1991), and Sean Howe, *Marvel Comics: The Untold Story* (New York: Harper Perennial, 2013).
2. Steve Holland, introduction to *The Steel Claw: Vanishing Man* (London: Titan Books, 2005), n.p.
3. Ibid.
4. Lew Stringer, "Tales Before Dreddtime," in *2000AD Action Special* [ed. Richard Burton?] (London: Fleetway, 1992), 40–41.
5. Steve Moore, foreword to the unpublished collected edition of Johnny Future stories, cited by John Freeman in "It's Fantastic: Johnny Future Flies in from the Sixties" Down the Tubes, at http://downthetubes.net/?p=2492.
6. Lew Stringer, "Britain's Forgotten Heroes," *Comic Heroes*, no. 4 (Bath, UK: Future Publishing, 2010), 31.
7. Holland, *Mushroom Jungle*, 60–61.
8. Chris Heath, ed., *Pet Shop Boys, Annually* (Manchester, UK: World International Publishing, 1988), 16–17.
9. Alan Moore, "A Short History of Britain," in *Captain Britain: The Siege of Camelot*, vol. 4 (Tunbridge Wells, UK: Panini Publishing, 2010), 137.
10. Bob Budiansky, *Captain Britain: A Hero Reborn*, vol. 2 (Tunbridge Wells, UK: Panini, 2007), 9.
11. Moore, "A Short History of Britain," 137.
12. Dez Skinn, at http://dezskinn.com/marvel-uk.
13. David Thorpe, in *Captain Britain: The Siege of Camelot*, vol. 4 (Tunbridge Wells, UK: Panini Publishing, 2007), 8.
14. Jeremy Briggs, "The 'Lost' DC Thomson Art of Dave Gibbons in *Hotspur* and *Wizard*," *Spaceships Away* , #36 (2015): 17.
15. Ibid., 22.
16. David Bishop, *Thrill Power Overload: Thirty Years of 2000AD* (Oxford: Rebellion Books, 2007), 8–18.
17. Dave Hornsby, e-mail correspondence with author, August 9, 2015.
18. Ibid.
19. Terry Hooper, at http://hoopercomicart.blogspot.co.uk/2015_05_01_archive.html.
20. Ibid.
21. Dave Gibbons, in personal correspondence with the author, 2016.

Chapter Five

1. Chris Murray, "These are not our Promised Resurrections . . . ," in *Alan Moore and the Gothic Tradition*, ed. Matt Green (Manchester, UK: Manchester University Press, 2013), 215–34.
2. DeZ Vylenz, dir., *The Mindscape of Alan Moore*, film (The Disinformation, 2008).
3. Alan Moore, "Behind the Painted Smile," in *V for Vendetta* (New York: DC Comics, 1990), 270.

4. Mark Garnett, *From Anger to Apathy: The Story of Politics, Society, and Popular Culture in Britain since 1975* (London: Vintage, 2008), 119–64.

5. Martin Pugh, *Britain since 1789: A Concise History* (1997; Basingstoke, UK: Palgrave, 1999), 223–24.

6. Andy McSmith, *No Such Thing as Society: A History of Britain in the 1980s* (London: Constable and Robinson, 2011), 12–13.

7. Alan Moore, Introduction, *V for Vendetta*.

8. Brendan McCarthy, e-mail discussion with the author, January 28, 2016.

9. Peter Milligan and Brendan McCarthy, *The Best of Milligan and McCarthy* (Milwaukie, OR: Dark Horse, 2013), 10.

10. Ibid.

11. Brendan McCarthy, e-mail discussion with the author, January 28, 2016.

12. Peter Milligan and Brendan McCarthy, *The Best of Milligan and McCarthy*. Milwaukie, OR: Dark Horse Comics, 2013, 179.

13. Grant Morrison in "Arkham's Architect," an interview by Mike Maddox, in *Amazing Heroes*, #176 (Seattle: Fantagraphics Books, 1990), 27, 33; and Jim Gillespie, dir., *Halfway to Paradise—Grant Morrison*, film (Big Star in a Wee Picture Production, 1988).

14. Grant Morrison in "Arkham's Architect," an interview by Mike Maddox.

15. Grant Morrison and Steve Yeowell, "Zenith," "Interlude: Peyne," in *2000 AD #559* (London: Fleetway, 1988).

16. A. O. Potter, editorial, *The Alpha Omega Collection*, Kindle ed. (Alpha Omega Editions, 1988).

17. "Kevin O'Neill on Fighting the Comics Code & Working with Alan Moore," CBR TV, SDCC 2014, at http://www.youtube.com/watch?v=E7×2sg6iZhQ.

18. Dave Elliot and Garry Leach, editorial in *A1*, #1 (London: Atomeka Press, 1989), 4.

19. Gillespie, dir., *Halfway to Paradise—Grant Morrison*, film.

Chapter Six

1. Dominic Sandbrook, *The Great British Dream Factory: The Strange History of Our National Imagination* (London: Penguin Books, 2015), 114–15.

2. Garnett, *From Anger to Apathy*, 355–57.

3. John Freeman "Roads Not Taken: *Renga*, DC Thomson's Abandoned Rival to *2000AD*," on Down the Tubes, at http://downthetubes.net/?p=23501 (accessed June 30, 2015).

4. Chris Ryan, "Comic Book Illustrator at CM Comics, at http://hostcat.co.uk/biography/comic-book-illustrator (accessed January 9, 2014).

5. Paul Grist, introduction to his *Jack Staff Volume One: Everything Used to be Black and White* (Orange, CA: Image, 2003), 7.

6. Rob Williams, "Cla$$war Returns With a New Artist," in Newsarama, at http://www.newsarama.com (accessed June 23, 2003).

7. Garth Ennis, in James Hoare, "Why Garth Ennis Hates Superheroes and Loves War," at http:www.scifinow.co.uk/interviews/why-garth-ennis-hates-superheroes-and-loves-war (accessed July 24, 2012).

8. Warren Ellis, "Supergod," at http://www.avatarpress.com/titles/supergod (accessed July 29, 2009).

9. Grant Morrison, interviewed by Warren Ellis, in *Come in Alone*, no. 28, at http://www.comicbookresources.com/?page=article&id=13349 (accessed June 9, 2000).

10. John Lees, e-mail correspondence with author, July 21, 2014.
11. Gary Bainbridge, interviewed by Gavin Jones, in "Daniel Clifford Writes . . . ," at http://danielclifford.co.uk/post/4184074140/sugar-glider-stories-interview-12-gary-bainbridge (accessed 2011).
12. Martin Eden, in "Spandex: The Idea," at http://titanbooks.com/blog/spandex-idea (accessed February 13, 2012).
13. http://www.comicvine.com/retro-active/4060-59704.
14. John Ferguson, e-mail correspondence with author, July 23, 2014.
15. Ibid.
16. Grant Morrison, in *Comic Heroes*, #23 (Bath, UK: Future Publishing, 2014).
17. Jon Drever, e-mail discussion with author, January 13, 2016.
18. Ibid.
19. Ibid.
20. Ibid.

Conclusion

1. See Murray, *Champions of the Oppressed*.
2. Chris Murray, "Signals from Airstrip One: The British Invasion of American Mainstream Comics," in *The Rise of the American Comics Artist: Creators and their Contexts*, ed. Paul Williams and James Lyon (Jackson: University Press of Mississippi, 2010), 31–45.

BIBLIOGRAPHY

Anglo, Mick. *Nostalgia: Spotlight on the Fifties.* London: Jupiter Books, 1977.
Ashley, Mike. "Weird Tales—English Style," at http://www.sfcovers.net/Magazines/GGS/index.htm.
Barker, Martin. *Comics: Ideology, Power, and the Critics.* Manchester, UK: Manchester University Press, 1989.
———. *A Haunt of Fears: The Strange History of the British Horror Comics Campaign.* 1984. Reprint, Jackson: University Press of Mississippi, 1992.
Baxendale, John, and Christopher Pawling. *Narrating the Thirties: A Decade in the Making: 1930 to the Present.* London: Macmillan Press, 1996.
Bishop, David. *Thrill Power Overload: Thirty Years of 2000AD.* Oxford: Rebellion Books, 2007.
Black, Lawrence. *Redefining British Politics: Culture, Consumerism, and Participation, 1954–70.* Basingstoke, UK: Palgrave Macmillan, 2010.
Boyd, Kelly, *Manliness and the Boy's Story Paper in Britain: A Cultural History, 1855–1940.* Basingstoke, UK: Palgrave Macmillan, 2003.
Bristow, Joseph. *Empire Boys: Adventures in a Man's World.* London: Harper Collins Academic, 1991.
Bulwer-Lytton, Edward. *The Coming Race.* 1871. First Hesperus ed. London: Hesperus Press, 2007.
Burch, Martin, and Michael Moran, eds. *British Politics: A Reader.* Manchester, UK: Manchester University Press, 1987.
Burk, Kathleen, ed. *The British Isles since 1945.* Oxford: Oxford University Press, 2003.
Callahan, Timothy. *Grant Morrison: The Early Years.* Edwardsville, IL: Sequart, 2007.
Campbell, Joseph. *The Hero with a Thousand Faces.* 3rd ed. Novato, CA: New World Library, 2008.
Carpenter, Kevin. *Penny Dreadfuls and Comics.* London: Victoria and Albert Museum, 1983.
Carrier, David. *The Aesthetics of Comics.* University Park: Pennsylvania State University Press, 2000).
Chambliss, Julian C., and William L Svitavsky. "The Origin of the Superhero: Culture, Race and Identity in US Popular Culture, 1890–1940." In *Ages of Heroes, Eras of Men: Superheroes and the American Experience.* Edited by Julian C. Chambliss, William L. Svitavsky, and Thomas Donaldson. Newcastle upon Tyne, UK: Cambridge Scholars Press, 2013.
Chapman, James. *British Comics: A Cultural History.* London: Reaktion Books, 2011.

Clark, Alan. *The Dictionary of British Comics Artists, Writers, and Editors*. London: The British Library, 1998.
———, and Laurel Clark. *Comics: An Illustrated History*. London: Greenwood, 1991.
Coogan, Peter. *Superhero: The Secret Origin of a Genre*. Austin, TX: MonkeyBrain Press, 2006.
Daniels, Les. *Batman: The Complete History*. London: Titan Books, 1999.
———. *Comix: A History of Comic Books in America*. New York: Outerbridge and Dienstfrey, 1971.
———. *DC Comics: Sixty Years of the World's Favourite Comic Book Heroes*. London: Virgin Books, 1995.
———. *Marvel: Five Fabulous Decades of the World's Finest Comics*. London: Virgin Books, 1991.
———. *Superman: The Complete History*. London: Titan Books, 1998.
———. *Wonder Woman: The Complete History*. London: Titan Books, 2000.
Denson, Shane, Christina Meyer, and Daniel Stein, eds. *Transnational Perspectives on Graphic Narratives: Comics at the Crossroads*. London: Bloomsbury, 2013.
Dierick, Charles, and Pascal Lefèvre, eds. *Forging a New Medium: The Comic Strip in the Nineteenth Century*. Brussels: VUB University Press, 1998.
Donnelly, Mark. *Sixties Britain: Culture, Society, and Politics*. Harlow, UK: Pearson Education, 2005.
Dunae, Patrick. "Penny Dreadful: Late Nineteenth-Century Boy's Literature and Crime." *Victorian Studies* 22, no. 2 (1979): 133–50.
Dziemianowicz, Stefan, ed. *Penny Dreadfuls: Sensational Tales of Terror*. New York: Fall River Press, 2014.
Eco, Umberto. "The Myth of Superman." In his *The Role of the Reader: Explorations in the Semiotics of Texts*, 107–24. London: Hutchinson, 1979.
Edwards, Owen Dudley. *British Children's Fiction in the Second World War*. Edinburgh: Edinburgh University Press, 2007.
Eisner, Will. *Comics and Sequential Art*. Expanded ed. Tamarac, FL: Poorhouse Press, 1996.
———. *Graphic Storytelling and Visual Narrative*. Tamarac, FL: Poorhouse Press, 1996.
———. *Shop Talk*. Milwaukie, OR: Dark Horse Comics, 2001.
Elliot, Dave, and Garry Leach. Editorial in *A1*, #1. London: Atomeka Press, 1989.
Feiffer, Jules. *The Great Comic Book Heroes*. 1965. Reprint, Seattle: Fantagraphics, 1997.
Ferris, Paul. *The House of Northcliffe: The Harmsworths of Fleet Street*. Letchworth, UK: Garden City Press, 1971.
Fiske, John. *Understanding Popular Culture*. Rev. 2nd ed. London and New York: Routledge, 2010.
Frayling, Christopher. *Spaghetti Westerns: Cowboys and Europeans from Karl May to Sergio Leone*, 1981. Rev. paperback ed. London: I. B. Tauris, 2006.
Freeman, Arnold. *Boy Life and Labour: The Manufacture of Inefficiency*. Rev. ed. New York: Garland, 1980.
Freeman, John. "It's Fantastic: Johnny Future Flies in from the Sixties," on Down the Tubes, at http://downthetubes.net/?p=2492 (accessed August 2, 2009).
———. "Roads Not Taken: Renga, DC Thomson's Abandoned Rival to *2000AD*," on Down the Tubes, at http://downthetubes.net/?p=23501 (accessed June 30, 2015).
Garnett, Mark. *From Anger to Apathy: The Story of Politics, Society, and Popular Culture in Britain since 1975*. London: Vintage, 2008.

Garriock, P. R. *The Art Form of the Comic*. Newcastle: Northern Arts, 1973.

———. *Masters of Comic Book Art*. London: Aurum Press, 1978.

Gifford, Denis. *The British Comics Catalogue 1874–1974*. London: Mansell Information, 1975.

———. *The Encyclopaedia of Comic Characters*. Harlow: Longman Group UK, 1987.

———. *Happy Days: One Hundred Years of Comics*. Rev. ed. London: Bloomsbury Books, 1988.

———. *Super-Duper Supermen*. London: Greenwood, 1993.

———. "Pow! Splat! Bop! Make Way for Another Superman," *TV Times* 91, June 8, 1978.

———. *Victorian Comics*. London: George Allen and Unwin, 1976.

Gilbert, Martin. *A History of the Twentieth Century*. Vol. 3, *1952–1999*. London, HarperCollins, 1999.

Gillespie, Jim, dir. *Halfway to Paradise-Grant Morrison*. Film. Big Star in a Wee Picture, 1988.

Goulart, Ron. *Comic Book Culture: An Illustrated History*. Portland, OR: Collector's Press, 2000.

Gravett, Paul, and John Harris Dunning. *Comics Unmasked: Art and Anarchy in the UK*. London: The British Library, 2014.

Green, Matthew. *Alan Moore and the Gothic Tradition*. Manchester, UK: Manchester University Press: 2013.

Haining, Peter. *The Classic Era of American Pulp Magazines*. London: Prion Books, 2000.

———. *Sweeney Todd: The True Story of the Demon Barber of Fleet Street*. 4th ed. London: Robson Books, 2007.

Hansen, Peter. "Mickey Mouse Weekly, or How WE Brits turned an American Icon into Staple of British Comicdom!" *Crikey!*, #8. Manchester, UK: Sequential Media, 2008, 30–35.

Harvey, Robert C. *The Art of the Comic Book: An Aesthetic History*. Jackson: University Press of Mississippi, 1996.

———. *Children of the Yellow Kid: The Evolution of the American Comic Strip*. Seattle: Frye Art Museum, 1998.

Hassler-Forest, Dan. *Capitalist Superheroes: Caped Crusaders in the Neoliberal Age*. Alresford, UK: Zero Books, 2012.

Hatfield, Charles, Jeet Heer, and Kent Worchester, eds. *The Superhero Reader*. Jackson: University Press of Mississippi, 2013.

Heath, Chris, ed. *Pet Shop Boys, Annually*. Manchester, UK: World International, 1988.

Henderson, Robert William. *Ball, Bat, and Bishop: The Origin of Ball Games*. 1947; First University of Illinois ed. Champaign, IL: University of Illinois Press, 2001.

Herdeg, Walter, and David Pascal, eds. *The Art of the Comic Strip*. Zurich, Switzerland: The Graphis Press, 1972.

Hewison, Robert. *In Anger: British Culture in the Cold War, 1945–60*. London: Oxford University Press, 1981.

Higgs, Mike, and Phil Clarke, eds. *The Great British Fantasy Comic Book Heroes*. Redditch, UK: Ugly Duckling Press, 2009.

Holland, Steve. *The Mushroom Jungle: A History of Postwar Paperback Publishing*. Westbury, UK: Zeon Books, 1993.

———. Introduction. In *The Steel Claw: Vanishing Man*. London: Titan Books, 2005.

Hooper, Terry. *The Amazing World of Alan Class*. Bristol, UK: Black Tower Comics Group, 2011.

———. Introduction. In *Back from the Dead*, by William McCail. 1st Black Tower ed. Bristol, UK: Black Tower, 2010.

Horn, Maurice, ed. *The World Encyclopaedia of Comics*. New York: Chelsea House Publishers, 1976.
Howe, Sean. *Marvel Comics: The Untold Story*. New York: Harper Perennial, 2013.
Hunt, Peter. *Children's Literature: An Illustrated History*. Oxford: Oxford University Press, 1995.
Hutcheon, Linda. *A Theory of Parody: The Teachings of Twentieth Century Art Forms*, 1985. Urbana: University of Illinois Press, 2000.
Hyam, Ronald. *Britain's Declining Empire: The Road to Decolonisation, 1918–1968*. New York: Cambridge University Press, 2006.
Inge, M. Thomas. *Comics as Culture*. Jackson: University Press of Mississippi, 1990.
———. *Great American Comics: 100 years of Comic Art*. Washington, DC: Smithsonian Institute exhibition catalogue, 1990.
———. *Handbook of American Popular Culture*. 3 vols. Westport, CT: Greenwood Press, 1988.
Ingram, Tony. "The Rise and Fall of Marvel UK." In *Crikey!*, #9–12. Manchester, UK: Sequential Media, 2009.
James, Louis. *Fiction for the Working Man*. 1st Penguin Books ed. London: Penguin University Books, 1974.
Jones, Gerard. *Men of Tomorrow: Geeks, Gangsters, and the Birth of the Comic Book*. New York: Basic Books, 2004.
———, and Will Jacobs. *The Comic Book Heroes*. Rocklin, CA: Prima, 1997.
Kane, Bob, and Tom Andrae. *Batman and Me: An Autobiography*. New York: Eclipse Books, 1989.
Khoury, George, ed. *The Extraordinary Works of Alan Moore*. Raleigh, NC: TwoMorrows, 2003.
Kunzle, David. *The History of the Comic Strip*. Vol. 1, *The Early Comic Strip*. Berkeley: University of California Press, 1973.
———. *The History of the Comic Strip*. Vol. 2, *The Nineteenth Century*. Berkeley: University of California Press, 1990.
———. *Rodolphe Töpffer: Father of the Comic Strip*. Jackson: University Press of Mississippi, 2007.
LeMahieu, Dan. *A Culture for Democracy: Mass Communications and the Cultivated Mind in Britain between the Wars*. Oxford: Clarendon Press, 1988.
Lippard, Lucy, R. *Pop Art*. 3rd ed. London: Thames and Hudson, 1994.
Lofts, William Oliver Guillemont, and Derek John Adley. *The Men Behind Boys' Fiction*. London: Howard Baker, 1970.
Maddox, Mike. "Arkham's Architect." Interview with Grant Morrison, in *Amazing Heroes*, #176. Seattle: Fantagraphics Books, 1990.
Magnussen, Anne, and Hans-Christian Christiansen, eds. *Comics and Culture* Copenhagen, Denmark: Museum Tusculanum Press, 2000.
Marschall, Richard. *America's Great Comic-Strip Artists: From the Yellow Kid to Peanuts*. 1989. Reprint, New York: Abbeville Press, 1997.
Massey, Anne. *The Independent Group: Modernism and Mass Culture in Britain, 1945–59*. Manchester, UK: Manchester University Press, 1995.
McCleery, Alistair, and Benjamin A. Brabon. *Scottish Comics: A Celebration*. Edinburgh: Merchiston, 2010.
McCloud, Scott. *Reinventing Comics*. New York: Paradox Press, 2000.
———. *Understanding Comics*. New York: Harper Collins, 1993.

McShane, John. "Through a Glass, Darkly: A Revisionist History of Comics." In *The Drouth*, #23. Glasgow: The Scottish Arts Council, 2007.
McSmith, Andy. *No Such Thing as Society: A History of Britain in the 1980s*. London: Constable and Robinson, 2011.
Meaney, Patrick. *Our Sentence Is Up: Seeing Grant Morrison's The Invisibles*. Edwardsville, IL: Sequart, 2010).
———, dir. *Talking with Gods*. Film. Sequart, Respect! Films, 2010.
Melly, George. *Revolt into Style: The Pop Arts in the 50s and 60s*. Oxford: Oxford University Press, 1970.
Millidge, Gary Spencer. *Alan Moore: Storyteller*. London: Ilex Press, 2011.
Milligan, Peter, and Brendan McCarthy. *The Best of Milligan and McCarthy*. Milwaukie, OR: Dark Horse Comics, 2013.
Monkhouse, Bob. *Crying with Laughter*. 1993. Reprint, London: Arrow Books, 1994.
Moore, Alan, "Behind the Painted Smile." In *V for Vendetta*. New York: DC Comics, 1990.
Morris, Jan. *Farewell the Trumpets: An Imperial Retreat*. Vol. 3, Pax Britannica Trilogy. London: Faber and Faber, 1978.
Murray, Chris. *Champions of the Oppressed: Superhero Comics, Popular Culture, and Propaganda in America during World War Two*. Cresskill, NJ: Hampton Press, 2011.
———. "Invisible Symmetries: Superheroes, Grant Morrison and Isaiah Berlin's Two Concepts of Liberty." *Studies in Comics* 4, no. 2 (2013): 277–306.
———. "More Space Combat! An Interview with Grant Morrison." *Studies in Comics* 4, no. 2 (2013): 219–34.
———. "Signals from Airstrip One: The British Invasion of American Mainstream Comics." In *The Rise of the American Comics Artist: Creators and their Contexts*. Edited by Paul Williams and James Lyon. Jackson: University Press of Mississippi, 2010.
———. "Subverting the Sublime: Romantic Ideology in the Comics of Grant Morrison." In *Sub/versions: Genre, Cultural Status and Critique*. Edited by Pauline MacPherson, Chris Murray, Gordon Spark, and Kevin Corstorphine. Newcastle upon Tyne, UK: Cambridge Scholars Press, 2008.
———. "These are not our Promised Resurrections . . ." In *Alan Moore and the Gothic Tradition*. Edited by Matt Green. Manchester, UK: Manchester University Press, 2013.
———, and Vaughan, eds. *The Amazing Mr X*. Dundee, Scotland: UniVerse and DC Thomson, 2012.
Ndalianis, Angela, ed. *The Contemporary Comic Book Superhero*. London: Routledge, 2009.
Neuburg, Victor E. *The Penny Histories: A Study of Chapbooks for Young Readers Over Two Centuries*. London: Oxford University Press, 1968.
Orwell, George. "Boys' Weeklies," 1939. In *The Collected Essays, Journalism and Letters of George Orwell*. Vol. 1, *An Age Like This 1920–1940*. Edited by Sonia Orwell and Ian Angus. London: Secker and Warburg, 1968.
O'Sullivan, Judith. *The Great American Comic Strip: One Hundred Years of Cartoon Art*. Boston: Bulfinch Press, 1990.
Overy, Richard. *The Morbid Age: Britain and the Crisis of Civilisation, 1919–1939*. London: Penguin Books, 2009.
Pells, Richard H. *Not Like Us: How Europeans Loved, Hated, and Transformed American Culture since World War II*. New York: Basic Books, 1997.
Perry, George, and Alan Aldridge. *The Penguin Book of Comics*. Rev. 2nd ed. Norwich, UK: Penguin Books, 1971.

Pickard, P. M. *I Could a Tale Unfold: Violence, Horror, and Sensationalism in Stories for Children.* London: Tavistock, 1961.

Plowright, Frank. "Rule Britannia: A Hero History of Captain Britain." In *Amazing Heroes*, #52. Stamford, CT: Redbeard, 1984, 43–47.

Pugh, Martin. *Britain since 1789: A Concise History*, 1997. Basingstoke, UK: Palgrave, 1999.

Reitberger, Reinhold, and Wolfgang Fuchs. *Comics: Anatomy of a Mass Medium*, 1971. Translated from the German. London: Studio Vista, 1972.

Reynolds, David. *Britannia Overruled: British Policy and World Power in the Twentieth Century.* 2nd ed. Harlow, UK: Pearson Education, 2000.

Reynolds, Richard. *Superheroes: A Modern Mythology*, 1992. Jackson, MS: University Press of Mississippi, 1994.

———. "Masked Heroes." In *The Superhero Reader*. Edited by Kent Worcester, Jeet Heer, and Charles Hatfield. Jackson: University Press of Mississippi, 2013.

Riches, Christopher. *The Art and History of The Dandy.* Dundee, Scotland: DC Thomson and Waverly Books, 2012.

———, ed. *The History of the Beano.* Dundee, Scotland: DC Thomson and Waverley Books, 2008.

Robbins, David, ed. *The Independent Group: Postwar Britain and The Aesthetics of Plenty.* Cambridge, MA: MIT Press, 1990.

Rose, Margaret A. *Parody: Ancient, Modern, and Post-modern.* Cambridge: Cambridge University Press, 1993.

Rosenberg, Robin S., and Peter Coogan, eds. *What Is a Superhero?* Oxford: Oxford University Press, 2013.

Rubenstein, W. D. *Capitalism, Culture, and Decline in Britain, 1975–1990*, 1993. Reprint, London: Routledge, 1994.

Sabin, Roger. *Adult Comics: An Introduction.* London: Routledge, 1993.

———. "Ally Sloper: The First Comics Superstar?" In *Image and Narrative* (2003), at http://www.imageandnarrative.be/inarchive/graphicnovel/rogersabin.htm.

———. *Comics, Comix, and Graphic Novels.* London: Phaidon, 1996.

Samuel, Raphael. *Theatres of Memory: Past and Present in Contemporary Culture.* 2nd rev. ed. London: Verso, 2012.

Sandbrook, Dominic. *The Great British Dream Factory: The Strange History of Our National Imagination.* London: Penguin Books, 2015.

Shepherd, Janet, and John Shepherd. *1950s Childhood.* Oxford: Shire Publications, 2014.

Simon, Joe, with Jim Simon. *The Comic Book Makers.* New ed. New Jersey: Vanguard Productions, 2003.

Singer, Marc. *Grant Morrison: Combining the Worlds of Contemporary Comics.* Jackson: University Press of Mississippi, 2012.

Skidelsky, Robert. *Britain since 1900: A Success Story?* London: Vintage Books, 2014.

Stapleton, Olaf. *Odd John*. 1935. 1st Gollancz ed. London: Gollancz, 2012.

Stringer, Lew. "Britain's Forgotten Heroes." In *Comic Heroes*, #4. Bath, UK: Future Publishing, 2010, 28–33.

———. "A History of British Comics." In *The Comics Journal*, # 122. Westlake Village, CA: Fantagraphics Books, 1988, 57–67.

Thompson, Kenneth. *Moral Panics.* London: Routledge, 1998.

Thompson, Kim. "The British Invasion." *Amazing Heroes*, #52. Stamford, CT: Redbeard, 1984, 27–28.

Thompson, Victor, interview with Charlie Chaplin. "Exclusive: The Chaplin Story." *Daily Herald* (London), September 1957, 9–16.
Turner, E. S. *Boys Will Be Boys*. Rev. ed. London: Michael Joseph, 1975.
Vance, James. "A Job for Superman." In *Superman: The Dailies, 1939–1940*. New York: DC Comics, 1999.
Varnum, Robin, and Christina T. Gibbons, eds. *The Language of Comics: Word and Image*. Jackson: University Press of Mississippi, 2001.
Vaz, Mark Cotta. *Tales of the Dark Knight: Batman's First Fifty Years 1939–1989*. London: Futura Publications, 1989.
Vincent, David. *The Rise of Mass Literacy: Reading and Writing in Modern Europe* Cambridge: Polity Press, 2000.
Vylenz, DeZ, dir. *The Mindscape of Alan Moore*. Film. The Disinformation, 2008.
Waid, Mark. Introduction. In *Superman in Action Comics: The Complete Covers of the First 25 Years 1938–1963*. New York: Abbeville Press and DC Comics, 1993.
Worchester, Kent. "Superman, Philip Wylie and The New Deal." In *Comics Forum*, #6. London: Comics Creators Guild, Spring/Summer 1994, 26–31.
Wright, Bradford W. *Comic Book Nation: The Transformation of Youth Culture in America*. Baltimore: Johns Hopkins University Press, 2001.
Wright, Nicky. *The Classic Era of American Comics*. London: Prion Books, 2000.
Wright, Thomas. "On a Possible Popular Culture." *Contemporary Review*, #40 (1881).
Wylie, Philip. *The Gladiator* 1930. 1st University of Nebraska ed. Lincoln: University of Nebraska Press, 2004.

INDEX

Ace Comic, 89
Ace Hart, 93–94, 215
Acromaid, 88
Adam Eterno, 151–52
Albion, 243–44
All Star, 77
Alonso, Matias, 167, 169
Alpha, 260–63
Amalgamated Press (AP), 16, 23, 34–35, 37, 40, 42–43, 58–63, 65, 70–73, 76–77, 79, 95, 99, 103, 110, 142–43, 150, 155, 167, 171, 260
Amazing Mr X, 78–81, 94–95, 141–42, 214, 260, 264–65
America's Got Powers, 268
Anglo, Mick, 83, 87, 94, 97, 99–100, 108, 114–16, 127–29, 131, 134–35, 137–39, 163, 198–99, 215, 236
Apollo, Mr, 121–23, 126, 215
Archie. *See* Robot Archie
Argo, 77, 215
Authority, The, 245–47, 250–51, 268, 271

Bainbridge, Gary, 258
Bananaman, 111, 190–91, 264
Banger, Harry, 111–12, 190
Bat, The, 76
Batman, 3, 9–10, 14, 41, 49, 76, 82, 91, 99, 109, 116, 149, 152, 155, 190, 202, 220, 222, 226, 255–56, 273
Beano, The, 39, 58–59, 72–73, 93–94, 105, 141, 150, 159, 190, 264, 273, 279
Beeton, Samuel, 31
Bermejo, Luis, 159–60
Bicknell, Sid, 151

Big Chuckle Comics, 96
Big Flame Comics, 96, 121
Big Shot Comics, 96
Billy the Cat, 159, 214, 236, 264
Black Sapper, The, 44–47, 141–42, 151
Black Whip, The, 43, 48
Blake, Peter, 146
Blasco, Jesús, 144, 151
Boardman, T. V., 57–58, 60, 81, 83, 88, 107
Bolland, Brian, 134, 182, 244
Boys, The, 220, 246–48, 257, 277, 278
Boy's Own Magazine, The, 31
Boy's Own Paper, The, 32, 39
Brand, Nat. *See* Fullerton, Len
Brennan, Paddy, 91–94
Brett, Edwin J., 31
Brickman, 190
Briggs, Jeremy, 180, 182
Brit Force, 239–41
British Invasion, 4, 148, 192–232, 244–45, 256, 276–77, 280
Bulmer, Ken, 151
Bulwer-Lytton, Edward, 51, 215

Captain Britain, 174–80, 188, 193–98, 224, 241, 246, 256–57, 266, 269
Captain Hurricane, 151, 242
Captain Marvel (Fawcett), 9, 14, 36, 86, 94, 103–4, 106, 112, 116–17, 119, 121, 123–24, 126–29, 131–32, 134–36, 143–44, 149, 166, 182, 190, 198–99, 212, 235, 243, 252–53, 256
Captain Might, 86, 100, 102–3
Captain Miracle, 135–37, 215
Captain Q, 41

299

Captain Scotland, 218
Captain Universe, 127
Captain Zenith, 114–17, 119, 169
Cartoon Art Productions, 74, 87–93, 99, 106, 117, 124
Cast Iron Chris, 76
Cat Girl, 88
Champion, The, 37, 60, 72, 77
Cla$$war, 246
Claremont, Chris, 174, 177, 255–56
Clark, Alan, 63, 88, 91, 281
Clarke, Phil, 85, 91, 131, 281
Class, Alan, 140–42, 144, 150, 154–55, 158, 280
Clifford, Daniel, 258
CM Comics, 239–41
Colquhoun, Joe, 124–26, 215
Comic Adventures, 77
Comic Cuts, 22, 34, 39–40, 43, 58, 74, 143
Coming Race, The, 51, 212–13, 215
Coogan, Peter, 8, 16, 38
Cornell, Paul, 236, 256
Crisis, 220
Cursitor Doom, 225, 243

Dandy, The, 58–59, 72–73, 78, 80, 82–83, 85, 95, 105, 142, 150, 190, 260, 264–65
Dane Jerrus, 90, 94
Daredevils, 179, 194
Dark Knight Returns, The, 5, 198, 217, 222, 226, 229
Davies, Crewe, 89
Davis, Alan, 179–80, 194, 196, 198, 256
DC Comics/National, 9, 43, 49, 59–60, 66–71, 89, 112, 121, 124, 128, 140, 148, 154–55, 163, 166, 198, 202, 205–6, 215, 218, 222–23, 231, 239–40, 242, 247
DC Thomson, 16, 37–39, 41, 44–47, 58–60, 63, 73, 76–77, 79, 81, 91, 93–94, 99, 105–6, 111, 127, 141–43, 150–51, 154, 159, 162, 166–67, 171, 180–85, 191, 202, 214, 236–37, 242, 247, 259–60, 264–65, 279
Death Sentence, 266, 279
Delano, Jamie, 179, 197, 244, 247
Desperate Dan, 72–73, 76, 214
Dicky the Birdman, 39–40
Dillon, Steve, 180, 185, 197, 226, 228, 244–46

Doctor Who, 152, 161, 178–79, 194, 241
Dolmann, 151, 154, 243
Duffield, Paul, 249
Dynamic Comics, 83–84, 87
Dynamic Thrills, 121–23

Eagle, The, 96, 110, 111, 144, 150, 167
Eden, Martin, 258
Eisner, Will, 57–58, 79, 88
Electrogirl, 215
Electroman, 96, 116–21, 123–24, 126, 128, 215, 260
Ellis, Warren, 55, 188, 244–45, 248–50, 254, 257, 266, 268, 275–76
Ennis, Garth, 185, 220, 244, 246–48, 257, 277–78
Ewing, Al, 257
Excalibur, 224, 256

Falcon, The, 95, 143, 215, 258
Fantastic, 155, 158–60, 162
Ferguson, John, 264, 267, 278
Film Fun, 42, 56, 143, 150
Fleetway, 16, 142–44, 150–52, 154–55, 166–67, 171, 173, 180, 185, 211, 225, 227
Flex Mentallo, 234–35, 255, 278
Foldes Press, 93
Freakangels, 249–50, 268
Freeman, John, 224–25, 264
Fullerton, Len, 61, 62, 77, 88–89, 108, 215, 236, 260
Funny Folks, 22

Gadgetman and Gimmick Kid, 152–53
Gaiman, Neil, 185, 201, 209, 218, 222–23, 232, 244, 255–56
G-Boy, 88
Gerald Swan Ltd, 63, 75–77, 111–12
Gibas, Michael, 187–88
Gibbons, Dave, 4, 5, 15, 17, 27, 134, 143, 147, 181–82, 185, 192–93, 205–8, 221, 226–27, 236, 243–44, 260, 270
Gifford, Denis, 7, 62, 73–74, 76, 82–89, 94, 96, 99–100, 102–3, 114, 116, 123, 134–35, 152, 163, 215, 236, 260, 281
Gladiator, The, 38, 51–53, 213

Glass, Jack, 21, 44, 78, 79, 141–42, 260
Grant, Alan, 220, 236
Green Ray, The, 43
Grist, Paul, 240–42

Hairsine, Trevor, 246
Halcon, 77
Hamilton, Charles (Frank Richards), 36
Hamilton, Richard, 145, 147
Hansen, Peter, 56, 281
Harmful Publications Act (1955), 109, 110
Harmsworth, Alfred, 22–23, 33–35
Havoc, 224
Heath, George, 95, 143
Heggie, Morris, 94, 281
Henderson, James, 22, 34
Higgins, John, 225, 243
Higgs, Mike, 85, 87, 91, 131, 281
Hitch, Bryan, 244–45, 248, 250–51, 268, 275, 278
Holland, Steve, 96, 151, 161, 281
Home-Gall, Edward R. (Edwin Dale), 62, 106–7
Hooper, Terry, 93, 140, 188–89
Hornsby, David, 186–89, 239
How to Be a Superhero, 226, 228, 273
Hugo Hercules, 38, 238

Ibanez, Victor, 166, 172
Illustrated Chips, 22, 34, 41, 43, 58, 143
International Comics. *See* Cartoon Art Productions
Invisibles, The, 232–35, 237, 239, 249, 253
IPC, 43, 110, 141–43, 150–55, 163–67, 172–74, 180, 182, 215, 225, 242–43
Isabella, Tony, 173

Jack Flash, 93–95
Jack Staff, 240–44, 273
Jay, Michael, 161–62
Jaye, Bernie, 179–80
Johnny Future, 158–60
Jupiter's Legacy, 268–69

Kelly's Eye, 144, 152, 225
Kick-Ass, 209, 245, 252, 266, 268, 278

King Cobra, 183, 214, 236–37, 264
King-Ganteaume, 96, 116–18
Kirby, Jack, 57, 85, 100, 103, 116, 144, 149, 152, 155, 159, 161, 176, 188, 208, 223, 229, 254, 258
Knights of Pendragon, The, 224, 269

Leach, Garry, 193, 198, 200, 221
League of Extraordinary Gentlemen, The, 238–39, 249
Lee, Stan, 144, 149, 155–56, 174, 176, 178, 229–30
Lees, John, 257–58
Li, Yishan, 258
Lieber, Larry, 174
Lion, 106, 110, 150–54, 163, 165, 168, 215, 243, 264
Litening, 96, 121
Lloyd, David, 179–80, 193, 197, 201–2, 204
Lloyd, Edward, 26–27
Lopez, Solano, 144, 152, 154
Lovecraft, H. P., 210, 212, 222

Mallard Studios, 89, 93
Mark Tyme, 161
Marshal Law, 5, 218–21, 246–48, 252, 257, 277
Marsman, 91–93
Martin and Reid Ltd, 86, 114, 115
Marvel Boy, 253–54
Marvel Comics/Timely, 9, 43, 49, 144, 149–51, 154–59, 161, 171, 173–74, 176–78, 182, 186–88, 201, 212, 218, 220, 224–26, 229, 232, 240–41, 245, 251–58, 269–70, 278–80
Marvel UK, 173–79, 192–94, 196–97, 202, 224–25, 230, 239, 264, 269, 280
Marvelman/Miracleman, 94, 100, 104, 112, 128–36, 155, 190, 193, 195, 197–205, 208–10, 213, 215, 217–18, 221, 226, 246, 248, 260, 265, 278, 281
McCail, John (Jock), 59–60, 63–65, 72, 76, 121
McCail, William (Bill), 76, 89, 93, 260
McCarthy, Brendan, 208–10, 230
McDaid, Dan, 279
McGachey, Daniel, 264
McLoughlin, Denis, 108
McNeill, Hugh, 72, 103

McQueen, George, 91, 109
Meltdown, 224
Mickey Mouse Weekly, 56–58, 60, 83, 100
Mighty Apocalypse, The, 186–89, 239
Mighty World of Marvel, The, 173–75, 179, 194, 280
Millar, Mark, 55, 185, 244–45, 250–53, 268–69, 271, 275–76, 278
Miller, Frank, 5, 193, 197, 209, 222, 226, 229
Miller and Son Ltd, 81, 86, 94, 103, 106, 130, 199, 281
Milligan, Peter, 208–10, 244
Mills, Pat, 5, 124, 185, 197, 218–20, 230, 246–48
Modern Fiction Ltd, 86, 95, 100, 102
Monkhouse, Bob, 82–83, 87–88, 99–101, 111, 198, 236
Monty Nero, 266, 279
Moore, Alan, 5, 55, 112, 176–77, 180, 185, 188, 190, 193–209, 211, 213, 217–18, 221–23, 226, 229–30, 232, 237–39, 243–44, 246, 248–50, 255–56, 270, 275–76
Moore, Leah, 243
Morgyn the Mighty, 39, 78
Morrison, Grant, 5, 55, 78, 185, 188, 209, 210–18, 222–24, 230, 232–37, 244, 249–50, 253–55, 266, 270, 275–76, 278
Muscle, Mr, 83–84, 87
Mytek the Mighty, 225

Neary, Paul, 224–25
New Statesmen, The, 220
Night Hawk, 41
Night Raven, 179, 202

Oakley, Shane, 243
Odd John, 53, 213, 215, 249, 258
Odhams, 57, 150–51, 155, 157–60, 162–66, 170, 173, 243
Oh Boy! Comics, 82, 98–101, 111
Oink!, 226–27
Okay Weekly Comics, 57–58
O'Neill, Kevin, 5, 218–20, 238, 246–47
Ortiz, Jose, 167, 171
Ortiz, Leopoldo, 171–72
Orwell, George, 33, 37, 202–3, 247, 279
Overkill, 224–25

Paget, 95–99, 101, 161
Panini, 225, 280
Pansy Potter, 73, 82
Paolozzi, Eduardo, 145–46
Paradax, 201, 208–10, 213, 217, 257, 278
parody, 4, 13–15, 17, 39–40, 62, 64–65, 79, 81, 83, 91, 94, 96, 99–100, 103, 111–12, 120, 127, 145, 147–48, 186, 189–90, 203–4, 213, 215, 217, 226, 229–30, 234–35, 237–38, 240, 242, 245, 247, 257, 260, 270–71, 273, 275–77
Pax Americana, 270
penny dreadfuls/penny bloods, 19–39, 46, 48, 50, 91, 103, 109, 151, 180, 182, 195, 197–98, 204, 210, 238, 243
Phantom, The, 12, 38
Phantom Maid, 88
Philmar Ltd, 95
Ping the Elastic Man, 72
Planetary, 248–50, 257, 266
Plastic Man, 14, 58, 72, 90, 108, 120
pop art, 105–6, 145–48, 159, 161, 201, 209–10, 254, 260
Potter, A. O., 217–18
Pow!, 155, 157, 162–73, 183, 188, 217, 225
Power Comics, 155, 158, 162
Powerman (Dave Gibbons and Brian Bolland), 82, 183
Powerman (Dennis M. Reader), 88–89
Powers, Joshua B., 57
Prest, Thomas Peckett, 26–27
Pro, The, 246
Purple Hood, 161–62, 169

Quality Comics (US), 57, 72, 107–8
Quality Communications, 197, 200
Quesada, Miguel, 166
Quicksilver, Wonderman of the West, 93–94
Quitely, Frank, 234–36, 254–55, 270, 275, 278

Radio Fun, 72, 95, 143, 150, 215, 258
Ray Spede, 95
Reader, Dennis M., 87–91, 108, 215, 236
Red Flash Comics, 95
Reppion, John, 243
Retroactive, 260, 264
Reynolds, G. W. M., 27–28, 33
Reynolds, Richard, 8, 10

Robertson, Darick, 220, 246
Robot Archie, 110, 195, 215–16, 242–43
Romero, Enrique Badia, 169, 183, 184
Ross, Jonathan, 268
Rymer, James Malcolm, 26–27

Saltire, 264–67, 279
satire, 4, 13, 15, 52, 99, 145, 179, 190, 204–5, 217–18, 220–21, 226, 229–30, 235, 237, 240, 245, 247, 251, 256–57, 266, 268–71, 275–77
Scarlet Bat, The, 41–42
Scion, 95–96, 99–100, 116, 118, 121, 124, 161, 239
Scraps, 22, 34
Segrelles, Eustaqid, 171
Sexton Blake, 34–35, 37
Siegel, Jerry, 12, 65, 154
Skingley, Petra, 174
Skinn, Dez, 178–80, 192–93, 197, 202, 220
Smash!, 151–52, 154–55, 158, 163, 172, 243
Smith, Ron, 183
Softly, Maureen, 173
Soloway, 75, 77
Spandex!, 258
Speed Gale and Garry, 91
Spencer, John (Samuel Assael), 161
Spider, The (UK), 151, 154, 168, 195, 225, 242
Spider-Man Weekly, 173
Sports Cartoons Ltd, 128
Standard, The, 257–58
Stapledon, Olaf, 53–54, 215, 249, 258
Starlight, 268
Steel Claw, The, 43, 144, 151–52, 154, 195, 215, 225, 242
story papers, 19–20, 25, 32–51, 58–59, 65, 72, 95, 128, 154, 179, 197
Streamline, 83, 85–86, 91, 100, 124–25, 215
Streamline Comics, 83, 85–86
Stringer, Lew, 159, 190, 225–27, 281
Strip, 264
Stuporman, 99, 101, 111, 190
Sugar Glider, 258
Super Hombre, 135
SuperBob, 270–73
Super-Bumper Comic, 89
Supercats, 183–84
Super-Duper Comics, 87–88, 90–91

Supergod, 248–50
Superman, 3, 9–10, 12–14, 38, 51, 53, 59–60, 62, 74, 76, 78–79, 81–85, 87–88, 95, 99, 103, 111–12, 116, 119, 121, 127, 128, 133–34, 140, 143, 148, 150, 154–55, 167, 190, 205
Superstooge, 111–12, 190
Superthriller Comic, 93

Talbot, Bryan, 188
Tennant, Neil, 173
Terrific, 155, 158–59, 162
Thorpe, David, 178–79, 194, 256
Thrill Comics, 74, 76
Thunderbolt Jaxon, 103, 143, 243
Thunderhawks, 236–37, 264
Tornado, 185, 260
Tornado, The, 98–100
Transatlantic Press. *See* Cartoon Art Productions
Tri-Man, 163–64
Trimpe, Herb, 174, 176–77
Triumph, The, 37, 59–66, 68, 70–72, 74, 77–79, 81, 88, 95, 106, 143, 155
Tully, Tom, 151, 154
TV Century 21, 21, 96, 164, 174
2000AD, 167, 178, 180, 183, 185–86, 192–93, 197, 211, 217–18, 220, 224–25, 230, 236, 245, 248, 250, 257, 279

Ultimates, The, 245–47, 250–51, 268, 271
Union Jack, 174, 241, 256, 269

V for Vendetta, 193–95, 197, 202–8
Valentines and Sons, 89, 93
Valiant, 144, 151–52, 154–55, 163, 165, 173, 242–43, 264
Vertigo, 205, 222, 231, 248, 266, 279

Wagner, John, 185, 197, 220, 248
Wags, 57–58
Ward, William, 76
Warrior, 112, 193, 197, 200–202
Watchmen, 4–5, 180, 182, 192, 194, 198, 201–2, 205–8, 217–18, 221–23, 226, 229–32, 234, 239, 243, 248, 250, 252, 258, 268, 270, 278, 280
Watkins, Dudley D., 72, 93–94, 141–42

Wham!, 155, 157
Williams, Rob, 246
Winged Man, The, 39, 40–41, 258
Wonder Boy, 88
Wonder Woman, 9, 14, 73, 239, 248
Wonderman, 96–97, 99–100
Wonderman, 96–97, 100
Wood, Gerald, 161
World Distributors Ltd, 93–94
Wylie, Philip, 38, 51–52
Wyndham, John, 179, 249, 268

Yeats, Jack B., 39, 40
Yeowell, Steve, 5, 210–11, 215, 217

Zeccora, Nevio, 152–53
Zenith, 5, 209–18, 222, 226, 233, 235, 239, 242, 252, 257, 260, 265–66, 268, 273, 278